(*continued from front flap*)

Woodburn Chase, Frank Porter Graham, and William C. Friday. His book evokes for all who have been part of the Chapel Hill community memories of their own associations with the campus and a sense of the greater history of the institution of which they were a part.

Susan Mullally Clark

William D. Snider, retired editor of the *Greensboro News and Record*, is author of *Helms and Hunt: The North Carolina Senate Race, 1984*. He is a 1941 graduate of the University of North Carolina at Chapel Hill.

LIGHT ON THE HILL

William Richardson Davie.
(North Carolina Collection, University of North Carolina Library, Chapel Hill)

LIGHT ON THE HILL

A HISTORY OF THE UNIVERSITY OF

NORTH CAROLINA AT CHAPEL HILL

BY WILLIAM D. SNIDER

THE UNIVERSITY OF NORTH CAROLINA PRESS

CHAPEL HILL AND LONDON

*The publication of this book was made possible in part by a
generous gift of James Graham Kenan, class of 1932.*

Manufactured in the United States of America

96 95 94 93 92   5 4 3 2 1

Library of Congress Cataloging-in-Publication Data
Snider, William D.
Light on the hill : a history of the University of North Carolina
at Chapel Hill / by William D. Snider.
p.   cm.
Includes bibliographical references and index.
ISBN 0-8078-2023-7 (hard : alk. paper)
1. University of North Carolina at Chapel Hill—History.
I. Title.
LD3943.S63   1992
378.756′565—dc20   91-50789
CIP

For Flo and Jane and Mary

and Little Flo and Milly—

who learned about Chapel Hill

early and late

CONTENTS

ILLUSTRATIONS

MAP

From Salisbury to Chapel Hill

It was a coincidence, but rather an unusual one. In September 1967 my wife and I drove our eighteen-year-old daughter to enroll at Chapel Hill exactly thirty years after my parents took me on the same mission on a bright autumn day in 1937. It seemed even stranger, as we thought about it, that Jane's grandfather had embarked on the same trip from Salisbury (by train, not automobile) another three decades earlier, in 1906.

Other North Carolina families have encountered that same experience, even involving more than three generations. For nearly two centuries now, starting with Hinton James in 1795, Tar Heel sons and daughters have been journeying to Chapel Hill. They have come from small villages and large towns and the countryside of North Carolina—often out of the provincial backcountry—to discover Chapel Hill's charming window on the world. It was there, as William R. Davie envisioned it, that the youth of a pioneering society discovered that "education" is indispensable for "the happiness of a rising generation."

Davie sought to educate the children of the gentry, for the most part. That was how it was in those days. But even he realized that such education must be affordable, within range of the pocketbooks of all youth who sought it. These were the young men who would go home to run the government at their county courthouses, serve as judges in the courts, teachers in the schools, doctors, legislators in the General Assembly, merchants in the marketplace, farmers in the fields, and guardians of the state's life and liberties.

Chapel Hill has served that purpose for almost ten generations. In the earliest decade of this century my father was a schoolmate of Frank Porter Graham. In later years he recalled that Graham, then a sophomore, gallantly headed off a hazing expedition in which my father and other freshmen were targeted victims. Later as a banker and businessman who differed with some of Graham's views, my father never lost his admiration and regard for his friend.

That was the essence of education at Chapel Hill. Academic freedom meant freedom to differ, to wrestle with the complexities of searching for the truth, to tolerate error where truth was left free to combat it, all in the best Jefferson tradition.

In the late 1930s Chapel Hill became my window on the world. It exposed a seventeen-year-old youth from Rowan County to the glory years of an emerging international institution. The university's seeds of academic distinction had been planted on the brink of the twentieth century by leaders like Battle, Alderman, and Venable. They sprouted and came to fruit during the fertile regimes of Edward Kidder Graham, Harry Woodburn Chase, and Frank Porter Graham from 1914 to 1949.

But on that autumn day when Chapel Hill first unfolded before my eyes, I knew nothing of that history. For many of the boys from the North Carolina hinterlands the great buildings under the trees had a mysterious and magical quality; here were the doorways to an intriguing new world. In later years one of my classmates, Arthur Link, explained what it meant to a "country boy" going to Chapel Hill: "The grandeur and romance and glory of it and the intellectual excitement of that place. Intellectual freedom. Anything went. I mean it could be anything. Didn't matter. People were very accepting in their tolerance. . . . I remember the first two or three days. I'd just roam the campus and look at the buildings and all those books, like a banquet to me, and the excitement of scholarly minds and bright people and bright undergraduate students."

Link recalled how far a dollar went. His room cost about $60 a year, and meals at the student cafeteria in Swain Hall (called Swine Hole) came to about 15 cents for breakfast, lunch maybe 18–20 cents, and dinners always 25 cents. The "student special" included entree, two vegetables, bread, dessert, and drink. One could go through a year—room, board, everything—for about $300 with a little spending money left over.*

I arrived at Chapel Hill a little late for Horace Williams, "the gadfly of Chapel Hill," but in time for George Coffin Taylor's classic Shakespeare classes and Phillips Russell's "bring on the bear" in creative writing. As a young reporter for the *Daily Tar Heel*, with quaking knees I interviewed the great zoologist Henry Van Peters ("Froggy") Wilson in Davie Hall. I spent many a Sunday evening at Dr. Frank and "Miss Marian's" open house on East Franklin Street. Dr. Frank usually stood in the foyer introducing new

*Interview with Arthur Link by George B. Tindall on August 8–9, 1989, at Montreat, N.C.

students to each other and asking about members of their family back home. He had a way of holding your elbow and gently forcing you to participate in the conversation. He invited you to enter that warm glow of a circle of new friends. No wonder you never forgot it.

Unlike Thomas Wolfe, I never performed in "Proff" Koch's Playmakers, but his artistry pervaded the campus. The scholarly E. K. Zimmerman had a heavy German accent hard to understand. But he drilled us soundly in economics. The tart-tongued O. J. Coffin, head of journalism, used the King James Bible as his source almost as frequently as Bernard Boyd did in his illuminating courses in religion at Peabody Hall. The mild-mannered H. K. (Harry) Russell sent us soaring on the wings of literature, and even J. P. Harland's archaeology, which rumor had it nobody ever failed, introduced us to the glories of Greece and Rome with unexpected bounties. The sharp-witted historian Hugh Lefler recounted the saga, warts and all, of our native state. Fletcher Green, affable but exacting, expanded that history to southern regions and beyond.

As World War II unfolded, golden Chapel Hill became linked with bloody Europe. I glanced out my third-story window in Old East one morning to see a disturbing sight. Lee Manning Wiggins, Jr., a classmate, and some of his American Student Union associates had planted the lawn under the great trees of McCorkle Place with small white crosses. They symbolized the graves of American boys who would be slaughtered if we followed Franklin Roosevelt's counsel to protect Great Britain from Nazi Germany. At that time I was associate editor of the *Tar Heel.* Every morning we splashed across the top of the editorial page a banner reading Keep America Out of Europe's War. Unlike Dr. Graham, who had already followed William Allen White in championing the cause of European liberty, the *Tar Heel* remained unconvinced (myself included). We were unduly influenced, I came to believe, by those who knew less than Roosevelt and Churchill about the fragility of justice and freedom in the world. Despite the crosses on McCorkle Place, the news of Hitler's invasion of France and the lowlands swung me around 180 degrees. Some things, I concluded, could be worse than war. Allowing democracy to die in Europe became one of them.

Being exposed to such divergent views in those idyllic days gave students a chance to shape their own insights in new and provocative ways. Never again, for example, could I return to Salisbury (as I eventually did to work on the *Salisbury Evening Post* after military service in China-Burma-India) with the same provincial outlook of high school days.

Over two centuries other young Tar Heels encountered the same experience—from the aftermath of the French Revolution in the eighteenth century to the 1990 military excursion in the Persian Gulf. They represented that great surge of young people who, in Albert Coates's memorable phrase, "went out from Chapel Hill" to work and live and serve in North Carolina. Coates called the university a "magic Gulf Stream." Those of us who discovered its bounties in the rising springtime of its greatness on the eve of World War II knew precisely what he meant.

But the fascination of Chapel Hill never lay exclusively in what came out of the classrooms. A good portion of its magic arose from daily student life—the making of new friendships at Harry's, the exhilarating athletic contests, the weekend parties, the German Club dances, the visiting speakers. Being in the Tin Can for a Tommy Dorsey dance or settling into Kenan Stadium for a Saturday afternoon with "Choo Choo" left the aura of Chapel Hill indelibly stamped on the mind. Whether one was seeing Archibald Henderson, Helen O'Connell, or Rameses up close, it was an unforgettable experience.

I hoped, of course, that my daughter, going down to Chapel Hill thirty years after I did and living in a dormitory named for "The Woman Who Rang the Bell," Mrs. Cornelia Phillips Spencer, would absorb some of that same magic. I think she did. Carrying Jane's luggage into Spencer Hall that day, I saw the same portrait of Mrs. Spencer that hung there, above an antique piano, in my own time. There she was, a strong, intelligent woman arrayed in a lace kerchief, wearing silver eyeglasses and a stern demeanor.

Seeing her portrait again, I recalled something that Cornelia Spencer had written about North Carolina at a low ebb in the university's history, when its doors had been closed after the Civil War. There were only a handful of state leaders then, and she was one, who thought the university would ever be opened again. "When I think of North Carolina abstractly," Mrs. Spencer wrote, "there are a hundred things that go to make up her image in my mind—not only does there rise up her geographical figures—her profile from the sandbars to the mountains—not only a thought of her commercial and political status, not only a reminder of her history, or the proverbial character of her men and the fair fame of her women; but somehow mixed up with all these comes a vision of her humblest aspects—of her red gullies and her broomstraw, her persimmon trees. I recall her may weeds as well as her yellow jasmine—her sassafras as well as her white oaks."

Similar thoughts arise in my mind about the University of North Carolina on its two-hundredth birthday. They range from the momentous to the humble. They span the years from the remarkable William R. Davie, that son of the Calvinist upcountry who became a Halifax gentleman and founded the university, to Joseph Caldwell, David Swain, Kemp Battle, Francis Venable, Harry Chase, and the Grahams and Bill Friday on down to the chancellors of our own time. This noble company, along with a talented faculty, came to love and respect and serve this place and the thousands of students who passed this way. They never forgot, for long, its essential purpose: *Lux (et) Libertas* (Light and Liberty), the university's motto, which described what they intended to produce and preserve and what, in fact, they did during the course of two centuries. The story of their enterprise deserves recounting.

Greensboro, North Carolina
April 1991

ACKNOWLEDGMENTS

In writing this manuscript I have been generously assisted by John Sanders, director of the Institute of Government, and Matthew Hodgson, director of the University of North Carolina Press. They approached me about it in 1987, well before the university's two-hundredth birthday, and I began research in the fall of that year. They have been interested counselors and advisers during the last three years, and I value their assistance. John Sanders was especially helpful in research suggestions as well as in the critique of a work which, I am sure, he would have found pleasure in writing himself.

A great number of other North Carolinians also helped along the way. I especially want to note the advice and assistance of William C. Friday, Arnold King, William B. Aycock, Douglass Hunt, Carlyle Sitterson, James Godfrey, Henry W. Lewis, William Little, Christopher Fordham, Ferebee Taylor, Doris Betts, H. G. Jones, William Powell, David Parker, and Linda Sellars.

Greensboro, North Carolina
April 20, 1991

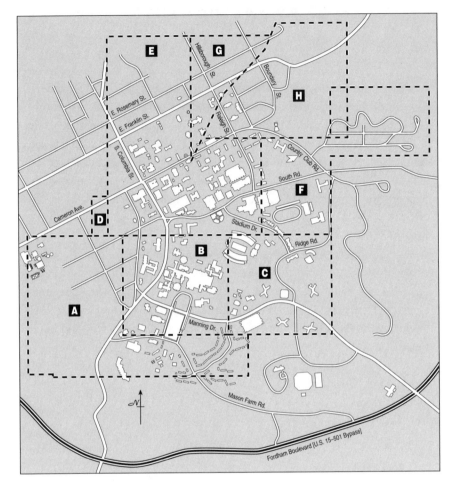

The University of North Carolina and the Town of Chapel Hill
Contiguous Land Donations, 1792–1806

A. Edmund Jones, 200 acres, 1796.

B. John and Solomon P. Morgan (heirs
   of Mark Morgan), 107 acres, 1806.

C. John Daniel, 107 acres, 1796.

D. James Craig, 5 acres, 1796.

E. Christopher Barbee, 221 acres, 1792.

F. Hardy Morgan, 125 acres, 1796.

G. Benjamin Yeargin, 50 acres, 1796.

H. Hardy Morgan, 80 acres, 1793.

Boundaries of donated tracts, based on research by L. J. Phipps in Orange County Registry,
superimposed on 1991 map of campus and town.

LIGHT ON THE HILL

In Chapel Hill among a friendly folk this old university, the first state university to open its doors, stands on a hill set in the midst of beautiful forests under the skies that give their color and their charm to the life of youth gathered here. . . . There is music in the air of the place. . . . Into this life, with its ideals, failures and high courage, comes youth with his body and his mind, his hopes and his dreams. Scholars muster here the intellectual and spiritual resources of the race for the development of the whole personality of the poorest boy. . . . Great teachers on this hill kindle the fires that burn for him and light up the heavens of the commonwealth with the hopes of light and liberty for all mankind.

FRANK PORTER GRAHAM

President of the University of North Carolina, 1930–1949

From his Inaugural Address, November 11, 1931, Kenan Stadium

The cagiest students—those who enter college resolved to avoid all mawkish display of loyalty—find their resolution shaken by the first football victory, stunned by the frenetic din of basketball season and drowned in the water-color tides of spring . . . that drench campus and village with magic.

FRANCES GRAY PATTON

Holiday, 1966

CHILD OF THE REVOLUTION,

1754–1795

The date was January 15, 1795. The weather was severe—the morning opened with a cold, drizzling rain—and the roads were almost impassable. The place was a wooded hill near the ruins of an old Church of England chapel at the intersection of two great roads meandering through the midlands of sparsely settled North Carolina.

To that lonely crossroads, known as New Hope Chapel Hill, journeyed a small delegation of Carolina gentry. Their leader, Governor Richard Dobbs Spaight, had "braved the discomforts of 28 miles of red mud and pipe clay and jagged rocks stretching from Chapel Hill to Raleigh [the new state capital]."[1] They had come to open the doors of the recently chartered University of North Carolina—to make it the first state university in the United States to admit students.[2]

But there were no students that day. The company, according to a Halifax newspaper, the *North Carolina Journal*, consisted of "several members of the corporation and . . . other gentlemen members of the General Assembly" (then in session). "The unfavorable state of the weather," the *Journal* reported, "disappointed many of our fellow citizens who wished to be present on that much desired occasion."

With the delegation was the new "presiding professor," the Reverend David Ker, a native of Ireland and a graduate of Trinity College in Dublin. Because financial resources were meager, the university's trustees had decided not to name a president. Even the new presiding professor had no tutoring assistant until later that spring—after the first students arrived.

What they saw that cold, drizzly morning must have been discouraging. Kemp Plummer Battle, the university's president eighty years later, reported:

As the sighing of the watery wind whistled through the leafless branches of tall oaks and hickories and the Davie Poplar, then in vigorous youth, all that met the eyes of the distinguished visitors were a two-storied brick building [Old East], the unpainted wooden house of the Presiding Professor, the avenue between them filled with stumps of recently felled trees, a pile of yellowish red clay, dug out for the foundation of the Chapel, or Person Hall, a pile of lumber collected for building Steward's Hall, a Scotch-Irish preacher-professor (Ker), in whose mind were fermenting ideas of infidelity, destined soon to cost him his place, and not one student.[3]

The delegation's only work that dreary morning was to hold brief opening ceremonies in North Wing (Old East) and to view the building and construction sites. They reported to a later trustees' meeting what they had seen and announced that "youth disposed to enter the University may come forward with assurance of being received."

The first student, the "precursor of a long line of seekers after knowledge," arrived two weeks later, on February 12, 1795.[4] His name was Hinton James, and he walked the entire distance from his native Wilmington to Chapel Hill to enroll. This same Hinton James became an energetic, enterprising student. His name appeared often on the faculty's roll of honor, his tastes following a scientific and practical bent. Among his essays were "The Uses of the Sun," "The Motions of the Earth," and "The Pleasures of College Life." James graduated in 1798 and became a successful civil engineer. Some of his work, stemming the floods and tides on the lower Cape Fear River, was still evident sixty years later.

How had these modest campus buildings, standing on a lonely hill in 1795, come to be? They had started in the earliest dreams of Scots and Scotch-Irish settlers, known as "dissenters" from the established Church of England, on North Carolina's western frontier. William Richardson Davie, the soldier-statesman who became father and founder of the university, spent his early youth in that region, reared in a Calvinist home. He arrived as a child from England with his parents to reside with his mother's brother, the Reverend William Richardson, a Presbyterian preacher, in the Waxhaws settlement on the North Carolina–South Carolina border.

The Waxhaws lay near the revolutionary hornets' nest of Mecklenburg County and the eighteenth-century frontier village of Salisbury. These pioneer people, largely Ulster Scot Presbyterians, Lutherans, and other Protestant sects, arrived mostly by way of the great road from Philadelphia. Some came through the port cities of Charleston and Wilmington. Sprinkled among them were older English settlers who migrated into eastern Carolina from Virginia and settled in the coastal plains, moving westward in succeeding generations.

These Presbyterians, according to one old chronicler, "kept the Sabbath and everything else they could get their hands on."[5] But their early preachers were also energetic schoolmasters, such stalwarts as the Reverend Samuel Eusebius McCorkle of Rowan and the Reverend David Caldwell of Guilford. Fleeing the religious tyranny of Europe, they brought their own austere pieties combined with a zeal for education. Whether that education should be state supported as well as church related became a hotly disputed question. It profoundly shook the university over the next two centuries.

The first attempt to establish a college at public expense occurred before the Revolution, in 1754. Part of a bill passed by the General Assembly and approved by Acting Royal Governor Matthew Rowan authorized a fund to support defense of Virginia against the French. It also aimed at promoting "order, Literature and True Religion in all parts of the Province."

As part of that program, the General Assembly earmarked £6,000 for "funding and endowing a Public School," subject to approval of the Crown. A year later, in 1755, the fund that had been set aside for education was "borrowed and employed for His Majesty's Service" for military purposes. Throughout the following decade Governor Arthur Dobbs and the legislature repeatedly sought to recover the fund for its original use. The Crown never concurred. When Parliament repaid Virginia and North and South Carolina for their support against the French, North Carolina's General Assembly tried to use some of the funds for "purchasing glebes" and "errecting and establishing a free school in each County." But the Royal Board of Trade and the legislature could never agree on this expenditure, and the plan died.[6]

The second attempt occurred in 1770. The Presbyterians of Mecklenburg County persuaded Royal Governor William Tryon, who had succeeded

Dobbs, to recommend legislative establishment of a "public seminary in some part of the back country of this Colony for the education of youth." The General Assembly passed such a bill on January 15, 1771, entitled "An Act for establishing and endowing of Queen's College in the Town of Charlotte in Mecklenburg County." The act would have created a board of trustees with power to select officers and tutors and to adopt rules "to be as near as may be agreeable to the Laws and Customs of Oxford and Cambridge or those of the Colleges of America."

But this charter failed to survive. It was granted in violation of a royal instruction to Governor Tryon that no schoolmaster from Great Britain should be permitted "to keep school" in the province without the license of the lord bishop of London. Governor Tryon tried to ease this concern by stipulating that the new president of Queen's be a member of the "Established Church of England." But that did not suffice.

Another part of the plan annoyed the Crown more: Financial support was to come from private sources and public taxation. The latter included "duty of six pence per gallon placed on all rum and spirituous liquors." Governor Tryon made a strong plea for this project, but neither Whitehall nor St. James would agree. In rejecting the plan, they charged that such an establishment would give "great and permanent Advantage to a sect of Dissenters from the Established Church who have extended themselves over the Province in very considerable numbers." Secondly, the Crown feared that such a tax would hurt "the consumption of British Spirits" and that it would be unfairly levied in only one colony.

The Crown sharply criticized Tryon for letting the project progress before obtaining approval. It was disallowed on April 22, 1772, but a year passed before action was certified to Governor Josiah Martin, Tryon's successor. Martin publicized the king's decision and warned that it be heeded. In the meantime the trustees of Queen's had already opened the college.[7]

What they did demonstrated the educational zeal of those backcountry folk, foreshadowing the approaching rebellion. They simply changed the institution's name from Queen's College to Queen's Museum and continued to operate it without benefit of charter or tax until 1777. Then it was rechartered under the name of Liberty Hall, in the spirit of the times, and moved to Salisbury.

The outbreak of the American Revolution in 1776 dramatically changed the rules. Acts of the legislature of North Carolina no longer needed the approval of the Crown. When the fledgling state's voters in 1776 held elections to select delegates to a congress at Halifax to frame a state constitution, those from the hornets' nest of Mecklenburg were instructed to "endeavor to obtain a law to establish a college in this county and to procure a handsome endowment for the same."

No detailed record of the action at Halifax survives, but the influence of four members of the constitutional convention, all former trustees of Queen's College, must have been substantial. Historians credit Mecklenburg's Waighstill Avery, a graduate of the College of New Jersey, later Princeton, as the architect of Article 41—the education article—of North Carolina's first constitution. R. D. W. Connor believed Avery, or others, borrowed almost verbatim from Pennsylvania's constitution, adopted forty-five days before the Halifax Convention. Delegates had before them the language of that constitution when they drafted Article 41, which read: "That a school or schools be established by the Legislature, for the convenient Instruction of Youth, with such Salaries to the Masters, paid by the Public, as may enable them to instruct at low prices; and all useful Learning shall be duly encouraged and promoted in one or more universities."

Those "golden words" (Battle's phrase) may have reflected Benjamin Franklin's influence. They became the constitutional foundation for North Carolina's university and, later, its public schools. The university, as a child of the Revolution, emerged directly from these eighteenth-century thrusts toward political liberty and public enlightenment.

Several conflicting forces were at work among the people of North Carolina in those days. On one hand the colonists, of varied European backgrounds, sought to free themselves from the political and religious domination of England and its established church. Convictions about separation of church and state were strongly reflected in one provision of the Halifax constitution of 1776: "That no clergyman, or preacher of the gospel, of any denomination, shall be capable of being a member, either of the Senate, House of Commons or Council of State, while he continues in the exercise of the pastoral function."

At the same time, the first impetus toward public education originated among the very Protestant congregations, mostly from the west, whose pastors were proscribed from holding public office. Davie, living in his uncle's home, grew up among these influences. His neighbor Rev. Samuel Eusebius McCorkle in Rowan became a singular champion of a public university.

Vigorous support, for another reason, also came from the landed gentry of the east. By background and education they had been closely associated with Church of England traditions. Their sons attended northern colleges, or even Eton and Oxford. They naturally sought better schooling opportunities nearer home. As mostly well-to-do Federalists, they feared the fervor inspired by the French Revolution stirring among the dissenters of the west.

The important leader in whom these diverse elements merged was William Richardson Davie, General Nathanael Greene's dynamic chief of cavalry against Lord Cornwallis. In his biography of Davie, Professor Blackwell Robinson sounded a theme which was to echo continually throughout the university's history: "In Davie," he wrote, "there were to converge the two forces in the state striving to provide the means of education for its people—the Ulster Scot Presbyterians of the Mecklenburg-Rowan region and the landed gentry of the East. These dual forces already had to their credit two tangible achievements, the founding of a college at Charlotte [Queen's] and the provision in the Revolutionary Constitution of 1776 for a state experiment in higher education."[8]

Davie's uncle, William Richardson, the Presbyterian pastor, served as a Queen's College trustee. Later Davie's father-in-law, General Allen Jones of Northampton County, and his more famous brother, Willie Jones of Halifax County (where Davie moved after the Revolution), were among eighteen members of the committee which wrote the constitution of 1776 containing the crucial Article 41.

In 1771, at the time of his moody uncle's death, Davie, then fifteen years old, had an unfortunate experience with religious zealotry. Robinson believes this episode influenced the young man's decision not to become a minister, as his uncle had planned.[9] After graduating from Princeton, Davie went instead to read law with Judge Spruce Macay at Salisbury, where Andrew Jackson later studied. Then he migrated east to Halifax to practice law, met his future wife, Sarah Jones, and went on to fame as founder of the university, governor of North Carolina, and an envoy appointed by President John Adams in 1800 to help stave off war with France.

Reared amid the revolutionary fervor of the Waxhaws and fired by his rebellious classmates at Princeton just prior to 1776, Davie strongly espoused the Patriot cause. Though influenced by his close association with the Presbyterian clergy, he broke with that faction. When he moved from the Calvinist west to Halifax, he became an enthusiastic Federalist, a deist, and a rationalist freethinker.[10] His doubts about the clergy were reflected in his relations with early Presbyterian leaders.

Moving from the west to the east, Davie quickly encountered the already deeply engrained sectionalism of North Carolina. It surfaced in the bitter fight over ratification of the federal constitution. It dominated the divisive struggle to build a university.

By all reports General Davie, who had once employed thirteen-year-old Andy Jackson as a battlefield messenger, was a splendid military officer. President Jackson considered him a model soldier. One of Jackson's biographers described Davie as "swift but wary; bold in planning enterprises but more cautious in execution; sleeplessly vigilant; untiringly active; one of those cool, quick men who apply masterwit to the art of war; who are good soldiers because they are earnest and clear-sighted men."[11]

For the young attorney in Halifax, striving to charter a public university became a difficult undertaking. Even after the surrender of Cornwallis, the evacuation of Wilmington, and the restoration of civil authority, North Carolina's resources and energies were so nearly exhausted that formal education became a low priority. Eight years passed before an attempt was made to comply with Article 41. Governor Alexander Martin, a popular public officer, sounded the first note in his opening address to the General Assembly of October 16, 1784: "Your schools of learning . . . are great objects of legislative attention which cannot be too often . . . held up to your view, that the mists of ignorance be dissipated and good morals cultivated."

The first recorded attempt to implement Article 41 came during that 1784 session of the General Assembly. William Sharpe, a representative from Rowan County, introduced a bill to establish "a University in the State to be distinguished by the title of the President and Trustees of the North Carolina University." The Reverend Samuel E. McCorkle, the Rowan County Presbyterian pastor and later the only preacher-teacher on the university's original Board of Trustees, helped draft the bill.[12] It was intended that Spruce Macay, under whom Davie read law, would introduce it, but he was riding circuit and was delayed.

Sharpe also introduced another bill, one to incorporate the Salisbury academy. The academy bill passed, but the university bill failed. "This might be attributed," historian Robinson thought, "to the fact that the conscientious Presbyterian divine, eschewing such mundane devices as a tax on spirituous liquors employed by Queen's College and the New Bern Academy as a basis for revenue, had devised a scheme by which a . . . tax was to be levied upon professional men, merchants and county officials and upon salaries." Its defeat was also due to the financial woes and general debilitation of the times, the scarcity of hard money, and fears of the more radical Republicans that a university would be used as "an engine of political propaganda and as a bulwark of aristocratic privilege."[13]

The same arguments arose in the ensuing years as Davie, by then a respected legislator, took the leading role in two major accomplishments: ratification of the federal constitution and chartering of the university. They took place at Fayetteville within twenty days of each other in 1789. Davie was at the helm of both, introducing the legislative bills and campaigning successfully to get them approved.

Davie had been a North Carolina delegate to the Philadelphia Constitutional Convention of 1787. There, as a figure of great strength and gifted with a sonorous and powerful voice, he spoke persuasively for forging a compromise on one deeply divisive question: whether slaves should be treated as property or as persons. Settlement of that issue became crucial, coalescing a favorable vote for the constitution.

Davie returned to North Carolina as an enthusiastic supporter of Federalism. North Carolina's mood still reflected fear of aristocratic control and centralized authority. State delegates rejected constitutional ratification in 1787. Only after the document was approved by all other colonies except Rhode Island—and after it seemed likely that a bill of rights would be added—did North Carolina convene a second convention and agree to enter the union, on November 23, 1789.

Davie proved equally adept at steering the university bill through the General Assembly, then also in session at Fayetteville. Elegantly graceful and commanding in manner, he sought the help of Governor Samuel Johnston and James Iredell, two influential Federalists. Together they worked to win a majority. Much of the anti-Federalism stemmed from fears that a university would be controlled by the eastern gentry. Many legislators had never enjoyed the benefits of education. Among the unschooled the plan was seen as a step toward a permanent aristocracy. For others the expense appeared burdensome.

Yet Davie used a combination of logic, satire, and eloquence to carry the day. Anti-Federalist sentiment eroded as other states joined the union. North Carolinians began to see that unless they changed their stance, they would be cut off from neighboring states and left in isolation. The very factors that pushed the state toward ratifying the Constitution also helped shape a majority for the university bill. Within four days of its introduction, Davie wrote Iredell: "The university bill will certainly pass."

On December 11, 1789, the General Assembly approved it. In the bill's preamble Davie expressed his views about the role of education. "In all well regulated government," he wrote, "it is the indispensable duty of every Legislature to consult the happiness of a rising generation and endeavour to fit them for an honourable discharge of the social duties of life, by paying the strictest attention to their education." It followed that a "university supported by permanent funds and well endowed, would have the most direct tendency to answer the above purpose."

The bill stipulated that the university's site not be within five miles of the seat of government or any place holding court. (Battle later speculated that this was aimed at avoiding "rowdyism and drunkenness during court week.") To a governing board that would be self-perpetuating it named forty of the prominent leaders of the state, headed by Governor Johnston. The legislation described various officers of the university and set forth their duties. It encouraged gifts and subscriptions by providing that anyone donating £10 within the next five years would be entitled to have one student educated free of tuition. Buildings might also be named for benefactors.

Following passage of the chartering legislation, the university's backers realized they had no funds for acquiring a site, erecting buildings, or hiring a faculty. So Davie, on December 22, 1789, sponsored and got enacted yet another bill, the University Endowment Law, better known in later years as the Escheats Act. It vested in the Board of Trustees "all monies due and owing the public of North Carolina either for arrearages under the former or present government" up to January 1, 1783. The act excepted monies or certificates due for the purchase of confiscated property, but it included "all the property that has heretofore or shall hereafter escheat to the state."[14]

This legislation described vast tracts of land in Western Carolina (later Tennessee) that had been warranted to revolutionary soldiers in return for wartime service. (For example: General Nathanael Greene received 25,000 acres.) But while such property provided great bounties in the long run, it also became a source of tedious litigation, creating hostility toward the university.

R. D. W. Connor wrote that its "liberal provisions" made the university "potentially one of the most richly endowed institutions of learning in the American Union, but many years were to pass before the trustees were able to turn these resources into ready cash."[15] President Battle commented that "the gift of the unclaimed land warrants was for years to the university like the cool waters near the parched lips of Tantalus." By vouchsafing such property, warriors who had lost their lives not only gained liberty for their country but became "unintentional benefactors of a great institution of learning."[16]

At its first meeting, on December 18, 1789, the Board of Trustees welcomed its first major endowment. Davie announced that General Benjamin Smith, a revolutionary officer of Brunswick County and later state governor, had donated to the university warrants for 20,000 acres of land in Tennessee. This ushered in decades of litigation between the university, the state of Tennessee, and the federal government over land ownership. Some lands had been deeded by the new federal government to the Cherokee and Chickasaw Indians, even as the state of North Carolina and its new university protested.

For a public university that remained otherwise unfunded by the state for almost a century, these land warrants and escheats monies became financial salvation.

But the university's sponsors remained frustrated. They had collected no substantial funds for either the purchase of a site or for buildings. In vexing deliberations during the following year they struggled to obtain such money and resources. In 1790 Governor Alexander Martin, president of the Board of Trustees, requested a loan from the General Assembly for securing a site and erecting buildings. The board campaigned for more private donations. But it made little headway and at a meeting in December of 1791 heard woeful reports on financing.

Then Davie again took charge. At the General Assembly's session in New Bern he led the drive to obtain a legislative loan of £5,000 ($10,000). At the end of December 1791 that campaign was successful.

Davie's contemporaries described his leadership as "magnificent." Judge Archibald Debow Murphey, one of the university's early graduates, declared later: "I was present in the House of Commons when Davie addressed that body upon the bill granting a loan of money to the trustees for erecting the buildings of this university and although more than 30 years have elapsed, I have the most vivid recollections of the greatness of his manner and the power of his eloquence upon that occasion. In the House of Commons he had no rival and upon all great questions which came before that body his eloquence was irresistible."[17]

The battle for the loan was hard fought. Much later it was converted into a gift. As such it became the only appropriation made to the university from tax funds until after the Civil War.

The trustees lost no time making use of the General Assembly's largesse. At a January 1792 meeting at New Bern, they set up a committee "to examine the most proper and eligible situation whereon to fix the university in the counties of Wake, Franklin, Orange, Granville, Chatham (or) Johnston." The board had in mind placing the university near the center of the state to make it accessible.

But for reasons not known, the committee appointed in January made no report. Further action took place at an August 1, 1792, meeting at Hillsboro where twenty-five of the university's forty trustees were present. Battle considered this a remarkably large turnout—"Patriotic sacrifice of comfort in the heated dog days."[18]

At that meeting the trustees moved decisively on the site selection. They adopted a proposal by Willie Jones that "the board will not determine on any given place; but the ballots shall be taken for a given point." Then they placed in nomination the following areas: Raleigh, in Wake County; Williamsboro, in Granville County; Hillsboro, in Orange County; Pittsboro, in Chatham County; Cyprett's Bridge, over New Hope Creek in Chatham County; Smithfield, in Johnston County; and Goshen, in Granville County.

On the following day, August 2, 1792, the board chose the area of Cyprett's (or Cipritz's) Bridge, later Prince's Bridge, on the great road from New Bern by Raleigh to Pittsboro. No record shows which trustees supported this choice, but a committee, again with Davie in the forefront, prepared an ordinance authorizing selection of a university site within fifteen miles of the bridge. It also elected a site committee, with one member from each of the state's judicial districts, to meet in Pittsboro on November 1, 1792, prepared to visit all places nominated.

At the Pittsboro meeting six of the eight commissioners met, ready to make the selection and to obtain not less than 640 acres. They were also empowered to secure 1,400 acres to serve as a farm and source of firewood and timber. Senator Frederick Hargett of Jones County was elected chairman. Members present included Alexander Mebane of Orange, James Hogg of Cumberland, William H. Hill of New Hanover, David Stone of Bertie, and Willie Jones of Halifax.

Battle, from his vantage point a century later, conjured up romantic visions of the commissioners' labors, none of which are reflected in their brief journal entry. He imagined how it must have been

> among the wooded hills of Chatham and Orange in the early days of November, when forests were clothed with their changing hues of russet and green, gold and crimson, when the squirrels chattered in the hickories and the deer peered curiously through the thick underwood, and the hospitable farmers welcome them with hearty greetings, and the good ladies brought out their foamiest cider and sweetest courtesies, while on the sideboard, according to the bad customs of that day, stood decanters of dark-hued rum and ruddy apple brandy and the fiery juice of the Indian corn, which delights to flow in the shining of the moon.[19]

The commissioners reported none of these romantic embellishments. Rather, chairman Hargett's prosaic account mentioned visiting various areas near Pittsboro, Haw River, and Raleigh, listing the hosts and the land and cash donations offered, all over a period of several days. Then on November 5 "the committee proceeded to view New Hope Chapel Hill in Orange County." And that was the site it chose.

The commissioners' report indicated few reasons for the choice, aside from the large acreage and cash donations guaranteed by the landowners. But a concerted campaign for New Hope Chapel Hill had been waged by one of the commissioners, James Hogg, described by Archibald Henderson as an "early American captain of industry."

This "canny Scotsman and expert realtor" had migrated from Scotland to North Carolina. In 1774 he brought a shipload of 280 persons to America, a number of whom settled in Orange County. Hogg, who lived at Cross Creek (later Fayetteville), "determined to exert all his influence in favor of New Hope Chapel Hill which he had often visited and regarded as the ideal spot for the university's location." He persuaded his Orange County friends to make generous offers of land and money.[20] Battle described most of them as "plain, honest, unambitious stock, possibly more moved to their generosity by the hope of increasing the value of the broad acres retained by them than by love of letters and far-seeing patriotism."[21]

Although fourteen sites were put in competition, the commissioners unanimously chose New Hope Chapel Hill and recommended it to the trustees at New Bern on December 3, 1792. The gifts of landholders, all conditioned on the university being located there, totaled 1,386 acres and £798 "or thereabouts." The donors were voted the "respective privileges of having one student educated at the said university free from any expense of tuition."

Among the twelve major donors of land and money were many of the leading residents of Orange County: Colonel John Hogan, Benjamin Yergan, Matthew McCauley, Alexander Piper, James Craig, Christopher Barbee, Edmund Jones, Mark Morgan, John Daniel, Hardy Morgan, Thomas Connelly, and William McCauley. Some of their descendants would become closely associated with the university.

But the donations of land and cash were not necessarily the only factors that attracted the commissioners to Chapel Hill. The intersection there of the great roads from Petersburg to Pittsboro and from New Bern toward Salisbury made it rather accessible. Equally alluring was the wild beauty of that hilltop forest described by Battle as situated on a "promontory of granite, belonging to the Laurentian system" and extending "into the sandstone formation to the east, which was once the bed of a long sheet of water stretching from near New York to the center of Georgia."[22] In the late nineteenth century the spacious depression east of Chapel Hill appeared to be the former bed of a "triassic sea," and local specimens from this primeval ocean bed revealed "ripple marks of the waves and of the prints of plants and animals found in its shallows."[23]

Davie himself, although not a member of the site committee, became enchanted with the place. In a vivid description, written the following September, when the trustees announced the sale of lots in the proposed adjoining village, the father of the university wrote:

> The seat of the University is on the summit of a very high ridge. There is a gentle declivity of 300 yards to the village, which is situated on a handsome plain, considerably lower than the site of the public buildings, but so greatly elevated above the neighboring country as to furnish an extensive and beautiful landscape, composed of the heights in the vicinity of Eno, Little and Flat Rivers.
>
> The ridge appears to commence about half a mile directly east of the buildings, where it arises abruptly several hundred feet. This peak is called Point Prospect.*
>
> There is nothing more remarkable in this extraordinary place than

*Point Prospect (site of Gimghoul Castle) has become Piney Prospect over the years. "In old times 'point' was pronounced 'pint' and the change was natural, especially as the hill has pines growing on it" (Battle, *History*, 1:26).

the abundance of springs of purest and finest water, which burst from the side of the ridge, and which have been the subject of admiration both to hunters and travelers ever since the discovery and settlement of that part of the country. . . .

The University is situated about 25 miles from the city of Raleigh, and 12 miles from the town of Hillsboro, and is said to be the best direction for the road. The great road from Chatham, and the country in the neighborhood of that county, to Petersburg, passes at present directly through the village . . . being the nearest and best direction.*

This town being the only seat of learning immediately under the patronage of the public, possessing the advantages of a central situation, on some of the most public roads in the state, in a plentiful country and excelled by few places in the world, either for beauty of situation or salubrity of air, promises, with all moral certainty, to be a place of growing and permanent importance.[24]

Davie's graphic description gave rise in later years to a purely apocryphal story that it was the university's distinguished father who "discovered" Chapel Hill. On a warm summer day, so the story goes, Davie and a group of trustees, exhausted by their search for a suitable site, sat down to rest beneath a giant poplar standing on the crest of a ridge near New Hope Chapel. Beneath its branches the weary trustees regaled themselves with "exhilarating beverages" and after a picnic lunch and a "refreshing nap" unanimously decided, under Davie's urging, that it was useless to proceed further. They settled on that spot. To commemorate this story, Cornelia Phillips Spencer in the late nineteenth century allegedly christened the tree Davie Poplar. Its antiquity, if not its association with Davie, is attested by Governor William D. Moseley, who in 1853 referred to it as "The Old Poplar" in a reminiscence of his days at the university in 1818.[25]

Even before the site had been chosen, the trustees began planning the university's first building. In August of 1792 they pondered building a three-story structure, but this plan was not then adopted. On December 8, 1792, they appointed a seven-man committee to supervise the erection of the building and to lay off and survey a town containing twenty-four lots of

*The great roads crossed just south of the site of the Carolina Inn. On the latter site, once the home of the Graves family, the ruins of a "rough little edifice" (New Hope Chapel) could still be seen in the Graves garden as late as 1826, according to the wife of Rev. James Phillips, who lived there (Henderson, Campus, p. 23).

two acres each and six lots of four acres each and "to sell and dispose of said lots at public vendue on 12 months credit."

In those days the professional architect had not yet emerged in America. As Dr. Henderson noted, all buildings were erected by contractors who bore the name "undertakers" (because they undertook the contract). After the board adjourned, four of the commissioners lingered to discuss the "most practicable and expeditious way to procure lime or shell" essential for making mortar for the building. They concluded that the best way was to transport it in boats up the Cape Fear River from Wilmington to Fayetteville. James Hogg, the trustee-merchant whose brother lived in Wilmington, was asked to attend to this.[26]

By April of 1793 the committee had contracted with George Daniel of Orange County to deliver 350,000 bricks for 40 shillings ($4) per thousand. On July 19 after considering a number of proposals by different contractors, they engaged James Patterson of Chatham County to build a 2-story brick building 96 feet, 7 inches long and 40 feet, 1½ inches wide for the sum of £2,500 ($5,000). The university would furnish the brick, sash weights, locks, hooks, fastenings, and paint. The contract stipulated that the building, to contain 16 rooms and 4 passages, was to be finished by November 1, 1794. According to the initial master plan, it was to be one (the north) wing of a larger building and "was placed accordingly."

Henderson provided another interesting insight about the first building. The original design of what is now known as Old East, drawn up by John Conroy at a cost of £10, "indicates a preoccupation with Oriental ideas in consonance with Moslem *mores*. In the East it was customary to bury the dead with head directed toward the east, to face toward the east in crying the *muezzin* (call to prayer) and to build temples and mausoleums fronting toward the rising sun."

Henderson speculated that the fashion of "Orientalization," as it was called in architectural circles, "doubtless had its origin in the Masonic Order and Conroy may well have been influenced in his design by Davie who became Grand Master of Masons in North Carolina in 1792." Conroy's original plans called for an avenue to stretch eastward from the east front of the "main building" all the way to Point Prospect.[27]

With building plans under way, the committee on August 10, 1793, met at New Hope Chapel Hill and laid out the sites both for the university buildings, offices, avenues, and "ornamental grounds" and for the adjacent village. They used a map, which is preserved in the university archives, provided by John Daniel, a surveyor. For the sum of £100 ($200) the commissioners purchased eighty acres of land owned by Hardy Morgan that "ran up angularly" into the donated holdings.

In the meantime the trustees busied themselves with procuring teachers, even before the first building had been finished. A notice in the *North Carolina Journal* of Halifax on December 12, 1792, set forth the courses of instruction: "The study of languages, particularly the English; History, ancient and modern; the Belle Lettres, Logic and Moral Philosophy; the Knowledge of Mathematics and Natural Philosophy, Agriculture and Botany, with the principles of Architecture. . . . Gentlemen conversant in these branches of Science and Literature, and who can be well recommended, will receive very handsome encouragement by the Board. The exercises of the institution will commence as early as possible after the completion of the buildings of the university which are to be contracted for immediately."

Simultaneously, groups of trustees worked to encourage private donations. Davie and his uncle-in-law, Willie Jones, who had led opposing Federalist and anti-Federalist forces in the fight to ratify the federal constitution, joined hands to solicit contributions in Halifax matching the nearly £1,000 of gifts in Orange County. In "a plea for donation" in the *North Carolina Journal* of January 9, 1793, they emphasized that "a liberal education of the youth of any country must tend to promote the happiness and prosperity of the people."

Their plea produced £804 by summer, but it also aroused critics. One, an evidently literate gentleman with a caustic pen, in letters to the *North Carolina Journal* signed IGNORAMUS, expressed surprise that Jones and Davie ("the greatest characters in this state") should endorse a university. Writing that such higher education was premature (and could be procured for those who desired it elsewhere in the country or Europe), IGNORAMUS proposed instead a "public school to be established and supported in every county by a general tax on the inhabitants." He also criticized the university as a place where "students of moderate prospects will endeavor to keep pace in appearance and extravagance, with the sons of our Nabobs who are born to affluence."

Neither Jones nor Davie replied directly to these attacks. But a response did come from a protégé of Davie, William Hill Brown, the Boston-born "first American novelist" who had been visiting relatives in Murfreesboro and, since the preceding summer, had taken a course of legal instruction in

Davie's office. Writing under the pen name COLUMBUS, Brown, in a letter to the *North Carolina Journal* on July 10, 1793, expressed surprise that learning should be opposed in a "young Republican country" since the "experience of mankind . . . exhibits . . . the truth that knowledge must be the guardian of liberty."[28]

Another, more comprehensive and eloquent letter called on all friends of learning, religion, and liberty to support higher education. "Learning," wrote this FRIEND OF THE UNIVERSITY, "is friendly to religion. It corrects prejudice, superstition and enthusiasm and gives right views of God. . . . Friends to a republican government! Give. A republican government is founded on virtue. It demands an equal and general diffusion of knowledge, without which it cannot exist. Where ignorance prevails, there prevail savage ferocity and despotism. Where learning is confined to a few, there is, or will be, a proud imperious Aristocracy, or the government of Kings."[29]

This debate continued as the trustees moved toward opening the university's doors. By July 22, 1793, commissioners Davie, Mebane, Alfred Moore, and Thomas Blount were able to announce that the village lots would be sold on the premises on Saturday, October 12, the same day as the cornerstone laying for North Wing (later Old East).

Davie, ever in the forefront, organized the university's first major public event. How carefully he planned the ceremony, which since 1877 has been observed as the university's birthday, is evident from his letter of invitation to his old friend and law teacher, Judge Spruce Macay of Salisbury: "As one who sat at the feet of Gamaliel in the intermission between tours of duty in the field, I write to press for your attendance at Chapel Hill in Orange on October (12)—laying of a cornerstone, great doings of the Masonic brethren, with your correspondent wielding a silver trowel and setting a stone in mortar. All are expecting our worthy and learned friend Dr. [Samuel Eusebius] McCorkle, *pater benignus*, who got up the first University bill. It is right and proper that he would now stand atop the Mount of Fulfillment and solemnly invoke blessings upon this embryo college."[30]

Dr. McCorkle, a graduate of Princeton and proprietor of Zion-Parnassus Academy at Thyatira Presbyterian Church near Salisbury, played an interesting role in the university's birth. Besides "getting up the first University bill," he became the only preacher-teacher on the Board of Trustees. Unlike his contemporary Dr. David Caldwell and other clerics, he saw roles for both private and public education in North Carolina. His Thyatira church congregation made the only recorded contribution from a religious group to the "embryo college" in its infant years. The trustees asked him to make the cornerstone-laying address on that first October 12.

Battle hailed the event, occurring on a bright autumn day when "the maple trees flamed red in the eager air," as one of the greatest in North Carolina's history.* Archibald Henderson ranked it with the Halifax Resolves of April 12, 1776, and the ratification of the federal constitution on November 21, 1789. By all reports, including Davie's own, it was a proud and inspiring moment.

On that day, in Henderson's account, a procession of dignitaries, stately in mien and conscious of the far-reaching importance of the occasion, wended its way eastward among the great trees and the gently undulating slopes of New Hope to the "spot destined to become eternally historic." Notable among the trustees in that procession were the commissioners who located the site and planned the town: Alfred Moore, small in stature, neat in dress, graceful in manners, and six years later to receive appointment to the U.S. Supreme Court; John Haywood, able, genial, and beloved for forty years as treasurer of North Carolina; John Williams, founder of Williamsboro, judge of the highest court in North Carolina, and representative in the congress of the confederation; William Henry Hill of Wilmington, graduate of Harvard, first district attorney of the U.S. for North Carolina, and member of the U.S. Congress; General Thomas Blount, commissioner to locate both the state capital and the state university and representative in the U.S. Congress; General Alexander Mebane, opponent of ratification of the federal constitution and member of the U.S. Congress; and Colonel Frederick Hargett, long a state senator from Jones County.

But two figures dominated the scene: Davie, who had guided the chartering legislation through the General Assembly and had raised funds for getting it started; and McCorkle, the orator of the day, who had helped prepare the first university bill and was the preacher-schoolmaster who espoused public education. Henderson described McCorkle as more than six feet tall "with light hair falling on his shoulders and clear blue eyes, a living replica of Thomas Jefferson in his later years."

At his side, the resplendent Masonic regalia of North Carolina's grand master contrasting with Dr. McCorkle's somber ministerial black, marched "the handsome William Richardson Davie, one of the most gifted and

---

*The autumnal colors do not appear in full as early as October 12.

Davie lays the cornerstone of Old East, 1793.
(Yackety-Yack sketch, North Carolina Collection, University of North Carolina
Library, Chapel Hill)

cultured men on the continent." He was the star of this first ceremonial event of the university.[31]

Davie's account is less colorful. It appeared in two North Carolina newspapers with varying details, but Battle tells us it was written "by Davie himself, the chief actor."

"On the 12 inst.," Davie wrote,

> the Commissioners appointed by the Board of Trustees of the university of this State, met in Chapel Hill for the purpose of laying the cornerstone of the present building and disposing of the lots in the village. A large number of brethren of the Masonic order from Hillsborough, Chatham, Granville and Warren attended to assist at the ceremony of placing the cornerstone; and the procession for this purpose moved from Mr. Patterson's at 12 o'clock in the following order: The Masonic Brethren in their usual order of procession, the Commissioners, the Trustees not Commissioners, the Hon. Judge Macay and other public officers; then followed the gentlemen of the vicinity. On approaching the south end of the building, the Masons opened to the right and left and the Commissioners, etc., passed through and took their place. The Masonic procession then moved on round the foundation of the building and halted, with their usual ceremonies, opposite the southeast corner, where WILLIAM RICHARDSON DAVIE, Grand Master of the Fraternity, etc., in this State, assisted by two Masters of the Lodges and four other officers, laid the cornerstone, enclosing a plate to commemorate the transaction.*

The Rev. Dr. McCorkle then addressed the Trustees and spectators in an excellent discourse suited to the occasion. . . . He concluded with these observations:

"The seat of the University was next sought for, and the public eye selected Chapel Hill—a lovely situation—in the center of the state—at a convenient distance from the Capital—in a healthy and fertile neighborhood. May this hill be for religion as the ancient hill of Zion; and for

---

*Sometime during the decade 1865–75 "the cornerstone was despoiled and its contents removed." The plate disappeared for forty years. In 1916 Thomas Foust, class of 1903 and proprietor of a foundry in Clarksville, Tennessee, recognized the name "Davie" and recovered the plate from a scrap heap. It was returned to Chapel Hill and is now preserved in the North Carolina Collection at Wilson Library (Connor, *Documentary History*, 1:242).

literature and the muses, may it surpass the ancient Parnassus! We this day enjoy the pleasure of seeing the cornerstone of the University, its foundations, its materials and the architect for the building; and we hope ere long to see its stately walls and spire ascending to their summit. Ere long we hope to see it adorned with an elegant village, accommodated with all the necessaries and conveniences of civilized society."

This discourse was followed by a short but animated prayer, closed with the united *amen* of an immense concourse of people.

The Commissioners then proceeded to sell the lots in the village; and we have the pleasure to assure the public that although there were but 29 lots, they sold for upwards of 1,500 pounds, which shows the high idea the public entertains of this agreeable and healthful situation.[32]

Along with his other splendid traits, the father of the university obviously lacked no personal pride in his own accomplishments. Battle, writing much later, showed equal fervor for the other principal figure in the ceremony, McCorkle. "We thank thee," he wrote, "for thy golden words, venerable father of education in our State."

McCorkle's references to Zion and Parnassus as the university's antecedents vividly described the two major forces shepherding it toward birth. Presbyterian preacher-schoolmasters and laymen provided the thrust for instilling the aim of education in North Carolina's first constitution. Then Federalists and Republican factions east and west joined hands, under Davie's leadership, to put public education ahead of sectionalism and political strife.

Neither Davie nor McCorkle could have fully foreseen what they wrought. But they may have had some inkling. Davie, as Henderson noted, was not an educator by profession, but he grasped the cardinal fact that the training of public leaders in a democracy could be accomplished only through "the establishment of first-class academies and a state university." He knew that self-government and liberty, attained through revolution, could not be preserved without education, and his university was the child of that dream.

While ever the devout cleric, McCorkle rose above the conventional wisdom of his day to perceive that religious learning alone was not enough—that Zion must be accompanied by Parnassus—in the ongoing enlightenment of the human spirit.

THIS EMBRYO COLLEGE,

1795–1804

The harmony evident on that festive October day at the cornerstone-laying ceremony did not long prevail. For, as Battle noted, the university was born "in troublous times." Its struggles "were not only with want and penury, but with ignorance and prejudice and a wild spirit of lawlessness."[1]

"The rage of party" gripped North Carolina. Jeffersonian Republicans sympathetic with the French Revolution found themselves arrayed against Hamiltonian Federalists whom they called "British bootlickers." Political passions ran high. The largely Federalist gentry who founded the university soon splintered in party strife that erupted among members of the Board of Trustees and the faculty. Sectional feeling—pitting east against west— exploded with a vengeance.

When the eastern-dominated Board of Trustees came to consider who should become the university's first administrator, the Reverend Mr. Mc-Corkle, the Princeton-educated Presbyterian schoolmaster from the piedmont, seemed the logical choice. As one of the original trustees (*pater benignus,* in Davie's description), he was a spirited supporter of public education, highly qualified as an innovative instructor of youth. His Zion-Parnassus Academy near Salisbury included a department for teachers that, according to Dr. C. Alphonso Smith, was "the first normal school in America."[2]

Yet the Thyatira schoolmaster failed to win the support of the one person whose influence overshadowed all others. Davie respected McCorkle's erudition but distrusted his executive ability. There was a story about his farming—that the pastor carried his theological books into the fields to read between intervals of manual labor. "A man on business found him stretched out, deep in his tomes, while the Negro plowman was asleep under a tree and the mule was cropping the corn tops."[3]

Davie's lukewarm opinion of McCorkle stemmed from other differences. The general distrusted preachers, perhaps a reaction against his Calvinist upbringing in the piedmont. Davie refused to follow his uncle's urgings that he become a minister. Instead, after finishing his legal education at Salisbury, he moved to Halifax where his Federalist sentiments became strong. When he married into the well-to-do Jones family, he became part of the monied plantation society of northeastern Carolina and plunged into politics. Like Benjamin Franklin and other fathers of the U.S. Constitution, he became a deist. He and McCorkle differed on the doctrine of revelation.[4]

Those who detected "freethinking" in the general's makeup cited a letter of condolence he wrote his friend John Haywood on the occasion of Haywood's wife's death: "I regret the various causes which produced your absence from the Board," he wrote. "However, as the Arabs say 'God would have it so and man must submit.' Under misfortunes like yours there is no comfort because nothing can be substituted. The only recourse for the human mind in such cases is a kind of philosophical fortitude, the calm result of time, reason and more reflection."

In another letter Davie criticized the influence of preachers: "Bishop Pettigrew has said it [the university] is a very dissipated and debauched place. Some priests have also done us the same good office to the westward. Nothing it seems goes well that these *men of God* have not had some hand in." Battle was disturbed by Davie's views and feared he had "imbibed some of the skepticism so prevalent among the educated class."[5]

There was another difference. Davie and McCorkle disagreed on whether the classics or science should predominate in the curriculum. McCorkle had chaired a trustee committee in 1792 which drew up the university's preliminary education plan. It was strongly classical. In December 1795 Davie offered a new plan, after working on it for at least a year, placing more emphasis on the sciences, and it was adopted. Latin and Greek were not mentioned. "Too much of a pragmatist to throw out classical studies," Connor wrote of this document, "Davie solved the problem by placing the 'bourgeois' sciences on an equal plane with the 'aristocratic' classics."[6] Battle later expressed surprise at Davie's liberality. His plan was far ahead of its time, he noted, and anticipated the work of Jefferson at the University of Virginia.[7]

In addition to philosophy, the languages, mathematics, and history, the curriculum included the study of chemistry, the philosophy of medicine, astronomy and geography, and agriculture and mechanics. "The scientific interests and the liberality of the curriculum appear to be even more advanced than the plan proposed by Franklin or any other man of the time. Science, English and history were to be the core of the curriculum. The classics, although offered, were to be the electives."[8]

When the trustees met on December 21, 1793, following the Old East cornerstone-laying ceremony, there were no applicants for the job of presiding professor. No records of the board's deliberations exist, but seven men were placed in nomination, including McCorkle. At least six of the seven, Davie's sentiments to the contrary, were ministers, probably because men of the cloth had the most acceptable academic credentials in those days.

At a meeting early the following year the board selected as the university's first presiding professor the Reverend David Ker, a thirty-six-year-old Ulster Scot graduate of the University of Dublin who had emigrated from Ireland to the United States in 1791. Most recently he had been a Presbyterian pastor in Fayetteville, also conducting a high school there. Ker's tenure at Chapel Hill survived only eighteen months. Because of his strong Jeffersonian views, he became a man of controversy. Archibald Henderson described him as a person of "high character, a learned classical scholar." But he also quoted others as saying Ker was "like Napoleon, grand, gloomy and peculiar."

We get another glimpse of Ker through the letters of Charles Wilson Harris, Princeton graduate and the university's first tutor (of mathematics), in the spring of 1795. Harris wrote to his uncle, Dr. Charles Harris, a Concord physician, that Chapel Hill was a lonely place. "My only resort is to Mr. Ker, who makes ample amends to me for the want of any other. He is a violent Republican and is continually deprecating the aristocratic principles which have lately prevailed in our executive [President Washington]."[9]

Ker faced frustrating duties. Following Hinton James's arrival on February 9, 1795, other students began to show up as news of the university's opening spread across the state. Some were delayed by the bad roads of a bitter winter. Chapel Hill's forest wilderness revealed only one building completed and several others under construction. It was a humble beginning.

As more students arrived, Ker divided them into four literary classes. The costs of tuition varied but seemed, overall, modest: $8.00 a year for reading, writing, arithmetic, and bookkeeping; $12.50 for the languages, geography, history, and the belles lettres; and $15.00 for the sciences, including astronomy, natural philosophy, moral philosophy, chemistry, geometry, and agriculture. Two-thirds of these fees went to Ker, who, as professor of humanity, also received a salary of $300 a year plus residence in the president's house, then under construction on the site of the present Swain Hall on Cameron Avenue. Charles Harris, the first tutor, received $100 annual salary plus one-third of the tuition money, free board at Commons, and use of a room in Old East.

Students were allowed, but not compelled, to live in Old East and board at Commons. The first steward's house arose beside Old East, and the trustees appointed John Taylor of Raleigh as first steward. Taylor, commonly known as Buck, was a veteran of the Revolution, a "man of strong character and resolute will, of pronounced eccentricity and grim disposition."[10] His wages were $30 per student per year. He was allowed the use of ten acres of the old field adjoining the steward's house for gardening. He also had permission to "cut up and use for fuel" timber that was blown down but not to "fell a tree" without permission of the trustees.

The board directed Taylor to provide for the tables a "clean cloth every day." Breakfast was at 8:00 A.M., dinner at 1:00 P.M., and supper "before or after candlelight at the discretion of the faculty." The trustees decreed that breakfast include a "sufficient quantity of good coffee and tea or chocolate" with "warm roll or loaf of wheat or corn flower" and a "sufficient quantity of butter." Dinners were to consist of a "dish or cover of bacon and greens or beef and turnips, also a sufficient quantity of fresh meats or fowls, or puddings and tarts, with wheat and corn bread." For supper the students got coffee, tea, or milk with bread or biscuit and potatoes, and all other kinds of vegetable food as available.[11]

Whether the boys got this fare regularly became a matter of controversy. There was abundant room for differences between the steward and his hungry patrons. The *North Carolina Journal* commended the food as having "exceeded the expectations both of students and of strangers." But this did not coincide with reports from Davie's own sons, Hyder Ali* and Allen, who were accustomed at home to the best fare of the land. They complained. So did the Pettigrew boys, John and Ebenezer, sons of the Reverend Charles Pettigrew. They criticized exorbitant prices for bed and board.

---

*Davie's oldest son, Hyder Ali, was named for an anti-British Oriental potentate, a custom of the times.

Drawing of Old East by student John Pettigrew, 1799.
(North Carolina Collection, University of North Carolina Library, Chapel Hill)

Although Buck Taylor was not easily deterred by criticism and knew how to put down mass revolt with a strong hand, he gave up the stewardship after three years and was succeeded in 1797 by another veteran of the Revolution, Major Pleasant Henderson. The new steward served four years, during a period of bitter faculty-student controversy. The students protested against Henderson's fare. The trustees' visitation committee reported that the steward "invariably serves mutton and bacon too fat to be eaten," which had "nearly starved the boys." Henderson was outraged and defended his food. He said little mutton was served, but the amount provided was due to the shortage of beef, shoats, and chickens. He deplored the charge that the middlings should have been discarded and insisted on "the golden mean of fat along with lean."[12]

The trustees established stringent rules for student behavior and duties. The steward saw to it that the boys' rooms were swept and cleaned once a day and that fresh water was brought from the spring four times a day. "No drink other than water" was authorized. Students paid $30 a year for board and $5 for room rent. The steward furnished tables and bedsteads, but the students provided their own bedding as well as wood and candles for their chambers.

Despite being passed over for presiding professor, McCorkle seemingly took no offense and continued to perform important duties as university trustee. He wrote bylaws which the board adopted on February 6, 1795. They required student attendance at prayer "thrice a day," including services at sunrise. The presiding officer was to examine students each Sunday evening on questions given them previously "on the general principles of morality and religion." Monitors were appointed to make sure there was no profane language or gambling or "any disrespectful remarks about religion or any religious denomination." McCorkle's bylaws included a phrase typical of the traditions of the day: Students were to "treat each other according to the *honor due each class*" and to "cleanse their beds and rooms of bugs every two weeks." Saturday afternoons were left open for "amusements."

The trustees decreed that punishments would consist largely of suspension (for from two weeks to six months), depending on the infraction. But, as Battle noted, this was like throwing Brer Rabbit into the briar patch— "injurious to scholarship but jolly for the offender." Often the suspended student engaged board a few miles from Chapel Hill and had a good time "rusticating, reading novels, hunting or fishing."[13]

During the first term, in the spring of 1795, tutor Charles Harris wrote his uncle optimistic letters about the curriculum. "We have begun to introduce, by degrees, the regulations of the university and as yet have not been disappointed," he wrote in April. "There is one class in natural philosophy and geography and four in languages. The constitution of this college is on a more liberal plan than any in America. . . . The notion that true learning consists rather in exercising the reasoning faculties and laying up a store of useful knowledge, than in overloading the memory with words of a dead language, is becoming daily more prevalent. It appears hard to deny a young Gentleman the honor of a College after he has with much labor acquired a competent knowledge of the sciences."

But this optimism proved short-lived. Vast numbers of students, it was discovered, had come ill-prepared. Archibald Henderson thought this failure was due mostly to the disturbed conditions following the Revolution when there were few secondary academies. Before 1800, North Carolina led the states in chartering academies, but not all of the two dozen established before 1795 were still in operation. Such education was not readily available.[14]

As a result, by the end of the first academic year in July 1795, when the enrollment had risen to forty-one, about half the students could not continue their education without remedial instruction. Accordingly, the trustees established a preparatory department. First they rented and then built a house for a "grammar school" and advertised for additional teachers. Eventually the school was located on the edge of the campus near the intersection of present Henderson and Rosemary streets (near the present post office).

By December 1795 Davie had presented a new curriculum plan for the grammar school. During two decades of operation, it was "one of the most efficient and well conducted classical schools in North Carolina," and "some of the ablest and most representative North Carolinians were prepared here for the university. . . . The discipline was strict and rigorous, and corporal punishment freely practiced."[15] Its graduates were admitted to the university without examination. But as the number of academies grew, its enrollment steadily declined, and the school was discontinued in 1819.

Even while Ker and Harris struggled to get classes started, the trustees had other projects under way. The industrious Davie chaired a committee that designed a new seal for the university. The committee "chose the face of Apollo, the God of Eloquence, and his emblem the rising sun as expressive of the dawn of higher education in our state."[16]

As work progressed on the president's house and the chapel, named for General Thomas Person, the trustees authorized plans for the "principal building." First named Main and later South, it was to be built adjacent to Old East and to have three stories containing twenty-four lodging rooms, a hall, a library, and several classrooms. But financing and construction moved slowly, and it was not completed until 1814.

In the summer of 1795 Charles Harris reported to his uncle the launching of a museum. The only "curiosity yet received," he noted, was "an ostrich egg from Judge Williams." Later Davie and other trustees enlarged the collection, which eventually was located in Person Hall. Probably the first piece of scientific equipment owned by the university was a compass given by the legislature on December 21, 1789. Among Davie's contributions were two medals from Bonaparte "in bronze representing him at the Battle of Marengo," the tooth of a mammoth, various Indian ornaments, and coins and paper money of all descriptions.

The trustees allocated $200 to Dr. Hugh Williamson for buying books. He was the trustee and College of Philadelphia graduate whom Battle credited with emphasizing the curriculum's scientific bent. At the same time, Davie took charge of organizing the first library. Several trustees donated books. Davie himself gave more than a dozen, including Gibbon's *Decline and Fall of the Roman Empire* and Hume's *History of England.*

Charles Harris had a hand in establishing the university's famous dialectic and philanthropic literary societies. As a student at Princeton, he had admired its renowned Whig Society. Harris's name appeared first on the list of signers of the articles of incorporation of the Debating Society founded on June 3, 1795. Its first president was James Mebane of Orange County.

The founders described as its purpose the cultivation of lasting friendships and useful knowledge. Each session featured a debate followed by discussion. The society had elaborate rules, including an admission fee of 25 cents and a prohibition against wearing hats. The first motion made after the society's founding was for purchasing books.

Later that month it was agreed that the society would be divided and enlarged. Students established a new organization called the Concord Society. Battle surmised that this involved an element of party feeling. He associated the name *Concord* with Jeffersonian democracy as was the name later adopted, *Philanthropic,* and the addition of the word *liberty* to the society's motto.

In 1796 the societies chose new Greek names, probably because it "occurred to members that English names were not of sufficient dignity."[17] Thus the Greek equivalents of *Debating* and *Concord* became *Dialectic* and *Philanthropic.* For a while students might join either group, but eventually the Di became the society for students from the west, the Phi for students from the east. In 1848, the Di occupied a new debating hall in Old West, the Phi similar quarters in Old East. After the construction of two new buildings in the mid-nineteenth century the societies moved from Old East and Old West and made their headquarters there—the Di in New West, and the Phi in New East.

The societies became influential on the campus. They had a member designated as Censor Morum who inspected the conduct and morals of members—such matters as inattention to studies and behavior reflecting "disgrace" on fellow members. Among the early questions debated were "Is suicide justifiable in certain cases?" (decided in the negative), "Is dueling consistent with the laws of honor and justice?" (decided in the affirmative), and "Is the use of tobacco pernicious?" (decided in the affirmative).

Philosophical differences within the university family intensified soon after Ker's appointment. In a letter to his friend John Haywood, written in November 1794, before the university's doors opened, Davie commented, "*Entre nous,* the institution should be committed to other hands than our present professor of humanity."[18]

From the beginning Ker's views troubled the board's religiously pious members, led by McCorkle. They believed Ker was developing into a "furious Republican" and an "outspoken infidel." Battle put it this way: "It was a great misfortune that Ker the next year went off into infidelity and wild democracy, thus raising up two sets of enemies in the Board of Trustees, Christians and Federalists, so that he deemed it prudent after 18 months to resign his charge."[19]

David Ker's later career proved he was a man of considerable ability. After becoming a merchant in Lumberton, he turned to the study of law, migrated to Mississippi where he became a clerk of the superior court and was appointed a territorial judge by President Jefferson. He became known as a fine classical scholar and an able and impartial judge.[20]

Even before Ker resigned under duress, the trustees had decided that McCorkle should replace him. In January 1796 they elected the Thyatira schoolmaster professor of moral philosophy without first informing him of their hope that he would become presiding professor after Ker resigned. But when they discussed their plans with McCorkle, he demanded certain terms of employment. He requested assurances of a house allowance equal to that of the president's, should he later be replaced by someone else. The board refused those terms and in July 1796 named Charles Harris to take temporary charge until the next board meeting. (Harris had already informed the board that he intended to resign and seek instruction in the law.)

Davie, still opposing McCorkle, bore the responsibility for refusing to accept his rather modest terms. The general's stand soured relations with his friend and co-Federalist, General John Steele of Salisbury, who was an uncle of McCorkle's wife. In a scathing letter to Davie written when the latter was leaving for his mission to France in 1799 (and quoting an earlier epistle of similar opinion), General Steele declared that he himself had "no sons to educate" and that his nephew, McCorkle's son, was "relieved of the humiliation of acquiring an education at an institution whose outset was characterized by acts of ingratitude and insult toward his father."[21]

Davie and Steele later resolved their differences. As it turned out, Ker's eventual successor, the Reverend Joseph Caldwell, who came to Chapel Hill later that year from Princeton, had strong classicist and religious views resembling those of McCorkle. On both these subjects Davie remained adamant. His education plan, which the trustees adopted as a replacement and enlargement of McCorkle's, was progressive for its time. It emphasized the sciences and utilitarian pragmatism. Davie wrote in its preamble: "In every free government the law emanates from the people. . . . The people should receive an education to enable them to direct the laws, and the political part of this education should be consonant to the Constitution, under which they live."

Ker's ideas were part of the emerging Jeffersonian Republicanism of the times. They shook the Federalist trustees' confidence in his leadership and marked the beginning of a period of political tension on the campus. Tutor Charles Harris, who had become presiding professor as Ker departed in July 1796, had already announced his intentions to pursue the law. It was intimated that he, too, had been attacked by the virus of skepticism.

Harris became the link with Princeton that brought Joseph Caldwell to Chapel Hill. Harris remembered Caldwell's character and reputation in the class ahead of him. It was on Harris's recommendation that the trustees asked the twenty-three-year-old Presbyterian minister to become tutor of mathematics and eventually presiding professor. The trustees discovered that meager financial resources made it difficult to attract mature personnel.[22]

Caldwell, a youth of scholarly reserve and sturdy Calvinist views, had no idea what troubles lay ahead when he packed his bags toward the end of October 1796 and departed from Princeton for Chapel Hill by way of the great road through Petersburg. When offered the job of presiding professor, he accepted only "with great reluctance."

Shortly after reaching Chapel Hill, Caldwell visited the legislature at Raleigh where he watched Davie in action. The general appeared to him as a "man of good abilities" and "like a parent struggling for the welfare and happiness of his children." To the young Princeton tutor North Carolina seemed to be "swarming with lawyers. . . . Religion is in so little vogue and such a state of depression, that it affords no prospects sufficient to people here to undertake its cause." One reason it has so little influence, he wrote a friend at Princeton, "is that it is taught only by ranters with whom it seems to consist only in the power of their throats and the wildness and madness of their gesticulations and distortions."[23]

Caldwell's Princeton friend John Henry Hobart expressed strong opinions of his own: "It is hoped," he wrote, "that the rays of light from your university, the Sun of Science, will illuminate the darkness of society, and chase away ignorance and vice. . . . With all due respect to the faculty of the University of North Carolina . . . they seem to constitute as motley a group as I have lately heard of. Presbyterians and Arians, infidels and Roman Catholics. Bless me, what a collection. The Age of Reason has surely come."[24]

Hobart's comments were directed at the university's small staff of scholars who were embroiled in bitter controversy among themselves. Samuel A. Holmes, first a tutor and later a professor of languages, carried his Republican views to an extreme, encouraging his students to defy faculty authority. By expounding his atheistic notions, he so horrified his colleagues, including Caldwell, that he was forced to resign. Nicholas Delavaux, the French Catholic teacher in the grammar school, likewise resigned because of differences with his fellow professors, although trustee James Hogg had a high opinion of his "grammatical accuracy" and Davie complimented his teaching ability.

Despite their clash over education and religion, Davie and Caldwell came to respect each other. Caldwell supported the traditional classics curriculum based on Princeton's. He considered the concept of free mass education, designed for public leadership, impossible to achieve. In 1803, prior to being named president of the university and a short time before Davie moved to South Carolina, Caldwell wrote: "The university early excited expectations which were unfortunately too sanguine and premature to be realized. Though the attainment of knowledge may be rendered comparatively easy, it is chimerical to propose that it shall be universally, or totally, without expense."[25]

Caldwell reported to his Princeton friend a conversation with Davie about the "evidences of Christianity," but he did not say whether the general was much impressed.[26] However, the savage turn of events in France, the reign of terror after the French Revolution, persuaded Davie to revert to some of the Calvinist views of his youth. In a letter to James Hogg in August 1797, he opposed the presentation of "plays" at Chapel Hill. "Acting a whole play is absurd. . . . If the faculty insists upon this kind of exhibition, the Board must interfere; our object is to make the students *men* not *players*. I wish you would mention this matter to Mr. Caldwell."[27]

Debates among students in the university's societies reflected the decline of the nation's friendship with France. In 1795 they had endorsed an American alliance with France in its war with Britain. By 1798 the issue had become American war against France.[28] Commenting on these shifting views Connor wrote: "No wonder the Republicans of North Carolina bitterly denounced the university as a stronghold of Federalism."[29]

While Davie became disillusioned about the drift of national politics, his support for the university never flagged. He continued his activities in its behalf after his election as governor in 1798 and during the following year, when he accepted President John Adams's appointment as a commissioner to The Hague to negotiate with Napoleon over threatening war with France.

Despite his interest in deism, Davie pushed for completion of the university's chapel, later named Person Hall. It became the nation's second-oldest permanent building on a state university campus. While the exact date of the chapel's completion is unknown, it was probably used at the university's first graduation exercises in July 1798.

Davie also encouraged work on Main (or South) Building, which was slowly rising near Old East. It had progressed enough by April 14, 1798, for the laying of the cornerstone. "The Most Worshipful General Davie, Grand Master, assisted by a respectable number of the craft" again performed the ceremonies assisted by trustees, council of state members, judges, members of the bar, the grand jury from Hillsborough, and 116 students.[30] Professor Caldwell delivered the prayer and dedicatory address.

After Davie returned from Europe, he discovered that university finances were more hard-pressed than ever. The Jeffersonian revolution of 1800 encouraged university critics in the General Assembly who repealed the 1794 statute which gave all unsold confiscated land to the university, as well as the Escheats Act of 1789. The confiscated property act had been due to expire in 1804, but the loss of escheats would have been catastrophic. By a stroke of good fortune the state supreme court in 1805 invalidated the legislative act withdrawing the escheats, and they came to furnish 69 percent of the university's total revenue during its first fifty years.[31]

Despite these difficulties Davie pushed ahead. A week after the inauguration of President Jefferson he met with Haywood to see what could be done about construction on the campus. "This valuable institution," he declared, "must not be immolated at the shrine of vandalism in the 19th century."[32]

About this time a vitriolic letter was published castigating the university as a bulwark of aristocratic Federalism and opposing construction of South Building as a useless extravagance. The writer, signed CITIZEN, denounced "the palace-like erection, which is much too large for usefulness and might be aptly termed the 'Temple of Folly', planned by the Demi-God Davie."[33]

Besides academic quarrels and meager revenues, other troubles vexed Davie and Caldwell. Church groups around the state criticized the university's reputation for skepticism and free thought. They saw Chapel Hill as a haven for dissolute sons of the affluent. Reports of student outbursts against faculty members, destruction of property, fighting, drinking, and other vices made the rounds. The Reverend Charles Pettigrew, whose sons John and

Ebenezer were students, upbraided the administration in letters from Tyrell County. "An education without the fear of God," he wrote, "may suit those who confine their views to *this world* and to the *present* life only, but to one who expects his Children are to survive the ruins of time, in a state of immortal and endless existence . . . such an education must be very shocking."[34]

Not six months after his arrival at Chapel Hill, amid all these tribulations, Joseph Caldwell came to have doubts about his ability to carry on as presiding professor. He notified the trustees of his intention to resign. The records of the time show that Caldwell was scrupulously conscientious and threw himself into his difficult tasks with determination. In addition to his chief administrative duties, he taught twenty pupils reading in the grammar school. Trustee James Hogg, in a letter to Davie, highly praised Caldwell. "The more I get to know (him)," he wrote, "the more I am pleased with him. I think him a respectable character and well qualified. . . . I am sorry that he has notified his determination to leave us. He seems to think that his constitution is too weak to undergo the anxiety and fatigue of the president's place."[35]

But the trustees persuaded Caldwell to remain as professor of mathematics. They did so by installing James Smiley Gillaspie of Guilford County as principal professor. Davie had been informed that Gillaspie (of whom little is recorded) was "attached to a studious academic life and would probably remain long with us." The general shortly discovered that such was not the case. Battle reported that Gillaspie's first year was "fairly successful" but that the term preceding the 1799 commencement became "especially stormy."

In the spring of 1799 a week-long student revolt broke out against campus regulations and certain members of the faculty. It centered on Gillaspie, who had become personally obnoxious to the students. They not only beat the principal professor; they waylaid and stoned other faculty members and made violent threats.[36]

This "Anarchy & Confusion," as reported to the trustees, led to the withdrawal of many students from Chapel Hill. Enrollment dropped from 115 to about 70. Many declared, as they departed, that they would never return. Trustee Willie Jones reported to the trustees that "the University totters, the Reputation of it is gone. But it may be recovered & made to shine with brighter Lustre than it has hitherto done."

How that could be brought about sorely troubled the trustees. Three of the worst student offenders were dismissed, and Gillaspie himself decided to depart. At that time Davie had resigned the governorship to take up his diplomatic duties in Europe. Jones and other trustees sought a successor for Gillaspie, even acting on one recommendation from President George Washington, but all to no avail. Finally they turned again to Caldwell. The rebellious students themselves had suggested that he should reassume authority. As they searched for an individual able to perform the demanding duties of directing what was, despite its imposing name, only, in Davie's term, an "embryo college," the trustees agreed with Willie Jones that it was absolutely essential to find a "Man skilled in the Sciences, of polished manners with dignity in his Appearance & established Character—and also an able professor."

Available close at hand on the campus, they discovered, was the individual they sought. Joseph Caldwell agreed to try again. He questioned his own capabilities, but he was too harshly self-critical. After General Davie left the state in 1805, Battle reported, Joseph Caldwell "acquired a commanding influence in the university's affairs," assuring its survival and shaping its destiny.

JOSEPH CALDWELL,

CHARACTER IS DESTINY,

1804–1835

Twenty-three-year-old Joseph Caldwell came to Chapel Hill driving his stick-back sulky through the countryside from Princeton, New Jersey, in 1796. Eight years later he became the university's first president.

The son of a physician born in Northern Ireland and a Scotch-Irish, French Huguenot mother whose family settled near Oyster Bay, Long Island, Caldwell entered Princeton when he was fourteen and after graduation studied for the ministry. He was a tutor at Princeton when he received the unexpected offer to move to Chapel Hill as a mathematics teacher.

As we have seen, the university was for him at first a "scene of severe suffering and trial." Taking over as presiding professor from the departing David Ker and Charles Harris, he found himself involved in continuous academic and political turmoil. His first inclination was to yield to his modestly diffident nature and retire from "the perplexities of his situation to the less responsible and humbler station he had left."[1] Several times he submitted his resignation. But the trustees somehow persuaded him to stay.

That was fortunate, for the university's founding father was about to retire to his South Carolina plantation. As Davie let go the reins, the fate of the struggling institution fell increasingly on Caldwell's shoulders. Cornelia Phillips Spencer, the nineteenth-century professor's daughter who became a celebrated chronicler of the university, concluded that it was the force of Caldwell's "private and personal character" that gave him the reputation he ultimately achieved. "Character is destiny," she wrote of this conscientious youth. He persisted in his exacting duties to become recognized as a leader of "high public spirit" and "inflexible integrity and fidelity to principle."

Caldwell was not gifted as an orator or a writer. In a society that Cornelia Spencer described as "given over to French Philosophy, or open Atheism, to the card table, the race track and the punch bowl," the straitlaced schoolmaster "had no such social graces as fitted him to shine."[2] Moreover as an ordained Presbyterian minister who deplored the loose morals and growing Republican enthusiasms of the day, he insisted on stern retribution for student misbehavior. Dr. Caldwell believed in "caning" and other forms of corporal punishment. Of "sinewy physique" and slight build with penetrating dark eyes and bushy eyebrows, he was strong of arm and swift of foot. In Battle's words, "He thought it not undignified to engage in a wrestle or race with midnight disturbers."[3] Some students nicknamed him Old Joe, others Old Bolus (from diabolus or devil).

Caldwell's clash with the growing Republicanism of the General Assembly required more than footraces or wrestling. As Thomas Jefferson won the presidency in 1800, animosity toward the Federalist-dominated university induced the General Assembly to repeal both the escheats and confiscated lands statutes of 1789 and 1794. These constituted the institution's lifeblood. With no other regular sources of revenue, it would wither on the vine.

The bill outraged Federalist leaders. Colonel William Polk, a trustee, protested the "demoniac rage . . . about to be exercised against education of youth." Congressman Archibald Henderson wrote to Walter Alves, "Alas! Alas! The Legislature of North Carolina [is about] to wage war against the arts and sciences. I blush for my native state."[4] A letter from a "Gentleman in Raleigh" to the editor of a contemporary journal declared: "(The university) now languishes. Mr. Caldwell's anti-Republican love of literature, and not the emoluments of his office, induces him to preserve in existence, and by his influence, even the shadow of a college. He is assisted by only one tutor; the funds do not permit the employment of more."[5]

Even as the trustees despaired and began to talk of finding new leadership, their "pugnacious young Scotch-Irishman" dug in his heels. He became, in Battle's words, "a fighting member of the church militant." He refuted the legislature's criticism that Chapel Hill was a hotbed of aristocrats and a costly trinket of the wealthy. He championed the cause of educating the state's public leaders at home as a means of avoiding the dangers of elitism. "If education should become easy . . . among us," Caldwell declared, "we

The Reverend Joseph Caldwell, first president of the university.
(North Carolina Collection, University of North Carolina Library, Chapel Hill)

shall preserve our public liberties from the grasp of those who would otherwise engross all merit and abilities and knowledge to themselves."[6] Student uprisings at Chapel Hill, he insisted, were the work of a few wrongheaded young people.

In his zeal to defend public education, Caldwell sometimes lashed out with invective that caused his opponents to label him a "bitter partisan." "Be assured, gentlemen," he wrote on one occasion to the legislators, "the stupidity of your politics will be known. . . . It is such men as you who rob a people, when you once get the sway into your hands."[7]

Yet as the debate continued in the legislative halls, sentiment for the university improved. One cause of its disfavor among anti-Federalists had been the self-perpetuating nature of the Board of Trustees, allowing Federalists to remain dominant. By 1805 a compromise statute restored the university's right to escheated lands in return for allowing the General Assembly to appoint additional trustees and to fill future vacancies. This restored a prime source of funding and simultaneously guaranteed stronger legislative control.[8]

By 1804 the trustees, impressed by Caldwell's leadership, decided to promote him from presiding professor to president. Caldwell's proven devotion to education and his steady attachment to the university were praised. His salary was increased to $1,000 a year. Within the university family he was seen as a man of "enlarged views, fearless and indefatigable in the discharge of duty and skillful in the administration of discipline, inspiring respect and confidence."[9]

Caldwell's promotion came just before Davie's decision to retire to South Carolina. Following his defeat for Congress in the 1802 elections, the founder of the university became convinced that the country was declining under Jefferson. He was disillusioned by the downfall of Federalism, the trials of the university, and the social and economic backwardness of North Carolina. In a letter written on June 9, 1805, on the eve of his departure he declared: "Men of science in other states regard the people of North Carolina as sort of semi-barbarians, among whom neither learning, virtue nor men of science possess any estimation."[10]

Davie never again returned to North Carolina for any length of time. As a remarkably successful leader in many spheres, he had accomplished seemingly impossible tasks—among them rallying his aristocratic colleagues to create an educational institution suited to republican government. He received the university's first honorary degree (doctor of laws) in 1811.[11] The U.S. Army appointed Davie a major general during the War of 1812. Davie died on November 5, 1820, and was buried in the Old Waxhaws Presbyterian Church yard, across the Catawba River from his plantation, Tivoli, near Lancaster, South Carolina. He left a net worth of $32,000 and 116 slaves.

Davie's departure enhanced Caldwell's authority at Chapel Hill. At the time of his promotion in 1804 he had been elected to the Board of Trustees, and gradually its members eased their practice of interfering in administrative matters. At the time, Caldwell served as professor of mathematics and also temporarily taught the classics. These times were marred by the death of his wife, Susan Rowan, and their only child, Anne, which left him alone in the president's house. Caldwell later married the widow of William Hooper. Helen Hooper was a daughter of trustee James Hogg and had moved to Chapel Hill from Hillsboro when her son became a university student. Caldwell strengthened his ties with Chapel Hill by moving to his new wife's home on East Franklin Street.

Caldwell continued to restore the classical curriculum, which Davie had amended. Latin had become a required subject in 1800, and in 1804 Greek was added. The trustees decreed that the president should wear a black gown at commencement and reported that seventy students were enrolled in 1805.

Not long after his promotion, Caldwell received an offer to become professor of mathematics at the College of South Carolina, at an annual salary of $1,500, with chances of moving to the presidency at $2,500. There was much consternation among friends of the university. Trustee John Haywood, the venerable state treasurer, wrote a letter begging Caldwell to stay, recalling the "fatherly part you have taken . . . in the days of (the university's) greatest trials and adversity."[12] Members of the senior class appealed to him in affectionate and laudatory terms, noting that "you have been the director of our youthful pursuits, our guide, our teacher and our friend." After the trustees passed resolutions commending his leadership, Caldwell agreed to stay. He wrote to a friend in Connecticut, saying that he had found his attachment to Chapel Hill growing.

Described as "something of a prig in his earlier years," Caldwell demonstrated a capacity for growth and an implacable will that "enabled him to weather the transition of the state's control from Federalist to Republican."[13]

Among Caldwell's objectives as he surveyed the university's needs was completion of South Building, which had remained roofless and half-finished because of a shortage of funds. Davie laid its cornerstone in 1798, but construction languished despite several money-raising campaigns, including two lotteries in 1801 which produced more than $5,000. In the interim, students, crowded and living four to a room in Old East, improvised living quarters in the roofless structure. They built cabins and shacks in its corners. "As soon as spring brought back the swallows and the leaves, they emerged from this den and chose some shady retirement, where they made a path or a promenade"—doubtless south of the building where numerous paths wandered through the hardwoods and where there was more than one spring.[14]

Caldwell was especially annoyed by the university's critic who described the unfinished building as a "Temple of Folly" planned by the "Demi-God Davie." He fired back: "Here are 56 persons huddled together with their trunks, beds, tables, chairs, books and clothes into 14 little rooms [in Old East], which by the excessive heat of summer are enough to stifle them and in the winter scarcely admit them to sit around the fireplace. . . . No Northern college has more than two persons in each room. . . . If rooms sufficient were here we would have 100 students and our nation would have, not a Temple of Folly but a monument of glory to herself and a pledge of utility and worth to all succeeding generations."[15]

When funds continued in short supply, Caldwell got in his stick-back sulky and traveled across North Carolina in 1809, and again in 1811, soliciting money in person. Eventually he raised about $12,000, which helped South Building get its roof and furnishings. Construction was not completed until 1814.

Almost simultaneously with Caldwell's elevation to the presidency the campus was shaken by a bad outbreak of student unruliness. The president bewailed the commission of annoying offenses ranging from stealing bee hives, removing gates, stoning houses, and damaging crops to firing pistols and staging duels. These students of "the frontier spirit," Phillips Russell observed, believed in "violent amusements and privately owned more pistols than books."[16]

In 1805 the trustees cracked down, empowering monitors to preserve order, limiting freedom of speech, and organizing military discipline at meals. Their ordinance required monitors to take oaths that they would uphold order. Even responsible students responded to this iron rule with anger and determination not to submit. They began leaving school in what was termed a "great secession." "The crisis is awful," steward Pleasant Henderson wrote a board member.

"The situation into which the imprudence and ill-directed conduct of the seceding students has thrown the institution is truly distressing," trustee William Polk wrote Caldwell. The president was deeply stirred. He was not originally responsible for the ordinance; it was supposedly written by attorney Archibald Debow Murphey. But he tried to enforce it and denounced the students' conduct.

One student leader, Henry Chambers of Salisbury, wrote General Steele: "Every friend to science must lament the injudicious conduct of the trustees in passing so odious a law. It is very objectionable in theory but much more so in practice. It banishes all harmony. . . . What young man of feeling would be willing to place himself in such a situation as this? Who would suffer himself publicly to be called a perjured villain?" Chambers was one of the best students in the class.[17] Other students joined his protest.

Caldwell thought that amending the ordinance's language—eliminating *oath* and substituting *pledge of honor*—might make it more palatable. But that proved unsuccessful. The protests continued. General Davie, in his last official act before departing for South Carolina, stepped in to quell the trouble. In a letter to John Haywood on September 22, 1805, he criticized "the ill-advised ordinance," noting that a similar one had been rejected by the trustees some years earlier. The principle, he said, of making monitors "real spies" in a literary institution is wrong. "Human nature revolts from the principle of espionage in every shape."[18]

Davie counseled absolute repeal of the ordinance. But he stoutly opposed the students' conduct. The ringleaders, he said, should not be readmitted. He blamed the real cause of the trouble on "the deficits of domestic education in the Southern States, the weakness of parental authority, the spirit of the Times." He suggested that the long-range remedy was better facilities, fewer written laws, and a different vacation schedule.

The repeal of the obnoxious ordinance in December 1805 did not bring back the seceders. In 1805 there were only three graduates; in 1806, four. Caldwell and the trustees had learned a lesson. But the problems of student discipline did not disappear. In a letter to a professor he was seeking to hire, Caldwell wrote that, though tempted by the offer of a higher salary and a more congenial chair (the South Carolina offer), he had "foregone all temptations with the view of still sustaining our tottering institution, assailed as it is by outward foes and rent as it has been lately by an explosion of inward insubordination, rashness and profligacy."[19]

The trustees were chagrined by their defeat. Disgruntlement over episodes of insubordination and misbehavior continued. In 1808 when a group of trustees tried to go over Caldwell's head by reinstating certain rebelling students, the president responded in fury and again threatened to resign. The trustees retreated. Although not essentially of a bellicose nature, Caldwell had acquired a sternness of demeanor as a weapon for difficult times. While he frowned on hardened vice, he could be forgiving and had an "open heart and hand" and "no want of sympathy with youthful feelings."[20]

Caldwell's reputation as a leader began to receive recognition beyond Chapel Hill. In addition to the offer from the College of South Carolina, in 1807 he was selected by North and South Carolina to serve as astronomical expert on a commission to finish running the boundary line between the two states and Georgia. His work satisfied the commissioners, and eventually their legislatures approved the recommendations.

Caldwell's love of mathematics, and scholarship in general, exceeded his interest in the presidency. "He longed for a time when he could complete his work in geometry," Battle reported, and "perfect his knowledge of astronomy and use of astronomical instruments."[21] Thus in 1812, as troubles at the university diminished, he proposed that the trustees name a new president and allow him to withdraw completely to the chair of mathematics.

Naturally the strong-minded president had a successor in mind. Also naturally he chose another Presbyterian schoolmaster, this time the Reverend Robert Hett Chapman, a graduate of Princeton then serving as a minister in New Jersey. Replying to Caldwell's offer, Chapman accepted reluctantly, regretting that he would be relinquishing "the dearest object of my heart, the advancement of the cause of our Glorious Redeemer" but confessing that his salary as preacher was "utterly inadequate to the expense of a growing family."[22]

The trustees named Chapman president on December 12, 1812, at a salary of $1,200 a year and retained Caldwell in the mathematics chair at $1,000 annually. The new arrangement failed. While devoted to piety, strong principle, and the spread of religion, Chapman became a "peace Federalist" at a time when the war spirit against Great Britain stirred deeply among students and friends of the university.[23]

Both England and France had confiscated U.S. ships and impressed sailors. "The devil himself," Congressman Nathaniel Macon declared, "could not tell which government, England or France, is the most wicked." President Madison and Congress challenged England largely because, with no navy to speak of, the United States could more easily attack neighboring Canada and at the same time diminish the Indian threat. New England's Federalists, with whom Dr. Chapman agreed, drank toasts to "the world's last hope" while Mr. Madison's war made the United States an ally of Napoleon, the greatest despot of the age.[24]

The war was over almost before it began, with Madison's war hawks defeated in Canada and the U.S. Capitol burned by British troops in Washington. In the minds of most North Carolinians, including students at Chapel Hill, the word Federalist was synonymous with *traitor*. President Chapman, being in this camp and too honest to conceal his views, lost favor quickly. Students directed a series of annoying pranks and property destruction at the president's house. This led to retaliatory action, promulgated primarily by Caldwell. He proposed examining all students under oath, not realizing that such "general warrants" were unconstitutional. Justice of the Peace Pleasant Henderson refused to carry out such procedures. "But," he explained, "the fiery doctor could no more easily be deterred from his purpose than a well-trained blood hound from the tracks of a fleeing criminal."

Caldwell amended the warrants by inserting the names of five students and a solemn court was held. The charges included entering a stable and cutting the hair from a horse's tail, stealing and secreting a cart, entering the premises and throwing down an outhouse, and carrying away a gate. These examinations violated all rules of evidence. Chapman received an anonymous note saying that his gatepost had been "decorated with tar and feathers" in order to "deride Toryism."

Chapman came under more fire when he excised phrases of a strong political character favoring Republicanism from a student's oration and ordered him not to deliver it. When the student, William Biddle Shepard, insisted on speaking anyway, students in the audience supported him and passed resolutions commending his conduct. The faculty retaliated by ordering forty-six students to appear before them. Shepard was suspended for six months along with George C. Dromgoole, another student leader. Others were punished. Still others who refused to apologize were expelled.[25]

Battle, who talked to some of the participants in later years, concluded that President Chapman was at fault in this affair by not allowing Shepard to have his say. The upshot was Chapman's resignation on November 23, 1816. The university's second president returned to the ministry and served churches in North Carolina, Virginia, and Kentucky. He was the recipient of a doctor of divinity degree from Williams College in 1816. During his four years at Chapel Hill he was one of the chief organizers of the Chapel Hill

Presbyterian Church and required the study of the Bible by all university students.

Caldwell sought, without success, a successor for Chapman. On December 14, 1816, he was again elected president by the trustees and answered "with diffidence, I will accept." The university gave him an honorary degree that year.

As Caldwell returned to the helm, the trustees looked beyond the familiar environs of Princeton for faculty enrichment. In 1818 they hired two young graduates of Yale, Denison Olmsted and Elisha Mitchell, who achieved distinguished careers in later years. Congressman William Gaston, a trustee, discovered Mitchell as a replacement for Caldwell in the mathematics chair. A twenty-four-year-old native of Litchfield, Connecticut, already licensed to preach in the Congregational church, Mitchell brought to North Carolina a keen interest in natural philosophy, botany, and mineralogy. Olmsted, Mitchell's classmate at Yale (1813), became professor of chemistry.

Together they formed the nucleus of an antebellum faculty of increasing quality. While Olmsted returned to Yale in 1825, Mitchell remained at Chapel Hill for thirty-nine years. Mrs. Mitchell, who was Maria North, daughter of a physician, left a vivid account of the trip she and her husband made in late 1819 from Connecticut to Chapel Hill by way of Philadelphia, Baltimore, Norfolk, Edenton, and Raleigh, most of it either by steamer or carriage. Mitchell preached his first sermon in Person Hall on the Sunday after their arrival on December 29, 1819. Mrs. Mitchell wrote her mother a colorfully detailed description of a Carolina dinner given them by President and Mrs. Caldwell, listing the menu: "Roast turkey with duck, roast beef and broiled chicken, Irish and sweet potatoes, turnips, rice, carrots, parsnips, cabbage, stewed apples, boiled pudding, baked potato pudding, damson tarts, current tarts, apple pies and whips."[26]

The Olmsted and Mitchell families lived together in the old president's house on Cameron Avenue in the early years. The Olmsteds later purchased the widow Puckett's house across from the president's home on East Franklin Street and sold it to the university when they left for Yale in 1825. Mitchell then moved to fill the chemistry chair and was replaced in math by James Phillips, the capable and well-educated Englishman who came from New York and founded a family dynasty that influenced the university well into the twentieth century.

The arrival of Mitchell and Olmsted marked a gradual diminution of the classical curriculum emphasized by Caldwell. Caldwell himself came to have similar nonclassical interests. However, in 1819 when another faculty opening occurred, he again selected a Princeton preacher-schoolmaster, Shepard K. Kollock of New Jersey, whom he hired as professor of rhetoric logic and moral philosophy. This stirred criticism around North Carolina about the faculty's strong Presbyterian flavor. Of five faculty members, four were Presbyterians, only William Hooper being an Episcopalian and, in Battle's words, "tottering toward the Baptists."

Presbyterians, mostly Princeton-educated, had managed university affairs starting with Davie and McCorkle. Joseph Caldwell kept them in charge throughout most of his regime. An early twentieth-century historian noted that "from the Constitutional Convention down to the present time (1937), with a few rare exceptions, the Presbyterians have shown a marked, almost paternal interest in the University of North Carolina." This was attributed to the fact that "Presbyterians have been more thoroughly devoted to education than any other denomination. It has meant life as well as light to them; it has made them independent and patriotic, strong and noble. They were really our first teachers, and during the latter part of the 18th century, they were well nigh our only ones."[27]

Some Presbyterians were annoyed, however, because the university's Board of Trustees contained few clergymen. In 1820–24 they sought to found a second state institution somewhere southwest of the Yadkin River. Presbyterians of Mecklenburg, Iredell, and adjoining counties launched the campaign. Its failure resulted in the establishment of Davidson College in 1837. This coincided with the rise of other denominational colleges—Wake Forest, Trinity (Duke), and Guilford.

A religious revival swept the state from 1800 to 1811. Waves of evangelism followed. They produced sharp differences between those who thought that higher education was a function of the church, even its "imperative obligation," and those who feared that religious institutions might again become a threat to republican government. Davie considered the university primarily a vehicle for training able public leaders, politicians, and servants of the state. The struggle between public and private higher education, heated from the beginning, flared repeatedly throughout the next two centuries.[28]

As the only institution of higher learning in the state, Chapel Hill trained a coterie of outstanding alumni who became state and national leaders. The class of 1818, for example, which numbered fourteen, contained men of considerable distinction. James Knox Polk, who won highest honors in his class, was later governor of Tennessee, Speaker of the U.S. House of Representatives, and president of the United States. William Mercer Green, who won second-highest honors, became bishop of Mississippi and chancellor of the University of the South. Robert Hall Morrison, Doctor of Divinity, served as president of Davidson College; Edward Jones Mallet became paymaster-general of the United States; and William Dudley Moseley, governor of Florida. Robert Donaldson of Fayetteville and New York City became a successful businessman, patron of the arts, and benefactor of the university.[29]

In 1824, as additional funds were anticipated from Tennessee land sales, the trustees embarked on ambitious building ventures. They proceeded over protests of the faculty, who thought money should be invested in books and laboratory apparatus for science courses. (In those days the orthodox science course was called natural philosophy in order to avoid controversy with those who supported a purely classical curriculum.)

The trustees' plan included a third-floor addition to Old East and construction of a twin dormitory called Old West and a new chapel. They first borrowed $10,000 for this purpose, pledging bank stock as collateral. Two years later they borrowed another $20,000. Dr. Mitchell took the lead in championing books and equipment. "The first impression of enlightened strangers [of the university] is uniformly favorable," he wrote to the trustees. "But when we show them our library and inform them that we have little or no philosophical apparatus, we sink even more than is reasonable in their estimation."[30]

Caldwell joined in this campaign, comparing a "bookless professor to a lawyer without a legal library, to a shoemaker without awls or lasts, to a printer with insufficient types." As a result the trustees compromised. They pursued their building plans but authorized Caldwell to take what turned out to be a successful, ten-month trip to Europe, where books and apparatus cost much less than in America or England.

Caldwell modestly paid his own personal travel expenses, but the trustees gave him $6,000 for spending money. He returned with 979 books and scientific apparatus which, Battle noted, was still in use at Chapel Hill seventy-five years later. He overran his $6,000 budget by $1,238 but was later reimbursed by the trustees.

Caldwell was not impressed by the grandeur of Europe, as described in a long, prosaic letter written to Professor Olmsted from Scotland in August

1824. The "wonderful sights of the Old World," Battle observed, did not "quicken the heart-throbs of the backwoods mathematician."[31]

Caldwell purchased the best apparatus of the day. When part of it was lost by shipwreck, he offered to replace it at his own expense. On the president's return to Chapel Hill, faculty and students welcomed him with a "brilliant illumination" of university buildings. Students flocked to his home. One of them, Paul C. Cameron of Hillsboro, who became a dedicated benefactor of the university, remembered "the splendor of that night and the procession of students to his residence and his stepping out upon the floor of the back piazza—the cheer after cheer that was given the dear old man."[32]

Caldwell never wrote much about his European trip. Instead, after his return he produced a "laborious" series of newspaper articles about the need for internal improvements in North Carolina, especially the need for a railroad between Beaufort and the mountains. He did, however, bring back a marked interest in astronomy and mounted a telescope on the roof of his house. In his backyard he installed a sundial and two "meridian pillars" pointing to the north. They still stand today in a little court in the rear of the president's house on East Franklin Street, restored in the twentieth century by former professor James Lee Love.[33]

With the help of Mitchell and Phillips, the president built in 1831 a small structure to house the astronomical instruments purchased in Europe. It became the first observatory connected with a university in the United States. The building, only twenty feet square, stood near the village cemetery, but it rapidly fell into decay and the instruments were removed after Caldwell's death in 1835.[34]

Meanwhile the appearance of the campus began to improve. Mitchell supervised construction of sturdy walls along some of the campus walks, mostly consisting of fieldstones piled one upon another, New England style. Professors Mitchell and Olmsted roamed widely across the state. Olmsted, who became a noted scientist, made the first geological and mineralogical survey of North Carolina. Mitchell, of whom it was said "nothing organic or inorganic was alien to him," took his students on long tramps through the beautiful forests adjoining the campus. On one of these trips a student named Zeb B. Vance, later governor, asked as they approached the site of Barbee's Mill: "Doctor, you reckon this old mill is worth a dam?" The reverend doctor's reply was not recorded. Mitchell became superintendent of property for the university, bursar, and acting president during Caldwell's long illness. Mitchell died in 1857 after suffering a fall on Mount Mitchell, which was named in his honor. On one occasion he wrote home to his family: "The prosperity of the university is dearer to me than any earthly thing besides my wife and children."[35]

The trustees' high hopes for money from the Tennessee lands diminished after the Panic of 1825. Money became scarce and student enrollment fell. Old West had been completed, a third floor added to Old East, and renovations made on South Building. William Nichols, building contractor for these projects and architect for the old State House in Raleigh, had to halt work on the new chapel. It was not finished for another decade.

Caldwell reported that declining enrollment was due to factors other than the economic malaise. He attributed it to the opening of new colleges in adjoining states and migration to the West. Cornelia Phillips Spencer, a child in those days, later wrote that one of her earliest recollections was seeing "long processions passing through town of white covered, one-horse carts or wagons, full of beds, buckets and babies, with lean men and women, tow-headed children and 'yallar dogs', walking alongside. 'Movers', we children called them, and we always made a rush to front door or gate to stare at the exodus; 'going out West' was the invariable reply to all queries."[36]

By 1830 the university once again faced financial ruin. Trustees were forced to borrow money to pay faculty salaries. After considering and rejecting a proposal to sell some of the unimproved land adjoining the developed campus, they decided to ask the General Assembly for help until more of the Tennessee lands could be sold. In reply to an eloquent petition written by Chief Justice Thomas Ruffin, the legislators declared they would only advance a $25,000 loan in return for placing the university under full control of the state with liens drawn up on all its property. The trustees rejected that arrangement and instead borrowed $4,000 from the U.S. bank at Fayetteville, which eased them through the crisis.[37]

One of the enduringly romantic campus stories had its genesis in 1831 when a student named Peter Dromgoole entered the university. The young man, a native of Virginia, took offense at the remarks of a professor, dropped out of school, and disappeared. A story sprang up that he was killed in a duel and that his body was buried beneath a large rounded rock on the summit of Piney Prospect. Certain stains of iron visible on the rock were said to be his blood. By tradition his sweetheart, Miss Fanny, had hurried to stop the duel but had arrived too late. She supposedly pined away, lost her reason and health, and was buried by Dromgoole's side. Students named the spring at the foot of the hill Miss Fanny's Spring.[38]

In 1832 trustee William Gaston delivered a memorable commencement address in which he advocated the ultimate abolition of slavery. "Disguise the truth as we may," he declared, "and throw the blame where we will, it is slavery which, more than any other cause, keeps us back in the career of improvement. It stifles industry and represses enterprise; it is fatal to economy and providence; it discourages skill; it impairs our strength as a community and poisons morals at the fountainhead."[39] Students cheered his words. Chief Justice John Marshall commended them. Gaston's bold language did not weaken his standing in the state. Six months later the General Assembly elected him a justice of the state supreme court, although it was ostensibly barred from doing so because he was Roman Catholic. Gaston later led the fight to remove that disqualification from the state constitution.

By 1833 the trustees, seeking completion of the half-finished new chapel, decided to sell 14,000 acres of land bequeathed the university in 1797 by Major Charles Gerrard of Edgecombe County. Major Gerrard's will directed that the property never be sold, but after obtaining legal advice, the trustees "with sorrow" voted to proceed. They used $2,000 from the funds, completed the structure in 1837, and named it Gerrard Hall in honor of its benefactor. Gerrard succeeded Person Hall as the focal point for campus gatherings over the next four decades, including addresses by Presidents Polk, Buchanan, and Wilson.

Cornelia Phillips Spencer described Person Hall, the old chapel, as the headquarters for "all itinerant preachers, lecturers, showmen, ventriloquists, Siamese Twins and the like." It was used, in turn, for a variety of purposes, ultimately becoming a fine-arts building in the twentieth century. When there were rumors that it might be demolished, Dr. Mitchell came to the rescue, calling it "not a splendid but a very neat Edifice."[40] Archibald Henderson later wrote that "if any hall on the campus deserves the title Zion-Parnassus, it is Person Hall, which began as a chapel and ended as a school of the fine arts."[41]

One of the other early campus buildings, Steward's Hall, where most of the students boarded and where commencements and commencement balls were held in the early years, had in 1816 been closed as university commons and rented by a series of individuals who provided meals for students. For a time Dr. Mitchell used a portion of the hall as his laboratory, and it later became a private residence. In 1847 it was dismantled.

The 1833 commencement took place without the attendance of President Caldwell, whose declining health had required a trip to Philadelphia. After that, it became known that he had been afflicted with an "incurable disease." The president, however, did not begin to lay down his burdens until December of that year when he requested that the senior member of the faculty be empowered to act when he was unable to perform his duties. Dr. Mitchell became that person. Another assistant, Professor Walker Anderson, was hired as adjunct professor of natural philosophy and astronomy.

As his painful illness intensified, Dr. Caldwell drew up bylaws covering regulation of student conduct, one of his last official acts. He also worked on curriculum changes.

Cornelia Phillips Spencer recalled as a child attending the last service at which Dr. Caldwell preached. It was on a bitter cold Sunday early in January 1835 in the village schoolhouse, site of the present Chapel Hill Presbyterian Church. She had, she wrote, been compelled to go and "shivered with the rest of the audience, for there were no stoves." Dr. Caldwell preached on the Twenty-third Psalm. Mrs. Spencer "retained for many years a vivid recollection of his strongly-marked benignant countenance as it appeared over the desk of the square wooden pulpit. . . . Before the month had ended he had passed through the dark valley."[42]

Joseph Caldwell died in the parlor of the president's residence on East Franklin Street on January 27, 1835. Dr. Mitchell officiated at the funeral. The first president of the university was buried in a grave that he himself had prepared in the village cemetery. The following November his remains were exhumed so that a plaster cast of his features might be made. When his widow died in 1846, she was buried beside her husband at the foot of a monument that had been erected to Caldwell on the campus north of Davie Poplar.

The pious young schoolmaster who arrived at Chapel Hill thirty-seven years before in his stick-back sulky left an impressive record. He had been appointed presiding professor of a weak and poorly supported institution buffeted by political and religious strife and internal controversy. He kept it afloat and solidified its foundations. His own indomitable character became part of campus tradition. He gained the trust and admiration of the state.

The university "struggled through a very feeble infancy," Professor Walker Anderson declared in his 1835 commencement oration honoring Caldwell, "until a development of its resources and the zeal and energy of its friends brought it to a condition of more maturity and stability." Dr. Caldwell's labors and splendid reputation helped bring this to pass. He saw it rise from a mere grammar school to a high and honorable station among the universities of the land.[43]

DAVID L. SWAIN,

DIPLOMAT AND PEACEMAKER,

1835–1868

After Joseph Caldwell's death in 1835, a surprising candidate for the presidency appeared. Thirty-four-year-old David Lowry Swain, governor of North Carolina, approached Judge Frederick Nash about Swain himself succeeding Caldwell. Nash, a trustee, was thunderstruck. But when he consulted another member of the board, ex-judge Duncan Cameron, the latter waxed enthusiastic. "As governor, Swain has always swayed and managed men so perfectly," Cameron said. "Perhaps he is the man to do as well with unruly boys."

On December 5, 1835, the trustees chose Swain as the university's third president. The appointment shocked some members of the faculty, especially those who were senior in age and teaching experience. The contrast between the scholarly, pious Caldwell and the unscholarly, worldly Swain was dramatic. Professor William Hooper, who had been considered a leading candidate for his stepfather's job, expressed outrage. Before resigning in 1837, Hooper declared: "North Carolina has given Governor Swain every office he has ever asked for, and now she is sending him to college to get an education."[1]

In some ways the differences between Caldwell and Swain resembled those between the courtly John Quincy Adams and the rough-hewn Andy Jackson who succeeded him in the White House in 1828. Swain, described as a tall, ungainly, shambling mountaineer, was a Whig and therefore identified with the Federalist political succession that had dominated the university from the beginning. As a student he left a good scholarly record at Newton Academy in Asheville, but he dropped out of the junior class at Chapel Hill after four months (because of a shortage of funds) and went to Raleigh to read law under Chief Justice John Louis Taylor. Then Swain opened a law office in Asheville and moved rapidly forward in his profession as attorney, legislator, judge, and governor.

Swain was born on January 4, 1801, in the Beaverdam section of Buncombe County near Asheville. His father, George Swain, a New Englander of some learning, had moved to Georgia where he worked as a hatter and farmer and served in the state legislature for five years. Migrating to the Carolina mountains for his health, George Swain married Caroline Lowry, widow of an army captain killed in an Indian massacre. Caroline was a sister of Joel Lane, who owned the property on which Raleigh was located.

As one of seven children, David Swain had to fend for himself. While in Raleigh he married Eleanor White, daughter of the secretary of state and granddaughter of Governor Richard Caswell. He served in the state legislature, became a superior court judge in 1830, and then was elected governor for three one-year terms. Near the end of his third term in 1836 he became interested in the university presidency. Swain was a Presbyterian layman. His appointment broke the tradition of naming Presbyterian preacher-schoolmasters to head the university. Swain was respectful of religion. He initiated the practice of making Bible study mandatory in the curriculum. "I love all those who show they are Christians," he said.[2]

It was as an enterprising administrator, both thoughtful and bold, that Swain made his reputation at Chapel Hill over the next thirty-three years. "His face was large and long of feature, his expression solemn and sheepish, though with a quizzical twinkle," one contemporary said of him. All through Swain's life, Cornelia Phillips Spencer wrote of him, "he showed sagacity in judging men, prudence in managing them and charity. . . . He saw clearly, he acted cautiously and he felt kindly." He had discreet financial judgment.

Students promptly nicknamed the new president Old Bunk (although that term had not yet become the symbol for inflated oratory). He was also known as Old Warping Bars for his loose-jointed frame. He knew the state and its people and had a splendid memory for names, faces, and family connections. Swain could tell most students more about their family history than they knew. "You see," he would say, "I know more about you than you know about yourself."[3]

President David Lowry Swain.
(North Carolina Collection, University of North Carolina Library, Chapel Hill)

Swain quickly overcame the academic bias evident when he was appointed. He won the trust of trustees and increased faculty autonomy. He employed an English gardener to lay out the campus and beautify the village. He supported Dr. Mitchell's campaign to build stone walls around the campus. Even though he was homely and homespun, the governor liked things done with elegance and style. He had a handsomely furnished home and good carriage horses, and he assisted his poor neighbors financially. He trusted students more than Caldwell and made college popular. "His aim was to turn out good material for lawyers and political leaders for the South and he under-rated high and deep scholarship."[4] While he was not an especially good public speaker, he was an engaging and witty conversationalist. He had an abiding interest in history, which led him to found the North Carolina Historical Society.

Swain broadened the foundations of the university. Before his appointment he had been a leader in the state constitutional convention of 1835, which gave the west better legislative representation and remedied some of the grievances of North Carolina's deeply ingrained sectionalism. At one point in the campaign, speaking of the westerners' cause, Swain declared: "Unless our demands are granted, unless our wrongs are righted, we will rise up like the strong man in his unshorn might and pull down the pillars of the political temple."[5] The convention amendments carried by 5,000 votes.

In his efforts to make the university acceptable to the broad populace east and west, Swain fought the perception that the campus was the exclusive stronghold either of Presbyterianism or of the newly dominant Whig party. The General Assembly criticized President Caldwell in his later years for devoting too much time to the Presbyterian church and refusing to appoint faculty members of other denominations. In a period marked by the rise of independent, church-related colleges and academies, Swain proposed regular faculty chaplains who should be rotated among Presbyterians, Episcopalians, Methodists, and Baptists. As they sought to attract students, private college leaders criticized low tuition rates at Chapel Hill and asserted that members of their own denominations contributed as much as non–church members to the university's support through taxes. They complained that the state failed to "provide properly for religion at Chapel Hill" even as they opposed "Presbyterian dominance."[6]

Yet tax funds were a meager part of the university's support, as Swain and others pointed out. Except for an early $10,000 loan later converted into a gift, the campus had survived on funds from escheated lands and arrearages, private benefactions, two lotteries, and tuition fees.

The Swain administration continued compulsory chapel for all students until 1848. Dr. Mitchell, known for his lengthy sermons, often officiated and was later joined by Professor William Mercer Green, an Episcopal clergyman who supervised construction of the first Episcopal church in

Elisha Mitchell, who discovered Mount Mitchell.
(North Carolina Collection, University of North Carolina Library, Chapel Hill)

Chapel Hill, the Chapel of the Cross, completed in 1848. Aside from the Presbyterians, no other denomination had a church in Chapel Hill. After 1850 the trustees allowed students to attend the church of their choice, but attendance was compulsory. Battle made a doleful comment about these religious customs: "There was no heating in chapel in the winter and in cold weather there was sad shivering in coats and cloaks. . . . The service lasted one hour and a half. Although Dr. Mitchell disapproved of forms, his long prayer was always the same."[7]

Swain steered the university through dangerous political currents as adroitly as he managed its religious problems. By the 1830s the Whig party had assumed firm control across the state. It maintained that dominance until the decade before the Civil War.

The Whigs deplored the rising tide of North-South sectionalism and emphasized national unity. Their opponents, the states' rights coalition called Democrats, with Andrew Jackson and the heirs of Thomas Jefferson at the helm, included most of the slave-owning planter class in North Carolina. Swain, though openly a Whig, "walked circumspectly and . . . emphasized that the university was for the sons of all parties."

Swain's nonpartisanship took some of the edge off party spirit. The student body never became a hotbed of sectional feeling as the Civil War approached. "It would be an untrue picture to paint the university as filled with young cavaliers ready to mount and ride away to a clash at arms," one historian observed.[8]

Swain also campaigned successfully for increased enrollment. The student body grew from about 89 at the time of his arrival to over 450 by the opening of the Civil War. Some of this upsurge stemmed from the state's burgeoning population and its expanding wealth, even in the uncertain economic fluctuations of a wholly rural state. Many students were sons of North Carolina families that had migrated to Tennessee, Alabama, Louisiana, and Mississippi.

However, Swain failed to obtain support from the General Assembly, no matter how hard he tried. The university, he soon learned, must live "on its own," as it had from its birth. The president managed to maintain a balanced budget and even developed one surplus. Faculty salaries remained meager, and there was little expansion of the physical plant. Scholastic standards were low and seemed to be kept that way as "if in appeal for more students."[9]

Even though the governor seemed more interested in the quantity of students than the quality of their instruction, changes gradually appeared in the curriculum. When Caldwell became president, he restored the primacy of the classics, but then he became interested in the sciences, especially astronomy. In his later years he published a textbook in geometry. The faculty members Swain inherited, such sturdy scholars as Mitchell and Phillips, promoted the sciences. Entrance requirements in 1810, in addition to reading, writing, and spelling, included a knowledge of *Aesop's Fables*. By 1850 a knowledge of algebra and ancient and modern geography as well as an approved exam in Greek, Latin, and English were also required. The lecture method became popular. Final exams were oral. "We had a considerable examination," one student wrote in 1837. "We had a great many spectators and sustained our exam tolerably well. It lasted two days."[10]

The 1845–46 college catalogue estimated annual student expenses at $170 to $185, including $50 for tuition, $5 for wood, $5 for candles, and $5 for servant hire. Student life still reflected the manners and morals of the raw frontier. The campus had no infirmary. The sick either remained in their rooms or moved to the village inn to be nursed by family or friends. Students used quill pens and homemade ink. Until 1850, when lamps became available, they studied by candlelight. Fireplaces were popular. The boys generally chopped their own wood, drew their own water, and disposed of their own wastes. Visitors were scarce and letters few since postage was expensive.[11]

Because the campus was secluded, life became dull and students stirred up commotion. One form of hazing forced freshmen to rob a hen roost or break into a stable and ride a professor's horse. Students patronized cock fights and horse races or attended murder trials, circuses, and theatrical performances at nearby Hillsboro. Some students had dogs and horses and liked to hunt. In 1856 freshman Huggins was admonished for "coaxing a dog after him into the South Building," which marked the start of an enduring tradition.[12]

As the influence of the Di and Phi societies waned, many small, secret clubs sprang up on campus. In 1838 there were the Ugly Club and the Boring Club. These groups, mostly social in nature, ended up creating disturbances. Young men disguised themselves with lamp black; insulted other students, faculty, and villagers; destroyed property; and engaged in pranks. One Ugly Club leader rode a horse through Old West. The Boring Club announced it would make its members familiar "with all the paths of vice in the college for fun and frolic—to gratify appetite and to study human nature."[13]

The arrival of chartered fraternities marked a decline of the secret societies, which the trustees banned in 1842. The first fraternity, the Beta chapter of Delta Kappa Epsilon (Dekes), was organized on April 5, 1851. By 1861 it had 118 members. Dekes were followed by Phi Gams, Betas, Delta Psis, SAEs, and Chi Psis. Dekes were known as polite gentlemen who disregarded dull textbooks, read "fashionable" literature of the day, used canes and gloves, and wore "ponderous chains."[14]

Earlier the Temperance Club had been organized (1829), a forerunner of the Young Men's Christian Association (YMCA) (1860). Religious revivals were held, encouraging many student conversions. The Alumni Association was founded on May 31, 1843, with Governor John Motley Morehead as chairman. Students organized the *North Carolina Magazine* in 1844.

Commencement week remained the most significant event of the year. "Houses of the village were thronged and crowded until they could hold no more," reported the *Raleigh Register* on May 28, 1833. Ceremonies continued for four days. They included the opening sermon, the salutatory delivered in Latin, the student oratory competition, addresses before societies and alumni organizations, declamations, reports, the valedictory, degree granting, and the commencement ball. The latter was first held at Steward's Hall; later, the event was moved to Smith Hall (which became the Playmakers Theater) after the belated completion of that building in 1851 as a memorial to Governor Benjamin Smith, the university's first major benefactor.

In the earliest days President Caldwell "danced in pumps and knee britches," but the most memorable commencement of the era occurred when President James Knox Polk visited the campus. The president, a member of the famed class of 1818, had promised such a visit before his election in 1844. He came afterward in the spring of 1847, and his own version of the event was recorded in his diary.

Polk's acceptance threw the trustees into a dither. Knowing he would be accompanied by his wife and Secretary of the Navy and Mrs. John Y. Mason (the secretary was an 1816 graduate), they ordered the repainting of college buildings and the enlargement of Gerrard Hall. Nancy Segur Hilliard, the engaging proprietor of the popular Eagle Hotel, paid the greatest tribute to President Polk. She built an addition to her hotel, located on East Franklin Street, and over the entrance placed a metal plate with the following hospitable inscription: "Erected to Receive Pres. Polk On The Occasion Of His Visit To His Alma Mater." The plate remained there until the hotel, then called the University Inn, burned in 1921.[15]

The president and his party stayed for the full four days of the exercises.

On commencement day, Thursday, the president wrote in his diary that "hundreds from the adjoining country had come in. As soon as I left my room in the morning I was surrounded by them." The ceremonies started between 10:00 and 11:00 A.M. and continued until 5:00 P.M. that afternoon, with a recess of an hour and a half for dinner. During his visit President Polk revisited the room he had occupied on the third floor of South Building. An observer noted that the president's "countenance was lined by labor, strain and suffering." He was lauded for his "total absence of ostentation, his sincere and unassuming courtesy."[16] Of President Swain's official greetings, student James Johnson Pettigrew wrote to his friend J. Bryan Grimes: "Swain was considerably frightened and made a rambling speech about the comparative merits of Tennessee and North Carolina." Of the whole occasion a reporter for the *New York Herald* was most impressed by student Matt W. Ransom's welcome to the ladies and the "ivory of 500 of the fair of old Rip Van Winkle."[17] Thirty-seven young men received their degrees that day.

Student dress in those days ranged from Zeb Vance's "home-made shoes and clothes about three inches between pants and shoes, showing his sturdy ankles" to the sometimes jaunty cap and blue jacket decorated with bright buttons, heavily starched pantaloons, snowy collars, gloves, and linen dusters of the fancier dressers. It was said that when "the Chapel Hill boys" arrived in an adjoining village on their "elegant steeds," they attracted the whole neighborhood's attention and horrified the ministers when they failed to attend church.[18]

As in all generations, the administration battled the problems of "disorderly houses." In 1839 President Swain sent a letter to the father of William Lea stating that his son "is the father of an illegitimate child in the village." In 1856 the faculty passed resolutions urging prosecution of "lewd women who are known to keep bawdy houses near Chapel Hill." Seniors found guilty of drinking were suspended until commencement, when they were given a private exam on "moral science" and, if they passed satisfactorily, received their diplomas.[19]

When this spirit of mischief got out of hand, "good Dr. Mitchell, who was kindly disposed toward errant boys, would often say, 'Let him go! Let him go! He is good legislature and trustee material!'"[20]

The education of women had no place on the campus in those days. The conventional argument prevailed that to educate women would deprive worthy men of the privilege and subject future mothers to evil influences.

But the Moravians had already opened the "single sisters" house in Salem in 1786 and Salem Academy (for women) in 1802.[21]

By mid-century Governor Swain's administrative talent had helped lift the university from the status of a small, provincial academy toward national reputation. William Horn Battle, member of a family closely linked with the university during the next 100 years, became professor of law in 1845, thus initiating what was to develop as an outstanding law school. The trustees established a chair of civil engineering in 1852, and Charles Phillips, son of the founder of another prominent Chapel Hill family, became its first occupant. The Reverend Fordyce M. Hubbard became professor of Latin language and literature. Also arriving were the Reverend John T. Wheat, professor of rhetoric and logic, and the Reverend Alfred M. Shipp, professor of French language and history. Benjamin S. Hedrick became professor of chemistry applied to agriculture and arts.

Swain continually emphasized the role of the university as trainer of public leaders. Steeped himself in the science of politics, he told Charles Manly in 1844: "I am and always have been anxious to render our course of instruction practical to the greatest possible extent."[22] By 1859 the faculty included nine professors and seven tutors.

The governor likewise encouraged admission of poor boys free of tuition and room rent, a policy that annoyed the religiously affiliated private colleges. Swain had a way with students. "It was generally understood in Chapel Hill that if you wanted to know 'what' anything was, you went to Dr. Mitchell," Governor Zeb Vance said in later years. "If you wanted to know 'who' anybody was you went to Governor Swain." Swain was tolerant of the follies of erring youth, so much so that the trustees confronted him at times over discipline and even passed a resolution of censure, which was publicly read by Governor Iredell. Swain arose at a trustees' meeting and defended himself with indignation and emotion.[23]

While Swain was greatly interested in history, his interest in books and intellectual pursuits was meager. He made no effort to restore the astronomical observatory after Caldwell's death and expressed satisfaction over the building's destruction. For the first twenty years of the Swain administration, according to the eminent lawyer and trustee Bartholomew Figures Moore, not a single book was purchased for the library. It was said of Swain, only partly in jest, that "he always kept the university library in the attic (of South Building) where the books were inaccessible and sure to be destroyed by fire."[24]

However, the president's views about books and libraries changed in the years following 1843 when he hired the distinguished architect Alexander Jackson Davis of New York to landscape the campus, enlarge Old East and Old West, and design a new building belatedly designated as a memorial to benefactor General Benjamin Smith.

The new extensions of Old East and Old West were turned over to the Di and Phi societies for meeting rooms and libraries to house their valuable collections of some 7,000 books each. This circumstance strengthened the custom that students from the west joined the Di and those from the east, the Phi.

Davis then designed what initially became the beautiful Smith Building and later the Playmakers Theater, a classical Greek-style temple. The major impetus for the building came after Steward's Hall, which was near the site and used for both student meals and commencement balls, was ordered removed. After completion of the building, Swain realized that, after two decades of total neglect of the library, it would never do for the people of North Carolina to suspect that a large sum of the university's money had been spent for the erection of a "ball room" used only once a year for commencement dances. "The books, some 3,600 of them, were transferred from the dusty and neglected shelves of President Swain's lecture room in the South Building to their new 'retreat.' "[25]

Smith Hall was remembered for its often lavish dances, but it later housed the Di and Phi libraries as well. During the Yankee occupation both Mrs. Spencer and President Battle reported that federal cavalry stabled their horses in South Building and Smith Hall.[26]

Swain's building activities were far from finished. As enrollment soared, he oversaw construction of two new buildings, New East and New West, built on either side of Old East and Old West. By 1858 the university had the largest enrollment of any college or university in the United States except Yale. Swain's last major building project was an infirmary, called The Retreat, built on the site later occupied by Spencer Hall on East Franklin Street. "There is intimation at once symbolic and prophetic in the arresting circumstance that the last building of the ante bellum university was a hospital," Dr. Archibald Henderson observed almost a century later.[27]

In the fall of 1856 Chapel Hill came under the first shadows of the impending civil war. Benjamin S. Hedrick, honors graduate of 1851 and a mild-mannered professor of chemistry, became a center of controversy when he innocently answered a student who wanted to know whom he would vote for in the national presidential election. Hedrick replied, "Frémont." John C. Frémont, leader of the Free Soil party, opposed extending slavery to the western territories. In the South, Free Soilers were known as Black Republicans, and no Carolinian had castigated them more vociferously than an Orange County youth, William Woods Holden, who had apprenticed himself to the printer-editor of the *Raleigh Standard* and had become the paper's editor.

Hearing about Hedrick's comment, Holden on September 13, 1856, published an article aimed at the professor although it never mentioned his name. "If there be Frémont men among us," it said, "let them be silenced or required to leave. The expression of Black Republicanism in our midst is incompatible with our honor and safety as a people. Let our schools and seminaries of learning be scrutinized and if Black Republicanism be found in them, let them be driven out."

The article inspired a letter signed "An Alumnus" written by Joseph A. Englehard, a former law student and staunch Democrat. It spoke of "poisonous influences" at Chapel Hill and of a "canker worm preying at the very vitals of Southern institutions." Word about Hedrick's sentiments spread. When he attended an education convention in Salisbury, a raucous gang followed him to his room, shouting insults and parading a mocking effigy. Hedrick's friends feared that the next step would be mob spirit at Chapel Hill.[28]

The professor then decided to write a letter of rebuttal to the *Raleigh Standard* outlining his views. He favored Frémont, he said, because he saw him as an "enlarger of science" and conqueror of California. His intent, he insisted, was not to "attack the institution of slavery," but in opposing its extension he shared the views of Washington, Jefferson, and Clay. Hedrick also argued that banning slavery in the territories would increase the wealth of North Carolina by keeping her slaves at home.[29]

The letter produced new rounds of denunciation. Hedrick was burned in effigy while the campus's old bell was "funereally tolled." Under this pressure the administration wilted. Swain appointed a faculty committee to study the case. After praising Hedrick's ability, it concluded that airing partisan political opinions was contrary to the "usuages" of the university. The trustees, endorsing the committee report, ruled that campus traditions forbade any professor from becoming "an agitator in the exciting politics of the day." By writing the newspaper letter, they said, Hedrick injured "the prosperity and usefulness of the institution." When the professor refused to resign, the trustees declared his chair vacant, whereupon Hedrick moved to Washington, D.C., and found employment in the U.S. Patent Office.[30]

Holden, the fiery advocate of secession, went on to switch sides, curry favor with President Andrew Johnson, and become provisional governor of North Carolina after Lee's surrender. Hedrick became influential in the Johnson administration, determining who should be pardoned among the Old Confederates and promoting black suffrage in North Carolina. Governor Holden used the militia to assert control of the university in the name of the new Board of Trustees and banished its old administration. He was ultimately impeached, convicted, and deposed.[31]

Swain's successful efforts to keep the university detached from political and religious strife began to fail as the Civil War approached. The university came under attack from southerners who opposed admission of nonsouthern students. In 1854 the senior class voted to invite Archbishop John Hughes of New York to deliver the baccalaureate sermon at commencement. Swain informed the class that its action was "indiscreet" and that Hughes's appearance would be painful to about one-fourth of the class and a majority of those at commencement. The executive committee of the trustees approved Swain's action, but the invitation was not withdrawn. The administration was relieved when the archbishop declined the invitation.

The incident ignited stormy comment around the state. Some charged that the university was about to become a Catholic institution. Others called the students individuals of "weak or ill-regulated minds." Swain tread softly to avoid political discord. Four years later Archbishop Hughes was invited again; he came and delivered a sermon which "pleased and instructed a numerous audience composed almost entirely of Protestants."[32]

When President James Buchanan accepted the university's invitation to attend the 1859 commencement exercises, he dined under the "lofty trees" in President Swain's front yard and later, in his address, warned of the evils of intemperance. When we so indulge, he declared, "we bring upon ourselves a greater calamity than is brought upon us by the yellow fever."[33] Neither the president nor his hosts realized that within two years an even greater calamity would engulf Chapel Hill and the rest of the nation. Mrs. Spencer described that "strange sad spring of 1861," which "besides innumerable violets and jessamines brought into bloom a strange enormous and terrible flower, the blood-red flower of war, which grows amid the thunders."[34]

Governor Swain initially sought to spare "the seed corn"—his term for the young students—from the ravages of fraternal strife. His kindly impulse proved unsuccessful, and in the emerging emotional fervor it "injured his credit with the war party." Old political differences between Whigs and Democrats were reawakened. Swain and his faculty were held by the Confederates to have no heart for the cause.[35]

Swain was strongly supportive of the moderate, nonsectional Whigs and insisted on keeping the university's doors open. Even as the students became fired with the zeal of joining the cause and began departing for home, Swain ignored petitions to suspend operations. Those who were left, a small number of faculty and students, carried on as best they could in a general state of gloom. The faculty accepted salary reductions. Only 5 trustees attended the 1862 commencement. The graduating class dwindled to 24 as compared with 125 in 1859. Mounting casualty lists contained the names of alumni and students. At the 1862 commencement Swain extolled the sacrifice of all, including James Johnson Pettigrew, grievously wounded at Seven Pines.[36]

Even though Confederate president Jefferson Davis heeded a plea from Swain in 1863 to grant draft exemption for some students, the Confederacy's declining fortunes did not stem the exodus. The university's contributions to the war effort on the civil and military side were substantial. They ranged from the top levels of the Confederate cabinet to all ranks of the military. "The sad tale of the fallen begins with Lt. William Preston Mangum at Bull Run and ends with Capt. John H. D. Fain and J. J. Phillips on the retreat from Petersburg," Stephen B. Weeks wrote in later years. "It includes five at Shiloh, 14 at Malvern Hill, nine at Sharpsburg, eight at Fredericksburg, five at Chancellorsville, four at Vicksburg, seven at Chickamauga, six at the Wilderness, five at Spottsylvania Court House, nine in the Atlanta campaign and 21 at Gettysburg."[37]

Both the campus and the village were devastated by the carnage. As the war reached its climax, President Swain found himself thrust forward as a participant in the surrender and peacemaking process. His was a difficult role, made more painful by the violent passions on both sides. The terms of the victor, however, had to be met, and whoever met them, or seemed to endorse them, risked becoming a victim of public distrust.[38] That became Swain's fate.

After the Confederate government's evacuation of Richmond, General Sherman moved up from Bentonville and began his ominous march toward

Raleigh. Governor Vance sent an embassy to meet the federal commander and obtain what terms he could for the surrender of the capital. He chose Swain and William A. Graham, both former governors and old-line Whigs, to be the emissaries. Vance thought that Swain, his old mountain friend, "would find plenty of acquaintances in the enemy's camp or at least prove that he knew the fathers of many of the officers."[39] Vance proved right: On his arrival at headquarters, Swain "not only claimed General Sherman as an old correspondent, a fellow college president, but immediately seized upon two or three members of his staff whose parents and pedigrees he knew and was soon at home among them."[40]

At the initial conference the commanding general, who had been superintendent of the State Military Academy of Louisiana, assured Swain, "as one college president to another," that the University of North Carolina, its buildings and property, would be safeguarded. On April 13, 1865, at the capitol in Raleigh, Swain met the federal officer charged with hoisting the Stars and Stripes over the building. Swain informed him of Sherman's promise that the state capital, with its libraries, museum, public records, and charitable institutions, would not be damaged. That afternoon, accompanied by Graham, President Swain personally delivered the keys of the capitol to General Sherman.[41]

The delegation's visit to Sherman's headquarters saved Raleigh and Chapel Hill. But it also spurred the hostility of more zealous Confederates against Swain and the university. The final sentence of Sherman's dispatch to General Kilpatrick in the field read as follows: "If you reach the University, do not disturb its library, buildings, or specific property."

The collapse of the Confederacy came soon afterward. As Wheeler's forces retreated northward, the first Yankee bluejackets reached Chapel Hill on a memorable Sunday, April 16, described by Cornelia Spencer:

> We sat in our pleasant piazzas and awaited events with quiet resignation. The silver had all been buried. . . . There was not much provision to be carried off. . . . Just at sunset a sedate and soldierly-looking man at the head of a dozen men dressed in blue rode quietly in by the Raleigh Road. Governor Swain, accompanied by a few of the principal citizens, met them at the entrance and stated that he had General Sherman's promise that the town and university should be saved from pillage. The soldiers replied that such were his orders, and they should

be observed. . . . The next morning, being Easter Monday, April 17, General Atkins, at the head of a detachment of four thousand cavalry, entered about 8 A.M. and we were captured.[42]

Mrs. Spencer added that "we in town were treated with the utmost civility," but the surrounding country was ransacked.

After General Joseph E. Johnson surrendered to General Sherman at the Bennett House near Durham, Swain again was projected into negotiations between the defeated Confederates and their conquerors. In May he was invited to Washington as one of three delegates to confer with President Andrew Johnson over the Reconstruction government of North Carolina. Johnson had in mind appointing a provisional governor and asked the delegation to make recommendations. Swain favored calling a convention of the people and was unwilling to propose any names. When he withdrew, the others suggested W. W. Holden, and he was appointed.[43]

Meanwhile at Chapel Hill, Cornelia Spencer reported that "the whole of this so lately flushed, defiant, scornful South lies prostrate, cowed, submissive." Of commencement week, she wrote in her diary: "What a sight for the old habitues of this place—four graduates. some 10 or 12 students in all, two trustees present. Pa [Dr. James Phillips] officiated in Governor Swain's place. The chapel audience was made up of villagers and children."[44]

President Swain's skill as conciliator and peacemaker faced an even more grievous and personal test. When Brigadier General Smith B. Atkins of Illinois, age thirty, and his brigade arrived to occupy Chapel Hill, the general called on President Swain and was politely received. Among the unintended receivers was Swain's attractive, twenty-one-year-old daughter, Eleanor Hope (Ellie). News of President Lincoln's assassination had just arrived and the assemblage was nervous. In the course of the conversation Swain, a history buff who wanted to show his military visitor General Cornwallis's order book, slipped into a side room and asked his daughter to get the book upstairs. She did and, as Mrs. Spencer reported, "threw up her head and marched in with great display of *hauteur.* An introduction was unavoidable which was more than the Governor had intended."[45]

Out of that meeting came the courtship and marriage of Eleanor Hope Swain and Smith B. Atkins. Every evening General Atkins sent the regimental band to play in President Swain's front yard. One day a Sherman orderly brought Swain a gift from the general, a fine horse. Then General

Atkins gave Ellie a riding horse. "Considering that these animals had doubt-less been swept from Southern stables," Mrs. Spencer wrote, "the accepting of these gifts was a great mistake."[46]

On the May evening after General Atkins and his command left Chapel Hill for other duties, Ellie handed her parents a note in which she formally notified them that she had accepted the general's proposal of marriage and nothing could change her mind. President and Mrs. Swain were deeply agitated but felt helpless. They scheduled the wedding for August. It was a handsome affair to which many were invited but few attended. Mrs. Spencer, among the guests, wrote in her diary that a good deal of bitter feeling was expressed in the village. "Invitations were spat upon in one or two houses. . . . The only way one can find an apology for it all is to believe honestly in the love which appears to have brought it about. Let us think and speak respectfully of a genuine love affair." Among the specialties of the wedding supper at the president's house that August evening was a large cake presented to the bridegroom with the compliments of "the colored people of Chapel Hill. They regarded the General at that time as their deliverer. The guests all crowded around this cake, placed on a small table apart and commented upon it with great good humor. I believe it was carried to Illinois intact."[47]

Even in the face of these blows Swain struggled to keep the university's doors open. The president's efforts to deal with "the enemy" were viewed as scandalous by many of his fellow North Carolinians. It was told from mouth to mouth and believed all over the state that Ellie Swain went to Illinois loaded down with finery and jewels stolen from the women of the South and given her by her husband.[48]

Swain, somewhat naively, thought that the war was over and that he and others could rapidly restore the antebellum status quo. He traveled to New York where he dined with Horace Greeley and associated with military notables on pleasant terms. He had been rather favorably impressed with President Johnson, and he even thought he could arrange loans for the fast-collapsing university with John Jacob Astor, which proved futile.

The university's sources of revenue had dried up along with its supply of students. When the trustees examined the financial wreck, they were appalled. Debts were $103,000 along with $7,000 arrears in salaries. The institution owned 2,000 shares of worthless bank stock, $25,000 in worthless Confederate securities, and a few other assets paying little interest.[49]

As for the students, they did not return in any great number after the war.

The economic collapse had reduced the priority of education. President Swain's activities as peacemaker had sullied the institution's reputation in many circles. There were fewer than 100 students between 1865 and 1868, while 700 students flocked to General Lee's new college at Lexington and the University of Virginia. Only three young men graduated in the spring of 1866. A great furor was aroused when the senior class sought to name conspicuous Confederate leaders, such as Jefferson Davis and General Lee, as "managers" for the commencement ball. The young ex-governor Zeb Vance, who had survived the war with an enhanced reputation, delivered the commencement address, "The Duties of Defeat." The university's future was bleak because it was torn by divided loyalties. "One faction, led by the new provisional governor W. W. Holden was denouncing the university as a center of aristocracy and rebellion. Another was accusing it of undue sympathy with Yankees and atheists."[50]

"Governor Swain's day was over," Cornelia Spencer wrote, "but he could not, would not, see that it was so; still less would he believe that there had been anything impolitic in his own management. The rudder had slipped from his hold, but he still thought to regain it."[51]

In 1867 the trustees and Swain succeeded in persuading the General Assembly to appropriate $7,000 to pay faculty salaries for the year. Simultaneously, they obtained additional funds through transfer to the university of the state's right to land script under the Morrill Act. But they remained in dire circumstances because student enrollment was slim, due to both economic paralysis and lack of confidence in Swain's administration. In a desperate effort to restore confidence the trustees appointed a committee, comprised of the young Raleigh lawyer Kemp P. Battle as chairman, William A. Graham, and Samuel F. Phillips, to study reorganization of the university's administration and curriculum. To assist in this effort President Swain and the faculty submitted their resignations, which were accepted in the fall of 1867. But the restructuring, which called for the creation of independent schools, higher scholastic standards, some electives, and less emphasis on the classics, while approved by the trustees, would not take effect until the 1868 commencement.

In the interim, President Johnson, who had spoken at Chapel Hill while visiting his old birthplace in Raleigh several months before, found himself in serious trouble. Congress overruled his moderate program for reconstruction and imposed its own harsher policies. Victory of the congressional reconstructionists eliminated all prospects for a compromised sectional peace.

It brought to the fore a politico-military regime governing under the tough Reconstruction Acts of 1867. In North Carolina this meant organizing the Republican party to carry out the will of Congress. The new party's constituents comprised what the old regime called "Carpetbaggers" and "scalawags" along with newly enfranchised blacks.[52]

In the forefront of this movement to reorganize the political and institutional life of the state appeared the shrewd and ambitious William W. Holden. Having been appointed provisional governor by President Johnson, he quickly moved to seize control under the new regime and won the governorship on his own initiative in 1868. Holden, born of a humble family near Hillsboro, had first been a talented, self-educated Raleigh editor, changing his politics as rapidly as the times demanded. He once told Swain: "I am, sir, like yourself, not a graduate of the university."[53]

Having begun his political life as a Whig, Holden shifted to become a Democratic champion of states' rights and secession when it seemed expedient. Then he shifted again to lead the "peace" party during the closing months of the war, finally joining the congressional abolitionists. Governor Vance observed of him: "Holden was for 10 years the great leader and teacher of secession."

Holden had already told friends he intended to "smoke out the old rookery at Chapel Hill." That was what he did after his election in 1868 when he became, ex officio, chairman of the university's Board of Trustees. The state's new Reconstruction constitution placed the university under the supervision of the State Board of Education. Holden had control of that board. At the 1868 commencement the old trustee board, anticipating its own demise, canceled its restructuring plans and reappointed Swain and his faculty. When the seventy-eight members of the new board were announced, only four had belonged to the old board, and only Swain, fast aging and growing deaf, failed to see that his presidency was ended. Even as the new board met for the first time on July 23, Swain thought it would need his experience and expertise to carry on. After attending the first meeting by invitation, Swain was shocked to learn that, at a second meeting the next day, the board had announced that his resignation of the previous year and those of the old faculty had been accepted. Swain addressed an eloquent letter of protest to Governor Holden, but he got no reply.[54]

To make his decisions clear and also to protect campus property, Governor Holden sent a squadron of militia to take control of the university. The last entry in Cornelia Spencer's diary for 1868 was abrupt: "Holden's Gov. has announced that the University shall *not* be re-opened on the 17th of July as Governor Swain had advertised. All is at an end."

All *was* at an end for those who had managed the university through the antebellum years. Some were not present to witness the death rites. In 1857 Dr. Elisha Mitchell had fallen over a cliff to his death while exploring the upper reaches of the mountain named in his honor. In 1867 Dr. James Phillips, the venerable professor of mathematics, toppled over in chapel where he had gone to deliver a sermon. A student, Alexander Graham, father of a future university president, Frank Porter Graham, eased his fall.

President Swain, shaken by the collapse of his administration, approached another August, the month he most dreaded. The year before, it had been the month of his daughter's marriage to General Atkins. On August 11, 1868, Swain hitched the horse that General Sherman had given him to a buggy and invited Professor Manuel Fetter to take a ride with him in the country. They drove six miles to a plantation owned by Swain. On the return trip the unruly horse bolted, a wheel hit a stump, and both men were thrown to the ground. Swain was so bruised that he was carried home on a stretcher. In a few days he was able to see friends in his bedroom. But he did not improve. The governor read much in his Bible and often rested with closed eyes. Before daylight he often chanted familiar hymns. On August 27 he sat up in bed and seemed stronger, but suddenly collapsed. Mrs. Spencer, who had been called, stood by his bedside. "I saw him pass," she wrote, "gently and without a sigh." Swain died in the same room where his predecessor, Joseph Caldwell, had died thirty-three years before.

Cornelia Spencer's brother Charles Phillips preached the funeral service at the Chapel Hill Presbyterian Church. David Lowry Swain was buried in the rear of his house "beside his gentle, deranged daughter, Anne, and his son David." "With him died the University," Mrs. Spencer wrote. "And with the University perished the prosperity of the town."[55] Within a few weeks the old faculty, the few that were left, met together, prayed solemnly in company, shook hands, and bade each other Godspeed.

COLLAPSE OF

THE PEOPLE'S COLLEGE,

1 8 6 9 – 1 8 7 1

But the university did not die when Governor Swain met his nemesis in the shape of a gift horse from General Sherman. Like the phoenix, it succumbed momentarily to the upheaval of war that ravaged all the South's institutions. For many, especially Cornelia Spencer and the old leaders, a golden era ended. During the antebellum years they built and managed a small academy educating the sons of the gentry for public service and professional careers. Slowly, as its clientele grew, including sons of expatriate North Carolinians from all over the South, the university expanded its horizons and became more than a minor college.

On the brink of the 1860s it had begun to build a national reputation. But civil war and its aftermath brought an end to all that. The resulting strife toppled the old leaders and broadened the campus's base. Commenting later on what happened, Governor Zeb Vance noted of Governor Holden and company that "the reformation, wherewith they reformed it, bore a strong family likeness to that with which Attila and his Scythian progressionalist civilized Italy."[1] Mrs. Spencer and her Whig associates considered Holden no better than Beelzebub himself.

Others, judging later in less emotional times, saw less rascality and more frustrated idealism in some of the reconstructionists. Holden thought he was defeating an outworn aristocracy. As a visionary and a pragmatist, he described his role as trying to broaden and democratize the university—to make it a "people's college." Whatever the man's motives, his opportunism, his ruthless tactics, and his inept lieutenants aroused justified hostility and doomed his efforts to failure.[2]

Holden's people's college began in January 1869 when he and his executive committee anointed a new president and faculty. The new president, the Reverend Solomon Pool, brother of U.S. senator John Pool, had been influential in persuading Holden to reopen "the old rookery." Solomon Pool, by a stroke of irony, was a second-honors, 1853 university graduate and a classmate of Cornelia Phillips Spencer's late husband, James. Her father, the Reverend James Phillips, taught Pool and made him adjunct professor of mathematics in 1861. Obviously he was no incompetent. Born of a Methodist family on a farm near Elizabeth City, Pool left Chapel Hill in 1866 to become deputy revenue appraiser in Raleigh, where he met and became a friend of Holden.

Those who knew Pool considered him a man of some ability. He was described by one of his critics as a "smallish, curly-haired man with pompous ways." There was gossip that his brothers, like Governor Holden himself, had to be "legitimized" in late boyhood.[3] Yet Pool was acknowledged to be an able writer and speaker, handicapped, however, by a lack of magnetism and a meager sense of humor. When he left Chapel Hill in 1875, he went on to teach school at Cary, near Raleigh, and to fill various ministerial vacancies in Methodist churches at Winston and Greensboro. When Pool died in 1901, he was a respected figure. His pastor said of him: "I profoundly believe that, take him all in all, he was the purest and best man I ever knew."[4]

For Cornelia Spencer, however, Pool was the devil incarnate. "Drop Mr. Pool into the boots of Dr. Caldwell or of Governor Swain and he may peep over the tops," she wrote in her diary. She noted his report during the 1868 state constitutional convention in which he charged the university with being under the undue influence of aristocracy and family connections. At that time Pool counseled, "Better to close it than have it a nursery of treason."[5] She also noted that Pool had commented, "Let the present board of trustees be superseded by a loyal board and the university will be a blessing instead of a curse."

Pool was by no means the administrator of "national reputation" Holden's group bragged it would choose. Neither were his five faculty associates, although one, Fisk P. Brewer, was a graduate of Yale and a brother of a U.S. Supreme Court justice. Brewer became professor of Greek language and literature. He supported the rights of blacks and, while principal of a school

The Reverend Solomon Pool, university president during Reconstruction.
(North Carolina Collection, University of North Carolina Library, Chapel Hill)

for blacks in Raleigh, shocked white society by inviting blacks to dine at his home.

David Settle Patrick, the Latin professor, was a native of Rockingham County and nephew of Judge Thomas Settle, an old Republican adversary of Governor Vance. He graduated from the university in 1856 and served as a school principal in Arkansas. He brought his family to live in the president's house across the street from Cornelia Spencer. He immediately aroused her ire by felling some of the oaks in the yard for firewood and looting the Phi Society hall, "carrying off velvet rug, carpet and handsome chairs in order to entertain the trustees at the President's house in all the rich splendor of pilfered furniture."[6]

The new head of the English department, James A. Martling, was a brother-in-law of S. S. Ashley, the state superintendent of public instruction. He came from Missouri, where he had been a schoolteacher. Little was known of his competency.

George Dixon, an English Quaker appointed professor of agriculture, immediately fell out with the old establishment when he destroyed a grove of trees south of South Building in order to establish a model farm. After a few months he visited his native Yorkshire and never returned to Chapel Hill.

The fifth member of the faculty, Professor Alexander McIver, struck the old guard as civilized. He was a native Tar Heel and a first-honors graduate of the same 1853 class as James Spencer and Solomon Pool. Davidson College had dismissed him from its faculty in a situation paralleling the earlier Hedrick case at Chapel Hill: He favored Ulysses S. Grant for president. An acknowledged Republican, McIver took the chair of mathematics vacated by the Reverend Charles Phillips, who moved into McIver's position at Davidson.

McIver, alone among what Nancy Hilliard described as the stump-tail faculty, decided to call on Cornelia Spencer and make his manners. She was at first dignified and aloof, but when McIver recalled her late husband, James, and spoke warmly of her father and Governor Swain, "she melted and was almost won over in one sitting." She wrote to Mrs. Swain in Raleigh: "He talked like a good man as well as a sensible one. He would have been much the best choice for president."[7]

Holden, Pool, and company prepared themselves for the fight of their lives. As the year began, the university and the village confronted advanced stages of deterioration. Members of the old faculty had packed their bags and departed. Judge W. H. Battle, Nancy Hilliard, and Dr. Mallett, the village physician, had moved to Raleigh. Grass remained uncut on the campus, and classrooms and the society halls were vandalized. Governor Vance lamented,

> This noble property of the State is fast sinking into ruin. Many of the grand old trees have been laid low for firewood. Doors are off their hinges and broken down, windows without blinds or glass, carpets torn up and carried off, the halls (Society halls) are measureably stripped of their furniture and adornings; and almost everything portable is either injured, destroyed or stolen. . . . An air of melancholy, of *ruin*, pervades everything where once there was so much active and intelligent life, where so much of North Carolina's moral and intellectual greatness were found and fitted for her advancement, where were centered so much of her hope and her pride.[8]

In January 1869 Vance's laments were heightened when he learned that Cornelia Spencer planned to move to Alabama. He wrote her an impassioned letter in which he said,

> I felt I could not let you go without expressing my regret. . . . Somehow I want you and all those who have labored to serve the dear old state, to feel toward North Carolina as I do—that we should not desert her in the day of her humiliation. I love her the more because of her sorrows and degradation. I should be greatly pleased to hear that the way has been opened for you to remain here and abet us in watching for the better day whose dawning we do not doubt. . . . Oh, how I sorrow for Chapel Hill! How worse than desolate it must look under the oaks! I don't know how you can live on there, thinking always of the past. How I miss my dear friend Governor Swain! Alas, alas, our pleasant village is broken up and destroyed indeed![9]

Largely as a result of this letter, Mrs. Spencer visited Governor Vance in Charlotte. While there, she arranged to write a weekly column for the *North Carolina Presbyterian* (at $400 a year). This income helped her decide to remain in Chapel Hill with her enfeebled mother and daughter. She did not return to her husband's home in Alabama.

Thus a half-deaf, grittily determined daughter of an English emigrant from Cornwall became the chief adversary of the Pool regime. Although widowed and alone, "when the dark was complete [she] lit a candle and polished her weapons."[10]

Cornelia Phillips Spencer, by all reports, was a "very remarkable woman."

Her strong intellectual interests, her knowledge of classical and modern literature, and her poise, taste, and courage would have "made her light shine anywhere."[11] When one of his friends declared that Mrs. Spencer was the smartest woman in North Carolina, Governor Vance replied, "And the smartest man too."[12] Cornelia Spencer's weapon was her pen. Immediately after the war, like her brother Samuel Phillips, she favored reconciliation between the North and South. But the arrival of the Holden-Pool regime transformed her from a Unionist into a rabid anti-Republican. Convinced that Chapel Hill would never again be as she fondly remembered it in the antebellum days, she launched a vigorous campaign of letter writing and sent signed and anonymous newspaper and religious magazine articles around the state. Forceful, vindictive, and headstrong, she aimed unerringly at toppling the new regime. As a skillful polemicist, she freely indulged in exaggeration and overkill, blaming every ill on the Republicans, no matter where it originated. In the eyes of most of her fellow Tar Heels, "her appeal was well-reasoned and profoundly emotional, a veritable *cri de coeur;* and therefore she poignantly touched the hearts of thousands of her readers."[13]

The people of the state imposed a virtual boycott on the Pool administration when the university's doors reopened on January 3, 1869. As at that earlier opening in 1795, not a single student was in evidence. One appeared for a day, but finding that he would be the entire student body and not welcoming that status, he disappeared.[14] Mrs. Spencer wrote to Mrs. Swain about this event: "As for poor Chapel Hill, the university opened on the 3rd [of January]. No students have appeared or can be detected with the aid of a magnifying glass. I am divided between exultation that it is so and sorrow for the poor village, so utterly dependent on the college for a living."[15]

That portion of the state press controlled by the conservatives unleashed a storm of criticism on the new administration. In the bitterness of defeat, most commentators were caustic and full of personal invective. Typical was a comment from the *Wilmington Daily Journal:* "We are still ready to yield to that institution [Chapel Hill] an earnest, honest, hearty and zealous support at the first moment in which we can send our sons there without degradation. This time will not arrive, however, until such pismires as now infest the place shall be swept away. . . . We do demand the appointment of a president and professors upon other recommendations than those of partisan malice, partisan prejudice, and family ties."[16]

Besides the poor response from students, Pool received no financial help from the Republican legislature in Raleigh. Already it was rocked by an orgy of corrupt bond issues and other dubious appropriations. As the old establishment watched the growing turmoil, Governor Vance wrote Mrs. Spencer words of encouragement: "Hold things in a sort of solution," he wrote, "and wait for the event. Don't hurry. They who can play the waiting game are winners in the end."[17]

In the meantime Cornelia Spencer established another journalistic connection that gave her views wider distribution. In April of 1869 she began a series of "Pen and Ink Sketches" in the *Daily Sentinel* (of Raleigh), an organ of the Democratic party, dealing with current affairs and personalities. She described her contributions as a "series of short spicy numbers giving a popular account of its [the university's] rise and progress . . . with, of course, poisoned arrows for the present incomparable incapables."[18]

Mrs. Spencer's poisoned-arrow articles, some of them written over the initials "H. H." or "Y. Y.," contained strong language, so much so that the Republicans assumed they were written by a man. In one she described Pool as an "arrogant prig, without two clear ideas in his brains beyond his own selfish aggrandizement and his own two-penny schemes."[19] In other articles she wrote rebuttals to her own criticisms, all in attempts to keep the university issue before the public.

One of her most stinging charges criticized Pool for hanging on to his tax collector job and providing jobs in his department for two brothers-in-law and installing his mother-in-law as postmistress. Pool did retain his old job for six or eight months after moving to Chapel Hill, and his mother-in-law served as postmistress.[20]

Holden, Pool, and the faculty did not endure these attacks quietly. In a slashing rejoinder published in the *North Carolina Standard,* Pool labeled the conservatives "biased and selfish-minded persons." He described Mrs. Spencer as a "daughter of a former professor in the university, and sister of another, who, together, have received as a salary, out of the treasury, at least $75,000."[21]

Leading citizens of Chapel Hill became alarmed over the decline of the university and the village, which, one said, was "withering to nothingness." They requested conservative newspapers not to criticize the university management too harshly until it could be demonstrated to be a failure. A village merchant, a member of Pool's own Methodist church, urged the president to resign, pointing out the ruin of the town. Pool replied: "I would not resign for $50,000. My course has never occasioned a regret or self-reproach."[22]

As commencement approached, Cornelia Spencer observed that "there are only three students, two Pools and a Guthrie. The rest are preps." She added in mid-June that the Pools planned commencement social functions, but "nobody came—or only a very few. Ten trustees and seven others."[23]

On the other hand the Republicans used the *Standard* to describe the 1869 commencement in glowing terms. They mentioned the beautiful buildings and grounds of "the people's university" open to all, no longer reserved "for the few." They attacked the conservatives' "prejudice and passion" as unworthy and as something that would pass.[24]

When President Grant failed to keep his engagement as commencement speaker, Holden himself served as substitute. While Professor McIver told Mrs. Spencer that Pool's inaugural address was "sophomoric, hifalutin' and commonplace,"[25] Holden's speech took a different tone. He reasserted his conviction that the institution was "the people's university" and pledged full support, morally and financially. "If parents and guardians who possess the means will not send their sons here, because of prejudice, or from resentment toward those who now control the institution, the people of the state will fill these halls with meritorious poor young men and will maintain and educate them at public charge."[26]

On that occasion Holden spoke forcefully of the need for educating newly freed slaves. He said the trustees had made the commitment to blacks for establishing their school elsewhere, but "it will be *one* university, the University of North Carolina. Education knows no color or condition of mankind."[27]

Holden referred to the trustees' never-consummated plan to open a state school for blacks at Raleigh. The new institution would have been a branch of the university. Later, however, the trustees, under political heat from the conservatives, prohibited "persons of color" from entering the university at Chapel Hill. Nevertheless, erroneous reports persisted that blacks attended the university and that a black was a member of the faculty during Reconstruction.[28]

The governor encouraged larger student enrollment and recommended that the General Assembly appropriate funds to provide free tuition for 170 students. These efforts failed.[29] By 1870 Holden and the Republican General Assembly were embroiled in the railroad bond scandals, which helped speed Holden's impeachment.

As Pool struggled to keep the university open, Cornelia Spencer continued her barrage of missives around the state. "Chapel Hill," she wrote, "is given up to pigs and pigmies who try to fill the seats of the mighty." By March of

1870 she was discouraged. "Chapel Hill was never quite so low," she wrote in her diary. "You may walk from end to end at 11 o'clock in the day and not see six people. I am writing letters. It is the only thing I can do."

Her letters were addressed to leading men of the state—Whigs, Democrats, and Republicans—asking their opinion about free, state-financed public schools and colleges. Adopting Holden's own idea, she championed the cause of free schools at all levels. This became part of a protracted campaign for university redemption and statewide common school education.[30]

One of her replies came from former governor William A. Graham, in which he suggested that there was "no hope" of reviving the university under the Pool administration. A convention to change the state constitution, he thought, would be necessary. Graham believed that the university should be funded first and then the common schools "if both were not possible," a view Mrs. Spencer did not share. "The grounds, groves, buildings, libraries, etc., of our university should not be allowed to lie in disuse."[31] Graham supported "educating downward" and did not think the state had money for both a university and common schools.

With only a handful of students and meager tuition funds, the administration's efforts were fast failing at Chapel Hill. Village stores refused the faculty further credit. Professor Patrick declared openly that he expected the old concern would bust up in June and that he wished it was now. In the *North Carolina Presbyterian* Mrs. Spencer noted that President Pool's second commencement (1870) was "an even more private affair than the one of 1869. Fourteen visitors, including children, went to hear the wisdom of King Solomon [Solomon Pool] and the music of the Fayetteville Brass Band."[32]

Holden's downfall, which also closed the university, stemmed from his unsuccessful confrontation with the rising terrorism of the Ku Klux Klan. The conservatives were determined to reestablish white supremacy, even if it meant lawlessness. They would not accept the Republican party's efforts to guarantee political and legal equality for blacks, which they considered an attempt to enforce social equality.[33]

The North Carolina Klan first appeared in the vicinity of Orange County in 1867. It featured brawls, night ridings, and whippings to instill fear in the populace. By 1869 its members began to ride openly in communities not far from Chapel Hill. Then one night they arrived in the village "clad in their usual uniforms of disguise," according to the *North Carolina Standard*. "They passed through the streets upon horses making *goosy noises*," the

Republican newspaper reported. During the fourth "riding," some 50 to 200 horsemen arrived one midnight "enquiring the whereabouts of the negroes and white radicals 'that were going to shoot K.K.'s if they interfered with them' and breaking into the house of Mr. Henry Jones, colored (knowing that he was from home) and rocking the residence of the notable November Esq. . . . (Then) they retired, as they would be pleased to have it, to parts unknown."[34] The "notable November Esq" was President Swain's black coachman, widely known as Dr. November.

Mrs. Spencer described the stoning of Dr. November's home as a "mistake." She believed that the night riders came from Chatham, not Orange County. Although disturbed by the outbreak of lawlessness, she did not write much about it.[35]

Pool, however, became greatly alarmed. The night riders, as he saw it, were intent on annoying and intimidating his faculty. He asked Holden for protection by the state militia. The governor, perturbed and cautious, told him to get the county magistrates to sign a petition requesting help. Pool never took such action.[36]

Holden launched a counterattack on the Klan in 1868. In a series of proclamations he expressed hopes for a peaceful solution. At the same time he reiterated his determination to provide equal justice for all. By March 1869 he dispatched a company of militia to Alamance County in a futile attempt to curb Klan activities. This action fanned the flames. Then black members of the Republican-sponsored Union League struck back by burning mills, barns, and homes of their former masters.[37]

The turmoil increased, resulting in the murder of an unsavory Caswell County Republican named John "Chicken" Stephens. Holden decided to organize a militia, one unit of which he placed under Colonel George W. Kirk, an aggressive Tennessee Unionist. Holden sent Kirk to restore order in Caswell County. In the process, as North Carolina moved toward the brink of renewed civil war, Kirk refused to release prisoners he had captured, even on habeas corpus writs signed by Chief Justice Richmond M. Pearson. Simultaneously, Holden brought companies of black troops into Raleigh.[38]

Then Holden's forces overreached themselves. They arrested the governor's chief critic, *Sentinel* editor Josiah Turner of Raleigh, a fiery conservative who had castigated the governor unmercifully. The governor's final undoing came when President Grant refused to sustain his use of military troops. "Once the issue had been placed before the courts, Grant seemingly lost all interest and stopped further support."[39]

Turner's arrest occurred the day after the crucial off-year state elections of August 1870. The Kirk-Holden war had so alarmed and frightened the state's conservative voters that they rose up and defeated the Republicans by a substantial margin. Samuel F. Phillips, who had become a Republican, was defeated in his race for attorney-general, and the Democrats won a comfortable victory in the state Senate and House.[40]

When the unexpected election results became public, a cry arose for Holden's impeachment. Within five months the General Assembly, working at top speed, arraigned, impeached, tried, and convicted Holden and banished him from his gubernatorial post, marking the first conviction upon impeachment of a governor in the United States.

The Democratic rebound encouraged those struggling to install new management at Chapel Hill. They renewed their efforts, but their task remained delicate. Threats of violence in the village had caused Holden to send troops to occupy the village all during the year preceding the Kirk-Holden war.[41] Even after the election, pillage of abandoned buildings continued. Cornelia Spencer reported that "gangs of Negroes spend the nights in the Old South Building, rioting, shouting, drinking. You have no idea of the degredation."[42]

Pool tried to keep the university open, but only fifteen students appeared for the new term in the fall of 1870. By December they had disappeared. With Holden's impeachment under way and no funds available, the trustees gave up hope. There was an abortive attempt to reopen classes on January 14, 1871, with an "average attendance" of four students. Exercises were postponed until January 29 when only two students remained.[43] As faculty members packed to depart, the collapse was complete.

William Joseph Peele, an honors graduate of 1879 and a member of the Raleigh bar, recalled later the scene when he arrived as a freshman at the reopened university in 1875: "I noticed that there was a subdued silence through the grounds. A few lonely-looking students could be seen going in and out of the old buildings, selecting their rooms, which were now musty from long disuse. Occasionally might still be seen relics and reminders of old student life. I saw written in chalk in one of the old recitation rooms a memorandum of that brief and disastrous attempt to continue the university after the death of Governor Swain by those unfamiliar with its traditions. It read: 'This old University has busted and gone to hell today.' "[44]

Scribbled below was the date: February 1, 1871.

RECONSTRUCTION AND REVITALIZATION,

1872 – 1875

Even though the governorship remained in Republican hands until later, the high tide of Reconstruction crested in the Kirk-Holden war and the resounding Democratic political victory of August 1870.

In Chapel Hill the roots of the university, which "had been planted and grown in conservative soil"[1]—starting with Davie's Federalists and continuing through Caldwell's and Swain's Whigs—began to stir again. Cornelia Spencer, who never quite accepted her brother's defection to the Republicans, began to see early signs of the dawn predicted by her friend Governor Vance. To Mrs. Swain, visiting her daughter Ellie in Illinois, she wrote: "It was indeed delightful to me to feel that the days of that party [the Republicans] were numbered. Chapel Hillians especially were bound to rejoice, you may be sure. Poor Miss Nancy Hilliard talks as if she already saw all the old faculty reinstated, and 300 students coming in. I doubt if any of the old faculty ever come back, and it will be long before prosperity is restored to an institution so degraded. I want the first step toward reform taken by the new legislature, by the reorganization of the University. I want this crew turned out."[2]

Mrs. Spencer got her wish. The Old Whigs, of whom she and Governor Vance were prime examples, merged gradually with the Democrats so that nothing was ever quite the same again. Most of the Whigs moved quietly into the newly energized Democratic party, where they served as a welcomed leavening in the stormy political times. This development kept North Carolina out of the hands of the irascible demagogues who later disgraced much of the Deep South. "It was a moderating influence, tending to dull the edge of Democratic Party bitterness."[3]

Among the emerging leaders sobered by the political chaos was Kemp Plummer Battle, a lawyer of impeccable Whig credentials. Faithful to the Confederacy as long as it lasted, he never relinquished hope that the old union would be restored. As a Raleigh attorney and banker, this son of the university's first law school professor, W. H. Battle, came near getting burned in the conflagration surrounding the railroad bond scandals that wrecked the Holden Republicans. On the edge of the nefarious ring headed by General Milton S. Littlefield, a carpetbagger, and George W. Swepson, an old-line southerner, Battle represented some of the Conservative party members who were paid off, in railroad bonds, to keep the skids greased for corrupt legislative schemes.[4]

Earlier than most of his contemporaries, Battle realized that a new day had arrived for the cotton culture South. The old plantation leadership, never strong in North Carolina, had been defeated. Immediately after Lee's surrender Battle saw the wisdom of welcoming new entrepreneurs with fresh ideas for a prostrate state. In a letter to Cornelia Spencer in 1865 he championed a hearty union with northern people, inviting and assisting immigration south, calling in capital, welcoming workers, and opening up every source of national prosperity.[5]

Battle, a nephew of Cornelia Spencer's sister-in-law, wrote Mrs. Spencer a letter of condolence after her brother's defeat in the August elections. "Mr. Sam [Phillips] was nominated by the honest element of the Republican Party led by Tod Caldwell. It was a bitter pill for Holden. I have not had such pain in years; but he is so truthful, honorable and noble that he will outlive the false impression of the present day."

Sam Phillips went on to become solicitor-general under President Grant in 1872, and Battle went on to become president of the newly reopened University of North Carolina in 1876.

In the interim another figure helped revive the college. Alexander McIver, the Pool administration's mathematics professor, succeeded S. S. Ashley as state superintendent of public instruction. One of his first acts in 1872 was to call a UNC alumni meeting in Raleigh to discuss reopening the university. Cornelia Spencer collaborated, urging influential friends to attend and gaining publicity through newspapers and magazines.[6] About fifty former students gathered for the first meeting in the state Senate chamber on February 1, 1872. "It was a sight to me that made tears lie very near the surface,"

Cornelia Phillips Spencer, who helped reopen the university after Reconstruction. (North Carolina Collection, University of North Carolina Library, Chapel Hill)

Mrs. Spencer wrote her mother. "There were Graham and his boys, and Barringer, and Battle and his sons, and the Binghams and the Haywoods, and many another familiar name and face."[7]

The group appointed a committee composed of Graham, Battle, and Barringer to confer with the trustees' executive committee. Meanwhile Cornelia Spencer's feud with Pool intensified as she lamented the sadly deteriorated conditions on campus. In a letter to the *Sentinel* she described a visit to the library of the Phi Society, where she discovered tattered books, dirty tables, shattered engravings, and the broken remains of the busts of university fathers. "Let there be at least one hand left in the state to take up these relics tenderly—be it only a woman's—and one heart to swell with kindly recollection of the past, and mourn that on these walls is inscribed Ichabod—for the glory is departed."[8]

This letter elicited a response from Pool. He accused several local boys of vandalizing the library under the direction of Mrs. Spencer and suggested that her statements "should always be taken with many grains of allowance." He added, "It is to be regretted that she selects such means of gaining access to the College Hall. There are those who believe she ought to be indicted."[9] Pool suggested that by moving out of a "woman's sphere" and becoming involved with the university, Cornelia Spencer emulated the activities of Victoria Woodhull, a notorious New York stockbroker and feminist who was imprisoned on charges of sending obscene material through the mail.

The *Sentinel* refused to publish Pool's letter, but it was published by the *Weekly Era*, a Republican newspaper, and caused a furor across the state. *Sentinel* editor Josiah Turner, Jr., launched a campaign to defend Cornelia Spencer's name. He assailed Pool's article as "vile calumny" and described him as a "monster" and a "fool."[10] Other newspapers and magazines joined the rebuttal. A protest meeting was held in Chapel Hill on August 16, 1873.[11] Mrs. Spencer's initiatives thus linked Pool indelibly with the oppressive Republicans and stirred up more support for redeeming the university.

During the same year, the General Assembly approved an amendment to the 1868 state constitution shifting authority to appoint university trustees from the executive to the legislative department, thus moving it from Republican to Democratic control. Governor Tod Caldwell, successor to the deposed Holden, cooperated with this effort, along with a bipartisan coalition. Caldwell, however, balked at what he held to be irregularities in the amendment technicalities, but its validity was upheld by a state supreme court decision in 1875.[12]

Meanwhile in 1874 the General Assembly authorized a new Board of Trustees, elected by joint ballot of the two houses. Of the sixty-four members, many were Old Whigs—men like W. A. Graham, Charles Manly, Paul Cameron, B. F. Moore, W. L. Saunders, D. M. Carter, Seaton Gales, Walter Steele, Rufus Patterson, Judge W. H. Battle, and his son Kemp. At its organizational meeting the board elected Graham permanent chairman and Kemp Battle secretary-treasurer. It directed a committee chaired by Steele to visit Chapel Hill and survey the physical plant and financial status of the defunct institution.

The committee found the campus a wreck—from untended buildings and collapsed walls and gates to demolished shrubbery and spoiled wells. Chairman Steele wrote of the "sadness that overpowered me when my eyes fell for the first time upon the ruined spot." Of the eight buildings described in the report (which confirmed that horses and cattle had been stabled in Old West), the only bright spot was the former Dialectic hall on the third floor of South Building. It was remarkably well preserved, especially the overhead plastering where "the gilded name and motto of the Society look[ed] as fresh and bright as they did over forty years ago."[13]

The university's financial affairs proved to be in an equal state of disarray. Before the board could seek operating revenue, it had to settle a crushing debt load. Treasurer Battle reported that, except for the bankrupt Bank of North Carolina, most of the university's creditors were not disposed to harass it. After tedious negotiations, including the sale of a portion of the university's property, the trustees gradually diminished a debt that at the end of the war included $20,000 owed to individuals and $90,000 due the bank.[14]

In order to achieve this objective, the board obtained a U.S. circuit court decision proscribing sale of buildings or equipment for debt. It assigned a commissioner to determine whether certain real property could also be protected. Ultimately the court shielded the university campus and 600 acres of land, most of it stretching from the southeast to the southwest of the campus. The 70 acres called Piney Prospect on the east, first mentioned by Davie eighty years before, were ordered sold, but they fell into friendly hands when trustee Paul C. Cameron, who became a university benefactor (and after whom Cameron Avenue is named), bought all the parcels offered.[15]

The $200,000 worth of North Carolina bank stock owned by the university, declared a valid debt by the court, had not been sold during the war apparently because university officials feared it might generate criticism from zealous Confederates. It was later scaled down to 25 cents on the dollar and repaid.

Once the major obstacles of entrenched debt had been reduced, the board turned to sources of operating income. After prolonged study the trustees saw their only hope in persuading the General Assembly to revalidate the agricultural and mechanical college Land Scrip Fund, obtained by Governor Swain from the federal government in 1867 under the Morrill Act. Governor Holden's trustees had invested this $125,000 fund in corrupt special tax bonds, later repudiated by the new Democratic legislature. The state remained responsible to the federal government for restoring the principal, but in a closely contested fight the General Assembly authorized the state to pay an annual sum of $7,500 to the university as interest on the money, provided the university offered agricultural and mechanical instruction.

Legislative sentiment split sharply over these payments. Many legislators opposed any such arrangement while the state budget was in disarray, especially one involving education for the sons of the formerly affluent. Others thought the debt should be ignored as so many other debts had been ignored at the time. Yet Treasurer Battle became a highly persuasive advocate of the university's cause. The bill, which had been introduced in the House on February 27, 1875, by Nereus Mendenhall, a member of the Society of Friends from Guilford, passed by a single vote. It passed the Senate by a larger margin, and the university's friends rejoiced.[16]

The General Assembly dispatched a special message to Cornelia Spencer, acknowledged leader of the redemption campaign. The date was March 20, 1875—her fiftieth birthday. She and her daughter, June, collected two neighborhood children, Susan and Jenny Thompson, and as a group departed for the campus. On the way they were joined by another faithful villager, Andrew G. Mickle, once the postmaster and university bursar. Mrs. Spencer led the group along the path through the Episcopal churchyard and across the campus to South Building, climbed to the belfry, seized the rope, and rang and rang the college bell. "She did more than ring a bell," her great-nephew Phillips Russell wrote three-quarters of a century later. "She rang out an old world of defeat and inertia and rang in a new world of hope and belief."[17]

University president Frank Porter Graham, during equally doleful years of the Great Depression, used the story of the woman who rang the bell in his report to the trustees in December 1930: "In the tragic era, Mrs. Cornelia Phillips Spencer, staunch champion of the public schools and University, received on March 20, 1875 a message from the committee in Raleigh that the University was to be opened again. For five years the bell had not rung in Chapel Hill. For five years she had worked and prayed for that day. She climbed the stairs to the belfry, and with her own hands rang the bell which has never ceased to ring to this day. The people of North Carolina were on the march again. Under God, we will not turn back now!"[18]

While the General Assembly arranged legislative financing for the university's reopening, Battle tackled the job of raising money from alumni and friends. He was amazingly successful in those poverty-ridden times. He obtained pledges for some $20,000 to help pay the university's grinding debt and start repairs. After the first exhilaration of the moment had passed, Cornelia Spencer threw herself into another project. She led a campaign to induce the women of North Carolina to outfit the scientific departments of the campus with new and improved apparatus and equipment. The same kind of project had been successful during the regime of Joseph Caldwell.[19]

Gradually a new climate of hope pervaded Chapel Hill. "You must come home to take care of . . . your dear generous mother," Mrs. James Phillips wrote to her granddaughter June Spencer as grass sprouted and flowers unfolded across the village in 1875. "She is pressed into service by public as well as private imposition. Everyone is repairing their front fences."[20]

The Phillips house, like others along Franklin Street, was pulsating with new life. "Important men in wide collars and broad white shirtfronts" were stopping by.[21] Word had come from the trustees that the university was to reopen in early September. News seemed good on every front. Trustee Paul Cameron, the rugged Scotsman of Farintosh Plantation near Hillsboro, was overseeing repairs. Using some of the funds collected by Battle, and much of his own, he spent $10,677 on general refurbishing of dormitories and classrooms and about $2,249 for gas works and piping. He planted new trees around the campus, especially along the avenue soon to bear his name.[22]

Cornelia Spencer had word that her brother, the Reverend Charles Phillips, was returning from Davidson College to rejoin the faculty. Not long afterward the trustees drew up a new curriculum and selected men who would administer it.

The plan eventually chosen called for reopening on the first Monday in September of 1875, with tuition at $60 and room rent at $10 per annum. There were to be six colleges (departments): agriculture, engineering and the mechanic arts, natural sciences, literature, mathematics, and philosophy. To fill these chairs the trustees selected Professor John Kimberly (agriculture), Professor Ralph H. Graves (engineering), Professor A. F. Redd (natural sciences), Professors J. DeB. Hooper and George Tayloe Winston (literature), Dr. Charles Phillips (mathematics), and Professor A. W. Mangum (philosophy).

Of this group Phillips, Hooper, and Kimberly had been members of the antebellum faculty. The trustees made sure that all major religious denominations were represented, recalling accusations of bias in favor of Presbyterians and Episcopalians. Dr. Phillips became chairman of the faculty. Ex-governor Graham, the man most often pushed for the presidency, moved that filling that position be postponed indefinitely. Graham, who suffered from an incurable disease and who had done valuable work toward the reopening, died on August 11, 1875.

Dr. Battle, writing in later years, decided that, among new students, Francis D. Winston of Bertie County won the honor of being the Hinton James of 1875. He arrived first on reopening day at the hilltop of Durham Road and reached the boundary of Chapel Hill before his brother Robert.[23]

Formal celebration of the opening took place on September 15, 1875. Cornelia Spencer and her ladies decorated the chapel with wreaths of evergreens and portraits of the "old worthies"—Davie, Caldwell, Swain, Mitchell, Phillips, Hawks, Badger, Ruffin, Graham, and Manly—borrowed from the two societies. Mrs. Spencer's own motto, Laus Deo, was prominent, woven in evergreen letters. The Salisbury Band played as the procession formed in front of South Building and marched to the chapel. Occupying the rostrum were Governor Curtis Brogden, Judge Battle, Dr. William Hooper, Governor Vance, Dr. Phillips, and Professors Mangum and Redd.

In his introduction of the governor, Dr. Phillips took care to emphasize that the university, while touched by "politics and religion," felt their influences only in the broadest sense. He warned that the faculty should carefully abstain from attempting to influence any students for or against any political party or religious denomination. Governor Brogden made an animated address stressing the importance of education as an ally of modern progress. After a felicitous introduction by Governor Vance, Judge Battle, in the words of a letter to the *Raleigh Times,* had the "tender task to awaken the echoes of memory and bid us remember, resemble and persevere."[24]

Finally, Professor Mangum paid tribute to the work of Mrs. Spencer and introduced her hymn written especially for the occasion and sung by the assemblage, accompanied by the band, to the tune of "Old Hundred."

KEMP P. BATTLE,

A ONE-IDEAL MAN,

1876–1891

"Kemp is surely the right man for this place," Cornelia Phillips Spencer wrote to Ellen Mitchell Summerell in 1876. "He brings an enthusiasm and a love for the university that no money could buy."[1] Mrs. Spencer referred to the unexpected elevation of the affable Raleigh lawyer Kemp Plummer Battle to the presidency of the university on June 17, 1876.

During the previous year, after Governor Graham had declined the presidency because of poor health, the trustees postponed the decision and named the Reverend Charles Phillips chairman of the faculty. In the interim they were torn by contending factions. One group, strongly devoted to the cause of the late Confederacy, favored an "old warrior" type similar to General Robert E. Lee, who had moved quietly into the presidency of Washington College at Lexington. These leaders sought a president "strikingly identified" with the South in the recent war—someone resembling Jefferson Davis, Joseph E. Johnston, or General Matt W. Ransom. The other faction, more representative of the unionist-minded Whigs, preferred a Tar Heel native already strongly identified with Chapel Hill, yet not so much an unredeemed Confederate and "therefore not offensive to men of the opposite party (Republican)."[2]

From the beginning of the war, many North Carolinians had profound reservations about secession. When it failed, they were less inclined than other southerners to indulge in dreams of what might have been. Arnold Toynbee, the British historian, wrote of this spirit prevalent in North Carolina in his *Study of History:* "North Carolina had not been inhibited by the idolization of a once glorious past; she lost comparatively little by defeat in the Civil War because she had comparatively little to lose; and, having had less far to fall, she had that much less difficulty in recovering from the shock."[3]

Toynbee's comment referred to North Carolina's reputation as the Rip Van Winkle State. The state was more poorly developed and less wealthy than its neighbors, contributed more privates and fewer generals to the war than did Virginia or South Carolina, and was less imbued with the cavalier tradition and the plantation culture. When that old culture was demolished, North Carolina had fewer "mummies," in Walter Hines Page's term—fewer zealous Confederates immobilized by defeat, looking to the past and vulnerable to bottom-layer demagogues.

Kemp Battle epitomized the distinctly independent Tar Heel tradition. His family sprang from an ancestor who fought in the Revolution. Elisha Battle, as a young man, crossed from Virginia into the Tar River section of North Carolina about 1744 and was the first of two or three generations who remained primarily interested in the land and planting. Later generations became townspeople and lawyers, mainly in Nash and Edgecombe counties, showing a capability for business and finance. Originally strict Calvinists associated with the Primitive Baptist church, they later became Episcopalians as their family fortunes rose. They had the earmarks in bearing, manners, and tastes of a "lesser gentry and an upper middle class."[4]

Kemp Battle, the fifth generation from Elisha, had the sturdy qualifications necessary to steer the university through the perilous post-Reconstruction times. His father, Judge William Horn Battle, had moved his family to Chapel Hill in 1843, primarily to become the university's first law professor and not incidentally to expose his family to the benefits of the campus. Kemp Battle entered the university when he was thirteen years old, won first distinction in all his studies, and was graduated in 1849 during the golden years of President Swain. He first became a tutor in Latin, then received his master's degree in 1854. Finally he studied law and opened his practice in Raleigh, riding the circuit and specializing in corporate and business affairs. He was a bank director, a road builder, and a railroad president.

Initially Battle had no overweening interest in politics, although he was gradually drawn into that orbit by the war. He became aligned with Old Whig conservatives, men like Governor William A. Graham, Judge George E. Badger, and Senator Willie P. Mangum, who sought to preserve

Kemp Plummer Battle, first president of the university after Reconstruction.
(North Carolina Collection, University of North Carolina Library, Chapel Hill)

the Union. Like others, including Governor Vance and Mrs. Spencer, Battle found his position difficult to sustain. During the early years of Reconstruction he was persuaded to become state treasurer (in 1866), then was swept out by Holden's victory in 1868. He served as a university trustee from 1862 until the Holden-Pool forces demolished the old structure in 1869.[5]

Battle never sought political office again after his term as state treasurer. He remained supremely devoted to the university and became, as he was later described, a one-ideal man. He spent most of his life struggling to restore the institution. He helped Governor Swain hold things together, then joined Mrs. Spencer and Governor Vance in their efforts to replace the Pool regime with something better. Never a dogmatist or firebrand, Battle believed in conciliatory leadership working to mollify hotheads. He believed the future would be shaped by the moderates.

Battle had a shrewd insight into his own strengths and weaknesses. He credited his own decision to become a candidate for the presidency with the pleadings of an old friend, Colonel Rufus Lenoir Patterson, a Republican of western North Carolina. "Kemp," Patterson told him, "you *must* agree to be president. There are some trustees in favor of electing a man on the war idea, of perpetuating feelings of hostility, which ought to be allowed to slumber. His influence will inculcate hostility to our party; his election will be considered an insult and the Republicans will be bound to oppose him. We have confidence in your fairness. You are not a bitter partisan. I feel safe in pledging my party to your support."[6]

Battle agreed with Patterson's assessment. He perceived the hazardous political and economic forces at work. He also realized he was not a profound scholar and therefore would have to work on his academic credentials. "His reading was diligent, though not coherent. He gathered facts like moss, but he never organized them into an effective pattern or placed them in due relationship. He had some flair for business management and business law and had some practical experience in these fields."[7]

On the personal side Battle exuded friendliness. This helped draw people into his circle. Of medium height and a very erect figure, he was conservative in dress, wearing a cape long after that garment had gone out of style. Possessed of a strong brow, blue-grey eyes, and a rounded beard, he had manners that were "uniformly frank and affable and touched with courtliness." He was a spritely conversationalist and of a lively and animated spirit. "His will to humor and wit was stronger than the results obtained." His comments were never meant to sting or embarrass. He was cheerful, energetic, and optimistic and reflected these virtues in all his contacts with colleagues, students, and friends.[8]

Thus Battle became the university's indispensable man. He "knew how to steer the craft without touching anyone's prejudices. . . . He had a great mission and fulfilled it by reason of his nature and training. All through this political turmoil he is said to have been a man all parties trusted as being honest and fair. He was disarming and conciliatory. A fight would have embroiled the feeble institution with its opponents and would have wrecked it again."[9]

After his election Battle wrote Cornelia Spencer and explained that he had tried to get her brother Charles elected president but illness had intervened. "When the trustees decided that I was the 'best man under the circumstances,' " he wrote, "I did not refuse. I have had opportunities. I have been student, tutor, trustee, before and after, secretary of the board, lawyer, politician, member of the Constitutional Convention, president of a railroad, banker, lobbyist and planter. These have trained me for the grandest of all trades perhaps. Time will show. If I succeed, it will be a crown of honor."[10]

Battle did succeed in nourishing and protecting the university. During the next fifteen years he maintained continuity with its past and slowly supervised its restoration and expansion.

As early as 1877 the president's father, Judge William H. Battle, then seventy-five years old, returned from Raleigh to reopen the law school. He oversaw its operations until his death in 1879. At that time President Battle personally took over supervision and managed until the arrival in 1881 of Judge John Manning. Under Judge Battle the school had taken on characteristics of a modern law school for its day, existing for the sole purpose of teaching. The old custom had been for youth to read law under established attorneys in an apprentice relationship. The embryonic law school at Chapel Hill had the sanction of the trustees and a place in the catalogue; but there was no exercise of financial responsibility by the state, and the school was dependent on its own income.[11]

Perhaps the greatest academic achievement of the Battle years was the establishment of a summer normal school at Chapel Hill, designed to train teachers for the undernourished common school system. In 1877 the General Assembly, working through the State Board of Education, appropriated $2,000 per year for that purpose. Teachers from around the state attended these six-week sessions. During the next seven years 2,500 teachers were enrolled. Simultaneously, the legislature established at Fayetteville a normal school for blacks preparing to teach in the public schools. The Chapel Hill summer school attracted as members of its faculty some of the nation's best educators. With Professor John J. Ladd of Vermont, a graduate of Brown, as its first superintendent and with support from the Peabody Education Fund, it became the first summer normal school launched by a state university.

It also established the precedent of admitting women, which created controversy. Women had been attending classes informally. Cornelia Spencer obtained permission to audit a series of classroom lectures during the regular term. The women who won this special privilege were Mrs. Spencer; her daughter, June; and her niece Lucy Phillips. The subject was botany, taught by Professor W. H. Smith. It was specified that the women occupy rear seats and remain quiet. [12]

The campaign for women's education moved slowly. Mrs. Spencer took up the cause immediately after the university reopened. "I think North Carolina ought to give the girls of the state some attention as well as the boys," she wrote to Ellen Mitchell Summerell. "When I think of what mere crumbs they have to pick up, I get angry."

Mrs. Spencer wrote about the subject in newspaper columns. One of her correspondents was Major R. W. Bingham, director of the well-known school for boys at Mebane, a few miles west of Chapel Hill. In a letter written early in 1876 the major was far from sympathetic: "More money is spent in North Carolina to teach girls to sing (to yell like hyenas) and tear the piano to pieces, both accomplishments being given up before the honeymoon is over in most cases, than would sustain ten first-class male schools of 75 boys each at $100 for tuition fees—and what a difference there would be in results upon the State, its interest, its programs, its glory!"[13]

These words failed to discourage a woman of Cornelia Spencer's determination. She pursued the cause with President Battle and others. Eventually she helped spearhead the movement led by Charles D. McIver that resulted in the founding at Greensboro of the State Normal College for Women, where one of its largest buildings was named Spencer Hall in her honor. Chapel Hill followed the example and named its first dormitory for women Spencer Hall.

In the first year's class at the summer normal school 128 students were men, 107 were women, and 42 counties were represented. The summer schools marked the start of a productive relationship between the university and the public schools, then beginning to revive after the war. Prior to 1860

Calvin H. Wiley launched North Carolina's public schools and became their first superintendent. The belief that education was a luxury slowly changed. A new generation of postwar leaders, most of them educated at Chapel Hill, championed the cause. They included the lively group of education enthusiasts led by Charles B. Aycock, Edwin A. Alderman, Charles D. McIver, Marcus C. S. Noble, E. P. Moses, and James Y. Joyner.

The summer normal school energized the education uplift. It spurred the academic awakening and attracted capable faculty members. The invigorated public schools provided a seedbed for the university along with the academies and institutes, once the sole source of college material.

In 1878 the teachers organized the North Carolina Teachers Association and encouraged a movement to improve the schools. The General Assembly of 1884, however, voted to regionalize the summer school and divided it into four parts. This eventually brought the program's temporary demise.[14]

At the 1877 commencement, which attracted the largest attendance since President James Buchanan's visit of 1859, Governor Vance, then chief executive for the second time, delivered an eloquent memorial lecture on the life of David L. Swain. At the request of President Battle the trustees established October 12 as an annual holiday to commemorate laying the cornerstone of Old East in 1793. The first ceremony was held that autumn in Gerrard Hall, and similar exercises continued throughout the next century.

By 1879 the university organized the beginnings of a medical department. Dr. Thomas W. Harris, an antebellum honors student (class of 1859), set up private practice in Chapel Hill. The trustees arranged to have him oversee a fledgling department comprised of himself and two other professors, one in chemistry and the other in botany and physiology. This arrangement, with no financial support provided by the university, continued until 1884 when it expired. The early ventures into law and medicine illustrated the process by which the university grew into various fields "by absorbing private enterprises set up around it."[15]

On September 23, 1880, the university launched the School of Pharmacy. The initial faculty consisted of Dr. Harris as professor of materia medica and pharmacy; Frederick W. Simonds, professor of botany; and Francis P. Venable, professor of chemistry.

Once the buildings of the old campus had been restored and the ten-mile railroad spur was completed between Chapel Hill and University Station near Durham in 1882, the trustees contemplated an expansion of physical facilities. The erection of a building to provide more room for public exercises ranked high on the priority list. At the suggestion of Governor Thomas J. Jarvis the trustees decided to build a hall as a memorial to President Swain. They hired Samuel Sloan, a Philadelphia architect, to draw up plans for a building to seat 4,000 persons. Work began at a site west of Gerrard Hall on a massive and what turned out to be an awkward and unattractive building, to be known as Memorial Hall.

The project was ill-starred from the start. Cost overruns discontinued work in 1883. President Battle and Professor George T. Winston took charge of a renewed fund-raising campaign, with help from the newly revived alumni association. The building's purpose was expanded to become a memorial not only for Swain but for all the university's fallen warriors of the recent war and for other distinguished citizens in whose honor memorial tablets were placed on the building's walls. The campaign lagged again, but with the help of bank loans and the support of interested friends, the hall was completed in 1885 at a cost of about $45,000.

Although the visiting committee hailed the building as "one of the most imposing auditoriums in America," the structure was far from that. As later described by Archibald Henderson, it "resembled a huge antediluvian monster of the turtle variety." Its price was also excessive, but it served until 1931 when it was declared unsafe and a new memorial hall was built on the same site.[16]

Trustee Paul Cameron came to the university's rescue again in the early 1880s. He bought up certain tracts of university property being sold to satisfy debts contracted as a result of loans obtained earlier for building purposes from his sister Mildred Cameron and the late President Swain. Cornelia Spencer had a hand in persuading Paul Cameron to buy the property rather than to allow it to be auctioned off to outside parties. The university was never able to repay its debts to the Cameron family, and at length its heirs took the money in scholarships. The Camerons bequeathed a few acres to Mrs. Spencer as a souvenir of her help.[17]

By the start of the 1880s Battle again perceived the university's precarious financial underpinnings. He renewed the difficult campaign to obtain regular state appropriations. From the start the campus had subsisted on escheats, the sale of unclaimed land grants, tuition receipts, and gifts. For eighty-five years there had been no regular source of income from tax funds, despite the university's constitutional mandate. The only regular appropriation came from the $7,500 annual interest on the Land Scrip Fund.

The success of the summer normal school encouraged Battle. It emphasized the university's mission to serve the whole state. "The souls of the teachers were made stronger by attendance on the great educational campus meeting," the president declared.[18] The problem lay in obtaining regular legislative tax support without arousing active opposition from private denominational colleges. Many had opposed, or had been decidedly lukewarm about, reviving the university after it closed during Reconstruction.[19]

Leaders of the private colleges launched an attack on the university some twelve months after its reopening in 1875. Criticism ranged from suggestions that the university's assets be sold to private institutions to having it give up its undergraduate education functions and concentrate on graduate and professional studies, thus becoming a "real university." The idea of "six colleges," into which the university was organized, generated ridicule. "Certainly nowhere else in the world can we find six colleges manned by less than a dozen professors," declared the *Biblical Recorder,* a Baptist publication that became, under Dr. T. C. Bailey and his son Josiah W. Bailey, a spirited critic of Chapel Hill. The Reverend Columbus Durham, another Baptist minister, called the university "poor kin" of a university and an "Episcopal college."[20]

Confronted by this opposition, Battle asked Dr. A. W. Mangum, a Methodist member of his faculty, to become chief spokesman for the defense. Battle sought to work "quietly and tactfully" with the university's critics. It was of utmost importance, he said, "that no acrimonious words should be used nor angry controversy engaged in. My plan was to confine myself to simple explanation correcting errors in good temper, or under the assumption that the adversary was under an honest mistake and would be pleased to know the truth."[21]

The controversy became acrimonious. Along with the trustees, Battle and Professor George T. Winston laid careful plans before petitioning the General Assembly. An alumni association meeting in June 1880 set the stage for a strong lobbying effort during the 1881 meeting of the legislature. Governor Thomas J. Jarvis initiated the campaign in his gubernatorial message of 1881. He recommended increasing the annual appropriation by an extra $7,500 and doubling the number of students admitted free of tuition (from one to two) for each county.

On January 26, 1881, university supporters sponsored a banquet at a Raleigh hotel following presentation of the university's needs by Battle and Winston at an alumni meeting in the hall of the House. After an address by alumni president Paul Cameron, no less than fifteen toasts were presented, including many by legislators and even heads of Davidson, Wake Forest, and Trinity colleges. They called the university "the mother of education in North Carolina." The trustees pledged to make "a sacred cause of education in the common schools, denominational colleges and the university, regardless of class, locality, sect, creeds, denomination or party."[22]

The Battle-Winston brief named seven occasions on which legislative support for the university had been mandated—at the constitutional conventions of 1776, 1835, 1861, 1865, 1868, 1875, and by the constitutional amendment in 1873. One of the university's missions, it stated, was essentially to undergird the public schools. The private institutions were engaged in good work, but that was no reason for the university to desert its traditional mission and step aside. To do so would cut it off from the mass of poor young people struggling to acquire a liberal education.[23] The brief noted that Virginia appropriated $40,000 annually for its university plus $65,000 to four other state institutions. South Carolina did even more than Virginia.

State newspapers joined the educational debate. The *Carolina Watchman* charged that the denominational schools were trying to control the state and to unite church and state contrary to principles of civil and religious liberty.[24] The *Wilmington Morning Star* thought there was room for all institutions, both state and denominational: "He is no friend of North Carolina who would rejoice in destruction of the university, and he is a vandal who would lay his unsanctified hands upon its hallowed halls and level them to the ground."[25]

The private institutions had their strong supporters. The Wake Forest faculty held a Raleigh meeting on February 9, 1881, in which Methodists and Presbyterians joined. They produced a memorial protesting the proposed appropriation as "inexpedient, unfair and unjust." Members of the three denominations pledged to resist legislation by every means in their power. They noted the greater needs of the common schools and excoriated expensive education at Chapel Hill aimed primarily at wealthier students.[26]

As the controversy grew heated, the Reverend J. D. Hufham, D.D., a Baptist clergyman not hostile to the university, offered a compromise which proved acceptable to both sides. He proposed abandoning the increase in free-tuition students and reducing the appropriation from $7,500 to $5,000 a year. President T. H. Pritchard of Wake Forest and others seemed pleased with the compromise, since they had been concerned about free tuition and the competitive advantage it gave the university. Friends of the university were happy because the principle of regular appropriations would be established. When Colonel William L. Saunders, secretary of state and an ardent supporter of the regular appropriation, heard about the compromise, he replied, "That settles the question—more will follow."[27]

Saunders was right. In 1885 Governor Jarvis urged an extra appropriation of $10,000 in state funds plus cancellation of other debts. Battle and the trustees decided to push for $15,000, plus $12,000 to pay a debt on a building. Lee S. Overman, a Trinity graduate and later a U.S. senator, introduced the necessary legislation plus a stipulation to double the free-tuition students from one to two per county. Again the denominational colleges balked. They were joined by some private academies which feared that the university was absorbing their students. Ultimately the Overman forces, aided by prominent Presbyterians, prevailed, adding an additional $15,000 to the $5,000 voted in 1881. This lifted total state appropriations to $27,500, including the $7,500 Land Scrip Fund. The proposal to double the number of free students was defeated, but the university was then better prepared to concentrate on additional faculty and higher standards.[28]

The second campaign for state funds pinpointed the need for raising academic standards and for making the campus a "true university." Extra revenue made it possible to enlarge the faculty from nine to fifteen members (two Baptists, one Methodist, two Presbyterians, and one Congregational-ist). It allowed the first offerings of postgraduate courses leading to earned degrees of master of arts, master of philosophy, and doctor of philosophy. It provided for the purchase of laboratory equipment and the merger of the libraries of the university and the two literary societies, aggregating over 20,000 volumes.[29]

The university's first Ph.D. was awarded to William Battle Phillips (1883), the first earned M.A. to Henry Horace Williams (1883), the first M.S. to John Edward Mattocks (1896), and the first Ph.M. to John Allen Moore (1896).

Enhancement of the university's resources in liberal arts produced other repercussions. It resulted in withdrawal of the $2,000 summer normal school fund and, in 1887, reassignment of the $7,500 income from the Land Scrip Fund to the newly established North Carolina College of Agriculture and Mechanic Arts (A&M).

Battle had tried to meet the needs of agriculture and engineering at Chapel Hill through what he called education of the "head and hand," but he never quite succeeded. With only meager resources he could not move much beyond the scope of a liberal arts college, giving some attention to scientific education in subjects "relating to agricultural and mechanical arts." Battle gave these subjects prominent note in the university's catalogue. He visited other states to discover what they were doing and influenced the General Assembly to set up an agricultural and fertilizer control station at Chapel Hill. The curriculum included a four-year course in applied science.[30]

However, this was not enough. The rise of the agrarian movement in North Carolina under Leonidas L. Polk, an ex-Confederate of Whig anteced-ents, brought substantial changes. Polk became the effective mover behind establishment of the state's agriculture department and served as its first commissioner in 1877. As early as 1872, while the university was closed, Polk championed the idea of an institution devoted solely to teaching practi-cal agriculture in an agricultural state. He favored reopening the university, but thought the Land Scrip Fund should be moved to a new, land-grant institution. In 1887 that new institution became North Carolina College of Agriculture and Mechanic Arts.[31]

Confronting competition from both church groups and farmers, the trust-ees and Battle decided to yield on the Land Scrip Fund, thus reducing the university's appropriation to $20,000 a year. Rising interest in science, however, led to renewed initiative in other areas, leading the university to build a top-flight engineering school and other departments specializing in applied science.[32]

In later years Battle described this period as "the most unhappy time" of his presidency. The loss of $7,500 was a serious blow. It forced dismissal of two full professors and one associate professor. Fortunately for the univer-sity, another legislative campaign to shave $7,500 off the annual appropria-tion failed.

Battle took his defeats with equanimity. Loss of the agricultural mission quieted intimations that the university was defrauding farmers and me-chanics by offering them less than they deserved. It allowed Chapel Hill to develop along the lines of the most advanced national universities—Har-vard, Yale, Columbia, and Princeton—without "being embarrassed by the constant demand to build stables and work shops, buy prize cattle and modern machinery." After the bill to establish the agricultural and mechan-ical college passed, Colonel Polk declared, "Now we will let Battle alone!" Battle felt that Polk kept his promise.[33]

The president's ingenuity and resiliency served well in resolving other problems less momentous than finances or church-state relations. The university had no organized sports during the antebellum years. This probably accounted for some of the explosive student aggression and pranksterism characteristic of the period. Interest in sports ran high, but the administration had other priorities. For almost a century the game of bandy or shinny, today called hockey, held first place in student affections. The open spaces west of South Building served as a playing field for this exciting game, played with curved sticks and a hard ball. Students engaged in other informal sports, such as weight lifting, target shooting, marbles, and ice skating. They enjoyed aquatic sports in nearby streams and lakes. While there were requests for a gymnasium, limited building funds went for other purposes.

In 1877, however, not two years after the university reopened, students organized an athletic association, with Julian M. Baker ('77) as president. The organization set up an outdoor gymnasium south of Gerrard Hall, complete with trapeze, horizontal bars, and swinging rings. Simultaneously students cleared an athletic field for baseball and football south of the old library, now the site of Bynum Hall.[34]

In 1884 the athletic association sponsored the university's first Field Day. Field events consisted of athletic stunts and contests, such as the five-mile race, the 100-yard dash, and the greased pig race. Student interest in baseball erupted early in the postbellum period. In 1867 Alexander Graham was elected captain of the baseball team. The team played several games with each of two independent clubs, the Crescents and the Stars. Baseball emerged again after the reopening in the 1870s, and university teams competed with several noncollegiate groups in nearby communities.

In the spring of 1884 the university played its first intercollegiate athletic contest (baseball) against Bingham Military School. Bingham won, 12-11. Applause was banned during the game, but afterward, "Our boys gave a 'huzzah for the Binghamites,'" and the response was a graceful "Three cheers for the university nine." Professor Francis P. Venable believed this was the first game featuring a university yell.[35]

The athletic association organized class teams in baseball and football in the early 1880s as intramural contests became popular. The two literary societies scheduled a hotly contested football game on Thanksgiving Day, 1887. President Battle saw organized athletics as a healthy outlet for pent-up energy and mischief. He called for erection of a gymnasium in his 1882 trustees' report. The trustees agreed to equip one if the alumni would build it, but the sagging campaign to raise funds for Memorial Hall postponed that project.

Ultimately Battle found a way to build his gymnasium and solve another problem as well. In the earliest days William R. Davie favored dancing on campus as a means of teaching his own sons good ballroom manners. But other university supporters of the Calvinist stripe opposed it. The controversy between the university and the private colleges resensitized the issue. Dr. L. S. Burkhead, president of the board of trustees of Trinity College, said standards at the private colleges were equal to or sometimes better than those at the university in every subject "except dancing."[36]

Battle knew that the annual commencement balls held in the university library aroused criticism. Thus he persuaded the trustees to ban dancing there after the spring of 1884 and organize a corporation to erect a building in Chapel Hill, off campus, to serve as both gymnasium and ballroom. Dr. Richard H. Lewis of Raleigh headed the fund-raising drive. Samuel Sloan, architect of the old Memorial Hall, drew up the plans. The wooden frame building, 118 by 45 feet, was built on Cameron Avenue, near the present site of Peabody Hall. Students emblazoned on the walls of the main hall: "We welcome the daughters of North Carolina to our own hall, on our own floor, where the critics of our pleasure have no rights nor power to deny us." The trustees leased the building from the gymnasium association for $300 a year and charged each student a gym fee of $2. Eleven years later, after the gym was converted into a commons hall, the administration used Memorial Hall as a gym until the erection of Bynum Gymnasium in 1905.[37]

The university's first intercollegiate football contest took place against Wake Forest in Raleigh on October 18, 1888, during State Fair Week. Wake Forest won 6-4. Shortly afterward a football association was organized with Lacy LeGrand Little as president, Stephen C. Bragaw as captain, and eighty-seven members.

In the autumn of 1889 the faculty, at the suggestion of Dr. John R. Mott, a YMCA leader, turned over direction of college athletics to the YMCA. Lacy Little became director of athletics and captain of the football team.

In 1884 Professor Venable built an excellent tennis court in Battle Grove, south of the president's house. In the fall of that year James C. Roberts became president of the newly organized University Lawn Tennis Association. The association laid out a number of tennis courts south of Gerrard Hall, and other courts were built on the campus and around the village.[38] During the 1890s Henry S. Lake gave the university a 100-yard straightaway cinder track and a sixth-of-a-mile oval cinder track. The university's first track team competed with teams from Vanderbilt, Texas, and Tulane.

In 1890, following disorders arising in the first intercollegiate football contests, the trustees barred all such games. As a result, interest in sports, even in track athletics, diminished, and the playing fields grew up in tough sedge grass and weeds. Enthusiasm for intercollegiate sports rose again in 1891 when the ban was lifted, chiefly through the influence of such faculty members as Horace Williams, Francis Venable, and Eben Alexander. The administration put athletics in the hands of an advisory committee consisting of one faculty member, one graduate student, and one undergraduate.[39]

The year of the university's reopening, 1875, marked the inauguration of a student honor system. Councils elected by the students themselves took over cases involving cheating and other rules infractions that had previously been the responsibility of the faculty and trustees. Each student was required to sign a pledge that he had neither given nor received aid during examinations.[40] In 1881 the two debating societies enacted a joint agreement to put a stop to freshman hazing. This prohibition worked fairly well for some years, but the practice was not entirely eliminated and later recurred with tragic consequences.

The university inaugurated its first regular student loan fund as the result of a small philanthropy in 1879. The Reverend Charles F. Deems, a former faculty member and pastor of the Church of the Strangers in New York City, gave $300 in memory of his son who fell at Gettysburg. Initially the fund was designated for sons of needy clergymen but later broadened. Dr. Deems contributed another $400 that was greatly enhanced in 1881 when his friend William H. Vanderbilt added a gift of $10,000. Both the principal and interest were used for student loans as the Deems Fund became a conspicuous benefit for indigent youths.[41] Other early scholarship funds included the B. F. Moore Fund (1878) and the Francis Jones Smith Fund (1885), derived from a gift of 1,440 acres of land in Chatham County by Mary Ruffin Smith and used for student aid.

In 1883 organization of the Elisha Mitchell Scientific Society, named for the professor who measured the height of Mount Mitchell, emphasized a growing interest in science on the campus. Professor Francis Venable, the society's first president, set forth its purpose as "to build up a spirit of research" at the university and to advance knowledge of the state and its resources. The society established a library and published a journal semi-annually.

During the 1880s and early 1890s the university attracted a coterie of talented professors who lifted its reputation in the academic world. These included, among others, John Manning, who succeeded the late W. H. Battle and Kemp P. Battle as head of the law school; F. P. Venable, chemistry; Joshua W. Gore, natural philosophy and engineering; Thomas Hume, English and literature; Walter D. Toy, modern languages; Joseph A. Holmes, geology and natural history; William Cain, engineering and mathematics; Henry Van Peters Wilson, botany; Eben Alexander, Greek; Richard H. Whitehead, head of the medical and pharmaceutical department; and Henry Horace Williams, mental and moral science.

From the beginning Chapel Hill had been prized as a primeval oasis detached from commerce, situated in a great hardwood forest and rather monastic in style. When President Swain arrived in 1836, the village had only one store, one practicing physician, and no pastor or lawyer. No other American university was surrounded by so many acres of natural forests, full of varied mountain and coastal flora.

Swain had called on the botanical skills of Elisha Mitchell for landscaping. Mitchell designed the rock walls of the campus and laid out other landscaping and gardening projects. In 1839 Swain obtained $3,000 from the trustees for these purposes. He began negotiations with university alumnus Robert Donaldson of New York City to hire the eminent architect Alexander Jackson Davis. These initiatives culminated in important additions—enlargement of Old East and Old West, improvements for Gerrard Hall, and erection of what is recognized as the most beautiful building on the campus, the old library and ballroom now known as the Playmakers Theater. Davis projected other plans for improvement of the grounds in the interest of utility and beauty.

Swain's association with Davis resulted in the hiring in 1848 of an English landscape gardener, John Loader, who was retained at a salary of $400 a year to acquire ornamental shrubs and flowers and supervise campus beautification. Loader remained until 1851 when he was replaced by a "burly Englishman of powerful frame," Thomas Paxton, reputed to be a relative of the duke of Devonshire's famous gardener, Sir Joseph Paxton.

Loader and Paxton trained assistants and executed some of the plans supplied by Davis. They were generally successful, but Paxton found it impossible to maintain walls and fences and prevent trespass by wandering livestock. In the year that Paxton resigned, the trustees "indignantly and mournfully" resolved: "That the Board of Trustees have seen with much regret the beautiful grounds of the Campus become the common pasture ground for the cows and hogs of the village. (And further) Resolved that the Bursar be directed to take the most effectual measures for expelling all stock from said grounds and keeping them away."[42]

After Reconstruction, President Battle became an equally dedicated champion of campus beautification. He guarded and preserved woodlands and forests far beyond the campus boundaries. These areas included what came to be known as Battle Park and Gimghoul Woods on the east and the large area around the south campus. In the early 1890s the Reverend and Mrs. James Pleasant Mason, descendants of Mark Morgan, one of the first campus benefactors, bequeathed the university their 800-acre farm. In time the university came to own University Lake, to the west of Carrboro, and its surrounding watershed and a tract of more than 1,000 acres to the north, the Horace Williams property, where the airport was built in the twentieth century.[43]

Battle was a nature lover and a great walker. He cleared many of the woodland paths in Battle Park with his own hatchet. He helped construct bridges and seats and introduced friends and students to favorite spots. Well into the twentieth century, some of his glens and dells retained names he gave them: Trysting Poplar, Woodthrush Home, Vale of Ione, Anemone Spring, Flirtation Knoll, Glen Lee, and Dogwood Dingle. At the summit of Piney Prospect in the 1920s the Order of Gimghouls built a memorial seat to Battle, using the rockpile he helped accumulate over the years. It is part of the "poignant charm which broods forever over the woods which surround the university town."[44]

Battle's love of the village dated back to the 1840s when as a twelve-year-old boy he moved to Chapel Hill with his family. His father, Judge W. H. Battle, built what became the family residence, Senlac, described by the president as "a charming tract of six acres with the university campus in front and the forest on two sides." Senlac, named for the hill on which the Battle of Hastings was fought, still stands. It is southeast of the site of the old president's home on East Franklin Street—the one occupied by Presidents Caldwell and Swain, which burned on Christmas morning 1886. Battle continued to live in Senlac until his death in 1919. A handsome new president's house was built on the Franklin Street site in 1907.[45]

In 1891 Battle's fifteen-year presidency closed serenely and triumphantly, unlike the retirements of his two immediate predecessors, Pool and Swain. Once Battle had confronted the loss of the Land Scrip Fund to the fledgling

North Carolina College of Agriculture and Mechanic Arts at Raleigh, he saw many of his more pressing problems recede. Agitation by the denominational colleges quieted. The university's financial condition improved because of larger state appropriations. Enrollment declined slightly, probably because of curtailment of free tuition for students from the various counties; but it soon bounded back, aided by growing public interest in education at all levels. Leaders such as Charles D. McIver and Edwin A. Alderman had much to do with this renaissance, which profoundly affected the state during the next two decades.[46]

President Battle resigned at the age of sixty while still in good health. The date of his retirement stemmed from events set in motion by the 1889 centennial of the university's chartering. The president and trustees planned special commencement ceremonies featuring the return of alumni from classes dating back to 1824. Dr. Armand J. De Rosset, sole living member of that class, attended, along with hundreds of others from Florida to Colorado. Sentimental fellowship and reunions of old friends culminated in a banquet held on June 5, 1889, in Gerrard Hall. Some 300 guests heard fifteen laudatory toasts to the university's dead and living benefactors and friends.

Out of these festivities came a resolution to endow a chair of history, a project which appealed to Battle. By the following year more than $25,000 had been raised. Battle himself visited alumni groups around the state soliciting funds.[47]

Early in 1891 the president made his decision to withdraw from his strenuous duties and to occupy the new chair of history. At that time the deaths of several close associates and friends—Dr. Charles Phillips, Professor Ralph Graves, Dr. William Peter Mallett, Professor A. W. Mangum, and Paul C. Cameron—seemed to signal the approaching end of an era. Battle attributed his resignation to his desire to "seek a position which would have cares less anxious than the presidency." He longed for quieter work, especially in history. The new chair "exactly met his wishes."[48]

Battle's tenure as president inspired universal praise. As one of the university's talented sons, he had accepted the reins of leadership at a crucial moment. He became the "spiritual heir of Swain but with a clear eye for some of Swain's mistakes." Always emphasizing the nonparty spirit, he shared Swain's penchant for friendliness with students and associates. He practiced sound financial management and knew how to operate on a shoestring budget when necessary. He "fitted the need [of the times] as the glove fits the hand."[49]

Bearing the presidential burdens "with patience and urbanity" had not been easy because Battle was essentially a sensitive man. While he had outwardly borne criticism and opposition with equanimity, "inwardly he had suffered, and in his modesty he had decided that the time was appropriate for someone else to take over." Besides restoring the foundations of the antebellum university, he attracted the nucleus of an unusual faculty—at first "a few able men, well-grounded in their subjects and willing to sacrifice adequate remuneration in the interest of ideals."[50] As the new century approached, these men, and others as they arrived, helped prepare the way for academic distinction.

ONE OF THOSE

RAZOR-SHARP WINSTONS,

1891–1896

Waiting in the wings when President Battle retired to teach and write his history of the university was his obvious successor, the energetic and enterprising George Tayloe Winston. The new president stemmed from an eastern Carolina family almost as closely associated with the university as the Battles. He quickly became known to faculty and villagers alike as "one of those razor-sharp Winstons."[1]

Winston's father, Patrick Henry Winston of Virginia, had been a planter and lawyer. After studying at Chapel Hill in 1844–45 and graduating from Columbia University, Patrick Winston moved to Bertie County to teach. He married Martha E. Byrd, built Windsor Castle on the banks of the Cashie River near Windsor, and reared a family of four boys and one girl. Two of his younger sons, Francis and Robert, arrived together as the first students to enroll at the reopened university in 1875. Earlier, in 1868, the university's closing sent the second Winston son, George Tayloe, to the Naval Academy at Annapolis. There his tendency toward seasickness caused him to transfer to Cornell, where he graduated with highest honors. After a year's tutoring at Ithaca he returned to Chapel Hill to become one of seven faculty members who helped Battle get things started again.[2]

Winston's succession seemed "in essence automatic and wholly natural." A lover of classics, especially Latin, and a fine teacher, he proved adept as an administrator in his early years. He served as Battle's right-hand man and assisted ably in the campaign for enhanced state appropriations. More aggressive and blunt than Battle and a skillful orator, he became a bold strategist very much "open to the new forces that were in the wind."[3]

Unlike Battle, Winston was not much interested in the nostalgic or the status quo. He had never been wedded to secession. Skeptical of religious orthodoxy, he accepted the growing secularization of the times and encouraged the university's break with denominational ties. Winston's younger brother Robert recalled that their mother never discussed religious matters with her college-bred sons. As a mid-Victorian, she was disturbed by "modern free thinkers. Yet she bravely held her own. When Brother George would put his arm about her and say, 'Now Mother, you know there is no such place as a fire-and-brimstone hell,' she would gravely reply. 'Never you mind, George, you just wait and see!' Whereupon there would be a round of laughter and brother would insist that mother would be unhappy without her hell."[4]

George Tayloe Winston delighted in challenges. A stern disciplinarian and keenly witty, he had a stubborn streak and a tendency toward the arbitrary. These qualities led to some of his thorny administrative problems in the presidency. As one historian noted, "Winston would have been a greater university president had he been willing to lead more and drive less."[5]

But Winston could not do that. The North Carolina of his day was poverty-ridden and backward, striving to rise out of the ashes of defeat. In that difficult struggle Battle trod a path of caution. He recalled only too well the miseries of Reconstruction, when time after time the university narrowly escaped destruction. As the private colleges—Wake Forest, Davidson, and Trinity—rose to prominence, public institutions felt more keenly the competition and the criticism of the state's religiously devout who charged that public higher education encouraged the works of the devil.

Winston's fellow North Carolinian and friend Walter Hines Page delivered the main address at the presidential inaugural ceremonies in 1891. As one of the forward-looking young turks of the postwar generation, Page thought North Carolina needed fewer "old mummies" gazing backward on the fallen glory of the Confederacy. In his inaugural address Page advised the new president to "renounce forever all servitude to ecclesiasticism and partyism," to remember that the "day of compromise was done," and to have nothing whatsoever to do with "every narrow ecclesiastical prejudice that shall demand tribute."[6] The university, Page declared, must exert "domineering influence over North Carolina's burgeoning industry, because without culture men get punier as they grow richer."

George Tayloe Winston.
(North Carolina Collection, University of North Carolina Library, Chapel Hill)

These bold words, spoken on a religiously conservative campus, challenged the old order and provided new ammunition for the university's critics who deplored its godless influences. In fact, the university, long managed by Presbyterian schoolmasters, had begun breaking old ties. Three of its early leaders—Gillaspie, Caldwell, and Pool—had been ministers, and many of its faculty members had religious connections; but that was not the order of the day in the last quarter of the nineteenth century. When Professor A. W. Mangum, a Methodist minister, died in 1890, Josephus Daniels, the crusading young Tar Heel editor, declared that it was not only not necessary to elect another preacher to the faculty but that a preacher ought not to be selected unless he was a man of great ability and promise.[7] The same rule prevailed for the Board of Trustees, where ministers had never been plentiful and were appointed even more rarely after 1891.

Newly inaugurated President Winston instituted no dramatic changes when he took charge, but behind the scenes he began to "fight with sharper weapons." With a student body of only 200, the university had not won the unconditional admiration of the state. Winston sought to keep its worthy attributes before the public. As an "adroit and forceful public speaker," ready in wit and reasoning, he believed the state and the university were destined to rise together.[8] Viewing the university as the capstone of the educational system, he saw the need for vigorous leadership from the top. Each branch should strengthen the other. "There is nothing narrow or restricted about university culture," he wrote in the *University Magazine* of March–April 1894. "It is as broad as life. . . . The university today imposes no rigid nor uniform curriculum of study. Within reasonable limits each student may select, to suit his taste, talents or necessities."

A new generation of educational leaders moved around the state proclaiming this message, among them McIver and Alderman at the new normal school in Greensboro and Polk and his agrarian leaders at the agricultural and mechanical arts college in Raleigh. This awakened interest in public education, inspired teachers' institutes, summer normal schools, and public education meetings.

The burgeoning movement, however, ran head-on into fierce opposition from church-related colleges fearful of the proliferating competition. While private college support had been growing, churchmen looked on the university's state support as unfair subsidization. An economic recession in the early 1890s—short crops, low prices, and financial distress—made student recruitment difficult. As new public institutions at Raleigh and Greensboro sought state funds, the church-state struggle erupted anew in the 1893 General Assembly. Private colleges deplored "the growing number of state institutions with their cheap rates and hundreds of scholarships." Baptists, Methodists, and even Presbyterians were fearful of a state monopoly in higher education.[9]

The various denominations rallied their forces to get a bill introduced in the General Assembly to "unify the higher education in the state and to elevate the university to the apex of all education in the state." While ostensibly praising the university, it sought to limit university offerings to graduate and professional studies and to eliminate undergraduate instruction entirely.

The audacity of the proposal shocked university supporters. They scarcely knew whether to take it seriously. Some treated it as a joke. An anonymous newspaper letter, credited to President Winston, pretended to assume that the bill would move the university from Chapel Hill to Apex, a small village in Wake County. The *State Chronicle* wryly noted that it would be cheaper to move the university to Apex than to do what was proposed. The legislation, it said, was "the wildest scheme we have known to be introduced in our experience of public affairs. . . . It should be entitled 'a bill to abolish the university.' "[10]

President Winston took the challenge seriously. He prepared an elaborate brief for the legislature's education committee. It asserted that all the major universities—Harvard, Yale, Columbia, and Johns Hopkins—have undergraduate classes. Only five postgraduates were studying at Chapel Hill at the time. The legislation would close the doors to the youth of nine-tenths of the counties of North Carolina.

The so-called Shearer bill—it was said to have been drafted by the Reverend Dr. John B. Shearer, president of Davidson College—was defeated. President Winston, as the master strategist, gained support of most of the state's secular press and many prominent laymen. University supporters circulated the insinuation that Wake Forest College, through its endowment fund, was a "sycophant of the Standard Oil Trust, and that Trinity, of the Methodists was on its knees to the American Tobacco Trust of the Dukes."[11]

When the 1893 General Assembly rebuffed the private colleges, they tried to generate a groundswell of public opposition to tax-supported higher education. President Taylor of Wake Forest wrote a series of articles for the *Biblical Recorder* ("How Far Should a State Undertake to Educate?") that were published as a booklet, and 25,000 were circulated around the state, underwritten by Dr. Columbus Durham.[12]

Meanwhile, the *Tar Heel*, the new student newspaper at Chapel Hill, sought to rally alumni and students. It urged them to stand by alma mater and hoped that the church colleges would lay aside their "nauseating whine."[13] President Winston spoke cautiously in public, but in private correspondence he was not so restrained. In September 1894 he wrote Cornelia Spencer, who had moved to Cambridge, Massachusetts, that the fight on the university had "degenerated into a war of wind and filth." He added that "we have already won. . . . Even the A & M. (State College) is ahead of W-F (Wake Forest); as soon as the A & M. football and baseball teams beat the W-F boys, as they soon will, the war will be over." Athletic rivalry became important in the struggle, reflecting the tension between public and private colleges.[14] In his annual report of 1893 President Crowell of Trinity mentioned how much Trinity's football victory over UNC "strengthened the self-respect of the college community." This rivalry became so fierce that football was banned between the two institutions for a number of years.

A renewed attack came in the 1895 General Assembly. The second bill to abolish all university appropriations called for increased tax funds for the common schools and curtailment of free-tuition scholarships for the university. Both factions lobbied for the support of Populist forces led by Marion Butler, publisher of the *Caucasian* and later U.S. senator. Butler eventually supported state aid, but the campaign was of "unexampled virulence."[15]

The university's friends held strategic posts in the General Assembly. They overcame heavy odds to defeat the bill and to persuade the legislature to sustain the university's $20,000 annual appropriation for the next biennium. President Winston told friends that if the bill had gone to a vote during the first two weeks of the session, it would have been defeated by a 3-1 vote. Even with the aid of alumni and friends, "we came near destruction. . . . The Baptist flood roared and surged and threatened us."[16]

Then the Baptists and Methodists rallied their forces again. Under the leadership of Dr. John C. Kilgo, the dynamic new president of Trinity College, and Josiah W. Bailey, editor of the *Biblical Recorder,* they continued their fight for what they called "the voluntary principle of education." Kilgo established his own newspaper, the *Christian Educator,* in 1896 to rail against taxation of the many for the few. C. H. Mebane, the state superintendent of public instruction, supported the Kilgo-Bailey group and wrote the Trinity president: "I shall not endorse any system of supervision that will open the way for the 'university gang' to control the public school system of North Carolina."[17]

The vitriolic contest continued through the closing years of the century with the university holding its own against church factions. Private colleges warned against dangers of pushing public education in a state with a large black population. They insisted that public institutions were debarred from emphasizing religious elements under the state constitution.

Opponents of the private colleges called their attacks on the university "heartless." The university, they contended, did not seek to crowd out religious institutions but only to perform services required by the state constitution. All civilized peoples recognized such services from the time of Moses and David to the time "when Jefferson founded the University of Virginia and Washington proposed a national university."[18]

Winston and his chief lieutenant, Professor Edwin Anderson Alderman, capitalized on a tide of popular support for higher education. Winston, "with his skill as a tactician, and Alderman, with his urbanity, ultimately isolated the enemy of state support. . . . By 1897 the battle was won. Kilgo and Bailey were discomfited and checked. Kilgo was to go on, drawing Trinity closer and closer to the source of its prosperity, the patronage of the Dukes of Durham. Kilgo went on to a bishopric, the fulfillment of his ambition; Trinity went on to transformation by Duke millions into Duke University, became a liberal institution of high quality, quite free from denominational restrictions or hampering jealousies."[19]

While the university's officials fought for its survival on the state political scene, the 200 young men who comprised its student body enjoyed the challenges and bucolic pleasures of an isolated Carolina village. Even by the turn of the century Franklin Street remained a primitive, unpaved lane, dusty or muddy through the changing seasons. Except where the land had been cleared for buildings, the mighty forest still enclosed much of the campus. Cameron Avenue, known as College Avenue before it was named for Paul C. Cameron, was hardly more than a simple path through the west side of the campus and remained unpaved until 1927.

Outside their classrooms students organized athletic teams, social organizations, and other extracurricular enterprises. On February 23, 1893, Charles Baskerville and Walter (Pete) Murphy, editor and managing editor, respectively, published the first issue of the *Tar Heel* as a project of the University Athletic Association. The weekly newspaper got competition the following year when a group of nonfraternity students objected to its "excessive coverage of sports" and launched their own publication, *White and Blue*. The new student newspaper succumbed the following year as the *Tar Heel* came into its own.[20]

As university football and baseball teams began intercollegiate competition, students went to work composing pep songs and engaging in other support activities. William Starr Myers, later a professor of political history at Princeton University, wrote the words for "Hail to the Brightest Star," sung to the tune of another old college song called "Amici" and performed for the first time by the University Glee Club in an 1897 concert at Gerrard Hall. Francis A. Gudger, the glee club's first tenor from Asheville, first sang what soon became "Hark the Sound." J. Maryon Saunders, for many years executive secretary of the UNC Alumni Association, discovered that the coda of "Hark the Sound" owed something to the old camp-meeting spiritual stanza that ran as follows:

> Baptist, Baptist is my name,
> And Baptist till I die
> When I am dead it can be said
> You've laid a Baptist by.[21]

Several years after Myers and Gudger left the campus, a university quartet picked up the tune of the song and, with slight changes in the first verse and chorus, began using it in public recitals. The quartet's members were Dr. Charles S. Mangum, then a young instructor in the medical school; Charles T. Woollen, later the university's business manager; J. C. B. Ehringhaus, governor of North Carolina from 1933–37; and Gaston G. Galloway, later a Charlotte businessman. Over the years it gradually became the official song of the university.

Members of the class of 1891 placed a stone on the Chapel Hill Cemetery gravesite of one of the university's first employees after it was reopened in 1876, Wilson Swain Caldwell. Caldwell, who had been a slave of President Swain before the Civil War, was known for his skill in lighting fires in student fireplaces before they arose on cold mornings and also "knew when to refrain from reporting a friendly game of cards." Caldwell and other servants provided fish and wild game for the tables, cleaned rooms and tended the campus, and provided transportation. Prior to the Civil War, George Moses Horton, called the "slave poet," even produced "affectionate poems for the students to send their ladies."[22]

Greek letter fraternities, which sprang up shortly after the university reopened, first published a university yearbook called *The Hellenian* in 1890. Initially it featured information only about members of fraternities and, later, group photographs and pen and ink sketches. In 1901 *The Hellenian* was replaced by the first *Yackety-Yack*, which represented all segments of the student body.[23]

Although Cornelia Phillips Spencer and some of her family members attended classes at the university after it reopened, it was not until 1897

South Building.
(North Carolina Collection, University of North Carolina Library, Chapel Hill)

that the trustees admitted women to postgraduate courses. Attendance by women averaged only about half a dozen a year in the beginning, President Battle reported in his history, but some of them were "brilliant." Mary S. MacRae was the first of five young women to register, and in 1898 Sallie Walker Stockard received the first earned degree awarded to a woman. Women organized the Women's University Club in 1907, and that year the editors of the *Yackety-Yack* took notice of their presence by means of cartoons. Their drawings suggested "that the men stood in awe of the female beauties, but that they were pleased nevertheless."[24]

As the religious controversies began to subside in the mid-1890s, President Winston was offered a challenge he could not resist. Trustees of the University of Texas, a much younger institution, asked him to become its president, doubling his salary to $5,000.

Winston looked back with considerable pride on five turbulent years at the helm of the university. In the early years his stern Roman discipline aroused strong student resentment, especially in what was regarded by many as "high-handed action in regard to athletics." One morning the campus awoke to the sight of the words *Winston's Military Academy* painted in vermilion letters two feet high across the face of Gerrard Hall. The president promptly

Gerrard Hall.
(North Carolina Collection, University of North Carolina Library, Chapel Hill)

ordered them removed or covered, but they were still dimly visible through successive coats of paint some fifty years later.[25]

Winston brought a new academic and political esprit to the campus. His administration added three new departments: history, biology, and education. Advanced instruction in one or more courses was offered in every department. The elective system was extended to cover two-fifths of the sophomore year, one-half of the junior year, and all of the senior year. Student enrollment rose from 200 to 500. Winston revived the summer normal school that had been successful for eight years under Battle. Edwin A. Alderman, then professor of the history and philosophy of education, became supervisor of its activities in 1895.

In 1894 Winston inaugurated a summer law school in collaboration with Professor John Manning. The chief justice of the state supreme court, James E. Shepherd, joined the faculty. Simultaneously (in 1894) a summer school in geology was established at King's Mountain in the western part of the state under a new and dynamic member of the faculty, Collier Cobb. This enhanced the university's awareness of the practical needs of the state.[26] In the same year Dr. Henry Van Peters Wilson, professor of biology and one of the university's emerging teachers of national reputation, launched a summer school in marine biology at Beaufort. This led to collaboration with

Smith Building (now Playmakers Theater).
(North Carolina Collection, University of North Carolina Library, Chapel Hill)

Johns Hopkins University, the Universities of Virginia, Georgia, and South Carolina, and the federal government in establishing the nationally financed Fisheries Biological Station at Beaufort.

Winston took care to reorganize and systematize internal affairs on campus. Under his influence the state appropriation rose from $22,500 a year in 1891 to $30,000 for 1893–94. All this was done despite the agrarian distress and the Populist uprising of the early 1890s. Winston strengthened the scientific curriculum and expanded the library. He brought a new aura of sophistication and a variety of course offerings.

Winston seemed to believe he might render the same kind of services at the University of Texas in a state "ready for pioneering" in higher education. Despite his ambitious goals and restless initiative, however, his tenure in Austin was short (1896–99). The University of Texas had been organized in 1883 with a large endowment in public lands (2 million acres). Winston's missionary zeal, while effective at Chapel Hill, was a "bit too polished and out of tune with Texas tastes."[27] The new president was arbitrary in personnel management. He spoke too much like an easterner, and "his knowledge of ancient Rome and his devotion to the image of a stern uncompromised Roman senator seemed out of place in a territory peopled partly by Mexicans, Indians, cowboys and ranch owners."[28]

When the opportunity presented itself, Winston returned to North Carolina to become head of North Carolina College of Agriculture and Mechanic Arts at Raleigh in 1899. Despite his lack of experience in agriculture and engineering, he increased the school's enrollment and endowment until his retirement on a Carnegie pension in 1908 to travel in Europe and the North Carolina mountains. Eventually he retired to Chapel Hill to live with his son, Patrick W. Winston, who was a professor of law. George Tayloe Winston died quietly there in 1932.

EDWIN A. ALDERMAN,

WOVEN IN THE LOOM OF JEFFERSON,

1896-1900

In the 1890s North Carolina again became embroiled in the bitter aftermath of war and reconstruction. Impoverished farmers and minority Republicans seized political power from Bourbon Democrats who retaliated with a vitriolic white supremacy campaign. Private denominational colleges heightened their attack against godless higher education at Chapel Hill. Simultaneously, an energetic coterie of young leaders, weary of war-generated quarrels, sparked a spirited appeal in behalf of the public schools.

Edwin Anderson Alderman, age thirty-five, a dedicated professor of education at Chapel Hill, became one of those young leaders. Tapped in 1896 to succeed George Tayloe Winston as the university's president, he brought fresh energy and zeal to the educational crusade then emerging in North Carolina. Born in Wilmington on May 15, 1861, a descendant of five generations of farmers, Alderman qualified as an authentic son of the valley of humility between two mountains of conceit. His people migrated originally from England to New Jersey and Long Island and then drifted to North Carolina. They lived in Duplin County where the first Daniel Alderman was a cabinetmaker and carpenter. Edwin's grandfather owned several hundred acres of land in New Hanover County. He married Flora McDuffie, daughter of Dougald, indubitably a Scot and strongly Presbyterian.[1]

Their son James, a timber inspector, elevated the family's fortunes by marrying Susan Jane Corbett, a small, vivacious woman seven years his junior. It was from the Corbetts, so the tradition went, that Edwin Alderman inherited much of his eloquence and intellect.[2] Susan was charming and austere, ambitious and enterprising. In Wilmington, where the family settled, they joined the Presbyterian church of which Woodrow Wilson's father was pastor.

In Wilmington Edwin Alderman became a friend of young Wilson, his contemporary. Later, Wilson's career greatly influenced Alderman's, and in 1924, during the last decade of his life, Alderman addressed a joint session of Congress in Washington memorializing the late president. In his speech he described Wilson's and his own philosophy: "He was of the group of young southern-born men who knew the contributions of the South to American history, who had no apologies to offer for its part in the great struggle, ennobled by so much valor and self-sacrifice, but who felt that the South must again become wholeheartedly a part of the Federal Union it had done so much to establish."[3]

Alderman, like his friends Charles D. McIver, Charles B. Aycock, and Walter Hines Page, espoused high educational objectives for the New South. After attending private academies in the Wilmington area and Bethel Military Academy in Virginia, he enrolled at Chapel Hill three years after its reopening and mingled with the state's young turks, who were more interested in exploring the future than in dwelling on the past.

Alderman studied Latin under President Winston and later married Emma Graves, a sister of Professor Ralph Henry Graves. Alderman took the philosophical course leading to a Ph.B. degree. He excelled in Latin. His grades influenced President Battle to say fifteen years later that he attained "the highest scholarship in his class."[4] He won a name for himself as a public speaker. He made lifelong friends at Chapel Hill, most of whom he encountered again and again in his productive career: Marcus Cicero Stephens Noble, Frank B. Dancy, Robert W. Winston, Charles B. Aycock, Locke Craig, James Y. Joyner, and Charles D. McIver.

In his memorial address for McIver a generation later, Alderman spoke of those golden days:

There was no better place, I think, for the making of leaders in the world than Chapel Hill in the late seventies. The note of life was simple, rugged—almost primitive. Our young hearts, aflame with the impulses of youth, were quietly conscious of the vicissitudes and sufferings through which our fathers had just passed. . . . A heroic tradition pervaded the place, while hope and struggle, rather than despair or

Edwin Anderson Alderman.
(North Carolina Collection, University of North Carolina Library, Chapel Hill)

repining, shone in the purposes of the resolute men who were rebuilding the famous old school. All of us were poor boys. Those who came
from the towns looked perhaps a trifle more modish to the inex-
perienced eye, but they were just as poor as their country fellows, and
had come out of just such simple homes of self-denial and self-sacrifice.
The unconscious discipline and tutelege of defeat and fortitude and self-
restraint had cradled us all.[5]

As a student young Alderman proclaimed his fealty to democratizing
education. In his senior year he used "corporate power" as the subject of his
prizewinning Mangum Medal speech. He thought it should be restrained.
Alderman came to be known for his elegant dress and oratorical grandeur,
but he was also recognized during his school days for his "pronounced gift
for fun." His friend Billy Noble noted that he had a characteristic quick step
and eagerness when he came forward to speak.

Many of Alderman's contemporaries thought this most promising orator
would embrace either the ministry or the law, professions in which Chapel
Hill graduates had excelled for generations. Yet Alderman's dedication to
education inspired him, in President Battle's words, to "devote all the
energies of heart and mind and soul to the uplifting of the children of the
land."[6]

Teaching had caught Alderman's fancy. He remained in Chapel Hill during some of the summer normal school sessions of the late 1870s and helped
organize a debating society. At one of those summer sessions he met Walter
Hines Page, later one of his mentors. On graduation, Alderman accepted an
offer from Edward P. Moses to help establish a new, graded school at
Goldsboro. When Moses left Goldsboro, Alderman, age twenty-four, took
over. He was associated there with Charles B. Aycock, then chairman of the
school board. After seven years this led to one of the important missions of
his life.

Alderman's reputation as a public speaker spread across North Carolina.
At a meeting of the North Carolina Teachers Association, held in Black
Mountain in June 1896, he was elected president. About the same time he
married Emma Graves. Their private life was marked by tragedy: Their
three children died within six years. As his biographer noted, Alderman "did
not realize that his memorable educational campaign was to be waged solely
for the children of others."[7]

Early in April 1889 Alderman received a letter from the State Board of

Education appointing him a state institute conductor. He and Charles D. McIver, former principal in the Durham public schools, joined forces to become North Carolina's educational evangelists of the new era. They stumped the state from one end to the other in the cause of tax-supported public schools. McIver, the robust young Scot fresh from the countryside, became the "most effective speaker for public education that Alderman had known in America." McIver never attained the urbanity of Alderman, but he was a natural leader. He conceived the idea for and helped found the state normal and industrial school for women at Greensboro.

Alderman served as his partner in this venture. They worked well as a team. Through institutes, public meetings, and school rallies with teachers and parents, they dramatized the wretched plight of public education, emphasizing the need for improved financing at the state and local levels. During the first year, Alderman traveled 3,100 miles, taught 3,600 teachers, and addressed 35,000 citizens. Their education campaign touched the lives of 160,000 people.

After three years, support for local and state taxation for schools of both races increased. Alderman and McIver won the allegiance of the powerful Farmers' Alliance, which became a strong force in the 1891 General Assembly and helped charter the Normal and Industrial School for white women and the Agricultural and Mechanical College for the Colored Race, both at Greensboro.[8]

But financial crisis arrived in 1891, and the political fusion fight curbed enthusiasm for education momentarily. The return of reconstruction issues ignited intense racial feeling, which reduced local tax support for schools. Enthusiasm for public education cooled until Governor Aycock revived it after 1900.

After three years on the educational gospel trail, Alderman joined McIver at the new Normal and Industrial School at Greensboro as professor of education. He and McIver refused to accept the inadequacy of schoolhouses, excessive size of classes, woeful shortages of textbooks, and incompetency of teachers. They believed with Jefferson that an enduring democracy must rest upon an educated electorate. That philosophy guided Alderman all his life. It led him to become a notable leader for public education in the South. It also influenced him in 1893 to join President Winston's faculty at Chapel Hill—as the newly appointed professor of education. In 1896 he became the obvious successor for the presidency when George Tayloe Winston departed for Texas.

Even though he had no graduate degree, Alderman's skill as a teacher was notable. Some of his students later recalled his mastery in the classroom. One said that under his tutelage she "saw history and literature as a succession of enthralling pageants." His "simple, strong Anglo-Saxon words" could have been understood by a little child, yet they seemed "as blocks of polished marble fitting into a temple wall."[9]

When he returned to Chapel Hill, Alderman succeeded Winston and then Professor James Lee Love and Professor Eben Alexander as custodian of the university's gradually expanding library. By that time dancing and other social functions had been transferred from Smith Hall to the off-campus gymnasium. Alderman supported the idea that the library should be coequal with other chairs of instruction, bearing a relationship comparable with that of laboratories to the natural sciences. He saw librarians as much more than clerks and deplored the inadequacy of the book collection. "The modern library," he wrote in an article for the *Alumni Quarterly*, "has become not only a storehouse of thought but a laboratory, a workshop, a mine, and inspiration for both professors and students."[10]

Alderman became superintendent of the revived summer normal school in 1894. These four-week sessions offered a broad curriculum and attracted a succession of distinguished educators from the faculty and from other institutions.

Alderman had a profound interest in history. He contributed to historical journals and spoke widely on both historical and educational subjects around the state. His criticisms of the limitations of antebellum society were sometimes sharp but less pungent than those of Walter Hines Page.[11] He believed that the Old South had many flaws. Speaking of the economic changes needed in the region, he declared, "We shall lose an element of charm and picturesqueness, but we shall gain in wealth and productive energy, and the change is inevitable."[12]

Returning to Chapel Hill at the age of thirty-two, eleven years after his graduation, Alderman became a figure of dignity and distinction. "In a period of frock coats," his biographer wrote, "he wore tweeds and colored neck ties. . . . At a later time it was whispered that his clothes were made in England. Undoubtedly he was often wondered at and sometimes laughed at, but unquestionably he was admired. Some may have doubted that such a natural aesthete could really have the common touch, but he had stumped the state in behalf of untrained teachers with the gusto of a countryman."[13]

Alderman became as much a natural successor for Winston as the latter had been for Battle. The trustees named him president on July 15, 1896, not long after the fourth personal tragedy of his life: the death of his wife, Emma, who had gradually declined following the demise of their three children. Alderman's election was "overwhelming and spontaneous." Regarded as the spokesman for a new era, he was inducted into office at Gerrard Hall by Governor Daniel L. Russell on January 27, 1897 (a ceremony planned for University Day, the preceding October 12, but delayed because of the autumn's heated political elections).

The General Assembly adjourned for the day, and many legislators traveled to Chapel Hill through sleet and snow on a special train. Nicholas Murray Butler, later president of Columbia University, brought greetings from sister institutions. President Emeritus Battle noted that for the first time the presidency was given to one "whose fame had come from arduous and successful labors for the teachers and the children of our public schools."

Aycock thought Alderman's inaugural address was the greatest he had heard. In it the new president declared: "The great war freed us all. Once we were aristocratic in government and education; now we are democratic in both." He characterized the university as "the mightiest single social engine for the direction and elevation" of the new social order. He criticized the legislature for limiting the institution's appropriations to $20,000 per year. This was "no fit sum" and compared unfavorably to the $333,000 supplied in Illinois and the $273,000 in Wisconsin. Among those working their way through college, Alderman listed a lengthy and specific roll call of self-help students: They included "three typewriters, two shoemakers, two haircutters, six printers, four clerks, a carpenter, twenty-two waiters, five woodcutters, a bookkeeper, a telegraph operator, four teachers in the village, twelve coaches of backward students, a lawyer and a dentist." This, Alderman declared, speaks for the "masterfulness of the race" and tells "the whole story of the passing of an old order and the birth of a new."[14]

Alderman thought the university should emulate the chief universities of the Midwest rather than those of the Northeast, as Battle had suggested. The university's prime function, Alderman said, was to gather in common effort all citizens without respect of creed or party and invigorate the public schools. Pure scholarship would have to bide its time. Under existing conditions it was more important to train "leaders and missionaries in the democratic crusade of arousing the intellect of the whole people."

In the beginning Alderman presented rather modest monetary requests. He sought a new water system, renovation of the library, and new chairs of political and social science and pharmacy. As it turned out, during his four-year presidency he became more a popular philosopher and evangelist of education than an "architect of institutions." He did less in prescribing forms than in instilling spirit. [15]

Yet the physical campus and the curriculum felt the influence of Alderman's touch. Looking out from his South Building office on the Old Well, a rather ramshackled structure, Alderman asked Professor J. W. Gore to help him do something about it. They ordered a modest reproduction of the Temple of Love at Versailles to be built over the Old Well at a cost of $200. In later years Alderman said of this project that he was "possessed with a great desire to add a little beauty (which after all is the most practical influence in the world) to the grim, austere dignity of the Old Campus." Some of his colleagues thought he was wasting money on "luxurious gewjaws" when other needs were more vital. [16]

During Alderman's regime the most expensive building, up to that time, was conceived and completed. Julian S. Carr, the wealthy tobacco financier whose family home once stood near the corner of Franklin and Columbia streets, contributed the bulk of a fund to construct a new dormitory east of Smith Building. Colonel W. H. S. Burgwyn ('68) formally dedicated the Julian S. Carr Building on Commencement Day of 1900 with an eloquent address. The building, built of gray brick and stone, had accommodations for eighty-four students and was outfitted with thoroughly modern conveniences. Later, however, it proved to be poorly constructed and required extensive renovations. [17]

Work began on a second, ambitious building project, Alumni Hall, early in the 1890s, using contributions from former students. Located on the east side of the north quadrangle, it was not completed until 1901 after protracted fund-raising efforts under the direction of President Francis P. Venable. [18]

Alderman achieved most of his objectives. Professor E. Vernon Howell became head of the new pharmacy department. The law school got a new associate professor. Smith Building was renovated to upgrade the library. A new waterworks was constructed and Gerrard Hall was refurbished. Enrollment increased markedly. Following Alderman's recommendations, the trustees voted on February 21, 1897, to admit women to postgraduate courses, but their attendance initially was only about half a dozen each year.

The professional schools did not grow notably during Alderman's presidency. Unlike during the decade before the Civil War, enrollment of out-of-state students, mostly from elsewhere in the South, remained meager. In

1857–58 every southern state had been represented, and students from other states made up about one-third of the student body. By the late 1890s the university's enrollment totaled about 95 percent in-state. The university had not yet established any conspicuous leadership in the southern region. That was to come early in the twentieth century.[19]

Alderman worried about these statistics. In several reports he emphasized the importance of graduate work. "Modern teaching," he wrote in his first report to the trustees, "is no longer a matter of dictionary and grammar grind. The key words of the new education are investigation, laboratory methods, research and discovery."

In the controversial 1897 session, the General Assembly increased the university's annual appropriations from $20,000 to $25,000. This vote of confidence marked a turning point in the bitter fight with the denominational colleges. Under the redoubtable leadership of Kilgo and Bailey, they continued their assault on state aid, but none of their three legislative bills passed.

Alderman received credit for doing much to counter the argument that colleges and universities should not be expanded until the common schools had been built from the bottom up. As an acknowledged champion of the public schools, Alderman argued that North Carolina needed both kinds of education. He went out of his way to praise private colleges for what they were accomplishing, but he warned that to rely on the voluntary principle exclusively in supporting higher education would lead to "aristocracy in education pure and simple."[20]

The furor over education resulted in increased appropriations for all public institutions of learning. The university and its friends won the battle over state aid. That was signaled by the fact that when the 1897 General Assembly came to fill vacancies on the Board of Trustees, no new ministers were included. This marked what historians noted as the complete secularization of university control.[21]

Alderman thought the bickering and sniping of the church-state controversy "demonstrated how much the South needed higher education." Even though his forces had prevailed in 1897, he found it necessary to rally them again in 1898. In that year, education support became embroiled in the vicious white supremacy campaign waged by the Democrats to retrieve power from the Fusionists. Furnifold Simmons, later a Democratic U.S. senator, made a deal with the Kilgo-Bailey faction to oppose increased education appropriations in the 1899 General Assembly in exchange for the faction's support for the white supremacy suffrage amendment. But with Alderman and McIver (called "a steam engine in breeches") leading the fight, the alliance never was consummated. Both the public colleges and public schools won enhanced funding in 1899.[22]

As the century moved to a close, Alderman became increasingly aware that crimped state financing imposed severe limitations on his vision for the university. His administration, he believed, did a better job on a smaller income than any other comparable institution in the South. Tulane, Texas, Vanderbilt, and Virginia had budgets two or three times the size of North Carolina's. The fact that the university did so well on a total budget of $50,000 a year amazed other educators. Over ten years the student body had increased by 150 percent, the state appropriations by only 25 percent. "This sort of struggle without adequate means cannot go on always," Alderman reported to the trustees. Mere enthusiasm and "mountain-removing faith" could not equip laboratories, add needed departments, provide new instructors, and retain old ones.[23]

Following his wife's death, Alderman boarded with her brother's family in a residence then located on the present site of the Carolina Inn. The trustees gave him three months' leave in 1897, which he used for a trip to the Holy Land and the Mediterranean. He became interested in fishing and took a number of trips to Canada with friends. Over the years Alderman acquired the nickname Tony, which remained with him the rest of his life. The name was not conferred because of his prominent nose or rather dark complexion or his large moustache, but rather because of his manner of dress. "Even in his more provincial days his predilection for smart clothes was pronounced. The adjective 'tony' then in common use . . . seemed particularly applicable to the showy young president."[24]

Alderman's expanding professional reputation spread far beyond North Carolina. He was called on to speak at educational functions all over the country. One of them, on the subject of scholarship, at the National Education Association convention in Chicago in 1899, extended his renown as a spokesman for the entire South. In discussing the region's tragic heritage, he declared that he doubted "whether any generation of Americans, save the men who made the Constitution and the pioneers who built the great West, deserved so well of their posterity as these bearers of war's burdens." He strove, he said, to hear the voices of statesmen but heard too many demagogues. He called for educational leaders who would strive to overcome the ignorance which self-seeking politicians found so easy to exploit.[25]

Old Well and students, 1892.
(North Carolina Collection, University of North Carolina Library, Chapel Hill)

Alderman's educational leadership generated in the spring of 1900 an event which seemed inevitable: The trustees of Tulane, at that time challenged only by the University of Texas in enrollment, elected him president. Alderman saw the decision as an important one: whether to move to a richly endowed institution, relatively independent of public clamor, as another step in his quest for democratic education. Tulane's income was twice that of Chapel Hill's.

To answer the question, Alderman sought advice from close friends. He went to Raleigh to confer with newly elected governor Charles Aycock and editor Josephus Daniels. The challenge of Tulane interested him. He did not see how he could obtain the financial backing he needed at Chapel Hill. "Do you think that the next Legislature will give the university an appropriation of $100,000? Could that be relied upon?" he asked Aycock and Daniels. They agreed it could not. Alderman decided to accept Tulane's offer. "A score of times in later years," Daniels wrote, "he [Alderman] referred to the conversation and said if any of the three [of them] could have foreseen the day when the Legislature would give the university a quarter of a million dollars a year nothing could have induced him to [leave]."[26]

News of Alderman's decision generated spirited efforts to keep him at Chapel Hill. The trustees promised more funds and eased duties as well as a

Sallie Walker Stockard, first woman graduate of the University of North Carolina, and class of 1898.
(North Carolina Collection, University of North Carolina Library, Chapel Hill)

$300 salary increase. Alderman's friend Nicholas Murray Butler urged him to move on. "There must be in the South somewhere," he wrote, "a strong, rich, well-equipped university. That cannot come in North Carolina in your time or mine for economic reasons."[27]

President Alderman's last commencement at Chapel Hill in the summer of 1900 also celebrated the twenty-fifth anniversary of the university's reopening. For the first time four university presidents, past, present, and future, sat on the platform: Kemp Battle; George Tayloe Winston, who delivered the chief address; Alderman; and his newly selected successor, Francis P. Venable.

In his departing words, Alderman praised his native state. He admitted that he had fretted because North Carolina was not moving as rapidly as he hoped it might, but he felt it was on the way. "I thank God for the inextinguishable breath of democracy breathed into me by birth in this state," he said. This priceless heritage was no "mere thing of ruggedness and homeliness. . . . It is the business of democracy to make out of itself an aristocracy. There is nothing too good for democracy. Surely its primal needs are strength and virtue and simplicity and freedom. Does it not also need beauty and dignity and grandeur, if you will, and all the things which minister to the spirit?"

North Carolina, he concluded, has been "clad from its hard-beset childhood in the garments of common sense and clear manhood." Alderman went on from Tulane to become president of the University of Virginia, where he built a notable reputation. As his biographer, Dumas Malone, put it, the mantle which he wore, though not native homespun, was "woven in the loom of Jefferson."[28]

FRANCIS P. VENABLE,

EXPANDING HORIZONS,

1900–1914

When President Alderman left Chapel Hill in 1900 for Tulane, no resident of the village summed up the succession more succinctly than the black barber, Thomas Dunstan, who spread the word to his customers on Franklin Street. "Dr. Venable is a very noble, Christian gentleman," Dunstan told them. "He'd make a fine president of the YMCA or presiding elder of the Presbyterian Church. But he ain't no orator. . . . He can't norate, he can't dilate, he can't prevaricate like Marse Ed."[1]

As far as he went, Dunstan was right. Francis Preston Venable was no orator. He ruled out formal inaugural ceremonies for himself and made as few speeches as possible during the fourteen years of his presidency. He had a skeptical view of what came to be known as public relations. He presented durable, airtight budgets to the General Assembly, but he never lingered around Raleigh to lobby for them. He viewed so-called university extension with a jaundiced eye. He believed the university's mission should be confined to the campus and should speak for itself. Surprisingly, for the most part it did.

Despite his occasional brusqueness and aloofness, Venable presided over the early stages of the transformation of a small, provincial college into a national university. Before his arrival there had been no administrative structure to tie the struggling graduate and professional schools—among them law, medicine, and pharmacy—into a coherent whole. The library had not been considered the heart of the university. Scientific research was practically nonexistent. The General Assembly had not provided capital funds for expansion. The faculty had only a small core of able teachers and scholars who were overburdened and underpaid. Financial management was haphazard and poorly organized. The trustees and faculty had not dealt with many academic and physical needs. As a result the curriculum was far from adequate.

Venable, whose father had been a mathematics professor and an aide to General Lee during the war, did not eliminate all these deficiencies. But he made a spirited start. Born in Prince Edward County on November 17, 1856, he graduated from the University of Virginia in 1879 and, after studying at Bonn, obtained degrees in chemistry (an M.A. and a Ph.D.) from the University of Goettingen in 1881. These European degrees gave him unusual distinction on a remote southern campus. Venable brought the university its first credentials of Old World scholarship. When called to Chapel Hill at the age of twenty-three by President Battle, he became a professor of general, analytical, and applied chemistry. He constituted the entire department except for a janitor who pumped water into a barrel in a library room above Venable's quarters in the basement of Smith Hall.[2]

As was the custom for bachelor professors, Venable took up residence in a room in Old East, then moved to the widow Puckett's house on East Franklin Street. On November 3, 1884, he married Sallie Charlton Manning, daughter of the head of the law school. His lecture room and one laboratory were in Person Hall, and his second chemistry laboratory was in Smith. By 1885 the number of chemistry students had increased to such an extent that a new laboratory was built as an addition to Person Hall. By 1892 still another wing was added, providing ten rooms for 200 students. The staff was increased accordingly with the arrival in 1882 of E. A. de Schweinitz as an instructor and in 1885 by William Battle Phillips as professor of agricultural chemistry and metallurgy. One of the assistants who came in 1892, Charles Baskerville, became Venable's successor when he left science to take over the formidable duties of university president in 1900.

Venable reached the president's office at an opportune moment. Bitter differences between the university and the denominational colleges had peaked in 1897 and gradually subsided. The political victories of Furnifold Simmons's organization in 1898 and 1900 banked the fires of racial discord momentarily. Democratic party supremacy eased the university's fears about its survival and independence. Newly elected governor Charles B. Aycock

Francis Preston Venable.
(North Carolina Collection, University of North Carolina Library, Chapel Hill)

chose to emphasize universal education, for blacks and whites alike. A crusade for public education swept the state.

The new president's Presbyterian affiliation, as one historian put it, "never marked him out as a true heir of the inner spirit of real Calvinism. God might not err, but his children could and often did. It was the duty of man to seek the good and perchance he might find it, but all were not in error who did not find it in Venable's way."[3] The university had eased its ties with denominational religion, and the new, young scientist-president did not reverse the trend. As a sturdy successor of Battle, Winston, and Alderman, Venable lacked some of their political shrewdness and oratorical flair. But as a dedicated scholar intent on building a first-rate university, he had no rival, and he became the man for the season.

From the start of his academic career Venable strove after his goals seriously, even austerely. He carried a full load of teaching and research, served as chairman of the committee on athletics, and was one of the founders of the Elisha Mitchell Scientific Society in 1883. This demonstrated his determination to encourage scientific research.[4]

One of the more interesting sidelights of Venable's teaching years, an example of his modest style, was his work with two talented chemistry students who later became benefactors of the university. John Motley Morehead, grandson of an antebellum governor, went to work in his father's cotton mill at Spray in Rockingham County after graduation in 1881. His father, J. Turner Morehead, hired John Motley at $3 a week to supervise construction of an aluminum production plant. The plant never produced aluminum. One series of experiments, however, produced a new material that nobody could identify. Major Morehead invited Professor Venable to visit the plant along with some of his students, among them William Rand Kenan, Jr. Venable and Kenan "made the key observation that identified the gas as not hydrogen but acetylene and thus determined that the material was calcium carbide."

After testing the mixtures with air for several months to yield a bright light, Venable invited Morehead and his associates to Chapel Hill to see the wonderfully bright flame. The new product, with the Moreheads and Kenan to the forefront, eventually became the mainstay of Union Carbide Company. Morehead's work led to full utilization of the "waste" material Venable recognized as calcium carbide. Morehead's associates applied for the patents, based on Venable's analysis. The Chapel Hill professor got none of the monetary rewards, which did not seem to concern him greatly.

The same pattern persisted in Venable's "classic refinement of the Bunsen burner for controlled air uptake and mixing," which he perfected. "The Bunsen burner achievement, published in 1887, is typical of Venable's finding satisfaction in the acknowledgement of his contributions rather than seeking financial reward. It was not worth the struggle with the forces of mammon to pursue extravagant recompense."[5]

Morehead and Kenan became associated in the Union Carbide Company's rise to prominence in the industrial world. Morehead later served as minister to Sweden and was awarded the gold medal of the Royal Swedish Academy of Sciences. A portion of his wealth returned to Chapel Hill in the form of benefactions, including the Morehead-Patterson Bell Tower (1931), the Morehead Planetarium (1949), and the Morehead scholarships (1950).

After graduation, Kenan worked for the North Carolina Geological Survey, taught in Virginia, and installed the first electric lighting system in Chapel Hill. Eventually he was employed by Union Carbide and set up plants for production of calcium carbide on five continents. He later met Henry M. Flagler, once associated with John D. Rockefeller in the Standard Oil Trust, and became part of his ambitious project to develop the east coast of Florida. Kenan also became a notable benefactor of his alma mater, his chief contributions being the Kenan Stadium and Field House and the Kenan Chemistry Library.

As a man of science, Professor Venable showed early signs of combining vision and practicality. In 1883 he became one of the incorporators of a small print shop ambitiously called the University Press. Set up in New West, it was designed to do commercial printing and issue official publications of the university. Like the schools of law, medicine, and pharmacy, it was established as a private enterprise, welcomed by the university for the convenient and inexpensive service it rendered and the training it provided for students.[6]

Even before his elevation to the presidency, Venable recognized the essentials of a good university. Publication was among them. While he generally refrained from speech making, he did speak effectively in a report to students, faculty, alumni, and trustees on University Day, October 12, 1907, about midway through his presidency. The very "heart and soul of an education institution," he declared, "lies in its teaching force, and I look hopefully forward to the time when in our ideal university the excellent faculty of the present shall have grown into a large body of strong, trained men, eminent scholars, skillful investigators, inspiring teachers."

From the start in 1900, Venable embroidered this chief goal with others designed to strengthen it. These included a strong administrative structure, classroom buildings and equipment, and efficient business management.

Venable's first task was to provide a durable administrative structure. He appointed Professor Eben Alexander to the newly created post of dean of the faculty. This honor graduate of Yale, former U.S. minister to Greece, and professor of Greek was ideally suited to become chief of staff for the kind of faculty Venable envisioned. In January 1901 Venable had the trustees bring the departments of medicine, law, and pharmacy wholly under the university's umbrella, with their heads made deans to work with Alexander. In June 1901 the trustees established the new School of Mines, later the Department of Applied Sciences (1904), with Professor Joshua Walker Gore as dean. Professor M. C. S. Noble joined this group as head of the summer school program.

Venable surrounded himself with capable associates. They championed his prime mission: good teaching. Simultaneously, he carefully selected professors to fill vacancies as they occurred or as funds became available through expanded largesse from the General Assembly and private benefactions. To the already solid core of professors assembled by his predecessors, Venable added individuals destined to attain national and international reputation.

Part of his success in starting this process lay in the legislature's growing generosity. In 1901 it increased its annual appropriation from $25,000 to $37,500. By 1913 it was $95,000. A stream of talented graduates emerged from the campus to become doctors, lawyers, businessmen, pharmacists, judges, and state and county leaders. Nearly every community in North Carolina had graduates of Chapel Hill. They encouraged the legislature to add further enrichments. Venable became the university's first president to benefit substantially from this relationship between the people and the university.

It would be difficult to name all the distinguished professors who enlisted under the Chapel Hill banner. Venable's funds were insufficient to hire many established academic luminaries. He attracted a few well-known professionals, then sought out young, potentially talented professors to start their careers at Chapel Hill.

Early in his presidency (1901) he found Louis Round Wilson, a fine librarian, who would make the library the heart of the university and serve as counselor to a succession of university presidents over the next half-century. Charles T. Woollen arrived as part-time secretary to the president and leader of the band, then became the university's business manager and athletic enthusiast. Dr. Charles Lee Raper became head of the Department of Economics and an associate in history, and William S. Bernard signed on as professor of Greek.

By the following year Venable had attracted Dr. C. Alphonso Smith as professor of English and Dr. William C. Coker, professor of botany; Edward Kidder Graham had already joined the English department. Other young scholars who arrived during those years included George Howe, Latin; J. G. deRoulhac Hamilton and Henry McG. Wagstaff, history; William M. Dey, romance languages; Marvin H. Stacy and Thomas Felix Hickerson, mathematics and civil engineering; and James F. Royster, John M. Booker, and Edwin Greenlaw, English.

Nowhere were the transformations in curriculum and development more marked than in the emerging professional schools: law, medicine, and pharmacy. The law school dated back to 1845 when it was established by Judge William H. Battle as an adjunct resource. Those were the days before the closed shop, when few barriers faced candidates seeking to enter the profession. Students read law, medicine, or pharmacy and worked under private professional guidance with varying standards and little or no certification.

By 1901 the law school consisted of two rooms, former bedrooms on the first floor of Old West. During that year the school moved to the first floor of South Building, former quarters of the physics department. In 1907 it moved to Smith Hall and then in 1923 to its new home, Manning Hall, on the south campus. The staff from 1845 to 1900 consisted of one person with occasional assistants. For a time, classes were conducted in a small building belonging to Samuel Field Phillips, still standing on the corner of the old Phillips property at East Franklin and Hillsboro streets. Judge John Manning succeeded Battle as dean in 1879 and was succeeded in turn by Judge Duncan MacRae in 1899, with J. Crawford Biggs and, later, Thomas Ruffin as assistants.

In the earliest years, a law license could easily be procured by any person twenty-one years old and of good character who had passed an exam offered by the state supreme court. These standards slowly rose, and by the time Lucius Polk McGehee became dean in 1910 a campaign was launched to establish a three-year law course. McGehee and his associate, Professor Atwell Campbell McIntosh, strengthened the curriculum, prescribed new standards for scholarship and publication, and established a law library and systematic teaching. The number of students varied, totaling 61 in 1900 and 131 in 1913. In 1911 the school admitted its first woman, Lillian Frye of Bryson City, who passed the bar and was licensed to practice. The *North Carolina Law Journal* was established in 1904 but survived only one year. The *North Carolina Law Review* was founded in 1922.[7]

The School of Medicine evolved in a similar fashion. Its advancement was more pronounced during the Venable years. The university trustees sponsored its first activities in 1879, when they appointed Dr. Thomas W. Harris of Chatham County, a physician of recognized ability, as professor of anatomy. The purpose of the new medical school, operating in association with the chemistry, botany, and physiology departments, was to prepare students for attendance at medical schools elsewhere. But Dr. Harris taught only on a part-time basis, and he received no salary. This arrangement expired in 1885 when Dr. Harris moved to Durham. It was revived in 1891 under Dr. Richard H. Whitehead and Dr. Charles S. Mangum, two able physicians. Dr. Isaac H. Manning joined the department in 1901 as professor of physiology. A dissecting hall and other laboratories were provided.

At the same time, the university opened a department of medicine at Raleigh to extend training offered for two years at Chapel Hill and to grant the degree of doctor of medicine (M.D.). This department, under the direction of Dr. Hubert Royster, utilized the services of ten practicing physicians. When Dr. Whitehead resigned in 1905 to become dean of the medical school at the University of Virginia, he was succeeded by Dr. Manning. Joining the faculty as well were Dr. William deB. MacNider, who became professor of pharmacology, Dr. L. B. Newell, Dr. R. B. Lawson, Dr. James Bullitt, and others as the department expanded. Completion of new classrooms allowed the department to move into Person Hall in 1906. By 1907 there was a new dissecting hall and a new infirmary providing health service for students. The construction of Caldwell Hall in 1912 gave the medical school its own home, which served until 1939.

Gradually, as funding increased, the medical school strengthened its curriculum, adding in 1909 a premedical year that required preparation in biology, chemistry, and physics. Admission standards were raised, and facilities and equipment were expanded along with the first medical library. Most students found ready admission to third-year classes of leading medical schools around the country. Dr. Whitehead did notable research in the anatomy of the brain, and Dr. MacNider became nationally recognized for his research on kidney disease. The medical department at Raleigh, which had served students unable to get further education elsewhere, continued until 1910 when it was closed because of the increasing complexity of medical study and a shortage of funds. During its seven years of operation the department graduated seventy-nine students of whom sixty-seven became practicing physicians in North Carolina.[8]

The School of Pharmacy, founded in 1880, discontinued in 1885, and revived in 1887, initially had quarters in New West. In 1901, in line with Venable's program of consolidation, it was brought under full supervision of the university with Dr. E. Vernon Howell as dean and a student assistant. During his long career, which ended in 1931, Dr. Howell helped raise state pharmaceutical standards, including stricter requirements for licensing. As the only school for pharmacists in the state during that era, it graduated fifty-five students, most of whom became practicing pharmacists in North Carolina.[9]

As a scientist, Venable sought to bring together all courses of applied sciences: mining, electrical and civil engineering, soil investigation, and pure science. First called the School of Mines and later the School of Engineering, it remained an important fixture at Chapel Hill until parts of it were transferred to North Carolina State College in 1938 as part of consolidation. Professor Joshua W. Gore, who had joined the faculty in 1882 and was known for his terrifying courses in physics, got it off to a good start.[*]

The staff of the School of Mines in its first years included, among others, Gore and J. E. Latta in physics and electricity; William Cain, Archibald Henderson, and M. H. Stacy in mathematics; Collier Cobb in geology; Charles Baskerville, A. S. Wheeler, and J. E. Mills in chemistry; and J. A. Holmes and Joseph Hyde Pratt in various aspects of mining. The work of the school was exacting. Some fifty of its early graduates served in the U.S. Geological Survey and in the Soil Division of the U.S. Department of Agriculture. Among these graduates were Hugh H. Bennett ('03) and Henry A. Allard ('05), who achieved international reputations. Upon Gore's

---

[*]Other dreaded courses around the turn of the century were Major William Cain's sophomore course in analytical geometry, Horace Williams's psychology course, and English composition courses taught by a changing group of instructors. "These instructors, at least in the student mind, lacked generosity in grading" (Wilson, *University*, pp. 72–73).

death in 1908, Dr. Charles Holmes Herty became dean.* In 1909 Andrew H. Patterson became professor of physics and, later, dean.

During the latter part of Venable's regime many new subjects were added, including mechanical drawing, soil investigation, and highway, medical, and military engineering. Two professors who added greatly to the school's strength in 1910 were Parker H. Daggett, associate professor of electrical engineering, and James Munsie Bell, associate professor of physical chemistry.[10]

Reorganization of the graduate school under Dr. C. Alphonso Smith in 1903 provided new direction and coherence. In many respects it was the most important accomplishment of the Venable administration. It ultimately helped transform "an excellent college" into a "well-organized, effective university." Here Venable's skill as organizer operated at its best. He began the process of systematically training experts dedicated to rebuilding the South twenty to twenty-five years ahead of other southern universities.[11]

Venable's appointment of an executive committee to supervise administrative matters, while successful in many ways, occasioned some faculty criticism until it was amended to include one representative elected by the faculty. Venable's "exacting sense of duty and unwillingness to tax others with duties to save himself" created problems and exacted a great physical and nervous toll on the president himself.[12]

As the administration reshaped degree programs, it saw the need for better preparation at the high school level if freshman standards were to rise. Largely as a result of poor training, only 18 percent of the entering class of 1901 was graduated. Professor Horace Williams and Instructor E. K. Graham organized the Order of the Golden Fleece in 1903, in part to emphasize high academic attainment. In 1904 the university secured a chapter of Phi Beta Kappa, the national scholarship fraternity, to help enrich academics. James Horner Winston became the university's first Rhodes scholar during the same year. Graham encouraged better scholastic achievement among the campus's burgeoning Greek letter fraternities.

Venable's regime continued the strong interest in training teachers for the

---

*Herty became promoter of what became known as the Herty Cup, a device used extensively in collecting resin in the turpentine industry, which he introduced from France. He resigned from the university in 1916 to become editor of the *Journal of Industrial Chemistry* and to continue to investigate slash pine for the manufacture of newsprint (Wilson, *University*, p. 74).

state's public schools. The Department of Pedagogy, especially under Professor M. C. S. Noble, who became dean in 1913, received top attention. Venable added Professor Nathan Wilson Walker to the faculty in 1905 and Dr. Harry Woodburn Chase, who would become president of the university, in 1910. In 1911 he obtained a $40,000 grant from the George Peabody Fund for the erection of an adequate home for the department. Named for Peabody, it stands today on the west side of the campus near the Carolina Inn.

Venable believed in generous leaves of absence for younger teachers. Despite less than generous salaries, he managed to keep faculty members stimulated and interested in their work. The president continued to teach chemistry along with his other duties. Of the first ten students to achieve doctorates in chemistry, six were his students. Venable, as already noted, also believed in publication. Under his leadership many new scholarly journals were founded along with clubs specializing in such subjects as economics, music, literature, and languages.

In addition to overhauling the administration, faculty, and curriculum, Venable capitalized on the rising interest in education to obtain a host of new buildings. The physical plant he inherited had been only slightly enhanced since Civil War days—Memorial and Commons halls were added under Battle, and Carr Dormitory and the start of Alumni Hall came under Alderman. By 1899 the campus had only 120 dorm rooms for 512 students, many of whom had rooms in townspeople's homes.

In 1905 the General Assembly appropriated $50,000 for construction of a new chemistry building, now Howell Hall, the first funds authorized for a state-financed building since Old East. This was followed in 1907 by $21,000 for an infirmary, now Abernethy Hall; in 1908, $35,000 for a new biology building named for William R. Davie; in 1910, $27,587 for a new power plant; in 1912, $50,000 for a new medical building named for President Caldwell; and also in 1912, $51,757 for a new three-section dormitory named Battle-Vance-Pettigrew, to honor notable alumni. Swain Hall, also named for a former president, was completed in 1914 at a cost of $46,654. Meanwhile, in 1907 the trustees authorized the use of $15,000 from escheats funds to build a new president's house on East Franklin Street. The sum spent on major buildings and additions between 1900 and 1914 totaled $359,500.[13]

This upsurge of financial support for bricks and mortar also came from the university's growing cohort of alumni and friends. Venable, who held the Mary Ann Smith professorship of chemistry before becoming president, recommended in 1900 erection of the Mary Ann Smith dormitory from that private benefaction. It was built for $16,000 on what was then the western edge of the campus.

In 1905 two major projects were launched: A $50,000 Andrew Carnegie Library on the old campus (later to become Hill Music Hall); and the $25,000 Bynum Gymnasium, a gift of Judge William Preston Bynum in memory of his grandson who had died as a sophomore in 1893. This served as the university's athletic center, providing facilities for swimming and basketball, among other sports, until the construction of the Tin Can in 1924. Later, Bynum became the home of the journalism department and the university press.

Simultaneously in 1907 the YMCA building was built, with solicited funds, adjacent to South Building and Gerrard Hall. It became the hub of student activities, housing both the book and student supply stores, but it was an unattractive building, out of harmony with campus architecture in that area.

As newly appointed director of the arboretum in 1903, Professor William C. Coker enhanced the beauty of the campus. As a professor of botany and a lover of flowers, he supervised drainage of the low-lying eastern area—an "uninviting crayfish bog"—and by laying walks and arbors and beds of flowers and shrubs produced "a garden of color and loveliness which (as Coker Arboretum) . . . has been an unending delight to the residents of Chapel Hill."[14]

In 1913 the United Daughters of the Confederacy contributed funds for erection of a bronze statue of a Confederate soldier, created by the Canadian sculptor John Wilson, honoring the war dead. Called Silent Sam by succeeding generations of students, it stands at the northern end of McCorkle Place in line with the Caldwell monument, Davie Poplar, and the Old Well.

During the Venable years the university acquired the site of the old University Inn near Franklin Street and eventually built the Graham Memorial there. It purchased the gymnasium at the corner of Cameron Avenue and Columbia Street that became the site of Peabody Hall. The number of buildings constructed during the Venable era totaled sixteen, and the valuation placed on the university's plant in 1914 totaled $1,008,400. Labor involved in these projects was formidable. Chapel Hill had no architects, contractors, or building suppliers, and it lay on a branch railway line. Venable, however, pushed the expansion "with grim Presbyterian determi-

William Rand Kenan, Jr., as a student.
(North Carolina Collection, University of North Carolina Library, Chapel Hill)

nation," seeing that every dollar was well spent and emphasizing simplicity and utility over luxury.[15]

Of all the building achievements of those years, none excelled the $55,000 library, endowed by Andrew Carnegie but essentially the brainchild of one of Venable's talented young faculty members, Louis Round Wilson. Imbued with the scientific spirit, Venable recognized the centrality of research in the creation of a topflight university. At Chapel Hill that required, first, increased faculty of outstanding quality and additional physical facilities. It was Wilson who tied into that vision the indispensability of a well-organized and well-equipped library, as both a storehouse of knowledge of the past and a resource for the future.

As early as 1903 Wilson campaigned for a new library building. This need either had not been perceived earlier or, at least, had not been acted upon. The library had a profound effect on the university as a working institution. Carnegie wisely stipulated that his gift be matched by endowment funds, which Venable and his associates collected by appeals to alumni and friends. Wilson's management of the new facility so firmly established the library as the "soul of the university" that the Carnegie Building was soon outgrown

Davie Poplar after the storm of 1903.
(North Carolina Collection, University of North Carolina Library, Chapel Hill)

and replaced some twenty years later by the $625,000 library on the south campus, which subsequently was named for Louis Round Wilson in 1956.[16]

Wilson's initiative had an impact on many aspects of campus life. The book collection grew from 38,593 volumes in 1901 to 72,295 in 1914. The university led the Southeast in number of library volumes for three decades. Wilson helped stimulate departmental libraries as well, helped organize the State Library Commission, expanded the North Carolina Collection, and encouraged numerous bequests from alumni and friends. He became first editor of the *Alumni Review* in 1912 and head of the university's extension bureau in 1913.

The arrival of Charles T. Woollen, age twenty-three, as registrar and part-time secretary to Venable and the trustees in 1901 marked the start of a remarkable thirty-seven-year career culminating in the overall business managership of the university. Woollen thoroughly overhauled bookkeeping and internal accounts systems. He set up indispensable instruments of budgetary control, well in advance of the state's own Executive Budget Act of 1925. He served as supervisor of buildings and grounds and as a keen liaison with the faculty and the legislature. He became an "exceedingly able business manager" and an "ingenious creative executive."[17]

The university's transformation under Venable brought problems in two areas where the president's own sterling qualities were sorely taxed. Troubles developed in athletics and hazing.

As a man of strong will and physique, Venable loved sports. In 1884, while still a professor, he supervised construction of the first tennis courts in Chapel Hill. He liked contact sports, especially football.[18] His insistence on purity of standards, however, clashed head-on with the popularity and growing competitiveness of intercollegiate athletics. Public and alumni opinion had not yet perceived the pitfalls of overemphasis, nor had the machinery of councils and conferences been installed to regulate standards and eligibility.[19]

As it grew in popularity, football at Chapel Hill began to suffer flagrant abuses. Faculty members and professionals played on campus teams. National sportswriters scorned the football programs of both Virginia and Chapel Hill. Their teams were not included on national ranking lists. The *Tar Heel*, the student newspaper, brushed off this criticism as evidently proceeding from "bad digestion and complete ignorance of southern athletics."[20]

Venable, who valued leadership qualities and team spirit developed on the playing fields, encouraged the university to join the Southern Inter-Collegiate Athletic Association in 1900. It installed the one-year rule whereby no student could play until after that period of enrollment; nor could a player miss more than five lecture days. The alumni strenuously opposed these rules. As a result, the university withdrew from the association after two years and established its own regulations. The university and the University of Virginia differed over sports policies, especially when Virginia won most of the football games between 1900 and 1914. By 1908 the eligibility rules had become a grievous issue.

The administration insisted on tightening loose regulations about gift giving and academic eligibility. Carolina's devastating 60-0 defeat at the hands of Virginia in 1914 produced new tremors and a watering down of rules. Gradually the university fell into the mainstream of national athletic practices. It joined the South Atlantic Inter-collegiate Conference of State Universities in 1915.[21]

Many changes developed in other areas. A class athletic field was built in 1907. Eight tennis courts were constructed behind Bynum Gymnasium in 1911. Baseball was already popular. The furor over athletics produced wear and tear on Venable, who strongly opposed hired players and professionalism. He was determined that athletics not overshadow academics. Some saw the president as overly rigid and puritanical.

Venable's greatest problem, however, arose in student government. The old "rule by faculty" system had gradually given way to self-government by students in certain areas, mostly in classroom infractions involving the honor system. By 1904 a student council was formed to administer student government. Its jurisdiction covered all areas of misconduct, inside and outside the classroom. The council sometimes differed with the faculty executive committee over discipline. Matters involving drunkenness and theft were not perceived in the same light. Often it was difficult for students to obtain information necessary to act on certain cases. All this came to a head in 1910 when the student government suspended a student who was later reinstated by the faculty. The incident created a campus uproar. Mass meetings were held. The *Tar Heel* lashed the faculty. Venable appeared in chapel to discuss the case. The trustees set up an appeals system bypassing the faculty executive committee, an action which produced renewed criticism. The student council resigned in a body. By tedious compromises, tensions were eased.

Yet controversy erupted anew following the death in the early morning hours of September 13, 1912, of Isaac William Rand, a freshman from Smithfield. Rand fell from the top of a barrel while being hazed by a group of sophomores, cut his jugular vein on a broken bottle, and bled to death. His death stunned the campus and the state. The coroner, the governor, and the press called for a full investigation. Venable appointed a special committee with himself as chairman. Following the committee's findings, the university dismissed the four sophomores found responsible. They were then arrested by county authorities and tried in Orange Superior Court. The court acquitted one defendant. It found the other three guilty of manslaughter and sentenced them to four months' imprisonment with the privilege of being hired out for four months instead of serving active jail sentences. They were hired out by their parents, who paid court costs.

The case led the administration to reopen several other hazing incidents. As a result the university expelled four other students, suspended twelve for one year, and reprimanded two. The committee's reports to the trustees and students reflected the anguish the Rand case had aroused. Venable termed the matter "one of the most disgraceful affairs that has happened here" and described in personal terms what he felt. "This humiliation of the institution that I have loved and labored for," he said, "has depressed me beyond words. Now that the attack seems to center upon me personally, it is better, for I am content to suffer for any blame which is justly due, and that which is not just cannot injure me."

As a result of Rand's death, the student council opened its records for public inspection and removed the veil of secrecy about charges made against student conduct. It also scheduled regular meetings. For a time, at least, hazing receded as a campus problem.[22]

The shock of these responsibilities took its toll on Venable. Even as the turmoil over the Rand case subsided, the president found his burdens heavier. As the summer of 1913 approached, he requested a leave of absence to recoup his strength. Over his protests the trustees granted him a year's leave with full pay ($4,000) and simultaneously appointed Professor Edward Kidder Graham to serve as acting president for the ensuing year. That summer, accompanied by his wife, Sallie, and two of their daughters, Louise and Frances, Venable sailed for Europe. There, thirty years after he had received his degree at Goettingen, he revisited old scenes of his youth. He renewed contacts with academic friends and lived leisurely in a congenial, scientific environment in Switzerland and Germany.

In the spring of 1914 Venable's health had not improved as much as he had expected. He wrote the trustees from London on May 7, 1914, that he would not be able to resume the presidency. At its meeting on May 28 the trustees accepted his resignation with regret and on the same day created the Francis Preston Venable chair of chemistry and elected Venable to fill it. At the same meeting they chose E. K. Graham as his successor.

Thus at the age of fifty-seven, Venable ended a notable administrative career, although he continued to teach for many years prior to his death in 1934. The modest scientist whose presidential tenure had spanned the years between the Spanish-American War and the First World War contributed markedly to the beginning of the university's rise from the ranks of small, inconspicuous colleges into national recognition. He fleshed out its administrative structure, attracted and developed an able faculty, expanded the curriculum, supervised a massive expansion of facilities, and managed the difficult controversies involving student athletics and self-government. While Venable's vision seldom ventured far out into the state and was sometimes poor on public relations, it did see to the founding of the extension bureau and revitalization of the alumni association.

The talented chemistry professor, as it developed, sacrificed a brilliant scientific career in order to serve the university. In making his decision to accept the presidency "at a time when his star was among the brightest in the firmament of American science," he made a turn which in later years he sometimes regretted. To one of his later students he confessed that he considered the years of his presidency wasted.[23]

But the opinion of most of his contemporaries sharply repudiated that judgment. In the words of his successor E. K. Graham, Venable was "the architect of [the university's] material rebuilding" and the patron of her "ideals of modern scholarship."[24] Speaking after Venable's retirement as William Rand Kenan professor of chemistry in 1930, President Frank Porter Graham referred to him as "being with us still in modest retirement . . . gathering flowers from his garden for his friends in the village where he once gathered truth from test tubes for all mankind."[25]

EDWARD K. GRAHAM,

SERVICE TO THE STATE,

1914–1918

Toward the end of the Venable years, in September 1912, a young Halifax County farm boy, Robert Burton House, arrived on the Chapel Hill Limited at Carrboro as an incoming freshman and hired a carriage for 50 cents to take him and his trunk to the campus. Writing fifty years later, House, who became chancellor in the mid-twentieth century, described his first view of Chapel Hill as he rounded the curve from Carrboro: "As I saw Franklin Street in 1912, it was a dusty red avenue cut through a forest of magnificent trees. The road dipped through a valley and then rose, but the trees dominated the scene and obscured any buildings that then existed on that section of Franklin Street. My first impression of Chapel Hill was trees; my last impression is trees."[1]

Under the trees, Bob House encountered the mystical ambience of a village campus which had already cast its spell over generations of Tar Heel students. In those days Chapel Hill remained a down-home sort of place, not fancy and still wedded to the personal touch. "Our dress was more conventional then than now," House wrote. "Everyone wore a coat and hat. Everyone tipped his hat to a professor and received in return a tip of the professorial hat. . . . I think it was Frank Graham [a later president] who started the hatless age on campus in my generation. Frank had a fine shock of hair and a theory that going bareheaded would prevent baldness."

Chapel Hill remained a man's world, too, although some women had been admitted since 1896. There were a few students in law, medicine, and pharmacy, but it was primarily a campus of undergraduates, living in a bucolic wilderness. Facilities were simple, even primitive. There was no hot water in the dormitories. Bathing and toilet facilities were located in Law Sub, the basement of Smith Building (now Playmakers Theater), and in Bynum Gymnasium. "It was good form to wrap a towel around your middle and, otherwise naked, to go down from your dormitory to the baths," House wrote. "Occasionally ladies would come on the campus. The old cry 'angel on the campus!' was not irreverence or satire. It was simply a warning to gentlemen in undress to duck."

House recalled "here and there an old open privy, unused but not as yet removed." But there was also a modern swimming pool in Bynum. "About one fourth of us were adequately financed," House wrote of himself and his fellow students.

> About one-fourth were able to get along by strict economy and self-denial. The other half had to take advantage of every sort of job the community offered, and since such jobs were few, they also had to borrow from university loan funds or privately at home. Their education was never far above the bread and butter line. Usually incomplete preparation and incomplete financing coincided in the same person. He was doubly handicapped. . . . It was wonderful to see doubly handicapped students, many of them, forge to the front and finish as leaders. The intangibles of brain and character are the secrets of the "quality education" we talk of so much today.[2]

There was a good deal of quality education at Chapel Hill. As Bob House arrived, a university president who strongly believed in brains and character was about to take charge.

His name was Edward Kidder Graham. He sprang from a family thoroughly steeped in the mission of teaching. One uncle had been founder of the Fayetteville public schools and was superintendent of schools in Charlotte, and another had operated a distinguished private academy in Warren County. Ed Graham's father was a banker, but he and his brothers had large families, most of whom had chosen teaching as life careers. Ed Graham's sister, Mary O. Graham, was president of Peace Institute in Raleigh.

A tall, pale, almost gaunt young man of thirty-seven, Graham was the son of Archibald and Eliza Owen (Barry) Graham. Many in his family were, or were to become, bonded to the mystique of Chapel Hill as enthusiastically as

Franklin Street, 1892.
(North Carolina Collection, University of North Carolina Library, Chapel Hill)

had the Phillipses and Battles of earlier generations. As with them, the place and the institution became the love of their lives.

Born on October 11, 1876, Ed Graham received his early education in the public schools of Charlotte. In 1894, at the age of eighteen, he entered Chapel Hill, graduating with a bachelor of philosophy degree four years later. He ranked second in his class and as a senior received the coveted Mangum Medal. From the start his career was marked by sound scholarship, high ideals, and a passion for fair play and square dealing.[3] At Chapel Hill Graham excelled as a debater and in tennis and baseball. He was editor-in-chief of the *Tar Heel* and a charter member of the Order of the Gorgon's Head. "During his undergraduate days," Archibald Henderson, a classmate, recalled, "by his stability of character, the dignity of his personality and the force which is an emanation of conscious power, he quickly won a position of acknowledged leadership among his fellows."[4]

Following his graduation, Graham returned to Charlotte to teach for a year in the Baird's School for Boys. In 1899 President Alderman, who had known and admired him as an undergraduate, recalled him to Chapel Hill as librarian. Next Graham became an instructor in English under Dr. Thomas Hume, and his ascent up the academic ladder began in earnest. He took the

President Battle beside Davie Poplar, Jr., 1918.
(North Carolina Collection, University of North Carolina Library, Chapel Hill)

year off in 1902–3 to win his A.M. in English at Columbia University. After more graduate study there in 1904–5, he became a full professor of English at Chapel Hill in 1907. By 1909 he was head of the department, succeeding Dr. C. Alphonso Smith, and shortly thereafter he became dean of the College of Liberal Arts, succeeding Dr. Eben Alexander. Thus Graham stood in line to become acting president when Venable took a year's leave in 1913 and to replace him when he retired.

Ed Graham epitomized for Chapel Hill in education what John F. Kennedy later epitomized for the nation in politics. As a gifted teacher and administrator, he died in mid-flight, cut down by the World War I influenza epidemic of 1918. The full scope of his potential was never realized, although his influence remained alive long after he departed. When Albert Coates, who as a student (1914–18) served as Graham's secretary, heard of his death, he said he "knew and felt that there had passed away a glory from the earth."[5]

The texts of Graham's speeches, sometimes complex and ponderous, by no means reflected the personality of the teacher described by his students. Graham's impact—whether in the classroom or in chapel where he seemed to be spellbinding—was personal. "He would take some campus event, a game, a debate, a noteworthy student achievement, anything," Bob House recalled. "He would reveal how the seemingly commonplace, if understood in its full significance, opened intellectual and spiritual vistas. To him the student and the university were in the center of the state, national and international affairs. He showed us ourselves in our deepest needs and opportunities and related us literally to the whole universe. He did not talk with us so much as he took us into his confidence and thought with us."[6]

Graham knew how to inspire people with "new visions of the perfectibility of man," Albert Coates observed. "By asserting that students were able and good, he helped make them able and good—inspired them to be better than they were. . . . He never sought to dominate or overawe, or subdue anyone, but to make every man his own master. . . . The men associated with him felt, not that they were working for him, but that he was giving to them a medium and opportunity for doing in the biggest way the thing they wanted to do. Around him men felt free."[7]

In the approaching shadows of world war, the Graham administration represented both an extension of the Venable priorities—good teaching and administration—and a new emphasis. Graham viewed the university as a vehicle to enhance the quality of life in North Carolina. He sought, in the words of Professor Henderson, to "release the educational principles and scholarly ideals of the university" into "channels of service and utility to the great masses of the people."[8]

In his inaugural address of April 1915 Graham declared that the "state university is the instrument of democracy for realizing all [these] high and healthful aspirations of the state. . . . Research and classical culture are as deeply and completely service as any vocational service." They are "too precious to be confined to the cloisters and sufficiently robust to inhabit the walks of man." He thought the "wealth of North Carolina should be turned to civic service."[9]

Graham sought to make the university's boundaries coterminous with those of the state. His goals were to interpret the campus to its constituencies and to make it a servant of the state in developing economic and social resources. Graham's speeches on the role of the university caught the attention of the press and the academic world. He launched a program to link the campus's activities with good roads, public health, city and county planning, rural economics, sociology, and civic problems. One of his first acts was to appoint a professor of economics as the nucleus of a school of commerce and business administration. Henry W. Grady prophesied such advances in the 1880s, but little attention had been given to his ideas in the South. "In these matters the university set a new pattern not only for herself but for other southern institutions, notably the University of Virginia and South Carolina."[10]

Graham's democratic spirit touched the faculty. He abolished the executive committee and provided for election of a faculty advisory committee by secret ballot rather than by presidential appointment. He sought better salaries and perquisites.

In this faculty enrichment thrust, the generosity of a family linked with the university from its beginning came to the fore. When Mrs. Mary Lily Kenan Flagler Bingham died in Louisville on July 17, 1917, she left the university one of the largest bequests ever made to a state institution at that time.

Mrs. Bingham's benefaction did not involve bricks and mortar. It specified a $75,000 annual endowment in perpetuity to enrich salaries of Chapel Hill professors in memory of her father, William Rand Kenan, and her uncles, Thomas S. Kenan and James Graham Kenan, all university alumni. The gift was so large that at first its size was not comprehended. Providing such an endowment required almost $2 million in principal. Once the scope of the gift became known, it was clear that Mrs. Bingham had provided an unprecedented opportunity. Applauding the benefaction, the *New York Sun* declared that it will "definitely put Chapel Hill on a real university basis, swelling the state income in proportions that will make things possible, and will doubtless break a broad way for future benefactions of great moment to the state and its venerable center of education."[11]

Mrs. Bingham's great-grandfather Christopher Barbee donated some of the original university land to the first board of trustees. In making her gift, she was influenced by her family heritage and several other factors. As an heiress of the Flagler oil, railway, and hotel fortune, she was in a position to be generous. She also responded to the idea of faculty enrichment advanced by her father-in-law, Colonel Robert Bingham (1857), headmaster of the Bingham School. A similar suggestion came from Robert W. Winston, a lawyer alumnus of the university and brother of the former university president.

Although he had not been instrumental in the bequest, President Graham recognized its significance. In his report to the trustees on November 20, 1917, he lauded Mrs. Bingham's recognition that the strength of an educational institution "depends absolutely on the strength of its faculty. This is the heart of the whole matter." He saw her benefaction as an opportunity to build a "truly great institution."

The Bingham gift aroused excitement among faculty, alumni, and friends. It set in motion visions and ideas about other enrichments. There were suggestions for endowing and expanding the law school. Even the university's old adversary, Josiah William Bailey, editor of the *Biblical Recorder* and later U.S. senator, wrote President Graham a note of congratulations. He could not resist one "word of advice": "I suspect our institutions too often in the appreciation of scholarship neglect the man; let the new professors be men first, scholars second."[12]

Dr. R. H. Lewis, a trustee, proposed a department of public health and a school of fine arts. A. W. McAlister (law student, 1886–87) suggested a department to meet an "increased demand from the counties of North Carolina for trained men for the position of county superintendent of public welfare." Lionel Weil (1897) called for training administrators for cities and towns in North Carolina. A. L. Brooks (1892) suggested that the university become actively interested in "social science"—a proposal that presaged the founding in 1924 of the Institute for Research in Social Science. Professor Eugene C. Branson also suggested a "Kenan School of Social Science."

Mrs. Bingham's bequest was a catalyst. It generated ideas which flowered in later years. The Kenan professorships, particularly, furnished "the impetus for the remarkable development of the social sciences at the university during the 1920s."[13]

President Graham hewed to the line of Mrs. Bingham's original idea: faculty enrichment. He sought to retain distinguished professors and to attract others. In his "Report of the President" for 1917 Graham described the potential of the Bingham gift. "It means," he wrote, "that the faculty may be given double its present strength; it means that the extent and the quality of this source of all its service may be so liberated from past restrictions that the youth of the state will have that quality of opportunity, judged by national standards, that equality of preparation and inspiration assures."

After requesting nominations from the faculty, Graham announced in early 1918 the first five Kenan professors. Citations showed that records of productive scholarship and inspired teaching were the major qualifications. The first five awards went to Dr. Francis P. Venable, the chemist and former president; Dr. H. V. Wilson, zoology; Major William Cain, mathematics; Dr. Edwin Greenlaw, English; and Dr. William deB. MacNider, pharmacology. The stipend called for a minimum salary of $3,500 annually. As an additional bonus, salaries of professors were increased by $250 annually. Initially the Kenan grant paid the professor's whole salary, thus releasing his former, state-paid salary to another professor. Now the grant is added to a basic, state-paid salary.

Because of tax complications involving the Bingham will, proceeds from the endowment were not received for several years, but the university provided funds from other sources until they were available.

Unlike President Venable, who was not much interested in off-campus activities, Graham associated the university with life in North Carolina. He championed revitalization of the alumni association. He supported the move to establish the *Alumni Review* in 1911–12. When the project faltered at the conclusion of the first year, he joined his cousin Frank Graham and Louis Wilson in signing notes to borrow money to keep it afloat. He spoke frequently and fervently at alumni meetings around the state and in 1915 pushed the creation of a loyalty fund similar to that at Yale University.

When the shadow of war began to touch the campus, Graham wrote hundreds of letters and postcards containing personal messages of cheer and pride to young alumni who had left the campus or their homes for distant military camps or foreign fields, always signing himself "Faithfully yours, E. K. Graham."[14]

Graham was adamant about securing more state funds. In his 1916 report to the trustees he declared, "If North Carolina needs and wants greatly to extend and deepen its educational activities, there is no issue of poverty involved. North Carolina is sufficiently prosperous. It is spending money for what it wants. During 1915 it spent more for the upkeep of automobiles than for the salaries of public school superintendents and teachers combined."

Graham's activities produced encouraging results. The General Assembly raised the university's appropriations from $95,000 to $115,000 a year in 1915, with an additional $30,000 earmarked for repairs; from $115,000 to $165,000 in 1917; and from $165,000 to $215,000 in 1919. In addition to the 1917 operating appropriations, it provided a bond issue of $500,000 for new buildings for a six-year period. These increases made it possible to secure more secretarial and support assistance for administrators and professors. Strong state backing enhanced faculty morale.[15]

In formally establishing the Extension Bureau under the leadership of Professor Louis Wilson in 1913, Graham dramatized the need for extending the university's mission beyond campus boundaries. To provide courses associated with state needs, he established academic chairs of rural social economics and rural education and appointed E. C. Branson and Z. V. Judd to serve in these positions. He chose Mrs. Thomas W. Lingle to collaborate with the North Carolina Federation of Women's Clubs and sponsor economic and cultural studies across the state. He assigned Professors Dudley D. Carroll and Frederick H. Koch to develop courses in business administration and community drama. He supported publication of the university *News Letter* and the *Extension Bulletin*.[16]

The Extension Bureau sponsored the North Carolina High School Debating Union. It offered the Aycock Cup as a prize and brought several hundred debaters and teachers to the campus in 1913. Wilson studied the work of extension departments at other universities, particularly Wisconsin. The university provided services for rural areas. It cooperated with Clarence Poe, editor of the *Progressive Farmer,* in sponsoring rural life programs. Graham became involved in the State Literary and Historical Association and the North Carolina Conference for Social Work. The Extension Bureau initiated correspondence courses, lectures, economic and social surveys, good roads institutes, and medical instruction seminars. In 1916 it launched a Newspaper Institute for the State Press Association, with visiting lecturers.

In all these activities President Graham planted seeds that flowered in the years beyond his own time. Professor Branson's work led to germination of Albert Coates's idea for the Institute of Government, to publication of significant books on county government and administration by Dr. Paul W. Wager, and to the two editions of *North Carolina, Economic and Social* by Dr. Samuel H. Hobbs.[17] Added to the John Calvin McNair Lectures in science and religion, begun in 1908, were the Henry and Solomon Weil Lectures in American citizenship in 1915.

Graham's extraordinary energy was ubiquitous. Members of the faculty noted that he frequently made notes in an odd-looking blank book bound in olive-green leather, which he kept on his desk. He listed here topics for chapel talks, reminders about university needs, and notes about new projects. The book became known as Graham's want book. But the wants were not for himself. They were always "for the university and through it for North Carolina and the nation."[18]

During the early presidential years Graham had the enthusiastic support of his wife, the former Susan Moses (daughter of Professor E. P. Moses), whom he married in 1908. The home of the president, his wife, and their son, Edward Kidder, Jr., became a focal point for campus gatherings and social life. Susan Moses Graham had been a student at Chapel Hill from 1898 to 1901 and had received her A.B. and A.M. degrees from Cornell. For two years she taught at two leading southern colleges for women, Sophie Newcomb and Sweet Briar. She encouraged her husband's campaign to enlarge the scope of women's activities. Edward Graham supported the expansion of women's opportunities at Chapel Hill. In the October 1917 issue of the *Alumni Review* he wrote, "The University of North Carolina offers to women the same opportunities in the two higher classes of the college and in the professional schools—law, medicine and pharmacy—that it does to men. . . . The advantages of university training will be increasingly sought by ambitious young women of the state." Susan Graham's death in 1916 robbed the president of a devoted helpmate during the last two years of his life.

While Graham could never be called a bricks-and-mortar president, several important campus projects were completed during his regime. In 1913 the president established a committee on buildings and grounds headed by Professor W. C. Coker with the help of George Howe, Collier Cobb, and, later, John M. Booker. This committee acquired the services of the noted landscape architect John Nolen and laid the groundwork for orderly campus

Judge Henry Groves Connor, President William Howard Taft, and
President Edward Kidder Graham, 1915.
(North Carolina Collection, University of North Carolina Library, Chapel Hill)

planning developed more fully during the Chase years. Swain Hall, the new
dining facility, was opened in 1914, and a new power plant was completed in
1917. Plans were made and construction was begun on a new building for the
applied sciences which, when completed in 1919–20, became Phillips Hall,
named for one of the university's noted families and located between Memorial and Peabody halls. Through the generosity of Baltimore's Captain Isaac
Emerson (1879), known as the Bromo-Seltzer King, the university in 1915
received a new athletic field and a modern grandstand to accommodate
baseball, football, and track athletics.[19]

Organized athletics, which came into prominence in American colleges
near the end of the nineteenth century, generated interest in the university's
activities among alumni. Toward the end of the Venable administration,
alumni created problems about who should control eligibility rules and other
regulations in intercollegiate sports. At a meeting in December 1912 the
alumni requested and received from President Venable and the faculty
greater authority to manage athletics. The athletic council collaborated in
the hiring of G. T. Trenchard, a former noted football player at Princeton,
as head football coach under a three-year contract. Trenchard introduced
spring football practice and inaugurated a contest among state high schools.

He also sought to liberalize the player eligibility rules. At a trustees' meeting on June 3, 1913, a rule was passed modifying the requirement that a student matriculate at the university for five months before being eligible for the football program. The new rule allowed attendance at summer school to count in the five months' residence requirement.

Opposition to this modification arose in the faculty. Differences between the faculty and the athletic council increased after plans were made in 1913 for resuming athletic relations with N.C. College of Agriculture and Mechanic Arts at Raleigh. Games had been suspended since 1906. When Coach Trenchard discovered that A&M had imported five or six players "whose presence on the team made prospects of Carolina's winning look very dim," he urged cancellation of the plans on grounds that A&M had violated its eligibility rules. This generated heated controversy in the state press, in which A&M, which had no five-month eligibility rule, charged that the university had watered down its own regulations.

President Graham asserted that the faculty and the administration, not the Alumni Athletic Council, should have primary control over athletics. In a strong letter to George Stephens, council chairman, he called the council's policy of working through trustees and undermining the faculty an "intolerable condition." After noting that the university's athletic regulations were "not one particle more rigid than those of Virginia," he insisted that policy-making be left to the faculty. The "athletic council," he said, "should distinctly and emphatically define a policy of cooperation and faith in the faculty." After thorough discussion at a meeting in early 1914 the trustees agreed.

As a result the faculty restored the five-month eligibility rule and restricted Coach Trenchard's authority until his contract expired in 1915. A new head coach, Thomas J. Campbell, a graduate of Harvard, succeeded Trenchard in March 1916. In the fall of that year both the university and Virginia tightened their athletic regulations. Under Campbell's leadership the university won its football game against Virginia that autumn.[20]

"The campus has become a military camp, the dormitories are barracks, the dining hall a mess hall. The YMCA has assumed the functions of a 'Y' hut, and the general program of the university conforms to strict military requirements," reported the *Alumni Review* in September 1918. World War I had arrived. In August the War Department issued General Order 79 establishing the Student Army Training Corps (SATC) at 565 American colleges and universities, including Chapel Hill. President Graham was designated director of the organization for the South Atlantic Division, embracing Virginia, North and South Carolina, Georgia, and Florida.

Unlike the situation when the Civil War erupted in 1861, the university "became officially a part of the nation's armed services, and the student-soldier-to-be of 1918 . . . retained his books, donned his uniform and began his service to his country within the campus instead of dropping his books and rushing from the campus to the battlefront."[21]

Graham redirected the university's goals toward winning the war as enthusiastically as he had strived for quality education. Before the nation's entry into World War I, he started a program of voluntary military training. A faculty committee organized military companies on the campus. Graham saw the issue as a fight between the "blood and iron" ideal of might makes right, bluntly stated by Bismarck, and the American ideal of rule by consent of the governed. He sought to enlist as a private and was "only dissuaded by a message from President Wilson delivered by Secretary (of the Navy) Daniels that as a soldier he would count only as one, whereas, in his post as president of the university, he would be the director and inspirer of a host of supremely needed trained men."[22]

The militarization of the campus had scarcely begun in the fall of 1918 when a devastating influenza epidemic struck the village. During October more than 500 victims flooded the infirmary. The overflow was assigned to the dormitories. Dr. William deB. MacNider, chief medical officer, quarantined the newly formed military corps for three weeks. The epidemic subsided by the end of the month.

But it exacted a fearful toll. President Graham himself, then forty-two, was its prime victim. On October 21 he contracted the disease, followed by pneumonia. On October 26 he died. The campus and the state were stunned. Tributes to the fallen leader poured into Chapel Hill. On October 31 the trustees appointed Dean Marvin H. Stacy chairman of the faculty and Dr. Harry Woodburn Chase acting dean of the College of Liberal Arts. Professor P. H. Daggett became successor to Graham as director of the SATC for the South Atlantic Division.

The armistice came on November 11, almost immediately following Graham's death. Demobilization of the student army corps took place during the first three weeks of December.

The Graham regime had lasted only four years, but its impact survived long after that. For many, Graham's influence was indefinable, something to be felt rather than described. "A stranger meeting Graham for the first time," Dr. C. Alphonso Smith said, "would be struck by the contrast between the flower-like frailty of his physique and the reasoned solidity of his convictions."[23] Dr. Louis Wilson described him as a "merchant of spirit." "Within a swiftly passing half decade," he wrote, "in spite of frailness of body and the turmoil of war, he transformed a previously cloistered institution into one fired with the creative spirit of scholarly attainment and beneficent service."[24]

Dr. Archibald Henderson provided one of the best descriptions of the fallen president: "No one who came into personal contact or association with this remarkable man could escape the pervasive influence of his personality or be blind to the simplicity, strength and dignity of his nature. Erect, tall, and fragile in figure; masterful in bearing; with challenging blue-gray eyes; a beautiful, delicate face, the face of a poet—he was a strange blend of frankness and exclusiveness, of gayety and seriousness, of whimsicality and gravity, of boyishness and maturity, of engaging outspokenness and invincible shyness."[25]

One of the vignettes long remembered by his student secretary, Albert Coates, occurred one morning in chapel when Graham talked to students preparing to leave for military service. He spoke of the landmarks of history—the Magna Carta, the Bill of Rights, the Declaration of Independence—and declared, "These are not empty phrases. Cut them and they bleed with the blood of men and women and little children." Then Graham read a letter just received from Robert B. House, a 1916 graduate and later chancellor:

> I am about to leave for France, aware what going there means, and glad to go. Before I go, I want to send my love to you and Carolina, because you two both send me and at the same time make me hate to go. You send me because you taught me ideals that won't let me stay here. You make me hate to go because I cherish you with the same love I bear my parents. I am not a single purposed man; if I have one dominant desire I don't recognize it. But the resultant of all my desires to live and serve is a purpose to come back and live and serve through Carolina.[26]

House returned to serve through Carolina. Like Edward Kidder Graham, who had been his teacher, he was inspired and energized by the university's noble mission.

HARRY W. CHASE,

NATIONAL DISTINCTION,

1919 – 1930

Harry Woodburn Chase became the university's tenth president on June 16, 1919. Journalist Gerald W. Johnson described him as "a damnyankee, a genuine, blown-in-the-bottle Massachusetts bluebelly."[1] Few more unlikely candidates could have been imagined. Chase, then thirty-six, modestly described his surprising appointment as having been "rather wished on me because I happened to be in the spot, rather than through any particular deserts of my own."[2]

That had something to do with it, but not everything. In the seven months between the death of Edward Kidder Graham and the June 1919 trustees' meeting, two other losses shook Chapel Hill. Marvin H. Stacy, dean of the College of Liberal Arts who was named chairman of the faculty on Graham's demise, himself succumbed to pneumonia on January 21, 1919. Then, two weeks later on February 4, Kemp Plummer Battle, eighty-seven, beloved former president who helped reopen the university in 1875, slipped quietly away at his home, Senlac.

In that period of jolting transition, Chase, who had joined the faculty fresh from Dartmouth and Clark universities in 1910, rose quickly to the top. His leadership during the emergencies, plus the respect he had gained on the faculty, played a large part in his rise. Not only was Chase a "damnyankee," a Republican, and a Congregationalist; he also happened to be only the third non–North Carolina native tapped, dating back to Venable and Caldwell. Even including Caldwell, university trustees traditionally favored chief executives seasoned in North Carolina.

As an impressive teacher and administrator, born and educated in the state, Stacy unquestionably would have won the job had he lived. The son of a Methodist minister of Burke County, Phi Beta Kappa graduate of UNC (1902), and member of the mathematics and engineering faculty, he worked closely in tandem with Graham. ("As president and dean, they labored together, planned together and almost died together.")[3] Stacy's wife, the former Inez Koonce of Trenton, remained at Chapel Hill after her husband's death in 1919 and became adviser and, later, dean of women.

Chase became dean of the College of Liberal Arts after Graham's death. A tall, slender, dignified New Englander, he had prematurely silvery hair that "gave him the effect of a halo" and a soft voice that seemed "admirably adapted to preaching to the birds."[4] Chase's grace and affability hid a firm backbone. He had a keen mind and, as events were to prove, an unrelenting dedication to progressive academic principles. Born in Groveland, Massachusetts, on April 11, 1883, the son of Charles and Agnes (Woodburn) Chase, he received both his A.B. and M.A. degrees at Dartmouth and then, after teaching school for three years, obtained his Ph.D. at Clark University in education, psychology, and philosophy. He married a Clark classmate, Lucetta Crum, a native of Minnesota. They had one daughter, Beth, and an adopted son, Carl.

Even though he stood in the line of succession, Chase had strong competition. At the same January 1919 meeting in which the trustees named Chase chairman of the faculty, they chose a presidential search committee which surveyed forty candidates. Among them were prominent North Carolinians who had substantial trustee support: Professor R. D. W. Connor; Dr. Howard Ronthaler, president of Salem College; and editor Josephus Daniels. When the committee reported, it submitted the names of two outsiders— Dr. Franklin L. McVey, president of the University of Kentucky, and R. J. Aley, president of the University of Maine—along with Chase's. Other candidates nominated from the floor included Connor, Daniels, Ronthaler, and Professors Archibald Henderson and Charles Lee Raper.

Both Connor's and Daniels's candidacies suffered because those men were members of the Board of Trustees. A statute prohibited members of governing bodies appointing their own colleagues to serve under them, and this applied to the university.

Chase led on the first indecisive ballot, then picked up the necessary

Harry Woodburn Chase.
(North Carolina Collection, University of North Carolina Library, Chapel Hill)

majority (forty-one votes) on the second, followed by his election. The choice received general approval from the university community and the state, although Chase was little known beyond Chapel Hill. In the interim between Stacy's death and his own appointment, he appeared ably before a General Assembly committee to defend the university's budget. He also quietly and resolutely assumed the faculty chairman's duties.[5]

As a professor of education initially (1910) and then of psychology, Chase had shown himself to be versatile and popular. He took over some of Professor Horace Williams's courses in general psychology in 1911–12 and published widely in scientific journals. He manifested an interest in North Carolina's public schools and was a much-sought-after public speaker. He spoke and wrote fluently, although with less eloquence than Graham or Stacy. His analyses, however, carried an aura of convincing logic, and he dealt more with principles than personalities. He was a man of dignity, patience, and tact. He was gracious in manner and set people at ease.[6]

The new president's first mission was to solve problems stemming from the devastating influenza epidemic, including better sanitation on campus. He was caught up in the transformation of the campus from its wartime footing and welcomed a new generation of students.

Some indication of Chase's concept of his own mission came during his inaugural address on April 28, 1920, in which he set forth his ideas about the university's role in the postwar South. Entitled "The State University and the New South," it projected the major themes of his stewardship at Chapel Hill.

After reviewing the tremendous advances of the South following recovery from the Civil War and World War I, he spoke of "years big with destiny for the South" and of the conviction that from all this creative energy, something "infinitely greater and finer than a giant essay in materialism" would take form. He spoke of a civilization blending "the best that is Southern by inheritance and tradition with the best that the new material freedom affords." This could be done, he declared, only through a "liberation of the spirits of men." The times demanded that the university "must press with new vision to set men really free, not from responsibility but through it." He saw "responsible freedom" as the "common business of education and the democratic state." He considered their common mission to be service to mankind. The university, he concluded, "strong as the oaks that guard her round about, kindly as the springtime that embowers her . . . sits upon this hill of pilgrimage for ceaseless generations of her sons."[7]

Chase's inauguration coincided with the postwar upsurge of optimism about North Carolina's future. As a poverty-ridden state emerging from war and reconstruction, it sought to move ahead economically, providing better schools, highways, and medical care. Even though a recession in the summer of 1920 toppled prices of cotton and tobacco and forced the General Assembly to cut expenditures, the following year produced a sturdy impetus toward renewal.

The number of high school graduates increased that year, causing the university to turn away 2,308 applicants. Campus enrollment swelled to 1,547 during 1920–21, overwhelming dormitories, boarding houses, classrooms, and laboratories. When the *Greensboro Daily News* published an editorial entitled "The Things We Lack" criticizing the fears and retrenchments of the 1920 special legislative session, Professor L. R. Wilson used its theme as the basis of a memo to President Chase. In it he endorsed the editorial's view that the state lacked leadership and should not back away from planning for expansion. He suggested a fund-raising campaign to secure $5 million from private sources and a public appeal to the people and the General Assembly for more state support for the multitudes of students seeking college education.

Chase responded by assembling a special faculty committee to discuss Wilson's ideas. The committee included Business Manager Charles T. Woollen, Alumni Secretary E. R. Rankin, News Bureau Director Lenoir Chambers, Dean of Students F. F. Bradshaw, and Professors W. S. Bernard, Frank P. Graham, and Wilson. It sent telegrams to 125 prominent alumni across the state, outlining the nature of the crisis and scheduling a meeting in Chapel Hill on October 2. Forty-three alumni met that day in a boarding house familiarly known as The Coop. Professor Bernard outlined the situation, noting the crowded dorms and classrooms and the shortage of funds to hold faculty together and attract new talent. President Chase declared that "nothing short of a revolution in higher education will handle the situation in North Carolina." Professor Graham, later director of the statewide campaign, said, "If the issue be the privilege of the few as opposed to the rights of all, we shall join the fight there. If the issue is taxes, we shall call it taxes and not beat around the bush of expediency. We will not tamely submit to the issue: More buildings or less boys. It is a question of the exemption of property or the redemption of youth. North Carolina will vote for the youth."[8]

The committee adopted six resolutions describing a vigorous plan of orga-

nization and enlisting support of other colleges. It recommended alumni
meetings in every county of the state. The committee launched the first
phase of the campaign on University Day, October 12, 1920. Descendants of
William R. Davie agreed to present a highly prized portrait of the general to
the university on that day. Chase used the occasion to compare the university founder's response to the educational challenges of his day with the
alumni response to current challenges.

The fund-raising campaign began at an educational conference in Greensboro on November 12. Governor Thomas Bickett (1894) championed the
cause. Businessmen under the leadership of A. M. Scales (1892) and J. E.
Latham presented nine individual gifts of $500 each as a nucleus. Other
meetings followed in Charlotte, Hillsborough, Wilmington, and Raleigh. A
second round of meetings occurred over the Christmas holidays.

The enthusiasm of alumni activities spilled over into the university's budget requests before the 1921 General Assembly. The trustees submitted recommendations for a $5,585,000 bond issue for upgrading the physical plant.
Requests of other state institutions brought the total to some $19,918,490.
When state senator James A. Gray, a trustee and member of the Budget
Committee, advised Chase to discourage "the campaign of propaganda
which appears to be under way in the state," Chase diplomatically but firmly
insisted that the university was at "an extremely critical period in its history." "In case the Budget Committee's report should not be such as to
meet these needs," he wrote Gray in Winston-Salem, "I do not well see how
I could avoid saying so to the trustees, and with their consent to the
Legislature."[9]

On the eve of the legislative session the trustees heartily endorsed Chase's
recommendations. But the Budget Committee's response was woefully inadequate—only $990,000 of the $5,585,000 requested for permanent improvements over a five-year period. Chase immediately issued a stirring
challenge to the alumni. "Never was the state faced by a greater crisis," he
wrote in the January 1921 *Alumni Review.* "The issue is simply and clearly
whether she shall save dollars or grow men. Shall she hide in a napkin the
greatest gift that God has given her—the gift of fine, clean young manhood,
youth of the sturdy old American strain? . . . Barred gates instead of an
open road to learning; youth cramped, denied, confined; future leaders
untrained, penalized for their North Carolina birth—will the great heart of
the state suffer these things to be?"

Chase's appeal inspired similar pleas in other areas. Professor E. C.

Branson, editor of the university *News Letter*, devoted several issues to describing the woeful plight of the state's colleges and the wealth available to meet those needs. Other publications, civic organizations, and the press joined in the appeals.

On February 23, 1921, A. M. Scales of Greensboro, chairman of the Citizens' Committee for the Promotion of Education, led a 500-member delegation from all parts of the state to testify before an open hearing of the House and Senate joint finance and appropriations committees in Raleigh. Unanimously, spokesmen for this group called for "an end to faintness of heart and expediency when the education of the youth, the one bright hope of North Carolina's future, is at stake."

The General Assembly responded by increasing the university's two-year maintenance budget from $850,000 to $925,000. But it took the position that it could not appropriate funds for permanent improvements for a period beyond the next biennium. To settle this difference Governor Cameron Morrison, who had thrown his support behind both good roads and education, took the initiative. He reached an understanding with legislative leaders that the budget for permanent improvements for all state institutions would be raised from $4,995,000 as recommended to $6,615,000 for 1921–23. Then, if these funds were well spent, the total $20 million would be provided by subsequent general assemblies.[10]

The push for higher education, one of the most impressive in the state's history, laid the groundwork for greatly enhanced funding of all state-supported institutions. It set the pattern used by Frank P. Graham and other university presidents for energizing alumni groups effectively in the decades beyond Chase's era.

Legislative underwriting of this enormous expansion enhanced the university's national reputation. Chase proved an ideal leader during this period. He had fresh ideas. Under his urging the General Education Board granted the university $50,000 for raising teacher salaries 25 percent. This enrichment, combined with settlement of the Bingham estate and funding of the first bequests for the Kenan professorships in 1922, became a providential tool. It helped hold an increasingly distinguished faculty against strong national competition.

Before his death in 1918, President Graham authorized appointment of the first five Kenan professors. Other campus funds temporarily financed these appointments, plus thirteen others made before final settlement of lawsuits generated by Mrs. Bingham's will. The first annual payment of

$75,000 arrived on January 18, 1922, thus providing an invaluable lifeline during a period of exploding growth and, as it turned out later, unexpected financial emergencies.

Chase moved toward restructuring the faculty shortly after becoming president. He divided the academic and disciplinary functions of the deanship of the College of Arts and Sciences by creating an office of dean of students. To these positions in September 1919 he appointed Dr. George Howe, professor of Latin since 1903, succeeding Professor Charles Lee Raper, and Frank Graham (1909), assistant professor of history. He also appointed a committee of deans to simplify the faculty's supervisory activities. In January 1920 Chase reorganized the business office and appointed Dr. Edwin Greenlaw, Kenan professor and head of the Department of English, dean of the graduate school. Chase informed the faculty of his keen interest in developing the graduate school. The minds and hearts of students and faculty are animated in laboratory and study, he declared, and this has "literally made modern civilization possible." Under Greenlaw's leadership the school entered a period of tremendous growth and impact.[11]

The postwar academic ferment proved ubiquitous. In 1920 the Department of Applied Sciences proposed a school of engineering, which was organized in 1922 with Dr. G. M. Braune, professor of civil engineering at the University of Cincinnati, in charge. The school provided a steady flow of electrical engineering graduates needed to develop the state's burgeoning public utilities companies. The new department became a seedbed for highway engineers needed by the State Highway Commission to construct highways authorized under the $50 million bond issue passed by the 1921 General Assembly.

The Department of Journalism flowered during the Chase years. E. K. Graham taught the first journalism courses in 1909 and was succeeded by James F. Royster (1910–14) and Richard H. Thornton (1914–18). After the war, Lenoir Chambers became head of the newly established news bureau and was succeeded by Louis Graves in 1921. Graves served as professor of journalism in the English department. When he resigned in 1924 to found the *Chapel Hill Weekly*, which became a village institution, he was succeeded by Gerald Johnson, associate editor of the *Greensboro Daily News*. Johnson became first head of the new journalism department and served until 1926, when he left to join the editorial staff of the *Baltimore Sun*. Johnson's successor, Oscar J. Coffin (1909), a colorful newsman of the old school, had been connected with several North Carolina newspapers. Under his vigorous direction the department expanded and became the School of Journalism in 1950. In the meantime Robert W. Madry (1918) became director of the university news bureau, where he served with distinction for many years.

To remedy woefully inadequate student health services, pinpointed by the influenza epidemic, Chase appointed Dr. E. A. Abernethy (1906) as university physician in the fall of 1919. Captain Thomas J. Browne became director of physical education. The duties of Dr. R. B. Lawson (1900), director of the gymnasium, were expanded to include supervision of remedial training and physical examinations.

Chase's regime initiated a thoroughgoing reorganization of the administrative structure of athletics. This began with the arrival in January 1921 of William K. Fetzer, assisted by his brother, Robert A. Fetzer, as director of athletics, and continued with the organization of the Southern Intercollegiate Conference. The conference provided new basic regulations for planning sports programs. [12]

A similar reorganization occurred in alumni affairs. The alumni association had been overhauled and revived in 1912 when the *Alumni Review* began publication under the editorship of L. R. Wilson. In 1922 the new plan of organization included a new constitution and a full-time secretary, Daniel L. Grant (1912). These changes took place under the administration of Walter (Pete) Murphy of Salisbury, who in his undergraduate days in the 1890s led the move to establish the *Tar Heel*. Grant became editor of the *Alumni Review* in 1924 and supervised publication of the *Alumni History of the University of North Carolina, 1795–1924*. In 1925 Grant resigned to join the Carnegie Foundation in New York and was succeeded by J. Maryon Saunders (1925), who began a long and successful tenure as executive secretary. The Alumni Loyalty Fund became responsible for some dozen benefactions during the 1920s, including completion of Graham Memorial and establishment of the Hanes Foundation for the Study of the Origin and Development of the Book and the Burton Craige professorship of jurisprudence and history. [13]

Chase's most important emphasis in curriculum centered on the social sciences. At Clark University he had studied with Dr. G. Stanley Hall, the noted professor of theoretical and social psychology. In his first report to the trustees in 1919, entitled "The University and the South," Chase summarized the material advance of the region and prophetically declared, "My own conviction constantly deepens that the next great creative chapter in the history of the nation is to be written here in the South. . . . Somewhere in the South there must inevitably grow up an institution . . . which typifies and serves and guides this new civilization. . . . My dream for the University of North Carolina is that she be nothing less than this."[14]

Chase moved first to encourage two projects initiated by his predecessor: a school of commerce and a department of music. He viewed the first as an instrument for directing the economic development of the region and the latter for artistic and spiritual enrichment. The commerce school began operation in September 1919 with an enrollment of 125 and with D. D. Carroll as professor of economics and acting dean. It was housed in Alumni Hall but moved to Saunders and then to Bingham Hall in 1929.

The music department remained largely unorganized until 1919 and consisted of occasional glee clubs and choral groups. President Venable brought Charles T. Woollen to the campus in 1901 to cultivate music in addition to other activities, mainly business affairs. The music department was formally organized in 1919 with the appointment of Paul John Weaver as professor of music. By the end of 1921 Weaver had reorganized the band and orchestra and developed the University Glee Club, which by the end of the decade was performing around the country and in Europe.[15]

Chase's strong interest in social sciences led him to develop a department of psychology, to reorganize the School of Education, and to establish the Department of Sociology, out of which grew up the School of Public Welfare and the Institute for Research in Social Science. The latter studied cultural and social life of the state and region; its work was similar to that of the Department of Rural Social Economics under Professor E. C. Branson.

Chase hired Dr. J. F. Dashiell, a graduate of Columbia University (1913), to succeed himself in psychology. The Department of Psychology brought to the campus several distinguished specialists, including Dr. Harry W. Crane of Michigan, Dr. Floyd H. Allport of Harvard, and Dr. English Bagby of Johns Hopkins. Dr. A. M. Jordan (Columbia, 1919) became professor of educational psychology in the School of Education in 1923.

The president's greatest find was his former classmate at Clark University, Howard Washington Odum, who became the South's first modern sociologist and stirred academic controversy all over the region. Odum, described by his admirers as a "warm-hearted, cool-headed, far-visioned, steady-armed man of dreams and action,"[16] came to Chapel Hill at Chase's bidding to elevate the university to the level of academic leadership both had envisioned. Odum, born on a Georgia farm and graduated from Emory in 1904, received two doctorates, one in psychology from Clark and one in sociology from Columbia University. When Chase recruited him, he was dean of the College of Liberal Arts at Emory.

Odum admired some of the advanced social legislation enacted in North Carolina, but he had no idea how much protest he would arouse when he began encouraging the state to confront its persistent social problems. He did not know, for example, that Chase had trouble getting approval for his appointment because some of the trustees couldn't "differentiate between a sociologist and a socialist."[17]

Odum arrived in Chapel Hill as Kenan professor of sociology on February 17, 1920, to help Chase launch the Department of Sociology and the School of Public Welfare. Over the next two decades Odum became, in the words of historian George B. Tindall, "the most perceptive observer of the southern scene during the first half of the century. He saw it whole, the old and the new, the folk and the academic, the agrarian and the industrial, the spiteful and the generous—and saw it all with a profound sensitivity and respect."[18]

Odum encouraged social criticism far more vigorously than did Chase or Branson. He came on like a whirlwind, eager to "turn out an army of eager welfare agents on the unsuspecting backwoods precincts of North Carolina." Launching of the Institute for Research in Social Science in 1924 greatly expanded the dimension of his work. Funded by a $10,000 grant from the Laura Spelman Rockefeller Memorial, it sponsored interdisciplinary studies in areas of southern life undergoing rapid change. One major project involved a "four-county plan," working with the State Board of Charities and Public Welfare. Using eight full-time research assistants, the study provided sustenance for fifteen scholars trained to "attack a multiplicity of pressing southern problems head-on."[19]

For this undertaking Odum attracted commanding academic figures—emerging scholars like Rupert Vance, Arthur Raper, Guy B. Johnson, Harriet Herring, Jennings J. Rhyne, George Mitchell, and Thomas J. Woofter, Jr. Working in allied fields were Roy M. Brown, Wiley B. Sanders, Gordon Blackwell, Katherine Jocher, H. D. Meyer, Paul Wager, Samuel Huntington Hobbs, Clarence Heer, Fletcher M. Green, Guion G. Johnson, and Julia C. Spruill. These scholars specialized in various fields, doing pioneer studies on the black family, the cotton culture, farm tenancy, labor relations, the mill village, the chain gang, rural illegitimacy, sharecropping, and the convict release system.

Odum's boldest venture began in 1922 when he launched the *Journal of*

Social Forces, in which many of the institute's studies were published. His objectives, he said many times, were to expose the facts, to encourage the organization of reform, and to smooth the course of social change or, as he put it, to make "democracy effective in the unequal places."[20] His studies had an electrifying effect on the academic world. Odum brought Chapel Hill national attention, encouraging national scholars to write for the *Journal.*

Odum's work had an impact on other evolving academic projects. The birth of the University of North Carolina Press sprang from the upsurge of creative research among university scholars. The press supported the belief that publishing local academic manuscripts would stimulate scholarship and creative writing. As early as 1918 Professor Louis R. Wilson had espoused such a venture. Dr. Edwin Greenlaw drew up a prospectus, and on January 28, 1920, the trustees authorized its establishment. The press began operation in 1922, with Louis Round Wilson as its first director. Dr. W. C. Coker's manuscript, *The Saprolegniaceae, with Notes on Other Water Molds,* became the first publication, followed by Professor Sturgis E. Leavitt's *Argentine Literature.* In December 1924 the press began accepting manuscripts from outside the university. Professor Wilson became first director, succeeded in 1932 by William T. Couch, who served with distinction for many years.[21]

Regional studies launched by Odum's coterie and publications by the UNC Press firmly established the university as the intellectual citadel of the South. During the 1920s and 1930s the press became recognized by academicians and historians as one of the nation's preeminent university publishing houses. Operating on a shoestring budget and dedicated to discovering manuscripts that would not otherwise see the light of day, it became, especially under the dynamic and provocative Couch, a target for those who charged the university with trying to overthrow the old economic order. Bitter attacks were directed at the monumental sociological studies of Odum and Vance that revealed the appalling poverty and ignorance of southern society and the need for uplift. When critics hurled the epithet "communist" at Chapel Hill, it was largely directed at the shocking revelations unearthed by Chapel Hill's scholars and revealed to the world by the UNC Press.

The School of Education achieved new vitality during the early Chase era. Marcus Cicero Stephens Noble, one of the state's education pioneers, had been dean. He was succeeded in the early 1920s by Professor N. W. Walker.

In 1926 the General Education Board made a $75,000 grant to the school for a five-year program of practice teaching in the Chapel Hill High School.

Another seed planted by President Graham's English department bore fruit. Professor Edwin Greenlaw, who headed that department from 1913 to 1925, took umbrage at Baltimore journalist H. L. Mencken's criticism of the vast intellectual and cultural wasteland of the South ("The Sahara of the Bozart"), especially the statement that the region had not "a single opera house, or a single theatre devoted to decent plays." From the University of North Dakota in 1918 Greenlaw lured a talented young teacher of dramatics, Frederick H. Koch. "Proff" Koch, a lovable little man dressed in a Norfolk jacket, with a big briar pipe and a small dog Patsy, "used to stride across the campus as if he were executing every errand on a direct order of God Almighty."[22] Koch's class in playwriting, English 31, attracted an array of ambitious would-be dramatists, including Paul Green and novelist Thomas Wolfe, whose play *The Return of Buck Gavin* became one of the first productions of the newly organized Carolina Playmakers.

Koch popularized the idea of folk drama. His Carolina plays toured North Carolina and the nation. Koch's pageant-drama, *Raleigh, the Shepherd of the Ocean*, presented in Raleigh in 1920, became the predecessor of Green's enduring symphonic dramas produced at Manteo (*The Lost Colony*) and elsewhere. Green, the Harnett County farm boy, joined the faculty and became an internationally known playwright. Wolfe became the celebrated author of *Look Homeward, Angel* and other novels in which Chapel Hill and North Carolina played prominent roles.

Plays written by Koch's students were produced for seven years in the auditorium of the Chapel Hill High School. When the law school vacated its quarters in Smith Building for Manning Hall, Koch's department moved in. The handsome structure, with its Corinthian columns surmounted by capitals composed of corn and wheat ears, became the Playmakers Theater, having served as library, ballroom, quarters for Sherman's horses, and classrooms since 1852. A Carnegie Foundation grant renovated the building and on November 23, 1925, it was dedicated by President Chase as the Playmakers Theater.[23]

One impressive indication of the university's recognition in academic circles occurred in 1922. The university became the twenty-fifth member of the Association of American Universities, an organization of U.S. and Canadian institutions achieving distinction in graduate study and research.

The university's rise, however, was accompanied by wrenching financial and political conflicts. As Chase pushed toward academic excellence in the mid-1920s, he ran head-on into economic pressures and a highly emotional controversy over teaching evolution in the public schools.

The General Assembly's generosity began to dwindle as the economy suffered setbacks. Initially Governor Cameron Morrison supported both good roads and good schools. But his ardor for the university cooled in the wake of the fight over the Poole antievolution bill. Angus W. McLean, an able but tightfisted Scot, succeeded Morrison as governor in 1925. He restructured the state's fiscal accountability program, establishing the Advisory Budget Commission and stringent budgetary controls. The gentleman's agreement on the $20 million permanent improvement program made by Morrison and legislative leaders with the university in 1921 never bore fruit. Partly because of bad economic times and partly because of McLean's conservative discipline, the struggle for funds became precarious. The legislature's appropriations committees rejected a special $500,000 request by the trustees in February 1923 for funding a four-year medical school, thereby "changing the course of medical history in North Carolina."[24]

Because of a move to a July-through-June fiscal year budget, an unexpected "deficit cash flow" loomed for 1925–27. The General Assembly passed a second bond issue for roads ($15 million) in 1923. With overdrafts and short-term notes, bonded indebtedness increased to $110 million and caused advocates of economy to clamor for stricter budget controls. McLean made frugality his successful gubernatorial campaign issue in 1924. The ruling Democratic party brought pressure on Chase to tighten budgets at Chapel Hill. To a letter from W. N. Everett, secretary of state, Chase replied vigorously, noting that the six-year permanent improvement commitment of 1921 and projects already under way—the new schools of commerce and public welfare—could not proceed without additional funding. "You are setting in motion reactionary processes that it will take, not two years, but ten, to overcome," Chase wrote. "Does any man want to see North Carolina develop its material life and choke its educational life? I cannot believe so."[25]

The 1925 General Assembly cut university expenditures. It also enacted a far-reaching executive budget act. In addition, it transferred income from the operation of the university's utilities service plant to the state treasury rather than letting the university use the funds as a supplement. These measures curbed expansion plans: Operating requests were slashed and capital improvement requests cut to the bone.

While money problems upset the university's plans and eventually affected Chase's decision about remaining at Chapel Hill, the 1920s stood as a period of remarkable growth. The university at the decade's end housed 3,017 students in a greatly enlarged dormitory system, providing them with expanded classrooms, laboratories, library, and faculty.[26]

The face of the campus changed dramatically. Professor Archibald Henderson believed the era of 1843–61 marked "the real beginning of an appreciation of nature and a sense of beauty" in campus development. He attributed much of this to the influence of the nationally renowned architect Alexander J. Davis, who worked for a decade in the antebellum period and did much to harmonize the style of the principal buildings and landscaping. The period from 1875 to 1913 was less striking in this regard, but Henderson saw the period from 1913 to 1930 as a return to "imaginative planning."

While Edward Kidder Graham got campus development under way before 1918, Chase supervised the great postwar expansion. His bold program centered on the south campus. It located classroom buildings at the center and dormitories on the eastern periphery. For this purpose the university requisitioned the services of architects Hobart B. Upjohn and William Mitchell Kendall of McKim, Mead, and White as well as A. C. Nash of Atwood and Nash. Plans had already begun for renovating Old East, Old West, and South Building, repairing several other buildings, and erecting two dormitories and a number of faculty houses on property owned in the village. Landscape architect John Nolen and Upjohn collaborated on the new dormitories and classrooms on the south campus.

All this brought early completion of Steele Dormitory south of Smith Hall, named for trustee Walter Steele, and a cluster of new dormitories, on the eastern edge of the campus, named Grimes, Mangum, Manly, and Ruffin in honor of other notables associated with the university. Three new classroom buildings south of Steele—named Saunders, Murphey, and Manning—comprised the eastern side of the new south quadrangle (named Polk Place) later balanced by the business school complex on the west and the new Wilson Library and Venable and Bingham halls on the south.

To transport building materials for these projects, the university constructed a railroad spur from Carrboro to the western edge of Polk Place. The initial contract for these operations, begun in 1921 and continuing until 1930, totaled over $1.1 million.[27]

Almost simultaneously trustee John Sprunt Hill and a group of alumni initiated another project that enhanced the beauty and comfort of the campus. On November 2, 1922, they presented a plan creating a nonstock corporation known as the Carolina Club Inn, Inc., to build a new hotel. Hill offered to donate an acre and a half of land, the lot occupied by the home of Mrs. Julia C. Graves at Columbia Street and Cameron Avenue, plus $10,000 to get the project started.

Since the destruction by fire in 1921 of the University Inn on the same site as Nancy Hilliard's Eagle Hotel on East Franklin Street, the town had had no adequate hotel. Trustees were enthusiastic about the project, but when the $50,000 needed to get it under way could not be raised, Hill built, at his own expense, what became the impressive Carolina Inn at an approximate cost of $200,000. The building, of colonial revival style, contained fifty-two rooms, a dining room, a ballroom, and a cafeteria, and its long porch on the Cameron Avenue side was obviously inspired by the porch at Mount Vernon. The inn opened in December 1924, and after maintaining it for more than a decade, Hill, on June 5, 1935, gave the entire property to the university. In his letter to Governor J. C. B. Ehringhaus he decreed that any funds over and above the cost of upkeep be given to the university, especially for the library's collection of books and papers known as "the North Caroliniana Collection."[28]

As student enrollment surged from 1,200 in 1920 to 2,529 in 1924, the building boom continued. Three new dormitories sprang up in the Battle Park area east of Raleigh Road—Aycock, Graham, and Lewis—again named for important figures in university history. Later, in 1929, Everett Dormitory was constructed, and Stacy followed in 1938 to complete the quadrangle. After a strenuous fight over an appropriation from the state, the first women's building, named for Mrs. Cornelia Phillips Spencer, was built in 1924 at the southwest corner of the intersection of East Franklin and Raleigh streets beside the new Chapel of the Cross. During this same year Venable Hall, named for an earlier president, was erected on the western edge of the south campus to house the burgeoning chemistry department.

Another building reflecting the new emphasis on harmony and beauty and named in memory of President E. K. Graham got under way soon after his death in 1918, but it was not completed until much later. Graham Memorial, designated as the student union building and located on the site

Howard W. Odum.
(North Carolina Collection, University of North Carolina Library, Chapel Hill)

Louis Round Wilson.
(North Carolina Collection, University of North Carolina Library, Chapel Hill)

Horace Williams.
(North Carolina Collection, University of North Carolina Library, Chapel Hill)

of the University Inn on the north campus, was a handsome, three-story building with an oak-paneled main lounge. The final fund drive was started in 1928 and completed in 1931 by an anonymous gift of $80,000, whose donor was later identified as L. Ames Brown.[29]

These bricks and mortar improvements, however, by no means equaled the academic achievements of the decade. Chase realized that North Carolina was moving away from its agricultural moorings into a new, industrial era without understanding the forces at work and ill prepared to deal with them. Through the work of Howard Odum and his corps of sociologists, Chase sought to collect and analyze the facts and present them to the public. The shocking truths about poverty and ignorance made such work politically controversial in a conservative state.[30] Thus the university, by fulfilling its mission of education, became a catalyst for change.

In earlier years the results of university research did not move much beyond the campus. But as monographs and studies were published in individual books or as articles in Odum's *Journal of Social Forces,* the disturbing findings began to reverberate around the state. Soon their impact became electric. Critics viewed the opinions expressed by researchers as threatening to conventional religious and social mores and to the conservative business establishment.

This concern came to a head in the bitterly fought struggle over the Poole antievolution resolution in the 1925 General Assembly. Poole's resolution, like the legislation that led to the Scopes trial in neighboring Tennessee, aimed at curbing the teaching of evolution in the public schools. Written and introduced by Representative David Scott Poole of Raeford, a Presbyterian elder, country editor, and schoolteacher, it declared that "it is the sense of the General Assembly . . . that it is injurious to the welfare of the people of the State of North Carolina for any official or teacher in the state, paid wholly or in part by taxation, to teach or permit to be taught as a fact either Darwinism or any other evolutionary hypothesis that links man in blood relationship with any lower form of life."

The resolution expressed the alarm, primarily among church people, that new scientific discoveries undermined religious faith. These worries were augmented by popular revivalists, among them "Cyclone Mack" McLendon, Mordecai F. Ham, and Billy Sunday. Ham, who repudiated the social gospel and engaged in anti-Semitic diatribes, accused philanthropist Julius Rosenwald of being party to a vice ring engaged in white slavery and prostitution. "Evolution," he declared in a Raleigh speech, "is a lie out of Hell that has never produced anything but infidelity. . . . The day is not distant when you will be in the grip of the Red Terror and your children will be taught free love by the damnable theory of evolution."[31]

Billy Sunday, the former baseball player, considered evolution, as well as alcohol and sex, a cardinal sin of the day. He linked it to Bolshevism, German militarism, materialism, and disintegration of the family.

Unlike the religious opposition encountered by the university in the 1890s, the outcry of the 1920s came mostly from the Presbyterian church, whose members largely founded the university in the eighteenth century and dominated its leadership during its first 100 years. When the private colleges launched attacks on public education in the 1890s, Baptists and Methodists were in the forefront. In the 1920s these congregations either supported the university or were mild in their opposition. Dr. William Louis Poteat, president of Wake Forest College, was a German-trained biologist. As an eloquent and highly regarded churchman, he strongly supported the idea of evolution. Duke's president William Preston Few, backed by his Methodist church and the wealthy Duke endowment, was a moderate and took little part in the evolution fight. It was the Presbyterians who castigated Chase and his faculty. They balked at the teaching of evolution and viewed the university as a center of atheism and infidelity.[32]

Two episodes enhanced the university as the object of Presbyterian wrath. One was publication in Odum's *Journal of Social Forces* of two articles by eminent New England academics implying that the Bible was myth and Christianity a superstition. The other was the caliber of speakers invited to deliver the McNair Lectures, an annual series endowed by an alumnus and designed to study the relationship of science and theology.

Governor Morrison, an outspoken Presbyterian who had supported university causes in the General Assembly, did an about-face on evolution. "If teachers of science use geology, biology and other sciences to unsettle the religious faith of our children, the Christian people of our country are not going to stand for it, and they ought not to stand for it," he declared.[33] As chairman of the State Board of Education, Morrison persuaded that body to reject two biology textbooks on grounds that references to evolution disqualified them. In a speech at Gastonia the governor insisted that North Carolina "has no room for so-called educators who are preaching and teaching the kind of evolution that holds that the human race sprang from a tadpole, developed into a frog, then into a monkey." The state, he said, has no money to waste on such "highbrow ignoramuses."[34]

The Reverend William P. McCorkle, a pastor-at-large in Orange Presbytery and a descendant of one of the university's founding fathers, the Reverend Samuel E. McCorkle, spoke out persistently against "modernist" teachings at the university. He charged that the McNair Lectures were a platform for "foreigners" to disseminate teachings contrary to the evangelical Christianity specified in the McNair bequest.

Opponents of Poole's resolution derisively called it the Monkey Bill. It caused sharp polarization among university alumni. Gerald W. Johnson, then professor of journalism at Chapel Hill and, earlier, associate editor of the *Greensboro Daily News*, lashed the evangelists, calling them witch doctors and "high-pressure peddlers" of psychological gimmicks who provided people an emotional escape and entertainment in their drab existence. Other newspaper critics, like Nell Battle Lewis of the *News & Observer* of Raleigh, and W. H. Saunders of the *Elizabeth City Independent,* bemoaned the artistic barrenness and intellectual inertia of the state's leadership.

As the legislative hearings on the Poole bill approached, Chase stepped forward as chief spokesman of the opposition. Odum, shaken by the outcry, offered to resign his professorship to spare the university embarrassment. Chase rejected his offer. He told President Poteat, "You have fought the battle long enough. Now we are going to do some fighting ourselves."[35]

Chase declined to let one of his science faculty members, Collier Cobb, speak at the hearing. "I am planning to go down (to Raleigh) myself," he said, "and I believe it would be better for me to be the goat . . . than for a man who is known to be teaching evolution to be put in a position where he might have to defend himself."[36]

When Chase's turn came to speak, a hush fell over the audience assembled in the hall of the House. Describing himself as a representative of an institution long respected for its intellectual honesty, Chase declared that he was "not here to discuss evolution as a biologist but to speak in behalf of human liberty." Both church and state are interested in the moral welfare of the individuals entrusted to their care, he said, yet the church is attempting to deny teachers a privilege that its ministers exercise without restraint. The Poole bill would prohibit the teaching of evolution in the classroom without interfering with the preaching of evolution from the pulpit. The measure is an abridgment of the freedom of speech guaranteed by the Constitution. "Shall we write into that article of the Constitution *except* for school teachers?" Chase asked. "If it be treason to oppose the bill offered in the name of tyranny over the mind for the purpose of abridging the liberty of one class of our people, I wish to stand here in the name of progress and make my protest."

When reminded later that the university's appropriations had not yet cleared the legislature, Chase responded: "If the university doesn't stand for anything but appropriations, I, for one, don't care to be connected with it."37

After three hours of emotional testimony from both sides, the education committee vote ended in an 11-11 tie. Chairman Henry Groves Connor of Wilson cast the decisive vote against it. The antievolutionists promptly submitted a minority report. Chase feared the cause was lost. However, he was assured by Wake Forest alumni that the institution's twenty alumni members in the General Assembly would oppose the bill, largely on grounds of separation of church and state. Poteat's boys, as they were called, remained firmly in opposition when the vote came on February 19, 1925.

Two well-known university alumni spoke up before that final vote. One was trustee Walter (Pete) Murphy of Salisbury, who declared that the Poole bill and its substitute were "pernicious measures likely to create more problems than they would ever solve." For Murphy, an Episcopalian, a man's religion was "strictly a matter between him and his God." A law attempting to regulate the relationship between theological and scientific beliefs would be the epitome of absurdity.

The other persuasive university supporter, the youthful Representative Samuel J. Ervin, Jr., of Morganton, later a celebrated U.S. senator, unveiled his sharp wit. "Such a resolution," he said, "serves no good purpose except to absolve monkeys of their responsibility for the human race."38

The university's supporters smothered the Poole bill. Its defeat brought rejoicing among university friends. Opponents were still disturbed. The *Greensboro Record* noted that the bill was "very properly killed" but warned that its defeat "did not allow a lot of little two-by-four professors to teach the sort of evolutionary doctrine that would undermine Christianity."39

Rather than becoming a license for liberality, the defeat encouraged caution on the campus. Odum curtailed editorials in the *Journal of Social Forces* and turned to other serious writing. During that period he published several enduring and influential books on the South, but they reflected new notes of moderation and ambiguity.

William P. McCorkle reiterated his attacks on Odum. After receiving a new petition from the Presbyterian Synod and McCorkle, Chase chose not to schedule a McNair Lecture in 1927. After various denominations tried to sponsor an independent school of religion at Chapel Hill in 1926, the university scheduled courses in the history and literature, including the Bible, of religions.

Chase knew that his regime remained under attack. He felt frustrated in his efforts to build a "truly great university." Associates noticed signs of weariness and irritation. Chase gave serious thought to an invitation to become president of the University of Oregon, but after strong pleas from academic associates and friends, he decided to remain at Chapel Hill. Professors R. D. W. Connor and Odum thought Chase's departure would create the impression that "fundamentalism pushed him out" and that the university was "not therefore a good place for big men."[40]

Antievolution rumblings continued, especially in Charlotte, the city of "roaring factories and snorting fundamentalists." Alone among the major newspapers of the state, the *Charlotte Observer* expressed delight at the possibility that Chase might resign. At a Charlotte meeting of the Committee of 100, speakers engaged in such abusive attacks that they aroused rebuttals by university alumni, among them Charles W. Tillett, Jr., Ed Broadhurst, and Robert Lassiter. They decried efforts to make orthodox Christianity a test for membership on a state college faculty.

The North Carolina Bible League sponsored an antievolution bill, again written by Poole, in the 1927 General Assembly, but it failed to pass. The public seemed to tire of the controversy and turned its attention to the emerging presidential campaign of Governor Al Smith of New York. H. L. Mencken visited Chapel Hill on the invitation of Howard Odum without creating a stir. Even the *Charlotte Observer* concluded that the "state has had enough of this monkey business."[41]

If doubt remained that the university had moved from the ranks of small, provincial colleges to the forefront of major academic institutions, it was dispelled by the defeat of the Poole bills. President Chase, the New England-born Congregationalist, had demonstrated courageous leadership in a conservative southern state. While neighboring Tennessee bogged down in the Scopes trial, North Carolina, with Chapel Hillians in the lead, staved off two emotional assaults on the freedom to teach and publish.

Writing from England in April 1925, where he was studying at the London School of Economics, Professor Frank P. Graham declared that the Poole bill had "raised issues older than the state of North Carolina. . . . The Inquisition, the Index and the stake are [its] unclaimed ancestors. . . . All honor to President Chase for speaking clearly and standing squarely on the issues raised. May we also salute with equal respect President William Louis

Poteat, who by his stand at Wake Forest has been for all the colleges the buffer state against unreason, the shock absorber of intolerance and the first line trench against bigotry."[42]

While Chase and his associates knew the margin of victory had been narrow, they nevertheless pressed forward with major objectives. After rejecting the presidential invitation from the University of Oregon, in 1926 Chase was given a leave of absence, which he spent with Mrs. Chase traveling in Europe.

The president did not depart, however, before setting in motion what was to become the crowning achievement of his administration: the new library. As early as 1924 Professor Wilson reminded Chase of the inadequacy of the Carnegie Library. In his annual report to the trustees that year Chase asserted that "the library is the heart of the intellectual life of a modern educational institution." In the budget of 1927 the General Assembly appropriated $625,000 for construction of a four-story building to be situated at the lower end of the sloping south campus quadrangle below South Building. Of late beaux-arts style, it was designed by architect A. C. Nash with the assistance of William M. Kendall. Kendall's firm, McKim, Mead, and White, designed the famous Seth Low Library at Columbia University. Kendall hoped to reproduce at Chapel Hill something "of the effect of the splendid facade and dome of that dominating structure on Morningside Heights."[43] The building was faced with limestone and surmounted by an imposing dome rising to a height of eighty-five feet. The interior reflected unusually artistic architectural treatment.

The library's dedication in 1929 marked the culmination of years of work by Louis Round Wilson. Professor Eugene C. Branson described Wilson as "one of the men who, in Sir Walter Raleigh's phrase, knows how to toil terribly. . . . He belongs to the royal order of brainsweaters. He is not brilliant, but he is something better—he is sane, safe, constructive and effective. He does not prance, he pulls heavy loads."[44]

Largely through Wilson's initiative, 1928 and 1929 were banner years for the library. The number of volumes reached 219,814. Private benefactions, announced at the library's dedication on October 19, 1929, totaled $146,000 from alumni and friends. Trustee John Sprunt Hill continued his generous endowments to the North Caroliniana Collection. The Southern Historical Collection, which began in the late 1920s, incorporated some of the materials handed down from the North Carolina Historical Society founded by President David L. Swain in 1844. Mrs. Graham Kenan of Wilmington gave

Mary Lily Kenan Flagler Bingham.
(North Carolina Collection, University of North Carolina Library, Chapel Hill)

$25,000 to the Southern Historical Collection. Professor J. G. deR. Hamilton became its director. Over the next quarter-century he supervised the collection of over 2.5 million items housed in spacious quarters provided in the library that was later named in honor of Wilson himself. [45]

While the state provided the bulk of the funds for the library's construction, alumni and friends moved in other areas. On November 13, 1926, William Rand Kenan, Jr., of Lockport, New York, announced a gift, in honor of his parents, of $275,000 for a sports stadium seating 24,000. This was the same Kenan who, with his classmate John Motley Morehead and their professor Francis P. Venable, had discovered carbide in 1893 and laid the foundation for the Union Carbide Company.

Eighteen alumni met earlier in 1926 to raise funds for a stadium. Their plans focused on a location in the natural valley of small streams running southeast beyond the new library and above the wooded spot known as the Meeting of the Waters. This natural amphitheater proved a perfect spot for the stadium, sheltered by a natural forest providing space for the oval lines of seat banks on either side of the field. When it was discovered that the original Kenan gift would not cover construction of the two-story stucco field house, Kenan provided an additional $28,000. The layout, designed by Atwood and Nash and built by T. C. Thompson Company, became a campus showplace for sports and academic ceremonies. [46]

Almost simultaneously in 1924 the trustees' building committee obtained funds for erecting another famous, if less elegant, sports structure. This was the indoor gymnasium, the successor to Bynum, known for generations as the Tin Can, located southeast of Wilson Library. It became a popular location for campus dances.

Another contribution to the beauty of the south campus was the addition of a portico on the south side of South Building, part of renovations in 1926–27. In 1929 the trustees added new stone walls and steps. Expenditures continued for overhauling power, water, heating, and sewer facilities during the era of prosperity.

Still another gift came from two old friends of the university. When John Motley Morehead failed to get permission to place chimes atop South Building, he and his cousin, Rufus Lenoir Patterson, joined forces to sponsor a $100,000 memorial bell tower. This monument, 167 feet tall and built of red brick and Indiana limestone, contained 12 bells ranging in weight from 300 to 3,500 pounds and cast by the Meneely Bell Company of Troy, New York. The bell tower was dedicated on November 26, 1931. [47]

John Sprunt Hill, John Motley Morehead, and William Rand Kenan, Jr.
(North Carolina Collection, University of North Carolina Library, Chapel Hill)

The 1929 budget contained an item of $25,000 for renovation of Memorial Hall, but that ungainly structure had suffered dry rot at the base of its tremendous trusses. The decision to raze it actually was not unwelcome. To replace it, a new building of colonial revival design with wide portico was erected on the same spot by the Nash and Thompson firms. The new structure included commodious stairwell and hall space for the memorial tablets honoring alumni lost in the Civil War and other notables. Benches of the old building, however, made in 1885 of the hardest North Carolina heart pine, remained for decades and offered "mute and painful evidence that the General Assembly of North Carolina believed there is virtue in discomfort for students."[48]

During this heavy construction period the south campus suffered. Unturned red clay and the rains and snows of winter left parts of the campus almost impassable at times. Cameron Avenue between Gerrard Hall and the west gate was difficult to navigate. It "swam in mud—soupey, goey, sloppy, oozey mud—three, four and five inches deep." When this situation brought criticism from students, the *Tar Heel* reprehended the administration with an editorial entitled "Real Mud and Cultural Mud." President Chase responded with a tongue-in-cheek letter recalling that mud was one of the oldest university traditions. "When Hinton James, first of university students, walked from Wilmington through the mud of winter to take up his residence at Chapel Hill," he wrote, "his feet trod the soil of Cameron Avenue, then a road cut through virgin forest. The mud of Cameron Avenue helped to make him what he became. Since his day, as the generations have passed, picture to yourself what feet . . . have trodden this sacred mud. . . . Shall we, in the name of progress, abolish one of the most typical of our inheritances—that fine, rich mixture of red earth and H_2O, the memory, and often the visible traces of which, university men carry with them to the ends of the earth?"[49]

During this period the skillful landscaping of Professor W. C. Coker continued. His Buildings and Grounds Committee, aided by donations from interested alumnus John Sprunt Hill and benefactor James Sprunt, constructed a carefully planned network of walks with brick gutters and plantings throughout the north and south campuses.

Completion of Wilson Library made it possible to remodel the Carnegie Library as a home for the Department of Music. Here again the generosity of Hill helped. Requesting in 1929 that his name be withheld from public identification, he underwrote the addition of a wing for an auditorium and a pipe organ for that facility at a cost of $70,000. This helped transform the old library into a fine facility for music, including a Reuter organ, all of which was dedicated on November 14, 1930.[50] In his dedicatory talk the university's executive secretary, Robert B. House, recalled the Old East cornerstone-laying address of Samuel E. McCorkle, who spoke of making Chapel Hill both a Zion for religion and a Parnassus for learning and the arts.

Teaching and investigation, incarnated in the persons of a devoted faculty, have spread their influences through the constantly augmented agencies of classroom, laboratory and press. Religion, literature and drama, housed in structures of beauty and dignity, interpret through the changing days the unchanging verities of the spirit. Athletics and sportsmanship rival in beauty of setting the glories of ancient Greece. Architecture and landscaping instruct us in the adaptation of woods and hills. Painting and graphic arts have made at least a wholehearted beginning. And music, having won its place already with a minimum of material equipment, comes into its own in this Hall of Music.[51]

As the Chase regime began, a fire on the northwest corner of the campus, called Fraternity Row, destroyed three of ten frame buildings occupied by the Sigma Nu, Sigma Alpha Epsilon, and Pi Kappa Phi fraternities. The fire threatened the Carnegie Library and led officials to purchase property on the west side of Columbia Street and to negotiate a swapping arrangement, moving the fraternities to a new location. This produced a new Fraternity Row, eight houses located along Columbia Street and Cameron Avenue and centered around two courts. The new houses encouraged expanded fraternity membership, which totaled some 17 percent of the student body in those days and rose during the next decade to about 25 percent. By the mid-1920s many of the thirty-two fraternities and two sororities were located in that area. Most of the new buildings contained meeting and living quarters for some of their members, along with dining facilities.[52]

In 1926 Chase appointed another Chapel Hill stalwart to his staff, Robert B. House (1916). House served as executive secretary and assistant until Chase's departure in 1930. Then following consolidation he became dean of administration (1934) under President Frank P. Graham and, ultimately, chancellor (1945). House served in World War I, received his master's degree at Harvard, and taught in the Greensboro High School and served as secretary of the North Carolina Historical Commission prior to returning to Chapel Hill.

Chase's restless ambition to enrich academic scholarship resulted in the expansion of the law and medical schools. The illness of Dean Lucius P. McGehee in the summer of 1923, followed by his death in October, focused the president's attention on pushing the law school to comply with the highest standards of American legal education. Specifically, North Carolina needed a three-year rather than a two-year school. It needed more emphasis on younger, more formally trained faculty members. Chase encouraged the law school to adopt higher entrance requirements and to employ faculty members who had teaching experience as well as training in the practice of law. He sought a dean who would reflect these qualities. The old practice of employing older attorneys to spend their latter years as teachers was fast passing.

In this case it became a struggle between those who favored appointment of a native North Carolinian in the old tradition and those who sought a young dean with extensive teaching experience. Chase outlined his views firmly and skillfully in a lengthy memo to the trustees. In it he declared that

the question at the root of the whole matter is whether it is the function of the University Law School to prepare an inferior brand of lawyers for law as a trade, or whether it shall prepare men for practice and leadership in law as a profession. It cannot do both. It is no answer to say that great professional success has been attained by men with little legal training. Times have changed. Not only has the existing body of law grown enormously, but the whole social and economic life of North Carolina is rapidly undergoing a transformation which affects legal problems as it affects problems in every other sphere of life.

In the ensuing discussions, Chase won the day for a three-year law school curriculum, stricter entrance requirements, and a dean, M. L. Ferson of the George Washington University Law School, who reflected youthful teaching experience. During this same period the law school moved into its handsome new building, Manning Hall, on the south campus. Upgrading of the *North Carolina Law Review* was accompanied by an increase in the law school library from 7,000 to 27,000 volumes by 1932.

Among the trained legal scholars who joined the faculty during those years were Maurice T. Van Hecke, J.D., of the University of Chicago and Robert H. Wettach from Harvard, both of whom later became deans of the school. Henry Groves Connor, the renowned judge of the federal district court of North Carolina, was appointed to the Ruffin lectureship, and Albert M. Coates (1918), the 1923 Harvard Law School graduate, began his academic career.[53]

While Chase's leadership spurred the law school to expanded accomplishment, it failed to enhance the medical school substantially. A plan to transform the two-year school into a four-year school with a 200-bed teaching hospital failed to materialize. At the heart of the medical school problems lay the fact that graduates of two-year schools found it difficult to gain admission to four-year schools as juniors to complete their education. Enrollment complications and curriculum differences enhanced these difficulties. Dean Isaac Hall Manning began to push for a four-year school as early as 1920. His recommendations cited the inadequate number of physicians and the shortage of general hospital beds in North Carolina.

By 1922 the trustees sought a four-year school and a teaching hospital, the latter to be located either at Chapel Hill or in a larger North Carolina town. A study committee recommended that the trustees approve such a request, but before President Chase could make his presentation, he was approached by Dr. William P. Few, president of Trinity College, with a special proposal. Few's plan suggested that both institutions and perhaps others raise $4 million for constructing a joint four-year medical school, the first two years of study to be located at Chapel Hill and the last two at Durham.

At first glance, the plan seemed to have merit. But old fears of conflict between state and denominational institutions arose again. A report circulated that if the proposal were rejected, Trinity would build its own school, using funds from the Duke family and the General Education Board. Ultimately the trustees rejected Few's offer, then moved ahead with their own unsuccessful request for funds from the General Assembly. This was a disappointing moment for medical school leaders. Dr. Manning felt that the university had lost its chances for a four-year medical school "perhaps forever." The two-year school continued to enlarge its faculty and curriculum, but full-scale expansion was not to come for another two decades.[54] Meanwhile, Trinity, on becoming Duke University, poured large sums into the launching in 1924 of the impressive Duke medical school.

In a related area the university established a program for training county health officers and public health nurses in cooperation with the State Board of Health. These projects planted the seeds for what later became the university's School of Public Health. The university inaugurated an improved public health program. Compulsory athletics became the order of the day. A unit of the Reserve Officers Training Corps was formed. The new four-year medical school, Memorial Hospital, and the new schools of dentistry and nursing and related facilities embraced in the Division of Health Affairs became part of the ambitious expansion immediately after World War II.[55]

When Harry Woodburn Chase submitted his resignation to Governor O. Max Gardner in a letter on February 20, 1930, the university reviewed a record of service matched but perhaps not excelled by any of his predecessors—including Caldwell, Swain, and Battle. In the words of one of his admirers, the journalist Gerald W. Johnson, he had "without the magic of a highly magnetic personality, without the aid of Bryanesque eloquence, without strong political or social or financial backing, with nothing in the world save courage, a level head and common decency" won "the confidence of his state to an extent that is matched by few of his colleagues in the country."[56]

Chase led the movement to transform a small, provincial college into a renowned university that, in his own words, "does not shrink from measurement by national standards." Evidence of this was visible in almost every area of the university's life—in its graduate schools, its enriched social sciences and liberal arts, its engineering school, and its scientific endeavors. Constantly attracting and retaining young teachers of promise and ability, Chase fought off serious efforts to curtail freedom of speech and inquiry. At the same time he persuaded the legislature and private benefactors to enrich Chapel Hill's faculty, curriculum, and physical plant. The result, even as the depression loomed, produced an institution firmly linked with its own roots but also in the front ranks of academic excellence. Building on the work of his predecessors, Chase addressed the higher education needs of a relatively poor state. Quietly and without flamboyance, he elevated the standards of the institution and enhanced its influence beyond state and region.

Chase went on to accept the presidency of the University of Illinois (1930–33) and the chancellorship of New York University (1933–51) before his death in 1955. He attained much of his national reputation at Chapel Hill, serving as president of many national educational and philanthropic organizations, including the Association of American Universities, and as a board member of the Julius Rosenwald Fund and the General Education Board. Offered the presidencies of several other outstanding institutions prior to his acceptance of the offer from the University of Illinois, Chase served almost half of his academic career at Chapel Hill.

In the final moments of Chase's last commencement exercises at Chapel Hill in June 1930, the university conferred on him its honorary degree of doctor of laws. During those same ceremonies Chase conferred the honorary degree of doctor of science on one of his own able predecessors, Francis P. Venable, who was retiring after fifty years of service as professor of chemistry and as president.

FRANK P. GRAHAM,

CHAMPION OF THE UNDERDOG,

1930–1949

The engine of the Roaring Twenties helped lift North Carolina's first university toward academic leadership. As the state outstripped its neighbors in industry, education, roads, and public health, the University of North Carolina challenged and surpassed the University of Virginia as the South's leading institution of higher learning.

Since 1904 the university at Charlottesville had been the only southern member of the prestigious Association of American Universities. Chapel Hill joined that company in 1922. In 1924 UVA's president Edwin A. Alderman, the former president at Chapel Hill, warned that "its [UVA's] pre-eminence is seriously threatened and will be destroyed in a period of five years unless something is done."[1]

North Carolina's emergence under Chase caught the attention of the academic world. Between 1918–19 and 1928–29 its faculty increased from 78 to 225, and its annual state support grew from $270,000 to $1,343,000. During the decade, it added a host of new departments, including the pioneering Institute for Research in Social Science, which exposed the South's economic and cultural deficiencies in disturbing detail. While North Carolina forged ahead by establishing a minimum six-month school term, a statewide highway system, and tax reform, the university founded a splendid publishing house (the University of North Carolina Press), added a greatly expanded research library, and sponsored Frederick H. Koch's creative initiatives in folk drama and playmaking.[2]

No one factor fully explains this spectacular flowering of Chapel Hill. Stimulating, creative people were assembled in an inspiring place at a special time of challenge and growth in North Carolina. But as the decade waned, a debilitating farm recession, a prelude to the Great Depression, swept the South. In the Hoover-Smith presidential election of 1928, "many voters for the first time permitted their convictions, moral and economic, to overcome the dictates of party regularity," one historian wrote. "Their decision seemed to open a new epoch of two-party politics in the South, but unforeseen events halted the process. . . . It was as if all the peculiar forces of the 1920s—prohibition, fundamentalism, nativism, religious bigotry and the nascent middle-class Republicanism—had united in one glorious and disastrous finale."[3]

The Great Depression had arrived. Its scope became painfully evident as President Chase submitted his resignation to Governor O. Max Gardner in February 1930. Gardner, a vigorous reformist, recognized the university's newfound eminence. "The election of a president of this university," he said, "is of more importance to North Carolinians than the election of any governor or any senator at any time."[4]

The trustees found no shortage of suitable candidates. The leading on-campus figure was the same R. D. W. Connor who had lost to Chase eleven years earlier. But a remarkable young history professor, Frank Porter Graham, age forty-three, with sturdy Chapel Hill family ties, touched the hearts and minds of Governor Gardner and the trustees' executive committee.

Graham, a cousin of the late president E. K. Graham, grew up in Fayetteville and Charlotte where his father, Alexander Graham (1869), served as superintendent of public schools. At Chapel Hill in 1905–9, Frank Graham was president of the senior class, editor of the *Tar Heel*, head cheerleader, and a successful student. As a five-foot-six-inch, 125-pound bundle of energy, he became president of the YMCA, taught Sunday School, and was described in the *Yackety-Yack* as "Frank, Laddie Buck, everyone's friend, confidant and playfellow."

From the start, Graham's ebullience and the vigor of his idealism impressed his associates. Known for his spunk on the baseball field, he also became a "self-appointed custodian of morals." He firmly opposed smoking and drinking but "considered religious doctrine unimportant." He was outgoing, unselfish, modest, and compassionate. During his senior year he was impressed by an address delivered at Chapel Hill on Robert E. Lee's birthday by the president of Princeton University, Woodrow Wilson. Wilson declared that "men need to become 'drunk with [the] spirit of self-sacrifice.'" Graham felt Wilson was speaking directly to him.[5]

During the latter part of his student years Graham boarded at the home of his cousin, Edward K. Graham, then an English professor and assistant to President Venable, and his wife, Susan. There Graham met and proposed to Susan Graham's sister, Mildred Moses, but was turned down. There also, among the student boarders, he made three of his closest friends, Charles W. Tillett, Jr., of Charlotte, Francis E. Winslow of Hertford, and Kemp D. Battle of Rocky Mount, all of whom became eminent North Carolina lawyers. Three of these friends graduated from the university's law school; but Graham studied only one year there, then turned toward teaching as a career.

The young law student considered his older cousin the best teacher he had ever encountered. In later years he described in Edward Graham certain qualities that mirrored his own: thoroughness and exactitude as a teacher, sensitivity to great language and literature, and noble idealism.[6]

After an interlude as a high school teacher and baseball coach in Raleigh, Frank Graham returned to Chapel Hill to become secretary of the YMCA. He drifted into teaching American history after taking courses under Professor J. G. deRoulhac Hamilton. In late 1914 Hamilton invited him to take over a class. Graham became fascinated with the subject. As some of his students later noted, he found a way to make history come alive. In 1916 he went to New York and got his M.A. in history at Columbia University. Inspired by President Woodrow Wilson's crusade to "make the world safe for democracy," he enlisted in the U.S. Marines and served two years. When World War I ended, he returned to Chapel Hill to accept the newly appointed President Chase's invitation to become the university's first dean of students. The job demanded the kind of administrative routine Graham never relished. After a year he returned to teaching history. Yet in 1920–21 Graham again became engaged in work beyond the classroom, this time helping Chase and his associates organize the statewide fund-raising campaign that launched an important era of expansion.

In 1925 Graham spoke out strongly against the General Assembly's controversial Poole antievolution bill by writing a letter from London that was published in leading North Carolina newspapers. The letter defended Chase and the search for truth. In it he wrote,

> Let us all close ranks solidly behind him [Chase]. He has raised the
> university standard to be seen by all our people. Freedom to think,

freedom to speak and freedom to print are the texture of that standard. . . . It is the cornerstone and motto of the first American university to open its doors in the name of the people—in a little North Carolina village. . . . *Lux Libertas* is cut with native chisel deep in the stones quarried from local soil. . . . It is a tradition of our people that they 'would have it a place where there is always a breath of freedom in the air . . . and where finally truth shining like a star bids us advance and we will not turn aside.' To preserve this spiritual possession of the people for the inheritance of their children, North Carolinians will fight against the false fear of truth and foes of freedom whatever be the power.[7]

Graham's courage and eloquence inspired numerous admirers. On his return he became firmly established in the faculty constellation. Shocked once more by North Carolina's backwardness and poverty, Graham devoted much time and energy to combating them. In 1927 he helped organize the North Carolina Citizens Library Movement, the first organization of its kind in the nation. In 1929 he persuaded newly elected governor O. Max Gardner to champion the Citizens Library Movement, which helped organize fifteen school libraries and, in 1929–30, six community libraries in towns across the state. In a letter to editor Josephus Daniels, a university trustee and friend, he wrote: "Daughters of the American Revolution should not become Daughters of the American Reaction. . . . It is my nature while drawing the line clearly on the great human issues, not to attack so much but to build on what is hopeful in any organization."[8]

Graham became president of the North Carolina Conference for Social Service and helped push passage of a workman's compensation law to improve working conditions. Under Governor Gardner's leadership in 1929 the state legislature passed such a bill, considered the most liberal in the South.[9]

The Loray Cotton Mill strike of 1929 helped project Graham as an outspoken supporter of embattled workers. Violence at the Gaston County mill, whose union had been organized by Communist leader Fred Beal, resulted in the death of Gastonia police chief Aderhold and four others, followed by the death of a twenty-nine-year-old worker, Ella Mae Wiggins. The deaths inspired murder charges on both sides.

Governor Gardner ordered out the National Guard. Graham joined a group seeking lawyers for those accused of murdering the police chief and the antistrikers. David Clark, a prominent editor of textile publications, and other industrial leaders criticized Graham's activism. "Mr. Graham," wrote Clark, "has no experience either in business or industry, but seems to consider himself an authority upon all industrial questions. . . . Everyone is proud of the University of North Carolina, and its able faculty, but it is well known that within that faculty is a small group of radicals who are in an insidious manner eternally fighting that which they frantically call 'capitalism.' "[10]

In the late summer of 1929 all the union leaders were sentenced to prison while none of the antiunion defendants were convicted. This led Graham to draft "An Industrial Bill of Rights," which he sought to publish over signatures of leading citizens. The document espoused "freedom of personality and equality of opportunity." It endorsed the right of labor to organize and to bargain collectively, a reduction of the 60-hour workweek, the abolition of night work for women and young people, and the improvement of child labor laws. Many of Graham's friends were torn by their recognition that the textile industry was tottering under the impact of the depression. One, Tyre Taylor, who was an administrative assistant to Governor Gardner, wrote Graham on February 6, 1930, "I very much fear that we are up against the most serious situation we have had to face in North Carolina since Reconstruction. . . . The economic situation among almost every class is nothing short of desperate." He questioned publishing the industrial bill of rights and advised that it "might be best to follow Governor Gardner's leadership and methods and do what can be done with the cooperation and good will of the [mill] owners."

Graham went ahead with his bill. It was released to the press in February 1930 and was signed by more than 400 people, including lawyers, college professors, newspaper editors, and women. Graham wrote to his friend Kemp Battle that he thought he would be vindicated by history.[11]

On February 20, 1930, three days after publication of Graham's bill of rights, President Chase submitted his resignation. Graham, R. D. W. Connor, and Archibald Henderson were immediately mentioned as possible successors. From the start Graham believed the job would never be offered to him because of his reputation. "But even if it were," he told friends, "I wouldn't accept." One of his outspoken supporters, Dr. William deB. MacNider, finally said in desperation, "Dammit, Frank, the university is going downhill fast, the budget has been cut to the bone and you stand there and tell me you won't help. I don't care what you say, I'm going to raise hell and fight for you to be president." Graham was shocked. "We've been friends for a long time," he replied, "and as a friend I ask you to promise me that you will respect my wishes and won't do anything." MacNider replied, "Frank, you're impossible." Later the physician wrote Graham a note of apology, saying, "When I feel about a thing keenly as I do your becoming president, I have to talk as I feel. I can't temper it and pussyfoot it. I feel you should do nothing to bind us and make us smart. The least you can do is to give our souls freedom."[12]

Graham's friends continued to organize support for him. Dr. Otho Ross, his Charlotte physician, became one of the leaders. In May, Charles Tillett prepared a mimeographed statement sent privately to all members of the Board of Trustees and others arguing that a democracy must use the leaders it has trained. When Graham learned of this campaign, he was angry. He dispatched telegrams to all involved, requesting that such activity cease. "I can best do my work for the university and the state as a teacher and citizen. Sincerely hope all will unite on Connor who is remarkably equipped to be a strong and progressive leader."[13]

As a result, Graham's name was not submitted by the nomination committee when the trustees met in Chapel Hill on June 9. But on the first ballot, Connor received twenty-six votes, Graham twenty, and Henderson ten, with the remaining twenty-seven divided among a dozen individuals. On the fourth ballot Graham received forty-seven votes, and his election was made unanimous.

The trustees had been meeting in Howell Hall near Davie Poplar. They adjourned, and many gathered outside under the trees while a committee was sent to bring Graham to the meeting. When he arrived, he approached the trustees still outside and begged for another ballot. Governor Gardner, Josephus Daniels, and Judge John J. Parker, among others, remonstrated with him. As the trustees reassembled in the hall, the protesting Graham could be heard saying, "I hardly know what to say. I want to remain a teacher. I want Mr. Connor to be president. Isn't there anything that can be done now to make him president and leave me free to go back to the classroom?"

In presenting Graham to the trustees as their unanimous choice, Governor Gardner declared, "I don't know of any process by which that can be done." "Well, with your help and with the help of God," Graham began in a low voice, then slumped into a front row seat. At that moment a friend spoke to him: "Be a marine; be a marine!" After the meeting as the trustees filed out, one was heard to say, "That's the sorriest acceptance speech I ever heard."[14]

Editor Josephus Daniels wrote in the Raleigh *News & Observer* the next day: "I have never seen an instance where the office more clearly sought the man. . . . He is one man of whom it may be said that the office not only sought him but had to throw him down and make him take it."[15]

Graham had scarcely taken office before the university was plunged into the fiscal crisis of the Great Depression. In the summer of 1930, as he took charge at South Building, financial pressures hit hard. From $894,000 in 1928–29, state appropriations fell by 25 percent in 1929–30 and careened another 20 percent in 1931. For one who had never put money high on his list of priorities, Graham faced a somber challenge. Almost immediately he fought back. Within weeks of his election he was speaking to service clubs, churches, farm associations, and patriotic organizations across the state. Depressions are temporary, he argued; schools and colleges are permanent sources of economic, social, and spiritual well-being. "If we turn back on public education," he declared, "we turn back all along the line."[16]

Graham requested $875,000 in 1931–32. The governor and the Advisory Budget Commission recommended $573,000. In January 1931 Graham became ill with a respiratory infection. Even after his doctor ordered him to bed with fever, Graham asked his driver, Hubert Robinson, to take him to Raleigh. While making a presentation before the joint appropriations and finance committees, he requested a drink of something for a stimulant. Charles Woollen, the university's business manager, said later, "Graham took one cup of coffee and kept the legislature in session for six months."[17]

The new president was a masterful persuader. Using comparisons of budgets at other universities, he made a cool but moving appeal. "We are now in the midst of a great depression," he concluded. "There are those who would conscientiously turn us back on the old road of ignorance, poverty and despair. . . . We must tighten up, but we must hold on. We must not throw away what we already have. We will say with Foch, below the Marne in his great depression, 'My right flank is broken and my left flank is beaten back. We will attack with the center.' With the school in the center, flanked by farm and factory, we will hold on now against the better day that is to come."

In his first major challenge Graham proved his resourcefulness. After his presentation that day, the joint committee raised the university's recommended appropriation from $573,000 to $800,000. The image of Frank Graham as a legislative lobbyist was somewhat startling to his friends. "Frank Graham still goes about without his hat," wrote the *Chapel Hill Weekly*, "but his trousers are better creased and his shoes are better polished."[18]

Graham's persuasiveness, however, could not sustain the budget's momentum in those dark days. That spring it totaled only $721,000. One month after the appropriation was approved, Graham was informed of another $175,000 slash. The president visited Governor Gardner's office repeatedly, seeking restoration. He was physically drained, but he did not give up. "I am going to resist with everything I have got any surrender to the dominant business interests in North Carolina which have adopted the false policy of trying to pinch their way out of North Carolina's critical situation," he wrote his friend Gerald Johnson in Baltimore. "We cannot pinch our way out. We have got to invest, build and create our way out."[19]

In the meantime, the fiscal crisis had its effect on the faculty. Within nine months after Graham's election, twenty professors had received offers from other institutions, sometimes at three times the salary they were making at Chapel Hill. Most of them refused to leave because of loyalty to the university and admiration for Graham. One professor said of him in later years, "He is the only university president I know who can announce a cut in salaries and receive a standing ovation."[20]

At his inauguration in Kenan Stadium on November 11, 1931, Armistice Day, President Graham made a seventy-eight-minute speech. He wrote much of it during his two-week vacation at Columbia University toward the end of the summer, after the budget battles had subsided. Graham decided not to mention those battles at all. Instead, reflecting on his readings from Bacon, Goethe, Milton, Mill, and Arnold, he presented an oration describing the kinds of freedom that must undergird the total life of the university. It was his favorite theme. Even though his address was long, Graham managed to hold the attention of his audience of about 5,000 gathered in the stadium's natural amphitheater set in "a forest like Arden" on the southern edge of the campus.[21]

Graham could not resist a touch of history. "Out of the past," he declared, "come figures, living and dead, to stand by us in this inaugural hour in the woods where Davie, the founder, stood under the poplar and raised the standard of the people's hope." Then he called the roll of presidents who had preceded him, identifying their contributions. Nor did he remain unmoved by the ambience of that autumn day. He spoke of the "friendly folk" gathered at this "old university" in the midst of "beautiful forests under cathedral skies," of the "friendships form[ed] here for the human pilgrimage," and of the "music in the air of the place." In the end he sounded the tocsin that had inspired his own generation and those that preceded it:

Frank Porter Graham.
(The University of North Carolina Alumni Association)

the vision of a "stronghold of learning and an outpost of light and liberty" for the people of a free state.[22]

It was clear, as his friend Kemp Battle put it, that the university depended on individuals like Graham to provide strong "spiritual leadership" to help maintain its "high level of distinction and of service" or else to "yield to the anemia of undernourishment and sink back into mediocrity."[23]

Frank Graham's vigorous leadership at Chapel Hill became paradoxical and controversial. Dragged almost handcuffed to the presidency, he ignited a spirit of genuine friendliness and hospitality in the president's office and home. Still unmarried at age forty-five, he asked his sister Kate Graham to serve as hostess and housekeeper. His engaging personality and dynamism attracted adulation. "Those who know him best love him most," Kemp P. Lewis said at the 1931 commencement luncheon. Louis Graves, the Chapel Hill editor, tried to explain it. "The love that Frank Graham has inspired in thousands—and their feeling toward him is nothing less—is due to an underlying essence that quite defies analysis," he wrote. "As near as I can come to explaining it, it is a combination of sincerity and sympathy with absolute simplicity in speech and manner. Of course he has courage and keen intelligence, and these win him admiration, but at the moment I am speaking not of these qualities that make people admire him but of those which make them love him."[24]

At the same time, Graham's liberal political and economic views alarmed many. He was careless about signing political petitions from radically leftist groups, and he never realized, as one of his admirers observed, that the "underdog can sometimes be wrong." When Howard Odum's sociologists revealed specific facts about harsh child labor practices and the stretch-out system, the state's industrial leaders were jolted and annoyed. When Graham championed the Loray Cotton Mill strike in 1929, he inspired public blasts from Charlotte's David Clark, editor of the *Southern Textile Bulletin*. Graham's industrial bill of rights, released publicly on the eve of Chase's resignation, led many, including Graham himself, to believe he would never be offered the presidency. Yet Graham's voice repeatedly rose above the critical clamor in its appeal to noble aspirations.

On July 21, 1932, the university president added an attractive new individual to his household when he married thirty-two-year-old Marian Drane, an Episcopal rector's daughter, of Edenton. Marian had been housekeeper for her father, the Reverend Robert Drane, rector of St. Paul's Church. Later Graham told friends, "They say that having gained experience in taking care of one old man, Marian married me to take care of another."[25]

The Grahams took a month-long wedding trip to Canada. Back at Chapel Hill, Marian joined the president's domestic entourage, which included Alice Neal, the cook; Hubert Robinson, the driver; and the perennial students who roomed upstairs. Graham never learned to drive an automobile, nor did he carry sufficient money in his pockets to take care of routine expenses. Graham's friends viewed these aberrations as the absentmindedness of one whose thoughts were fixed on weightier matters.

Among those weightier matters was university administration. It became the center of a fundamental change early in Graham's regime. Soon after the stock market crash of 1929, when banks closed, unemployment soared, and public budgets dwindled, Governor Gardner authorized a Brookings Institution study of state government, primarily to see where spending could be curbed. One of the report's suggestions, besides state administration of schools and roads, was that a study be made of the possible consolidation of the three major institutions of higher learning—the university at Chapel Hill, North Carolina State College of Agriculture and Engineering at Raleigh, and the North Carolina College for Women (Woman's College) at Greensboro. Without further investigation, and mostly for budgetary reasons, the governor announced he would recommend consolidation to the General Assembly in early 1931. Thus the stage was set for a major restructuring of university management.

At first Graham shared the view of many at Chapel Hill that consolidation would not be in the university's best interests. The other institutions were less well established and largely vocationally or technically oriented. Graham and others were highly skeptical about what consolidation might do to the university's broad educational mission.

Prior to the final Brookings Institution study Gardner approached the heads of the three institutions and discovered that Julius Faust of the Woman's College and Eugene C. Brooks of North Carolina State tentatively favored consolidation. Gardner told Graham that the General Assembly was thoroughly alarmed by the financial crisis and would support centralizing and conserving the state's threatened resources. It would be unfortunate, he said, if the university held out in opposition. "I am not the one in opposition," Graham replied. "I simply have many questions. One thing I am certain of: If it is not wisely handled, it will split the state wide apart." "How can that be avoided?" the governor asked. Graham suggested a careful study by competent people.[26]

In March 1931 the governor's consolidation bill began its way through what became "The Long Parliament" of the General Assembly. Faust favored it. Brooks opposed it. Graham described his attitude as "an open mind with a question mark." Largely because of the president's ambivalence, the faculty refrained from opposing the bill. On March 27, 1931, the General Assembly passed the legislation consolidating the three institutions. That summer a study commission began the tedious process of fleshing out the merger with specific changes. The three presidents served on it, but its work was mostly done by a panel of three educational consultants under the direction of Dr. George A. Works of the University of Chicago. Most of the consultants' recommendations shaped the new administrative structure. Its headquarters would be centered at Chapel Hill. The Woman's College would continue to operate at Greensboro. North Carolina State would become a junior or community college. Schools of agriculture and engineering would be anchored at Chapel Hill.

The commission's report caused little initial concern at Chapel Hill or Greensboro (which generally welcomed association with the university), but it generated fierce opposition at N.C. State College in Raleigh. Governor Gardner, a State graduate, had not intended consolidation to weaken his alma mater. After reading the report, he told State's outraged alumni that he would see that changes were made.

Without mentioning the more controversial parts of the report, Gardner urged the three presidents to agree on selecting a single presiding officer—at first called *chancellor* and later changed to *president*. The three presidents began work together smoothly. At Graham's suggestion Faust, age sixty-six, served as chairman of the group; but it quickly became evident that the trustees intended to name Graham president. By midsummer of 1931, when this choice was clear, David Clark wrote Brooks: "When Frank Graham becomes president of State College as part of the university . . . we shall be absolutely in (his) power and I see no future for us."[27]

Graham had some of the same reservations about the consolidated presidency that had plagued him earlier. He told friends he had not been enthusiastic about consolidation and did not want to become head of the three institutions. "My best work," he wrote one of his trustee friends, Leslie Weil, "is with human beings and not with an organization."[28] He also told Weil he felt he was "too controversial" and did not want to be forced on others. Weil replied, "Can you tell me plainly if you know of a man in the state to whom you would be satisfied to entrust this particular job?" Trustee Josephus Daniels was even blunter: "I say to you what I said on the day you were first elected president, that it is the duty of every man to serve where those who have the life of the university at heart think he can serve best. . . . The only thing for you to do is to say 'Aye, aye, Sir!' and quit this business of being over-modest. I think a man ought to be humble before his God and not before anybody else."[29]

The trustees elected Graham president in November 1932. From the start he was thoroughly determined to be fair to State and the Woman's College. In his acceptance statement he urged cooperation of all to the end that "we will be free and fair and intelligent in the long run with the best interest of the whole state in mind." Despite his own distaste for administration, Graham moved with a sure hand toward calming anxieties and inspiring cooperation. He saw to the appointment of planning committees and consulted patiently with faculty members, students, and alumni. He accepted the Raleigh and Greensboro institutions as part of his own family and won over many individuals who had been skeptical. David Lockmiller, professor of history and political science at State, credited Graham with "most of the successes . . . of consolidation." Graham, he wrote, won "national recognition" for his "able, fair and tactful administration."[30]

Initially the trustees elected sixty-one-year-old Eugene C. Brooks vice president at N.C. State and Julius Faust, age sixty-seven, to the same post at the Woman's College. The position at Chapel Hill was not filled, although it was later offered to Dr. L. R. Wilson, the librarian, who by that time had moved to the University of Chicago and was not available. Robert B. House, for ten years secretary of the university, became Graham's chief lieutenant at Chapel Hill in 1934 and stood gallantly and loyally in his shadow for many years.

Graham's identification as chief of operations at Chapel Hill kept the university on top of the state's educational hierarchy. But it created problems for the person working directly under him. Beginning with House, the job was more difficult than the other chancellorships because it was too near the system's president, who continued working in South Building and living on East Franklin Street. To the outside world Frank Graham was the "president of Chapel Hill" rather than the chief of a multicampus university. Both the presidents and the chancellors struggled with that circumstance as other institutions joined the system. Graham remained the de facto head at Chapel Hill because he wanted it that way, and so did most trustees, faculty, and students. The pattern he established long survived his administration.

Graham believed that consolidation could not "be a fact overnight but [was] by nature a long-run development."[31] At first Faust resented Graham working directly with his faculty at Greensboro and occasionally bypassing him. Later he became optimistic about consolidation. Graham worked hard to ease retirement for Faust as the matter became a source of tension. He encountered an equally taxing problem with Dean Brooks at State. Brooks had become ill and could not carry on his duties, although he refused to resign. Both Faust and Brooks retired in 1934. Graham and the trustees replaced them with deans of administration who were already familiar with the institutions: Dean Walter Clinton Jackson, who had served twenty-three years at the Woman's College, and Dean John W. Harrelson, who had been at State College since 1909.[32] House was named dean of administration at Chapel Hill at the same time.

Location of the engineering school became a point of contention in the consolidation struggle. Both Chapel Hill and Raleigh had thriving schools. When Dr. W. E. Wickendon, prominent engineer and president of the Chase School of Applied Science, made the survey for the Works Committee, he judged Chapel Hill's school the outstanding one of its kind in the South. The Works Committee recommended consolidating the two schools at Chapel Hill where Dr. H. G. Baity, the engineering dean, was nationally known. The school, in addition, had the support of strong science departments. Retaining it at Chapel Hill got enthusiastic support from the Board of Trustees.

Allied on the other side was a powerful coterie of state leaders, chief among them Governor Gardner. The governor had already pledged not to demote State as the scientific and technological nucleus of higher education. The legislative act of consolidation prescribed that "a unit of the university shall be located at Raleigh and shall be known as the North Carolina State College of Agriculture and Engineering of the University of North Carolina." On the same day it elected Graham president, the Board of Trustees passed a resolution declaring that there was "no intention to demote any of the institutions to the rank of junior college or to discontinue the school of engineering at Chapel Hill and Raleigh." This policy itself was contradictory.[33]

On November 14, 1932, the trustees tried to make their position clear, but they only confused it more. They again resolved to leave both schools intact. This violated the spirit and letter of the statutes of consolidation passed by the General Assembly, since engineering was the chief area of program duplication.

By the fall of 1933 Graham took the initiative by appointing another study committee. Its report, submitted in the fall of 1934, was split between those (six) who wanted the school consolidated at Raleigh and those (five) who favored retaining both schools with differing specialization on each campus. At this point Graham recognized the gravity of the stalemate. Moving carefully, he studied the situation for eight months, consulting with other universities and specialists. On June 11, 1935, in his annual trustees' report he addressed not only the engineering school impasse but the general principles and procedures of consolidation. This report became "a new charter of operations for the consolidated university" and a "historic document."[34]

The Graham report acknowledged that physical consolidation of institutions was impossible, but to leave the current situation unsettled would only intensify rivalries and promote duplication. The president recommended, instead, a third alternative: "Preservation of the locality, institutional integrity, historic traditions, values and loyalties around the basic purposes of each institution, but with no duplication of schools or curricula in the upper and graduate years."

Using this formula, Chapel Hill would move forward with all its schools and divisions except engineering, which would be transferred to Raleigh. State would become the technological institution minus its schools of science and business, which would be transferred to Chapel Hill. The Woman's College would be maintained as a first-class liberal arts college for women but without its school of library science (to be moved to Chapel Hill). When the formula was explained by Graham to former president Lowell of Harvard, he replied, "That is your answer, but I doubt if it will work. Faculty, alumni and vested interests will attempt to block you at every turn."[35] That prospect did not deter Graham, although the solution displeased many factions, especially those at Chapel Hill.

Graham not only set forth the principles; he proposed a plan of operation. Effective September 1935 there would be no new registration of engineering students at Chapel Hill or for the School of Science and Business at Raleigh. A general college—two years of basic courses in the humanities and sciences—would be established at North Carolina State as a foundation for the Schools of Agriculture and Forestry, Textiles, and Engineering. At the same time women students were denied enrollment in freshman and sophomore classes at Chapel Hill and Raleigh and channeled to Greensboro. A division of education for training teachers specified various types of instruction at each institution, with graduate work largely focused at Chapel Hill. New art departments were authorized for Greensboro and Chapel Hill.

This detailed plan reduced duplication and encouraged specialization. The report generated warm discussion at the trustees' meeting. Ultimately it passed by a vote of 58-11. Most of the negative votes came from the Chapel Hill faction led by trustees John Sprunt Hill and Walter (Pete) Murphy. The crucial vote occurred on a motion by Hill to retain the two engineering schools. It failed by a 50-25 vote.[36]

Sentiment for keeping an engineering school at Chapel Hill remained alive even after that. The Chapel Hill faculty joined a renewed fight by Hill and Murphy to save the university from "the politicians and educational idealists." After a seven-hour debate on May 12, 1936, faculty members voted 80-19 to request trustee reconsideration of the decision. They favored Professor Baity's plan to consolidate the two schools, placing professional and graduate engineering at Chapel Hill and technical and industrial engineering at State. This marked the first faculty opposition to a Graham policy decision. The resolution simultaneously praised the president's encouragement of faculty freedom and declared that differences on the engineering school question in no way implied lack of confidence in him.

The faculty's action, in turn, aroused renewed interest elsewhere. The State College alumni association, initially cool on consolidation, rallied behind Graham's position. Similar support came from the Woman's College. The state press presented the pros and cons of the issue but was split editorially. The *Durham Herald*, for example, referred to consolidation as a "pretty thing on paper but a well-nigh unworkable thing in practice."[37]

Opposing forces reflected the competitive spirit on three campuses. Majority sentiment supported the statewide vision of Graham and a coterie of trustees, many from Chapel Hill, who were convinced that to equivocate on the engineering school decision would spell consolidation's doom. In typical fashion, Graham, after taking his stand, remained calmly unmovable while the fight raged all about him.

Prior to the trustees' meeting in the spring of 1936, Graham sent the board a letter. Among other things he wrote, "After considering all points brought out in the faculty meeting and in the faculty statement, for which I have high respect, I am still of the opinion, in so far as I have any responsibility, that the recommendations made to the board last June are sound in principle, and despite temporary upsets and misgivings due to necessary readjustments, will in the long run prove to be in the best interests of the whole university and the whole state."[38]

At their meeting on May 30 in Greensboro the trustees heard impressive presentations from the three campuses discussing all phases of the issue. Graham again mentioned the need to hear "above the fears and sometimes clamor" of the hour "the call of the future of our state for a unified university." Then the trustees, with Governor J. C. B. Ehringhaus presiding and by a vote of 50-24, reaffirmed their previous recommendations.

Thus ended a decisive battle in the struggle for consolidation. It was the beginning of the "long process" foreseen by Graham. Out of it eventually came the multicampus system including sixteen degree-granting institutions across North Carolina. Graham's leadership proved crucial. Without it the movement launched by Governor Gardner as a response to the Great Depression might have failed and split the state, as Graham at one time feared. Relying on a sense of fairness and seeing the state whole, Graham embraced the sensible idea of specialization. Eventually the contending forces united behind that idea.

Even during the protracted fights over consolidation and state funding, other controversies swirled around the Graham regime. The president's bold espousal of free speech and human rights generated opposition even as it gave him a national reputation. When he and Marian returned from their Canadian honeymoon in the summer of 1932, they found piles of letters and newspaper comments about speeches made at Chapel Hill by Bertrand Russell and Langston Hughes. Russell, the British philosopher, had just published *Marriage and Morals,* and Hughes, the African American poet, had written a poem called "Black Christ" in which he declared, "Christ is a nigger on the cross of the South."

One hundred prominent citizens petitioned the governor to forbid "further predatory acts by so-called modern educators." Hughes was labeled "sacrilegious" and Russell "neo-pagan." Graham was held responsible for both. Confronted by demands for censorship and for his resignation, Graham wrote an Alabama critic: "The integrity, the moral autonomy and the intellectual freedom of this university are going to be preserved with faith and good will."[39]

In midsummer 1933 a student wrote Graham complaining that he had not been admitted to the medical school because he was a Jew. Graham called the student and, after a discussion, told him he would investigate the charge. When asked about the matter, Dr. Isaac Hall Manning, the highly respected dean of the medical school, confirmed the rejection. Manning explained that the two-year medical school had trouble placing Jewish graduates in four-year schools to complete their training. To lessen this difficulty, he said, the school had adopted a quota system whereby no more than 10 percent of the student body would be Jewish. This policy had been followed for many years.

The revelation shocked Graham's moral sensibilities. It clashed with his belief that the university should not bar a qualified student solely because of religion (although exclusion of blacks was taken for granted). When Manning finally convinced Graham that his considered judgment would not allow him to change the policy, Graham concluded, "In that case, Dean Manning, I will have to over-rule you and the young man will be admitted to your school." "Then I have no alternative," Manning replied, "but to resign as dean of the medical school."

The resignation had far-reaching effects. The *New York Herald-Tribune* supported Graham as did most of the state's newspapers. A number of physicians, however, protested, mainly about the loss of Dean Manning and the independence of the medical school. Replying to a group of doctors who had been critical of his decision, Graham declared, "I trust it is not necessary for me to express my deep appreciation of the character and service of Dr. Manning. . . . [He] and I understand each other and frankly and openly disagree on a matter of principle and policy. The position I have taken is simply that there shall be no discrimination on a quota basis or any other basis because a boy is of Jewish descent." After resigning from the deanship, Dr. Manning continued as a professor in the medical school.[40]

Almost as if to keep the controversy pot boiling, Graham in September 1934 offered to make bond for Alton Lawrence, a thirty-four-year-old former UNC student and secretary of the N.C. Socialist party. Lawrence had been arrested for trespassing as part of a "flying squadron" trying to close the Carolina Cotton and Woolen Mill of High Point. In his telegram of support, Graham wrote, "I am confident you have committed no crime." The bond was refused.[41]

While Graham's leadership prevailed on consolidation and most of the human rights issues he championed, it faltered badly on professionalism in athletics. Graham's interest in the subject was piqued by a 1934 Carnegie Foundation study of 112 campuses where "the recruiting and subsidizing of athletics" had become a subject of academic concern. The report recommended that college presidents take the lead in "rooting out" such evils. Graham, in typical fashion, accepted the challenge.

An enthusiastic supporter of college sports and a baseball player during his college days, Graham nevertheless believed financial interests had invaded intercollegiate athletics and were exerting a corrupting influence. After studying the situation, he produced what became the controversial Graham Plan for regulating intercollegiate sports. It decreed that college athletes should receive no special financial aid and should provide statements of their income. The faculty would control athletics, and no staff members would receive special remuneration except from the colleges. Recruitment would be limited, athletic accounts would be audited and published, and there would be no postseason contests.[42]

Graham knew that his plan would arouse vigorous opposition. He presented his general ideas to the November 1934 trustees' meeting without revealing details. "Is student life to revolve mainly around a circus subsidized and brought into the institutions?" he asked. "Or is it to center around, mainly, the teachers, library, classrooms, laboratories, historic buildings, shrines and traditions which are a part of the soil, the air and the spirit of the place?"[43]

Opposition immediately resounded in North Carolina and the South. University alumni chapters in ten North Carolina communities condemned the regulations. The university's athletic council rebelled and unanimously expressed its opposition. President W. P. Few of Duke University announced the opposition of his university. Sportswriters, coaches, and students added their criticism. Many of the coaches said it would mean the end of intercollegiate athletics. The Greensboro Daily News noted that whether an athlete got outside help should be a matter between the student and his sponsor, not the university administration. Trying to police athletic sponsorship would result in "lying and hypocrisy," and the "evils incurred and encouraged will out-distance the cure."[44]

While the furor grew, the presidents of six of the ten institutions in the Southern Conference met on January 11, 1936, and supported the Graham Plan. Two weeks later the university faculty at Chapel Hill, by a decisive voice vote, also backed it. Almost simultaneously, the Southeastern Conference voted overwhelmingly for open subsidization. Athletes who met academic requirements would be given scholarships. The conference argued that assistance would help worthy young men get a college education, and since subsidies were inevitable, it was better to bring them into the open.

The varied forces which opposed Graham's proposal became thoroughly visible at the January 31, 1936, meeting of the trustees. The president came to the meeting hoping to gain another endorsement for his athletic plan. But the proposal had triggered so much opposition across the state that it ignited renewed criticism among other groups already disturbed about consolidation, the medical school, and Graham's active sponsorship of liberal causes. It became clear to the president and his supporters that the Graham Plan would not be approved. A motion was made and passed to refer the matter to the faculty. "If we can't trust the faculty to control and regulate athletics," Judge John J. Parker declared, "then we ought to get a new faculty."[45]

The outcome of the trustees' meeting encouraged Graham's opponents to increase their pressure. In late February 1936 the *News & Observer* published a rumor that Graham's critics were planning to seek his ouster. The *Durham Herald* editorialized that despite Graham's "bullheadedness" on athletics and his questionable championing of radicals, he was "the biggest single asset the university has left."[46] David Clark, the most outspoken critic, declared that the ouster report was a "hoax" deliberately concocted to generate sympathy for Graham. He cited the exposure of a "cheating ring" among students at Chapel Hill as an example of the kind of at-home business Graham had ignored while "racing off to Washington to regulate the government."[47]

In January 1936 a freshman had exposed a cheating ring, headed by a graduate student, which had been in existence for more than two years. Guaranteed grades had been offered for sale in preparation of themes and, in some courses, in help in taking examinations. More than 150 students had participated, including the president of the senior class and members of Phi Beta Kappa and the Golden Fleece. When Graham became aware of the ring, he insisted that details be publicized and that student government take the lead in making amends. Students were suspended as a result. The probe added more ammunition for the president's opponents.[48]

Graham's friends became seriously concerned. Charles Tillett and Kemp Battle began studying university records to obtain facts for building a defense. Josephus Daniels, then ambassador to Mexico, offered to return to defend Graham. An organized ouster movement never developed, but the Graham Plan faded.

At a special meeting of the Southern Conference on February 8, 1936, the plan was adopted by a vote of 6-4. This produced renewed uproar among critics. Newspaper sports pages opened their columns to numerous letters from readers, many of them labeling the plan autocratic and Graham dictatorial. North Carolina State's football coach predicted that "football will be dead in two years." By the time the Southern Conference met again in

December the opposition had heightened. The University of Virginia, an original sponsor of the Graham Plan, announced its resignation from the conference unless certain revisions were made. The absolute prohibition of scholarship help for athletes was repugnant, the university said. It suggested amending it by adding a single word—*primarily.* That word would make the regulation read that special treatment to students would not have "accrued *primarily* because of athletic ability." The change was accepted. Faculty councils accepted it, including Chapel Hill's.

President John J. Tigert of Florida, who led the fight for open subsidization of the southeastern conference, commiserated with Graham. "I am sorry," he said, that "your noble experiment has failed." Graham took his defeat with grace, describing it as a "bitter fight" with practically "unanimous opposition." "Not being dictators," he said, "we will have to await the democratic process for the next struggle for the same principles in which I believe."[49]

In the minds of North Carolinians not wedded to New Deal liberalism, Frank Graham, "that man in Chapel Hill," had become as controversial as Franklin Roosevelt, "that man in the White House."[50] Both enjoyed the affection and respect of vast numbers of citizens at the grass roots. Both also generated strong negative sentiment in the conservative business establishment.

Roosevelt considered Graham a dedicated ally and repeatedly sought his services on responsible missions in Washington. In 1933 he appointed Graham vice chairman of the Consumer Advisory Board, which helped organize community consumers' councils to encourage economic recovery. In 1934, at the invitation of Secretary of Labor Frances Perkins, Graham served as chairman of the Advisory Council on Economic Security, which helped draw up the landmark Social Security program. Graham served on FDR's vocational education study committee as it pondered federal aid to education.

Graham never lost touch with social service missions in North Carolina and the South. His most troublesome organizational connection was the Southern Conference for Human Welfare (SCHW). This organization, established by a diverse group of southern liberals, held its first meeting in Birmingham in November 1938. Graham delivered the keynote speech and chaired a committee to designate the southerner who had "done the most to promote human and social welfare in line with the philosophy of Thomas Jefferson." Justice Hugo Black received the Jefferson Award, and Bull Con-

William MacNider.
(North Carolina Collection, University of North Carolina Library, Chapel Hill)

nor, the Birmingham police commissioner, castigated the conference for holding racially mixed meetings. Attacks came as well from U.S. representative Martin Dies, chairman of the House Un-American Activities Committee, who said the organization was controlled by Communists.

Against the advice of some of his friends, Graham became chairman of the conference and oversaw its activities for eighteen stormy months during which he tried to deter Communist influence and bolster an overly idealistic and sometimes inept board.[51] Graham openly broke with the Communist faction when he supported a resolution denouncing Soviet Russia introduced by W. T. Couch, director of the University of North Carolina Press. The Communist members then denounced Graham in the conference rooms and hotel halls as a "tool of Wall Street" and a "lackey of the mill barons." The resolution (denouncing both Communists and Fascists) passed; but the conference was shattered, and after Graham's term as president ended, it fell into the hands of more strident leaders.[52]

Even in the midst of controversy and setbacks Graham never lost his zest for the "good fight for the good cause." At the end of 1938 he helped the student chairman of the Carolina Political Union, Alexander Heard, persuade President Roosevelt, then at the height of his New Deal popularity, to

Archibald Henderson.
(North Carolina Collection, University of North Carolina Library, Chapel Hill)

visit Chapel Hill. Many years later Heard, who was to become chancellor of Vanderbilt University, recalled that when he drafted a telegram to the president, he put Graham's name first and his own second. When Graham saw the draft, "he immediately suggested that the names be switched. When the answer came, it came addressed to me. 'You see,' [Graham] said, 'that's why I wanted our names switched.'"[53] Roosevelt visited Chapel Hill on December 5, 1938. Speaking in the newly completed Woollen Gymnasium (named for the business manager and controller who had died the previous

Albert Coates.
(North Carolina Collection, University of North Carolina Library, Chapel Hill)

year), he praised the university's liberalism, defended his own, and received an honorary LL.D. degree.

Meanwhile, the university, like the nation, had been slowly recovering from the Great Depression. One of the notable achievements of that period, the brainchild of law professor Albert Coates and his wife, Gladys, was the Institute of Government, modestly launched in 1931–32 as a personal enterprise. The Coateses' early hope, drawing on memories of President E. K. Graham and Professor E. C. Branson, was to enlarge the scope of the law school by providing organized instruction, research, and training for public officials across North Carolina. Dean M. T. Van Hecke and the faculty of the law school thought otherwise. The Great Depression was on, the school's budget was being repeatedly cut, and there was no money for new ventures.[54]

Thus the Coateses founded the institute on their own. In many respects it was better able to fulfill its mission in the early years as an independent enterprise. With the help of several public-spirited citizens, among them Benjamin Cone and J. Spencer Love of Greensboro, they sustained it until 1942, when it was incorporated into the university. The institute's first headquarters was built on East Franklin Street, near the Presbyterian Church, largely with the help of Julian Price of Greensboro and Will Reynolds and Bowman Gray of Winston-Salem. The new building was dedicated on Thanksgiving Day 1939. After World War II the Coateses persuaded Mrs. Joseph Palmer Knapp, widow of the philanthropist, to give $500,000 to match a similar grant from the General Assembly. This provided funds for a newer and more spacious building opened in 1956 at the eastern gate of the university on Raleigh Road.

Professor Albert Coates himself became an institution at Chapel Hill. Over the next half-century the Institute of Government trained thousands of officials in the city halls, county courthouses, and state departments of North Carolina. Coates helped accomplish the goal his mentor, President E. K. Graham, envisioned before World War I: to plant the heart of the University of North Carolina in the heart of North Carolina.

During the same period, another division of the university enlarged its outreach. Dr. Charles Staples Mangum, who succeeded Dr. Isaac Manning as dean of the medical school in 1933, working with Dr. Carl V. Reynolds of the State Board of Health, helped secure state funds for the Department, later the Division, of Public Health in the School of Medicine. Dr. Milton J. Rosenau, recently retired as professor of preventive medicine and dean of the School of Public Health at Harvard, agreed to head the new enterprise. Dr. H. G. Baity, head of the Department of Sanitary Engineering and dean of the School of Engineering before consolidation, joined the department along with a corps of able young specialists in various fields of public health.

Dean Mangum, along with President Graham and Dr. William MacNider, secured a grant from the Public Works Administration, matched by funds from the legislature, to construct the first new building for the Schools of Medicine and Public Health. Prior to his death in September 1939, Dean Mangum, assisted by Dr. MacNider, played a key role in persuading the Council on Medical Education and the Association of American Medical Colleges to reverse their positions and thus temporarily save the two-year medical school. For accreditation purposes such institutions were continued as "schools of basic medical sciences" until after World War II, when the university was able to transform its school into a four-year institution.[55]

During the regime of Dr. William MacNider, who in 1937 succeeded Mangum as dean, another unsuccessful effort was made to expand the medical school. Funds were tentatively offered from the Bowman Gray Foundation if the school were moved to Winston-Salem. President Graham and other officials questioned the educational soundness of moving the school. As a result the Gray funds helped establish at Winston-Salem the Bowman Gray School of Medicine in Wake Forest College, a four-year institution, which graduated its first class in 1943.[56]

The university, which had been largely a child of the American Revolution and a victim of the Civil War, developed close ties with the national administrations of Woodrow Wilson and Franklin Roosevelt during World Wars I and II. As a result its resources were pledged to the war efforts and utilized accordingly.

The impact of the war on Chapel Hill became especially evident in the early 1940s. President Graham had worked closely with President and Mrs. Roosevelt on social service projects during the preceding decade. At the beginning of his administration in 1931, Graham, while always working for a "warless world," perceived that "modern democracies stand face to face with communist and fascist dictatorships." When Hitler's threat loomed in Europe, Graham promptly aligned the university with the view of Americans who proclaimed that "this is our war." In a contribution for a volume edited by Kansas editor William Allen White, Graham declared, "We favor immediate aid to the allies because the democracies, with all their injustices, frustrations and failures, give the world's people, including the German people, more hope of the opportunity to struggle for peace, freedom, democracy and humane religion as the basis of them all."[57] In his university convocation address on September 27, 1940, over a year before the United

States entered the war, Graham announced that by order of the trustees the university was "offering its total resources to the nation for the defense of the freedom and democracy it was founded to serve."[58]

On March 20, 1941, President Roosevelt appointed Graham a member of the eleven-member National Defense Mediation Board. The appointment was greeted with "shocked outrage" among some members of Congress familiar with the Dies committee's probe of the Southern Conference for Human Welfare. Lend-lease to the Allies had begun. Labor troubles were crippling the flow of war goods to the warfront. Almost all the cases involved union security or wages, and Graham found his eight-month service a time of learning. One of the bitterest cases involved a controversy with the colorful labor leader John L. Lewis. After Graham and other public members opposed his "closed shop" initiative, Lewis was enraged and called Graham "that sweet little son-of-a-bitch."[59]

After the Japanese attack on Pearl Harbor, the White House established a war labor board to handle problems of industrial production. Graham became a member and for almost three years held two full-time jobs. He never worked less than sixty hours a week, shuttling constantly on weekends between Chapel Hill and Washington, D.C. During that period he accepted a salary only from the federal government. While the individual campuses were managed by administrators on the scene, Graham tried to keep up with educational affairs as best he could. No major decisions were made without his active participation or concurrence.

At Chapel Hill the death of controller Charles Woollen brought to the fore an able and dedicated successor, William Donald Carmichael, Jr. In the spring of 1940 Graham went to New York City to persuade Carmichael to give up his seat on the Stock Exchange and his successful brokerage business to return to his alma mater. Carmichael, a 1921 graduate of the university and a campus basketball star, became a key administrative figure on the consolidated university staff under Graham and his successor, Gordon Gray. Along with Dean Robert House, Carmichael helped manage affairs at Chapel Hill while Graham was away, and he played a substantial role in the university's burgeoning growth after World War II.

Graham's close association with the Roosevelt administration played a part in the U.S. Navy's decision to place at Chapel Hill one of its four newly authorized preflight centers for the training of naval pilots. Carmichael helped negotiate this project, announced in February 1942. It was agreed that the university would supply facilities for housing and feeding and a program for 1,875 Navy preflight cadets. The center required a substantial program of new building and renovation. Included were the overhaul of ten dormitories in the upper and lower quadrangles, additions to Woollen Gymnasium and Lenoir Dining Hall (which had been completed in 1939 and replaced Swain Hall), and the construction of a new infirmary, a recreation center (called Navy Hall), and a new athletic field.

The Navy also maintained a Reserve Officers Training Corps (ROTC) unit and V-12 units on the campus during the war, which required an armory, an infirmary, and extensive barracks. The U.S. Navy brought the war to Chapel Hill in a sizable wave of expansion. University property increased in value by more than $1.5 million between 1945 and 1947, due to improvements made by the Navy.[60]

The task of managing the university became increasingly complicated as more Navy candidates arrived and as Graham's duties kept him constantly in Washington. While the civilian enrollment fell from 3,633 to 1,387 during wartime, more than 20,000 men attended the university in special military training programs over several years. Complaints grew about the president's absence from South Building. As early as July 1942, after Graham had served on the War Labor Board for six months, he received a letter from Professor MacNider saying he was needed for guidance and counsel. "It is important for us to know more of you here at home," MacNider wrote. This dissatisfaction increased until in the spring of 1944 the faculty unanimously adopted a statement that Graham's absence "has retarded unduly and inevitably the administration of affairs" and that the faculty lacks "cohesion and direction." A dozen years after consolidation the faculty still considered Graham their leader.

These criticisms ultimately led to Graham's resignation from the War Labor Board on December 31, 1945. By that time President Roosevelt had died, the war with Germany and Japan had ended, and a new president, Harry Truman, sought to involve Graham in other Washington missions. Graham accepted an assignment in November 1945 from Truman to serve on the Oil Panel Fact Finding Committee, but by the end of the year he was able to return to the campus full-time for the first time since the war crisis began in 1940.[61]

Returning veterans from World War II swelled enrollment and taxed housing facilities. The university's extensive expansion under wartime conditions helped take care of some of the overflow, but surplus army housing from Fort Bragg and other military bases was moved to Chapel Hill and converted into apartments for married students. Quonset huts, trailers, prefabricated houses, and even the Tin Can were utilized as living quarters. The residential complex south of the medical school became known as Victory Village and provided housing for hundreds of students and their spouses.

This was an upbeat time. The university's reputation in academic circles flourished. The attractiveness of the village became known all over the country. Chapel Hill felt the impact of the big bands and claimed one of their notable leaders, Kay Kyser, the former head cheerleader whose Kollege of Musical Knowledge became nationally renowned. Kyser, who had written the famous pep song "Tar Heels on Hand," along with his wife, Georgia, returned to live in the village when he retired at the peak of his success.

But a modest young football player set the tone of the post–World War II years and became the toast of the campus. The Charlie Justice era at Chapel Hill began in 1946 and lasted through 1949. During those years the talented Tar Heel athlete from Asheville captained coach Carl Snavely's Tar Heels and led them to thirty-two victories, seven losses, and two ties. The teams competed in three national, postseason bowl games and rejected an invitation to a fourth. Justice won first-string All-American honors twice and broke scoring, rushing, and passing records as a triple-threat operator. Justice became the "Lil David" who befuddled the giants. Fast, dramatic, and a breathtaking broken-field runner, he stunned audiences with his grace and pluck. "Remember we're talking about the era of the hero, not the anti-hero," said his classmate Billy Carmichael III in later years. "Charlie was every mother's dream—clean-cut, modest, generous, didn't drink or smoke. . . . He always gave generously of his time and he was always appreciative of what athletics had done for him. He's one of the few who gave as much as he got."[62]

On his full-time return to the campus in 1946 President Graham led the campaign to establish several new academic departments, among them city planning, mathematical statistics, radio and communications, and religion. John Motley Morehead, having noted that there were only five major planetariums in the nation and none on a university campus, informed Graham in 1946 that he would give $2 million to have one built. The chairman of Union Carbide and Graham selected as a site the property between Graham Memorial and the Episcopal Church on East Franklin Street.

The first postwar General Assembly treated the university well. A 50 percent increase in the maintenance budget underwrote development of a new salary scale. On March 28, 1947, the legislature agreed to the greatest single capital appropriation for Chapel Hill by funding at last the ambitious, four-year medical school complex.

The final drive coincided with the statewide Good Health Program triggered by the disquieting medical statistics revealed about North Carolina soldiers during the war. Governor J. Melville Broughton, Dr. William MacNider, Dr. Paul Whitaker, and Dr. William Coppridge, among others, led the early stages of this hard-fought project to improve medical care. Many doctors thought medical schools at Duke and Wake Forest were adequate to serve the state's health needs. Others feared the tax burden. Some sentiment developed for locating the new medical school in the piedmont, either at Greensboro or Charlotte, to take advantage of the larger population pools for the teaching hospital.

Governor Broughton got the campaign under way by appointing a fifty-member State Hospital and Medical Care Commission to study and publicize the state's health needs. The North Carolina Medical Society enlisted the support of physicians, although many were not enthusiastic. Incoming governor Gregg Cherry (1945–49) refused to support some phases of the comprehensive medical care program, but he endorsed the four-year medical school. William D. Carmichael, Jr., secured funds from leading industrialists to underwrite the campaign for the expanded medical school, the new hospital, and rural health centers across North Carolina as well as loan funds for students who would practice in rural communities. Kay Kyser, the popular band leader, became an enthusiastic supporter, stumping the state.[63]

The $3.79 million program approved in 1947 proved less comprehensive than university officials had first thought, but it met long-standing major medical school needs and assured location of the new 400-bed teaching hospital and medical center at Chapel Hill. The General Assembly approved at the same time a $6.25 million grant for building community hospitals and health centers around the state. At one point the program hinged on passage of the Hill-Burton bill for hospital construction, which was narrowly enacted by Congress. Graham and others helped assuage groups in Charlotte and Greensboro anxious to locate the medical school in their cities. Graham consulted officials in other states who convinced him that the medical school should not be separated geographically from the university.[64]

A number of physicians and leaders who initially opposed the medical center later became supporters. The Duke Endowment became a benefactor of North Carolina Memorial Hospital. The newly established Cone Memorial Hospital in Greensboro set up an affiliate program with N.C. Memorial Hospital, providing student medical training and a residency program for family physicians.

Meanwhile, Dr. William MacNider had resigned the medical school deanship in 1940 in order to pursue his research in the fields of nephritis and diseases of aging. Failing health caused him to restrict his academic pursuits in 1943, and he died in 1951. Dr. MacNider served the university for forty-eight years and was considered by many as "the most completely identified in mind, body and spirit" of any friend of the university of his era. Reared in a house on the site of the old post office, when Franklin Street was only an unpaved boulevard, he spent all his productive career at Chapel Hill. His mother's boarding house was a favorite dining place for veteran faculty members.[65]

Dr. W. Reece Berryhill, assistant dean of student affairs and director of clinical courses, succeeded Dr. MacNider. He became one of the guiding figures in supervising construction and management of the four-year medical center. Another dedicated medical stalwart, Dr. Isaac H. Manning, ended a thirty-nine-year career as professor of physiology and dean when he died in 1946. Dr. Manning had sustained the faltering two-year medical school in its moments of greatest need and helped assure its survival.[66]

President Graham's return to full-time duty proved short-lived. After his wartime stint in Washington ended, his reputation as a skilled negotiator and mediator survived. In December 1946 President Truman appointed him to the Civil Rights Commission, which submitted a far-reaching report recommending "elimination of segregation based on race, color, creed or national origin." The report, entitled "To Secure These Rights," became a landmark on the road to the elimination of segregation in employment, education, housing, health care, and access to public services. Graham agreed with the report's objectives but hesitated about using full government force in obtaining them. Graham never publicly approved a "frontal attack" on segregation but espoused education and religion as instruments to change segregation laws.[67]

Postwar demands on Graham's services went far beyond the Civil Rights Commission. In late September 1947 he was approached by Secretary of State George Marshall to serve as part of a three-member United Nations mediation team to negotiate the dispute between the Netherlands and republican forces in Indonesia, which threatened to erupt into warfare. A reluctant Board of Trustees granted Graham another indefinite leave. The departing president selected Henry Brandis, a UNC professor of law and one of his former students, as an assistant. They departed on a mission halfway around the world, which again left the consolidated university without full-time leadership and with renewed frustration. By the end of four months Graham and his fellow mediators had persuaded opposing forces to sign a truce agreement. Then Graham was off to report to President Truman at the White House and attend the United Nations Security Council debate at Lake Success, New York. The Renville Agreement, a significant start toward the independence of Indonesia, represented a forward step for the United Nations as a negotiating instrument in international disputes. Graham rejoiced over its constructive impact.[68]

Meanwhile, renewed stirrings of the House Un-American Activities Committee and alarm over the Soviet Union's technological advances in atomic energy rekindled criticism of Graham's association with Communist-front organizations. The university president had continued his affiliation with the Southern Conference for Human Welfare and served as its speaker at a 1945 convention honoring Eleanor Roosevelt. Roger Baldwin, head of the American Civil Liberties Union, criticized the SCHW for closing its eyes to risks of collaborating with fellow travelers and lack of diligence in excluding them from its membership. The *Charlotte News* published a lengthy probe of Graham's associations and cleared him of charges of collaboration with Communists. But trustee Thurmond Chatham, a textile manufacturer, declared, "Our university is regarded as radical rather than liberal. I don't like the atmosphere and as a trustee I want to protest against it."

Graham himself repeatedly denied Communist connections or indoctrination at Chapel Hill, saying there were no Communists on the faculty. He did, however, know avowed Communists among students, including Junius Scales, chairman of the N.C. Communist party, who later became the first individual imprisoned under the Smith Act.

The outcry against Graham's association with radical groups reached a new level of intensity in early 1949 after he was elected president of the board of Oak Ridge Institute of Nuclear Studies, sponsored by fourteen southern universities. In a series of seven broadcasts the radio commentator Fulton Lewis, Jr., charged that Graham was not a safe security risk. When the Atomic Energy Commission granted Graham "complete security clearance," it overruled its security advisory committee. Graham replied to Lewis's charges, citing his record of support of the policies of Woodrow

Wilson and Franklin Roosevelt and saying that he would not "renounce any stand I made for human freedom."[69]

Amid these circumstances, on March 22, 1949, newly elected governor W. Kerr Scott announced he was appointing Graham the new junior U.S. senator from North Carolina. When the announcement came at the end of an O. Max Gardner awards dinner in Chapel Hill, near-pandemonium erupted. Graham's appointment as a replacement for the recently deceased U.S. senator J. Melville Broughton stunned the state's political establishment. It inspired rejoicing among Graham's friends but jolted conservatives who considered Graham a well-meaning but dangerous political maverick.

Governor Scott, the cigar-smoking populist dairyman of Haw River, enjoyed political surprises. In 1948 he had overthrown the Gardner political organization by winning the governorship on a liberal, Go Forward platform aimed at paving farm-to-market roads and expanding rural electrification. With the names of as many as fifty possible senatorial nominees before him, Scott consulted liberal editor Jonathan Daniels of the Raleigh *News & Observer* (son of the former ambassador to Mexico), who suggested Graham's name and agreed to meet with the university president and help twist his arm. Scott had also consulted his wife, Mary, who told him, when he reached Graham's name, "You can stop right there. So far as I'm concerned, that's it."[70]

Graham, then sixty-two years old, once again became the reluctant appointee. He had many reasons to remain in his education post. But when Scott and Daniels insisted that serving as U.S. senator was his duty, Graham could not resist. Some of his friends feared he would get lost in the political mazes of Washington, but others felt that his friendships and associations across the state and his imposing academic reputation would prove unbeatable at the polls.

The appointment produced new critical outbursts in Congress as well as spirited accolades from friends. Among the latter was the eloquent Senator Wayne Morse of Oregon, with whom Graham had served on the War Labor Board. Morse called Graham "the most Christ-like man I have ever known" and included him on his list of the twenty-five "greatest living Americans." When "collaboration with Communists" charges against Graham were hauled out again on the floor of the U.S. Senate, his senior colleague, the courtly conservative U.S. senator Clyde R. Hoey, responded emphatically: "I cannot remain silent when these suggestions or insinuations are made against the loyalty of Dr. Graham."

Frank Porter Graham and William Friday, 1961.
(University of North Carolina Photographic Laboratory, Chapel Hill)

Frank and Marian Graham held their last traditional Sunday open house on March 27, 1949. More than 1,500 students and townspeople came to the president's house on Franklin Street to tell them good-bye. On March 29 in Washington he was sworn in as North Carolina's new junior senator.

Graham's service in the Senate proved brief. He had been appointed to Broughton's unfinished term, which meant he must mount a campaign to hold his seat the following spring. Graham's strong coterie of friends turned out enthusiastically and in great number to help him. But opposition proved equally fierce. It tapped the latent emotional fears of the times—Communism and desegregation.

As it turned out, the Democratic primary of 1950 polarized public opinion in North Carolina. It thrust a dedicated, sometimes naive idealist into the rough political marketplace. Graham's perennial tendency to trust the motives of the underdog and to champion justice for the dispossessed made him vulnerable to those practical-minded conservatives who, while acknowledging his good motives, often thought his judgment faulty and his concept of human goodness exaggerated.

One of Graham's opponents, former U.S. senator Robert Rice Reynolds, proved something of a laughingstock and was no threat. But the other, Willis Smith, a reputable conservative Raleigh lawyer and former president of the American Bar Association, successfully took the middle road and portrayed Graham as a dangerous leftist.

The efforts of Graham's organization often proved amateurish or ineffective and fell short of their mark. Meanwhile Smith's backers, most of them supremely hardheaded, exploited Graham's involvements with leftist, Communist-front organizations and stooped, at times, to racial smears and distortions. Smith himself was a man of character, but some of his associates could not resist demagoguery in the heat of political battle, and Smith never stayed their hand.

Graham led the ticket in the first primary when the Smith forces tried unsuccessfully to discredit him as a Communist collaborator. Then, assisted by U.S. Supreme Court decisions ordering racial desegregation and by his organization's distribution of defamatory racial leaflets and outright lies, Smith defeated Graham in the runoff by a narrow margin. It was one of the meanest political campaigns in North Carolina history.

In defeat Graham was as serene and magnanimous as ever. He never criticized his opponents, before or after the election. Utilizing his unusual talents as mediator and diplomat, he went on to serve the United Nations Mediation Service for almost two decades. He died on February 16, 1972, and was buried in the Chapel Hill Cemetery under a dogwood tree. On the stone, beneath the names of Frank and Marian Graham, were carved "words they together had chosen: 'They had faith in youth and youth responded with their best.'"[71]

Frank Graham influenced not only youth but the whole populace of North

Carolina. His impact on his times was profound, and he left a legacy of constructive achievement for the university he loved. Through his career, his friend Alexander Heard observed, "coursed his vision of the University of North Carolina as the instrument of the people's advance and as the exemplar, expositor and agent of Western culture."[72]

GORDON GRAY,

THE SECRETARY AND THE GENERALS,

1950–1955

Frank Graham's resignation in 1949 marked a sharp break with the past. For almost two decades he had symbolized Chapel Hill for university students, professors, and alumni. Even among those who disagreed with his liberal ideas and viewed him as an impractical idealist—or, on occasion, a dupe of Communist-front organizations—his personal magnetism, his integrity, and his devotion to democratic ideals remained authentic and persuasive. Across the state and in the academy itself his name and reputation inspired respect and praise.

. North Carolina State and the Woman's College had their chancellors, but Frank Graham epitomized Chapel Hill, even in absentia. Consolidation had not changed that relationship. The president's longtime assistant and secretary, Robert B. House, who became dean of administration in 1934, had remained in the shadow of his superior and was not named chancellor until 1945, when the heads of all three institutions gained that title.

The difficulties of this arrangement increased after Graham's departure. His successor, the forty-one-year-old secretary of the army Gordon Gray, had few of Graham's activist tendencies or his deep roots and associations with Chapel Hill. Gray brought a new aura of formality and businesslike precision to South Building. The new president had no experience with the diffuse authority and style of academic life. "Gray was as lacking in perception of what a university is as any person I've ever seen," one professor noted.[1] Gray himself wryly observed that the positions of secretary of the army and president of the university were somewhat alike, the main difference being that the faculty had no individuals below the rank of general.[2]

More than a year elapsed between Frank Graham's resignation early in 1949 and the arrival of the new president. During that time William D. Carmichael, the charming and industrious "Billy," who was the controller and a shrewd and genial spokesman for the university in many fields, became acting president. Not a few North Carolinians thought Carmichael should succeed Graham. But the business manager knew he lacked academic credentials. He was too smart not to recognize that his religious affiliation as a Roman Catholic was a handicap in a state still considered missionary territory by the Vatican. Carmichael openly joked about this with friends. When a prominent legislator approached him about running for governor in the early 1950s, Carmichael, as he told the story, thanked him in declining and said, "You know, I'm a Roman Catholic." His visitor looked thunderstruck and replied, "The hell you say!"[3]

Carmichael steered the trustees toward Gray, who, as a member of a wealthy Winston-Salem family, had already been approached about becoming head of the commerce school before President Truman named him army secretary. Some members of the trustees' executive committee had been disturbed by Frank Graham's liberalism and quietly leaned toward a successor less activist-minded. Gray fell into that category, although his Truman connections branded him in some quarters as a "millionaire liberal."[4]

Carmichael's interest in Gray stemmed in part from their rather similar backgrounds. Carmichael's father was an officer of Liggett & Myers Tobacco Company of Durham, while Gray's father, uncle, and brother served as chief executive officers of R. J. Reynolds Tobacco Company of Winston-Salem.

Gray, however, had career ideas beyond the tobacco business. After graduating first academically in his class of 1930 at Chapel Hill, he received his J.D. degree from Yale, where he was editor of the *Yale Law Review,* then practiced law in New York and Winston-Salem prior to purchasing the Winston-Salem *Journal & Sentinel* and radio station WSJS. He served three terms in the N.C. Senate and became president of the North Carolina Young Democrats. In 1942 he entered the U.S. Army as a private, was commissioned in 1943, and rose to the rank of captain before his discharge in 1945. On the initiative of Secretary of the Army Kenneth Royall, Sr., a North Carolinian, Gray became an assistant secretary in 1947, and when Royall resigned in 1949, President Truman gave him the top position. He thus became the first private to serve as civilian head of the army.

Gray's credentials and achievements were impressive. Reserved and modest in demeanor, he was keenly intelligent and ambitious. He had an appetite for work and a passion for accomplishment. Born to wealth and privilege, he prized excellence and, like an old Roman, sought it in public service. He reflected some of the qualities of his cousin Alice (Polly) Gray, who told him when he climbed behind the wheel of his first shiny roadster, "Now remember, Gordon, you never earned a cent of the money you're about to enjoy."[5]

The trustees' nominating committee, under the chairmanship of Victor Bryant, pondered its decision for ten months and reviewed 200 names. Gray's shortage of academic credentials was a negative factor, but the committee decided he had more than enough strength in other areas. When the appointment was announced in February 1950, the national press generally hailed it as continuing North Carolina's progressive southern leadership in the Frank Graham tradition. "UNC will gain a president of truly exceptional ability," the *Washington Post* predicted.

Gray, as it turned out, had little of the Frank Graham personal ebullience or missionary spirit. When he took office on September 23, 1950, he quickly perceived the organizational weakness of the consolidated system. It had never been fleshed out under Graham's informal management. Since he had no academic experience himself, Gray appointed a provost, Logan Wilson, dean of Newcomb College, Tulane University, in 1951 to be his spokesperson in faculty relations. Wilson's tenure was short; in 1953 he left UNC to become president of the University of Texas. Under Gray's direction the university hired a consulting firm to study the organizational structure and the needs of the consolidated office.

In his inaugural address at Raleigh's Reynolds Coliseum on October 10, 1950, the climax of three days of elaborate convocations in Greensboro and Chapel Hill, Gray praised Frank Graham for "skillfully charting the course and guiding the university through nearly two decades of successful consolidation in the spirit and letter of unity envisioned by O. Max Gardner, the father of consolidation." Graham, who had lost his Senate seat the preceding June, received a standing ovation when his name was mentioned.

Then Gray issued a warning. "We shall not knowingly allow any campus to become a workshop or laboratory or training ground for the operation of those who are committed to the destruction of American culture and institutions," he said. "Indeed, Communists are not welcome at any of our three institutions." But he added that the university would approach such problems "sensibly" and "with restraint" and would not be "over-absorbed" with them.

Gray, accompanied by his wife, the former Jane Boyden Henderson Craige, and their four sons, moved into the president's house on East Franklin Street, destined, the trustees hoped, for an extended tenure. He arrived at a moment when international security concerns, reflected in the Korean War and fear of atomic weapons and McCarthyism, were paramount at home and abroad. Only that spring former president Frank Graham had been defeated as he sought to retain his U.S. Senate seat, in a bitter campaign featuring anti-Communist attacks and trumped-up racial charges.

Gray had scarcely taken office before reports circulated that he would be lured back to Washington. Between his selection and his inauguration Gray served on President Truman's committee to study continuation of Marshall Fund aid to Western Europe. There was a rumor that he would be asked to succeed Dean Acheson as secretary of state.

When President Truman sought the president's services again in June 1951, less than a year after he had arrived, the trustees were disturbed. Reluctantly they authorized Gray to spend two days a week in Washington serving on the Psychological Strategies Board after Mr. Truman applied pressure by calling Governor Kerr Scott, chairman of the board. "I see no way other than to go along with President Truman when he says he must have [Gray]," Scott told the trustees. In an editorial comment, the *News & Observer* spoke of the "unraveling of Mr. Gray's presidency before it is well begun." L. P. McLendon, Sr., one of the trustees who helped select Gray, declared that "morale at the Greater University has reached a low ebb."[6]

After President Eisenhower's election in 1952, Gray's popularity in Washington remained undiminished. Initially he rejected all invitations, but by 1953 he had become a member of Eisenhower's Committee on International Information Activities. In 1954 he accepted a request to become chairman of the Personnel Security Board of the Atomic Energy Commission in the matter of J. Robert Oppenheimer. In a controversial 2-1 vote the board recommended lifting the security clearance of Dr. Oppenheimer, one of the fathers of the atomic energy program. When the Atomic Energy Commission adopted this recommendation, it created a stir in the academic community. The Gray committee confirmed Oppenheimer's "personal loyalty" but found him "less than candid" and "susceptible to influence." Gray called this "the most difficult assignment I ever had." Critics of Gray and the commission felt they erred on the side of caution at the height of the McCarthy scare when the U.S. senator charged, without verification, that the federal government was honeycombed with Communists. The fact that Oppenheimer's wife had been a member of the Communist party and that he continued his associations with fellow travelers led others to agree that the commission had taken "the only position it could take." But Gray lost support among academicians. This enhanced his restlessness at Chapel Hill.

During the early part of his five-year regime Gray devoted considerable effort to organizing an effective administrative structure for the consolidated system. An $80,000 management study by the consulting firm of Cresap, McCormick, and Paget, initiated in 1952, came in 7 parts, 28 chapters, and 367 recommended changes. The report suggested dividing controller Billy Carmichael's job overseeing business and finance and vastly reducing the number of individuals reporting to chancellors on each of the three campuses. At Chapel Hill the number reporting to House was decreased from fifty-six to six, providing, as the report noted, for clear lines of authority and greater efficiency. The Faculty Council had grave doubts about some of these modifications, but they were resolved in time. By June 1955 Chancellor House reported that 103 of the recommendations had been accepted and woven into the administrative structure.

These clarifications did little, however, to differentiate the duties of the consolidated university president from those of the chancellor at Chapel Hill. House again adjusted to his vexing situation with fortitude and patience. When Gray inquired about advice on handling invitations to ceremonies, such as inaugurations of presidents of other institutions, House informed him that such missives usually went directly to the chancellors at State and the Woman's College but were directed to Gray's office at Chapel Hill. Confusion arose over small and large issues. Gray and House differed at times over presidential approval of faculty appointments. The issue of fiscal control was a continuing problem.

House set forth the management dilemma in a statement responding to Gray's inquiry in November 1951. He declared that the problem was not one of "power" but rather of "function." "The chancellor cannot act as president, but the president can act as chancellor whenever he so desires," he wrote. "He has a difficult job in keeping from doing so at Chapel Hill because, being resident here, he sees immediately many more local affairs than he ever sees at Raleigh or Greensboro. . . . Time after time for 15 years in the former

William Rand Kenan, Jr., Robert House, and Gordon Gray, 1951.
(North Carolina Collection, University of North Carolina Library, Chapel Hill)

administration I observed the president function as chancellor in small matters as well as great. I say this not in adverse criticism of that great president (Graham). I say it to emphasize the exceedingly great difficulty of maintaining any distinction at all."[7]

With both the president's and the chancellor's offices housed in South Building, problems of divided authority continued throughout Gray's presidency. They were augmented by the impression that Gray did not have much confidence in House's leadership and sought to encourage him to retire.[8]

During the first decade of the post–World War II years, Bob House came to epitomize the down-home spirit transmitted by Frank Graham from the old regime. As a genial, pipe-smoking, harmonica-player elevated to the chancellorship, he never took himself too seriously and managed to charm both faculty and students. "He had the canny native wisdom of a country lad raised in the cotton bottomland of the Roanoke River valley," one friend observed. "He was unabashedly patriotic and proved his courage as a machine gun company lieutenant in the trenches of World War I."[9]

Although he had never been considered seriously as a candidate for the presidency, House labored with patience and loyalty in the second-in-command position under Graham and Gray. He was a first-honors graduate of the university and, like Senator Sam Ervin in the law and Thomas Wolfe in drama, went on to Harvard to get his graduate degree (in English). He devoted his career to the university. At the end of House's twenty-fifth year of service, Professor Albert Coates accurately pegged him as one of the significant leaders in the "magic gulf stream" of Carolina. Coates described House as "plain as an old shoe; honest as an old field pine; tough as a top sergeant; blunt as the crack of doom; impulsive to a hurt; generous to a fault; quick to fly off the handle and dangerous as an axe flying off an axehelve when he does; quick to confess he was not himself when he did though it is hard to imagine who he was, because God knows he could not be anybody else."

In describing House, Coates described himself and a whole generation of early twentieth-century scholars who grew up in the depths of the Great Depression and put the university first in all their endeavors. "Every North Carolinian worth his salt," House said of his compatriots, "was born in a panic, brought up in a depression, and buried on a debit balance."[10]

These singular Carolina personalities—including such professorial eccentrics as Horace Williams, George Coffin Taylor, Archibald Henderson, "Bully" Bernard, and "Fanny" Bradshaw—often gave way to more conventional successors; but some, like House, continued their postretirement careers in the classrooms "relating literature to life, history to current events, philosophy to facts (and) figures to folks." In many ways, especially for their students, they constituted the authentic legacy of Chapel Hill. Their inspiration could seldom be precisely measured. But it lit up the classrooms and memories of Chapel Hill.

George Coffin Taylor, the flamboyant professor of English, in writing of the 1920s, 1930s, and 1940s, recalled that at Chapel Hill "there was . . . a splendid yeast and ferment of ideas in almost all the departments. . . . History under Bob Connor and deRoulhac Hamilton was building the most distinguished of all the distinguished sections of the university. . . . Louis Round Wilson, head of our library, was fast becoming recognized as the leading university librarian in the United States. . . . The University of North Carolina was a most amazing mixture of Southern and Northern ingredients. It sprang into national fame because of the cosmopolitan groups of outstanding thinkers in their many vital contributions to the sum of knowledge."[11]

Thomas Wolfe, the novelist, speaking of Professor Horace Williams, explained how many rank-and-file youth pouring in from the North Carolina countryside viewed their exposure to the sophisticated yet down-home world beyond the red clay and sassafras. "We boys didn't know what the Old Man taught," he said, "and we didn't give a damn. He taught us to think and that was enough. He was the Hegel of the Cotton Patch."

The Eisenhower Fifties ushered in one of the golden eras of student life. One old grad remembers it as the era of "splendid formal dances in Woollen Gymnasium[;] . . . chartered buses of 'imports' from women's colleges; hayrides and parties at Hogan's Lake; convivial 'brews' at Jeff's; open stacks in the library; outdoor classes in fine weather near Polk Place; the almost luminous appearance of the old campus at sunrise and sunset; the sand-walks; the easy familiarity between undergraduates and even senior professors in an almost idyllic, secluded grove of academe."

Hugh Morton, owner of Grandfather Mountain, and Orville Campbell, publisher of the *Chapel Hill Weekly*, discovered a talented young graduate student and playmaker named Andy Griffith. They launched his show business career with a popular recording called "What It Was Was Football." Earlier Campbell had done much the same thing with the highly popular UNC football star Charlie Justice, who became the subject of the best-selling recording called "All The Way, Choo-Choo."

During the 1950s a Franklin Street bistro called the Rams Head Rath-skeller—better known as the Rat or even just Danziger's—became a favorite hangout for much of the campus. Edward ("Papa D") Danziger, an Austrian Jew who fled his homeland before World War II, ended up in Chapel Hill and opened Danziger's Old World Candy Kitchen. This coffeehouse-bakery brought a European flavor to the village. His son, Ted, added the Rat in the basement, with its pizzas, steaks, lasagna, and cold imported beer. It flourished as students, professors, and townspeople flocked to Amber Alley for the latest in good food and conversation.

The Rat became the thriving competitor to such noted Franklin Street institutions as the Porthole and Brady's. It managed to survive, along with the Carolina Coffee Shop, well beyond the World War II era.

The Gray presidency became heavily involved in the struggle over school desegregation. North Carolina's political and educational leaders strongly opposed admission of blacks to white colleges, even though the breakthrough had occurred at other southern institutions, notably the University of Virginia. By 1950 the U.S. Supreme Court was moving toward its landmark *Brown v. Board of Education* ruling. A decision by Federal Judge Johnson J. Hayes in the North Carolina middle district court in the fall of 1950 denied four black students entry to the law school at Chapel Hill. But the U.S. fourth circuit court on appeal reversed that decision.

Earlier, in 1939, the General Assembly had established a law school at North Carolina College for Negroes at Durham. North Carolina had traditionally provided more segregated higher education facilities for blacks than most southern states. As prospects for desegregation grew, Governor William Umstead and the General Assembly stepped up efforts to hold the segregation line. They made substantial grants to black institutions. Professors from Chapel Hill were assigned to organize the graduate curriculum at North Carolina College for Negroes, including new departments of pharmacy and library science. Professor Arnold King of the education department at Chapel Hill spent a year working on the project. Some $50,000 was spent for new books. [12]

These efforts could not be pursued, however, in medical education, since North Carolina had only one public medical school, at Chapel Hill. So it was not possible to provide a "separate but equal" alternative. On April 4, 1951, the trustees voted 61-14 to weigh medical students' qualifications "without regard to color or race." At the same time they reaffirmed their policy that "equal" facilities were available for law students at North Carolina College.

This modification opened the door for admission of black medical students at Chapel Hill. President Gray emphasized that the university could follow no other course. Opponents of the change called it an "opening wedge" leading to the breakdown of racial segregation. Trustee John Kerr, Jr., of

Warrenton charged the administration with "selling out" to Negroes. State representative Wayland Spruill declared it would "lead to bloodshed." Answering these charges, Major L. P. McLendon of Greensboro, author of the new policy, urged the trustees to face the issue squarely. It was not a question of what the university would like to do but what it had to do. "It is not in the character of the University of North Carolina to say we haven't got the courage to face this issue on the law of the land," he said.[13]

After the U.S. Supreme Court refused to overturn the fourth circuit court decision, the trustees followed Major McLendon's counsel. On June 6, 1951, they authorized admission of three (eventually four) black students to the law school. They were Harvey Beech of Durham, J. Kenneth Lee of Greensboro, Floyd B. McKissick of Asheville, and James Lassiter of Rocky Mount. The same kind of admission was simultaneously being authorized at the medical school, where Dudley Diggs, a thirty-year-old veteran of World War II and a premed student at North Carolina Agricultural and Technical College (A&T) at Greensboro, was enrolled for the fall term. Diggs had already been accepted by the University of Chicago and Meharry Medical College but preferred UNC, he said, "because North Carolina is my home."[14]

One of the first blacks to attend the university was Gwendolyn Harrison, who had an A.B. in history from Spelman College and a master's degree in Spanish from the University of California. A teacher at Johnson C. Smith University at Charlotte, she applied for the first 1951 summer school session after the trustees announced the new admissions policy in April. Since the summer school application form made no reference to race, Harrison was admitted to the first session, apparently by mistake, then not allowed to register. Eventually she was admitted to the second session, but only after she had filed a federal district lawsuit against the university. The trustees held an emergency session on July 16 and voted, after much controversy, to accept her application. The majority was influenced by trustee Victor Bryant's statement that he did not "think we should say we're willing to be ignorant rather than educate Negro children."[15]

In this manner the university reluctantly accepted desegregation. Despite its reputation for liberalism, it did not take the lead but trailed other state institutions in the South, among them Virginia and Louisiana. The *New York Times* declared that the university was "in a position to accept [desegregation] with grace. It has been a tower of enlightenment in the South."[16] The *Carolina Times*, a black publication of Durham, however, called President Gray a "slick lawyer" who was determined to "keep the Negroes down, but do it as quietly as possible," which "has been the way of the Old North State."[17]

Elements of segregation remained on the campus for a while. Blacks and whites sat together in the same student section at a football game on November 2, 1951. Four black students had been assigned seats in a separate section, but when one of them objected, they were allowed to move.[18] Initially black law students admitted during the summer session were housed together (separately) on the third floor of Steele Dormitory and were exempted from paying athletic fees, although they attended classes, used the library, and ate in the dining hall with white students. Chancellor House first balked at supplying student athletic passbooks to black students that autumn, saying football games were "social occasions." The Daily Tar Heel responded: "There should be no second-class students at the University of North Carolina. . . . It is regrettable that the university has used such poor strategy in a situation which would have passed with little comment had sounder judgment been used . . . Our task is not to fight grudgingly the new social situation in which we find ourselves but to make the transition as gracefully and smoothly as possible."[19]

When the law school voted to hold its annual dance in the spring of 1952, the chancellor again demurred, announcing that "no mixed social functions shall be held on the university campus." The Daily Tar Heel again protested, but the law school sponsored an all-day picnic in a state park that spring rather than a dance (which was resumed the following year). At first black students were not allowed in the university's swimming pool. One of them, Floyd McKissick, said he jumped in the pool with his clothes on one day just to be able to say that the university had an integrated pool.[20]

In February 1952 C. O. Pearson, an attorney for the National Association for the Advancement of Colored People (NAACP) in Durham, charged that UNC harassed black law students to prevent them from graduating and discouraged others from applying. He said black students received lower grades than they deserved, and some black students agreed. Law school dean Henry Brandis denied any discrimination. One of the black students, Kenneth Lee, said later that professors were not trying to discriminate but that deficiencies in their previous education made courses more difficult for blacks. An outside investigation supported the professors.[21]

Gradual acceptance of desegregation at Chapel Hill caused less stir among students than it did at South Building. Student government president Don

Fowler described the reaction of white students: "The presence of these Negroes causes so little interest that most of us are unaware they are here unless we happen to have a class with them. Nobody resents them, or if they do, they certainly don't show it."[22]

The university's most significant post–World War II project—expanding the medical school and the health affairs center—required elaborate planning and coordination. Even after the 1947 General Assembly approved funds for the four-year medical school, quick action was not possible. In 1948 trustee subcommittees began work and architects were hired. Collier Cobb, Jr., became chairman of the subcommittee on building, and trustee Victor Bryant chaired the subcommittee on staff and general policy.

The committees soon discovered that funds were not sufficient to cover increases in building costs and staffing needs. In addition, the State Medical Care Commission used some funds appropriated under the Hill-Burton Act for community hospital needs rather than the university's. By the time the 1949 General Assembly had made substitute funds available, contract awarding could not be completed until the autumn of 1950.

Planning was complex because it required coordination of both the expanded medical school and the new hospital as well as new schools of dentistry and nursing. The 1949 General Assembly appropriated funds for a 100-bed tuberculosis sanatorium as part of the new medical complex. In 1951, through the efforts of Representative John W. Umstead of the State Hospitals Board of Control, $1 million was allocated to provide care for psychiatric patients. By 1953 additional space for the basic sciences department required the addition of a south wing for MacNider Hall, matching the north wing.[23]

Simultaneously Dean Reece Berryhill began the arduous job of recruiting additional staff for the enlarged medical school and the new hospital (which was designated North Carolina Memorial Hospital by the 1951 General Assembly). After several delays the new facility opened with appropriate dedicatory ceremonies in September 1952. Former president Frank P. Graham was principal speaker.

In the autumn of the following year the Council on Medical Education and the Association of American Medical Colleges reviewed the programs of the junior and senior years, the adequacy of the faculty, the library, and the physical plant and approved certification of the four-year medical school. In 1954 for the first time since 1910, when the last class graduated from the medical department at Raleigh, all four classes, a total of 126 students, were in residence on one campus, and a new era in medical education had begun at Chapel Hill.

The campus's enhanced medical and health facilities soon created pervasive administrative problems. With numerous expanded services and functions it seemed wise to establish a division of health affairs to oversee all the departments, including the teaching hospital. Dean Berryhill, more a physician and teacher than an administrator, had initially been enthusiastic about this arrangement and, in fact, endorsed it. In 1950 Dr. Henry Toole Clark (UNC Med. '39), director of the Vanderbilt University Hospital, was named administrator. Dr. Clark, an able physician, turned out to be stronger in planning than in administration. By the same token Dr. Berryhill found it difficult to have one of his former students supervising his activities. The medical school and the hospital constituted a large part of the new Division of Health Affairs, although the School of Public Health, the School of Nursing, and the Schools of Dentistry and Pharmacy were also part of the complex. Varying views developed about how much attention should be paid to extending medical services to the people of the state and how much emphasis should be devoted to strictly on-campus teaching functions. As relations between individuals in charge of these departments worsened, the university trustees stepped in to propose a viable plan of administration. The developing pressures finally became so "overwhelmingly frustrating" that the trustees created a separate division for the medical school and the hospital in 1956.[24]

A project as important in communications as medical education was in its own field had its genesis during the early 1950s. Educational television became a reality in 1952 when the Federal Communications Commission (FCC) allocated 10 percent of all TV channels for noncommercial broadcasts. The consolidated university, with Vice President Carmichael in the lead, expressed an interest in securing one of these channels. President Gray convened a two-day conference on the subject in June 1952. The conference concluded that it was "desirable for the university to own and operate a station."

By May 11, 1953, the trustees had approved establishment of studios on the university's three campuses. Carmichael launched a successful appeal for private financial support. On September 30, 1953, the FCC awarded the university a permit to operate a noncommercial educational station on

Charlie Justice (# 22) in Kenan Stadium.
(North Carolina Collection, University of North Carolina Library, Chapel Hill)

channel 4, and President Gray announced the appointment of Robert F. Schenkkan as director.

The university bought a sixty-five-acre tract on Terrell's Mountain in Chatham County, about seven miles southwest of Chapel Hill, for the transmitter, and the station went on the air on January 8, 1955. The first presentation was a film followed by a live program of music and dancing from the Woman's College in Greensboro. The highlight, however, was live coverage of the Wake Forest-Carolina basketball game that evening, which Carolina won 95-78. The General Assembly later that year granted WUNC-TV its first state operating funds.[25]

The early 1950s marked the start of other ambitious campus expansions, among them the new School of Business Administration, which sprang out of the old School of Commerce established in 1919. William D. Carmichael, Jr., controller and vice president of the university, was the first student to receive a degree from the old department in 1921. He, along with graduate school dean W. Whatley Pierson and School of Business Administration dean Dudley D. Carroll, had much to do with launching the expansion of that branch of the university after World War II. They initiated the master of business administration degree (M.B.A.) in 1952 and pushed construction of a cluster of new buildings on Polk Place.

Carroll Hall, the central building facing Manning Hall across Polk Place, was named for Dean Carroll himself, founder and for thirty years dean of the School of Commerce. Hanes Hall, on the north side, honored the Winston-Salem family of industrialists and bankers. O. Max Gardner Hall, on the south, was named for the governor who initiated consolidation and provided funds for an annual award honoring the consolidated university member "contributing most to the welfare of the human race."

In 1953 the school established an executive development program based on similar ones at Harvard, Chicago, Columbia, and Northwestern. This brought groups of top business managers from major businesses and industries across North Carolina to the campus for an intensive six-month period of intermittent study. Dr. Willard Graham, manager of a similar course at the University of Chicago, became director.

By 1955 friends of the school had established a business school foundation, and prominent business corporations, among them Wachovia Bank and Trust Company, Burlington Industries, R. J. Reynolds, and Jefferson Standard Life Insurance Company, had endowed chairs. In 1956 Maurice W. Lee became dean, the business school had 750 undergraduate students, and 48 business leaders were enrolled in its executive development program.

The lure of Washington, which had repeatedly attracted Graham and Gray, again proved overwhelming in 1955. The death of Jane Gray in 1953, combined with the president's restlessness about academic affairs, made the invitation extended by the Eisenhower administration too inviting to resist. When Secretary of Defense Charles Wilson summoned Gray to Washington to become assistant secretary for international security affairs, Gray informed Governor Luther Hodges that he must accept this call to duty.

At a special meeting of the executive committee on June 10, 1955, Governor Hodges read a telegram from Secretary Wilson, and Gray told the committee that "the insistent requests of the national administration" had persuaded him to tender his resignation after "the severest deliberations." The executive committee, again disappointed and frustrated, voted to give Gray a six-month leave of absence. They then named J. Harris Purks, who had succeeded Logan Wilson as provost, to be acting president.

When Gray again submitted his resignation in November 1955 in a personal letter to Hodges, the trustees accepted it. Gray went on to serve as director of the Office of Defense Mobilization in 1956 and then as special assistant to President Eisenhower until the end of his term in 1961. When

Gray died in 1982 of throat cancer, his onetime assistant William C. Friday noted that "he was generous with his wealth but gave even more generously of himself." The *Chapel Hill Weekly* observed that Gray may have been overqualified for the presidency. Perhaps it would have been fairer to say that his qualifications lay in other fields.

Meanwhile, the trustees faced a major transition at a time when other campuses were challenging Chapel Hill's position as the state's capstone public institution.

WILLIAM C. FRIDAY,

STEEL UNDER VELVET,

1956–1964

One of President Gray's best decisions during his five-year tenure was the appointment of a capable young lawyer named William Clyde Friday as his executive assistant. Friday, a 1941 textile graduate of N.C. State, had become assistant dean of students at Chapel Hill immediately after graduation from the UNC law school.

Some thought Bill Friday would accompany President Graham to Washington after his appointment to the U.S. Senate in 1949. But three days before Graham left for his new job, as Friday later told the story, "we stood together at the Old Well. He [Graham] put his hand on my shoulder and said, 'It's better that you stay here.' "[1] Friday was to remain in Chapel Hill for the rest of a notable career. His rise up the administration ladder was phenomenal; less than a decade later he would become president.

Born in Raphine, Virginia, and reared in Gaston County, North Carolina, in a family of five children, Friday won the countywide declamation contest in school, became an enthusiastic baseball catcher, and dreamed of making the majors. When he finished high school in 1937, his father, who had been mayor of the small community of Dallas and who was a manufacturer of textile machinery, took him to Wake Forest in the family A-model Ford to get a $50 scholarship and enter college. The following year he transferred to N.C. State, where he became senior class president, met Ida Howell at nearby Meredith College on a blind date, and graduated with honors. By 1942 he had a new bride and an ensign's commission in the U.S. Navy. After

World War II the Fridays moved to Chapel Hill for Bill's law school studies. Following graduation in 1948, he briefly considered textiles, then, partly because Ida was pursuing her graduate studies at Chapel Hill, accepted Chancellor House's invitation to become assistant dean of students.

Friday's acceptance was fortunate both for him and the university. Quiet-spoken and steady, the young lawyer had a congenial personality and considerable steel under the velvet. Starting as an academic novice—growing up, as he put it, under the influence of Frank Graham—he became a fast learner. As Chancellor House observed in later years, many values are caught, not taught. Friday quickly caught the spirit of Chapel Hill. Modest but not timid, possessed of a mellow sense of humor and cool judgment, firm but sympathetic to the other person's point of view, and supremely generous, Friday rapidly gained the trust and respect of his peers.

At the time of Gray's resignation, the trustees' executive committee, a sometimes crusty and autocratic body, was encountering difficulties at the hands of the General Assembly. Since 1804 choosing trustees had been a legislative prerogative. Serving on the board had been viewed as a prestigious job. But the university's position as the flagship of higher education was being challenged by other institutions. During the steamy desegregation controversies of the early 1950s, the General Assembly failed to reappoint several outstanding trustees—among them Major L. P. McLendon and Mrs. Laura Cone of Greensboro, Dr. Clarence Poe of Raleigh, George M. Stephens of Asheville, Collier Cobb, Jr., of Chapel Hill, and J. G. Clark of Bladen.[2]

Thus the selection of Gray's successor came at a critical time for the trustees. By 1955 the need for higher education was growing throughout North Carolina and the South. The clamor of other state institutions for greater financial support goaded the General Assembly to establish the State Board of Higher Education (SBHE) to oversee ambitious former state teachers' and community colleges struggling for a place in the sun. The board's announced purpose was to "promote the development and operation of a sound, vigorous, progressive and consolidated system of higher education."

Initially the consolidated university trustees had supported the creation of the SBHE, viewing it as a vehicle for regulating only the nonuniversity institutions. Instead, it became their formidable rival. This rivalry developed at a time when there was growing criticism of the university's governance—its large, unwieldy board with 100 members and its domination by Chapel Hill alumni. Some saw the trustees' board as a "fifth wheel," no longer necessary if the SBHE were to be properly organized.

Immediately after acceptance of Gray's resignation on November 10, the trustees appointed a presidential search committee, while J. Harris Purks continued as acting president. In a surprise announcement at a special meeting of the trustees' executive committee on January 4, 1956, Governor Hodges, chairman of the trustees, announced that he had been requested to release Purks from the acting presidency to become head of SBHE. Hodges had also asked trustee Victor Bryant, chairman of the search committee, to prepare a report on candidates for the post of acting president. Bryant's committee recommended no one, although A. K. King noted that the possibilities were Vice President Billy Carmichael, whose doctors had suggested he slow down, graduate dean W. Whatley Pierson, who was nearing retirement age, and thirty-five-year-old Bill Friday, who had become Gray's assistant in 1951 and then secretary of the university in 1955. The board named Friday to become acting president on March 1, 1956. He plunged into his new job with vigor and skill.[3]

Meanwhile, the presidential search committee continued its search and discovered the hard facts of educational life. While the university offered $15,000 as an annual salary for the prospective president, comparable institutions paid as much as $25,000. Some potential candidates anticipated structural changes in the university system that might threaten a future president's position. Committee sentiment leaned toward a young president with potential rather than toward a seasoned educator. The executive committee in February had already directed that all administrative officers would retire on July 1 in the year after they reached sixty-five. At the same time it made provision for Chancellor House to continue his professorship in the English Department after he retired.[4]

Speculation on the presidential search continued until a special meeting of the executive committee on October 18 when Victor Bryant's committee recommended the nomination of William Clyde Friday, which secured the unanimous approval of both that body and subsequently the full board of trustees on October 26.

After he had been chosen, Friday made a personal statement to the executive committee. He acknowledged that he lacked a doctoral degree and teaching experience, and was only thirty-six years of age, factors that had concerned some search committee members. However, he had met informally with committee members and discussed his basic views about the office of president. These views and his basic principles he reiterated. He

Ida and William Friday.
(Photograph by Will Owens, University of North Carolina News Bureau,
Chapel Hill)

voiced full support for academic freedom and in a "tactful way" let it be known that pressure had been applied to have him "make certain appointments if he were elected president." He told the committee he had made no such commitments. He had spent time with the committee, he said, discussing not only the presidency but the provostship and the chancellorships, particularly at Chapel Hill. "I advised the nominating committee chairman [Bryant] that I felt it must be clearly understood that anyone invited to serve the university as its president must enter the office completely free of commitments," Friday declared, adding that it "must be understood that, within the broad policy declarations of the trustees, he has full and complete authority along with the full responsibility for the administration of the university."[5]

The executive committee, headed by Governor Luther Hodges, received these forthright statements courteously but without comment. Later at the full board meeting Chairman Bryant discussed problems facing the university; then he declared that the committee "had been impressed by Mr. Friday's integrity and fairness as he had gone about his duties as acting president. . . . In a trying time Mr. Friday has stood steadfast on all matters." The new president then received a standing ovation and made a "short and eloquent" statement of acceptance.[6]

Friday lost no time making presidential changes. At a press conference he said he would move his administrative offices from South Building to the former Institute of Government building on East Franklin Street, off the university campus, as soon as possible in order to "permit the chancellor more freedom" and provide more space for both operations. He said he would start the search for new chancellors at Chapel Hill and Greensboro and would seek higher faculty salaries, better library facilities, and more research funds. The presidency, he said pointedly, is a "full-time job" and he intended to devote his full energies to it.

Within a month President and Mrs. Friday and their two daughters moved into the old classical revival presidential mansion on East Franklin Street, the home of five previous presidents. State press reaction to his appointment was almost uniformly favorable. Commenting on Friday's age, Louis Graves, editor of the influential *Chapel Hill Weekly*, noted that six of the twelve presidents who preceded him were under forty at the time of their selection.

Friday's inauguration as third president of the consolidated university took place on May 8, 1957, in a colorful convocation at William Neal Reynolds Coliseum at Raleigh. Friday's two immediate predecessors, Frank P. Graham and Gordon Gray, were present. Also in attendance were more than 450 representatives of faculties from the three campuses, some 160 delegates from other universities and colleges, and 75 representatives of learned societies and educational organizations, along with trustees, state officials, and alumni. Chief Justice J. Wallace Winborne of the North Carolina Supreme Court administered the oath of office.

Friday was already acquainted with consolidated university administration. He realized that his first challenge involved his relations with the academic community. "I was never valedictorian of my class or Phi Beta Kappa," he said later. He recalled that a few months after he became president, he happened to be walking behind two faculty members on the Chapel Hill campus. "Unfortunately," Friday said, "I was close enough to overhear a mournful exchange as one said to the other, 'After 18 years of Frank Graham, Good Lord, look what we have now!' "

Friday's congenial personality, his insights on other people's problems, and his determination to "work collegially" won the allegiance of the academy. "He never tried to center everything in himself," one veteran faculty member said. "He assembled an able group of associates. . . . He became a past master at getting people to work together."

Friday's major assignment as his administration opened was to find chancellors for the Woman's College in Greensboro and for Chapel Hill. At Greensboro, Edward Kidder Graham, Jr., had resigned under unpleasant circumstances, and at Chapel Hill, Chancellor House was prepared for the transition after his sixty-fifth birthday. The trustees' Chapel Hill selection committee came up with a candidate who, as far as Friday was concerned, filled all the qualifications.

After World War II, among the young married couples housed in Victory Village near the site of the new medical school were Bill and Ida Friday and Bill and Grace Aycock, who became lifelong friends. Another young couple there was Terry and Margaret Rose Sanford. The young men, along with some half-dozen others who were to become university and state leaders, studied at the law school.

William Brantley Aycock was only a collateral relative of Governor Charles Brantley Aycock, but his dark, flashing eyes reflected the same vision and courage. Born at Lucama and reared in Selma (Johnston County), William Aycock finished high school in the depths of the depression, went to N.C. State College, where he was president of the student body, and received his B.S. degree in education in 1936. The next year he earned an M.A. in history at Chapel Hill, then worked briefly at Greensboro as a high school history teacher and assistant football coach (doing graduate work at Duke and Harvard during the summers). After serving as chief of project planning for the National Youth Administration, Aycock entered the U.S. Army in 1942, where he served with distinction in the infantry, emerging as a lieutenant colonel with the Silver Star for combat bravery in Europe.

Plucky but affable, sharply intelligent, and energetic, Aycock had much of Friday's geniality and common sense. In 1951 Graham had chosen this young UNC law professor to accompany him on his United Nations missions to India and Pakistan. Friday, Aycock's friend, saw in him qualities of leadership that made him the logical choice for chancellor. When he was named in 1957, Aycock said quietly of his law school classmate, "I mean to serve him well."[7]

That he served Friday and the university well over the next seven years as chancellor in a time of phenomenal postwar change can scarcely be disputed. Although Aycock was untested in administrative work, he quickly established his mettle. He did it because he was perceptive about personnel relations and understood the structure and interworkings of the university. He explained this rather candidly in a 1958 speech to the Faculty Club. "The development of this superstructure [the 'consolidated university'] leaves the executive head of this institution in the middle. He is the narrow neck in the administrative hourglass. . . . The executive head of an institution cannot provide flexibility in excess of that which is intrusted to him."[8]

It was a time of extensive long-range planning. From the outset Friday made it clear that he expected Aycock to take charge at Chapel Hill. In a letter to Aycock written on September 17, 1957, Friday declared, "In order that there be no misunderstanding as to our procedures, let me say that, from this point on, I am looking to you for the leadership in implementing the self-study of the university in Chapel Hill. I believe that the individuality of each institution should be recognized by the Consolidated Office, and this means you should be free to work with your faculty committees in setting up the study you wish to make, implementing the work that should be done, and making the decisions and recommendations that must be made."

Aycock took Friday's instructions seriously. He ordered a comprehensive self-study of the six administrative divisions of the university. It played a major part in helping absorb the some 500 additional students per year who poured into the campus over the next decade, raising enrollment from roughly 7,000 in the fall of 1957 to almost 11,000 by the fall of 1963.

Aycock confidently accepted the challenge of change. In his installation address on October 12, 1957 (University Day), he declared that the university had first obligation to accept additional students. The institution, he said, is "not only willing but eager to admit each qualified person, provided we are given resources to grow greater as we grow larger."

Under Friday and Aycock the university experienced a surge of expansion, swept up in the energies of the postwar years. Among the new projects was the Ackland Art Museum, made possible by a $1,395,000 benefaction long disputed among several universities. When he died in 1940, William Hayes Ackland, a Washington, D.C., lawyer, left a bequest to Duke University specifying that his remains be interred in the museum building with a recumbent statue on the sarcophagus. Duke's trustees declined the funds, allegedly because acceptance would threaten support by the Duke Endowment. Later in an article entitled "One Recumbent Too Many," historian Robert Durden reported that the trustees specifically objected because they felt the sarcophagi and recumbent statues of three Dukes in the Duke Memorial Chapel were enough. Ackland had named UNC and Rollins College as his second and third choices in an earlier version of his will. When Ackland's nieces and nephews sued to obtain the funds, the U.S. District Court of the District of Columbia handed down a decision in their favor that was reversed by the U.S. circuit court. The lawyers for UNC argued that Duke and UNC were "alike as two peas in a pod" in size, location, quality of institution, interest in art, and financial ability to advance its cause in the South.

After success in legal battles stretching over eighteen years, the Ackland Art Museum was built on a site on campus facing South Columbia Street and was dedicated on September 20, 1958. The building contains a marble sarcophagus beneath a recumbent statue of William Hayes Ackland.[9]

In another significant addition in 1959, the university accepted as a partial gift from the Sperry-Rand Corporation a 1103B computer valued at $2,285,000, which was installed in the new wing of Phillips Hall. This installation launched the computer age for the university with the U.S. Census Bureau purchasing time worth $700,000; other contracts were arranged with the National Science Foundation. William M. Whyburn, vice president for graduate studies and research of the consolidated university, and Professor J. Carlyle Sitterson, who had served as dean of arts and sciences and was named dean of the General College under Aycock, played leading roles in this acquisition.

Other new projects springing to life around the campus included the Joseph Palmer Knapp Building for the Institute of Government; the pharmacy building, Beard Hall; the School of Public Health building; Coker Hall for the botany department; W. M. Dey Hall for the foreign languages departments; apartments for married students; and five dormitories—Craige, Ehringhaus, Parker, Avery, and Teague. The latter occupied newly developed areas on the south campus near Kenan Stadium.

Emphasis on natural beauty, begun with the rock walls of Elisha Mitchell, the landscaping ideas of Robert Donaldson in 1843, and the arboretum developed by W. C. Coker at the turn of the century, continued in the 1950s and 1960s. In response to a proposal by Professor John Couch in 1952 the trustees approved a botanical garden on a seventy-two-acre tract of the Mason Farm property. Professor William C. Coker provided additional lands in 1953, and along with gifts from John Sprunt Hill, George Cooley, and Professor H. R. Totten, a new enterprise got under way. Other gifts, includ-

ing 103 acres of dramatic creek gorge and rhododendron bluffs from William L. Hunt, led to the appointment in 1961 of Dr. C. Ritchie Bell ('43) as
the first director of the North Carolina Botanical Gardens.[10]

A benefaction as important as the Kenan family's largesse after World War
I had its genesis after World War II when John Motley Morehead, the
eleventh member of his family to graduate from Chapel Hill, established the
Morehead Foundation. Morehead, who had been an industrialist and ambassador to Sweden, gave the university a handsome new building, located near
Graham Memorial, that incorporated a planetarium, a Copernican orrery, an
art gallery, a state dining room, and a rose garden.

An even more rewarding gift came from the foundation as the new
planetarium opened in 1950. The group's trustees founded the Morehead
scholarships, a remarkably generous endowment patterned after the Rhodes
scholarships. They initially provided $1,250 a year for four years to under-
graduates at a time when total student expenses averaged about $1,000 a
year. Trustees awarded the scholarships for merit and overall desirability,
not primarily for academic excellence. Financial need was not considered.
Robert A. Fetzer, the former head track coach and long-time director of
athletics, helped organize and directed the program. By the fall of 1958,
thirty-five scholarships were being awarded each year as Roy A. Armstrong,
former director of admissions, became director.

Morehead, who, as an undergraduate, had discovered calcium carbide
with William Kenan and Francis Venable, lived to be ninety-four and was
known as Uncle Mot to the 425 Morehead scholars he met personally before
his death in 1965. As the Morehead scholarships began in the 1950s, the
Greensboro Daily News wrote of John Motley Morehead that he had "become for North Carolina what the Medici and Borgia once were to Renaissance Florence—a patron of culture and enlightenment with few peers."[11]

The postwar years produced another successful enterprise that affected
not only Chapel Hill and the universities in central North Carolina but the
whole state and the South. As early as 1952 Dr. Howard Odum, founder of
the Institute for Research in Social Science, advocated creation of a research
institute located near the Raleigh-Durham airport. Romeo H. Guest, a graduate of Massachusetts Institute of Technology and president of a Greensboro
contracting firm, became convinced that the way to bring industry to the
South was to establish a high-technology center that would attract research
scientists. He called his project the Research Triangle. Guest thought it
should be located in the midst of the research universities at Chapel Hill,

Raleigh, and Durham. The university at Chapel Hill invited a panel of physicists from Princeton, Cornell, and Harvard to survey its Department of Physics and to make recommendations for improvement. In 1954 the panel recommended that "the opportunity should be seized to . . . build a strong center of pure physics, of physics technology and engineering physics" in the area because "the Chapel Hill-Raleigh-Durham Triangle has the potentiality to grow into the great physics center of the Southeast."

Out of these fermenting ideas sprang the Research Triangle. Early in 1955 Guest interested Governor Luther Hodges in the idea, and he became its enthusiastic advocate. Later that year Hodges appointed the Research Triangle Committee, chaired by Robert M. Hanes, the Winston-Salem banker and industrialist. By this time President Friday and his chancellors and President Hollis Edens of Duke had become involved. On Friday's recommendation George L. Simpson, Jr., a professor of sociology at Chapel Hill who was familiar with Odum's work, was named director.

The park began as a for-profit venture and failed. At Hanes's request, Archie K. Davis, chairman of the board of Wachovia Bank and Trust Company, took charge and converted the operation into a not-for-profit corporation. Working with officials of the three universities and a board of directors that included Governor Hodges, Davis spearheaded a fund-raising campaign that initially collected $1.5 million and reached $2 million by 1960.

A major part of this endeavor centered on establishment of the Research Triangle Institute, an organization devoted to high-level scientific research sponsored by government and industry. The institute opened on December 29, 1958, when George Herbert, former executive associate director of Stanford Research Institute in California, was named first president. The Atomic Energy Commission signed on with a $160,000 grant as one of the institute's earliest clients. In May, Chemstrand Corporation announced it would build a $1 million laboratory for research in chemical fibers. This was followed in October by plans for a $2.5 million laboratory for research in polymers provided by the Dreyfus Foundation.

Occupying the spacious greenbelt area among the state's major research universities, the Research Triangle moved slowly but steadily toward spectacular success. Six companies had facilities in the park by 1965, and sixteen more were opened by 1970. This number had risen to forty-three by 1986, with many of the nation's major industrial firms represented. The project thus became a priceless asset not only to the universities but to the whole state and its people—a "real park, not an industrial village." It wrought "not only a great scientific and economic revolution in central North Carolina but also a serious traffic problem."[12]

Intercollegiate athletics had already made its mark—sometimes for better, sometimes for worse—in the years before World War II. President Graham tried unsuccessfully to deemphasize rampant professionalism when it appeared in the 1930s. His successors, including Gray, Friday, and Aycock, encountered similar problems as basketball fever hit North Carolina after World War II. It began in 1946 when North Carolina State hired the popular coach Everett Case from Indiana. Case's success in producing championship teams pushed Chapel Hill to employ Frank McGuire, another colorful coach who had amassed a winning record at St. John's College in New York. Other colleges in the Atlantic Coast Conference (ACC) moved quickly to upgrade basketball as it attracted mass media attention on television.

In May 1954 the National Collegiate Athletic Association (NCAA) placed North Carolina State on probation for one year and halted its participation in the basketball championship playoffs for violating recruitment regulations. Two years later it again placed N.C. State on probation, for four years, for similar infractions.

In the meantime, UNC under coach McGuire began to produce highly talented teams, climaxed by a perfect season and the NCAA national championship in 1957. Then in January 1961 the NCAA placed the university's team on one-year probation for violating recruitment regulations. At the same time, in March 1961, evidence of a UNC athlete's participation in bribery reached Chancellor Aycock. The student was dismissed from the university "under circumstances other than honorable." After further investigation Aycock suspended another athlete who had received All-American honors that year. Simultaneously, N.C. State's new chancellor, John T. Caldwell, learned that members of State's basketball team had been involved in the briberies. Another student was dismissed, and two others were denied readmission. Rumors flooded the campuses, among them that St. Louis gamblers had threatened the lives of some players involved in point-shaving commitments. Much of the bribery activity swirled around the Dixie Classic, a popular athletic spectacle conceived by coach Case and held at N.C. State's Reynolds Coliseum over the Christmas holidays.

President Friday aired the matter before the board of trustees on May 22, 1961, after exhaustive study and conferences with Chancellors Aycock and Caldwell. Their joint recommendations were detailed and specific. Among them were a ban on player activities during the summer, restrictions on athletic grants-in-aid to two per year for athletes from outside the ACC area, and discontinuance of the Dixie Classic.

Public reaction was sharp. When trustees questioned the need for canceling the basketball tournament, Friday responded: "I will say to you . . . we have told you how we think the matter should be handled. The question, then, if you start getting into specifics, will be this: Are you ready to take over the administration of inter-collegiate athletics as a board of trustees?" Friday strongly deplored the strain on the academic reputations of the two campuses. The trustees sustained his judgment by a vote of 88-4. Two years later, representatives of the General Assembly sought to reopen the Dixie Classic, but Friday refused to change his decision.

Several years later the president and the chancellors agreed to lift restrictions on recruitment, grants-in-aid, and holiday tournaments. In the meantime in August 1961 coach McGuire, plagued by athletic scandal, left the university to become coach of the Philadelphia Warriors, a professional team. His replacement was a little-known assistant named Dean Smith.[13]

In 1959 the arrival of several military test pilots at the Morehead Planetarium to train for important projects in the U.S. government's burgeoning space program caused hardly a stir. The young astronauts, among them Donald "Deke" Slayton, Wally Schirra, Alan Shepard, Scott Carpenter, John Glenn, and Gordon Cooper, spent three or four days at a time in Chapel Hill. Anthony Jenzano, the planetarium's director, built them a mock space capsule in the big star room. "It was not boring at all," Schirra said later of the planetarium study sessions. "Tony made it interesting for us." The astronauts went on, in the words of one reporter, "from Carolina blue to the wild blue yonder." Many of them returned to Chapel Hill years later to help celebrate the Morehead Planetarium's fortieth birthday.[14]

Newly elected president John F. Kennedy visited Chapel Hill on University Day (October 12) 1961 and spoke to a large crowd in Kenan Stadium. Present for the occasion, along with President Friday and Chancellor Aycock, was North Carolina's symbol of new generational politics, Terry Sanford, the young governor who also served as chairman of the university trustees. In the 1960 election Sanford supported Kennedy over the opposition of old-line North Carolina Democrats. He also supported a vast enrichment program for public education, bringing changes even more pronounced than Governor Gardner's three decades earlier.

Governor Terry Sanford, William Friday, President John F. Kennedy, and
William Aycock, University Day, October 12, 1961.
(North Carolina Collection, University of North Carolina Library, Chapel Hill)

In 1962 the Governor's Commission for Education Beyond the High School—known as the Carlyle Commission, for its chairman, Winston-Salem lawyer Irving Carlyle—produced a comprehensive program for overhauling state-supported higher education. The commission responded to the rising number of college-age students stemming from the postwar baby boom. It recommended a statewide community college system, at the same time transforming public junior colleges in Charlotte, Wilmington, and Asheville into four-year undergraduate institutions.

Implicit in the commission's recommendations was the belief that the university should break out of its regional shell and provide an enlarged umbrella for institutions across North Carolina. President Friday and the trustees recognized the need for expanding the university's outreach. They also felt the pressure of the SBHE, which had begun, they believed, as a coordinating and advisory agency but was rapidly flexing its supervisory muscles. As early as 1958 the trustees balked when the SBHE sought to curb additional married student housing at North Carolina State, calling this "interference with the internal affairs" of the university. The trustees feared the SBHE would place the consolidated university in the same category as other state-managed colleges, reducing its appropriations and homogenizing its quality. In a

September 26, 1962, speech at Goldsboro, L. P. McLendon, SBHE chairman, attacked President Friday and East Carolina College president Leo Jenkins as part of a small group "grasping for more control of higher education."[15]

Challenged by the needs and alarmed by the SBHE threat, the university trustees on July 23, 1962, appointed a study committee under the chairmanship of Thomas J. Pearsall of Rocky Mount. The committee conducted exhaustive research, including visits to campuses at Charlotte, Asheville, and Wilmington and a special subcommittee trip to inspect the newly formed multicampus public education system at the University of California. From this study came a comprehensive plan to enlarge and reshape the university system.

The most revolutionary proposal called for expanding university supervision initially to Charlotte, Asheville, and Wilmington as these former community colleges met requisite standards. The committee recommended that all campuses (including the Woman's College) be coeducational and that a degree-granting program in the liberal arts be restored to N.C. State College at Raleigh. Women would be admitted in the freshman year at Raleigh and Chapel Hill. Under these changes the old allocation of functions, as conceived by the architects of the 1930s consolidation, would be drastically altered, not always for the better.

One recommendation created the most furor. It proposed new names for the three campuses. The committee contended that distinctive names for each campus unit hindered full development of a "spirit of unity and common purpose." The names proposed for two of the institutions—the University of North Carolina at Chapel Hill and the University of North Carolina at Greensboro—generated little initial opposition. But trying to meet objections of North Carolina State officials and alumni against being called the University of North Carolina at Raleigh resulted in a compromise that "evoked both ridicule and anger": "North Carolina State of the University of North Carolina at Raleigh." Eventually, in 1965, the Raleigh campus became North Carolina State University at Raleigh, but not without arousing deep feelings.[16]

Meanwhile, the 1963 General Assembly approved the Pearsall committee's overall proposals. However, it added two checks on the trustees. Any plan for adding a new campus must be approved by the SBHE and would be subject to "adequate financial support" from the legislature itself. These stipulations kept alive the controversy between the trustees and the SBHE. It was not to be quieted for another half-dozen years.

One important provision of the 1963 legislative overhaul explicitly made the university the only state-supported institution granting the doctorate. After 1945, separate graduate schools had emerged on the three campuses, but policy-making power was retained in an all-university graduate executive council. Various graduate programs were officially assigned to each campus. Chapel Hill retained graduate programs focused on humanities and liberal arts as well as the professional schools. Greensboro's graduate programs emphasized home economics and nursing. North Carolina State majored in technological education with emphasis on applied sciences, while Chapel Hill retained strong departments in physical and biological sciences and mathematics.

Events moved quickly after 1963, and three more campuses were added to the system. On trustee initiative Charlotte College became the University of North Carolina at Charlotte on July 1, 1965. The old Asheville-Biltmore College and Wilmington College came under the umbrella in 1969. Meanwhile, trustees and alumni of other state-supported colleges, the former teacher-education institutions, began to fear for their own survival. In February 1965 East Carolina College, under President Leo Jenkins, asked the SBHE to establish a two-year medical school at Greenville. By 1966 East Carolina College, Western Carolina College, and Appalachian State Teachers College petitioned to become "regional universities." The SBHE launched elaborate studies on this subject.

Once the path to university status had been cleared by Charlotte, political forces across the state guaranteed that other institutions would not be denied membership in the "university club." North Carolina, as one observer put it, had embarked on a program to create a system of "instant universities." The matter became a source of wry humor as well as alarm. During the late 1960s the General Assembly gave the designation *university* to nine other state colleges, naming them regional universities and granting all the authority to confer master's degrees and to provide extension service.

This demeaning of the label *university* appalled many at Chapel Hill and elsewhere. Efficient management of more than a dozen ambitious universities became an increasingly contentious issue and ultimately brought on the decision to restructure the university system.

Largely because of its liberal management, the university at Chapel Hill did not feel the rumblings of student unrest as quickly or as sharply as other campuses in the early 1960s. The lunch counter sit-ins launched by A&T

students at Greensboro in February 1, 1960, spread across the nation. Some observers thought Chapel Hill was "smug and self-righteous and so proud of the past that it has not really kept pace with the current situation. It has been . . . willing to live on the moral capital of men like Odum and Graham."[17]

The first noticeable civil rights demonstrations began in the town of Chapel Hill during the spring of 1963—simultaneous with the start of higher education restructuring and the enactment of the Speaker Ban Law by the General Assembly. In April John Dunne and Pat Cusic, two students who called themselves the Student Peace Union, picketed the College Cafe on Franklin Street with no appreciable results. By May a Committee for Open Business (COB) had been organized with the objective of desegregating all business establishments. During the spring and summer COB began holding regular marches, and on May 25 some 350 people participated in one demonstration. Some businesses opened their doors to blacks, but others remained segregated. In June COB tried, without success, to persuade the Chapel Hill board of aldermen to pass a public accommodations ordinance. The first Chapel Hill sit-in occurred with both black and white participation at the Chapel Hill Merchants Association office, where many were arrested and were later found guilty of trespass.

As opposing forces became more adamant, the Chapel Hill Freedom Committee, a more militant group, replaced COB. This new group gained broader community support, including students and professors from UNC and Duke, many nonwhite students, and several ministers, among them the Reverend Charles Jones of the Community Church of Chapel Hill. By December 1963 the sit-ins had become more pervasive. Police arrested more than 150 demonstrators before the Christmas break. In January 1964 violence occurred, and the Chapel Hill board of aldermen again rejected a public accommodations ordinance. Simultaneously the Congress of Racial Equality (CORE), led by James Farmer, announced that the town of Chapel Hill would be given a February 1, 1964, deadline to integrate. When the deadline passed without action, there were massive demonstrations in Chapel Hill. They included sit-downs on major highways around the town. Hundreds of protesters were arrested.

During this period when many students and faculty members were involved, no disorders took place on the campus itself. Chancellor Aycock, a keen lawyer, made it clear that he intended to enforce the law; however, he also said he would not interfere with any peaceful protesters. Some students came before the student honor court "for ungentlemanly conduct." None was disciplined, for which the honor court received some criticism from civil authorities.[18]

Civil rights activists urged the university not to do business with firms practicing segregation. Aycock replied that it "would be unwise to attempt to use the economic power of a state-supported institution to bring about social change. . . . The university will not knowingly make arrangements for public accommodations which would result in discrimination of our students, faculty, administration or guests. On the other hand, the university will not attempt a policy of boycotting businesses solely because they are not completely integrated in their service to the general public."[19] The disturbances continued until Congress passed the Civil Rights Act in June 1964. Then all places picketed by the freedom committee were opened to the public, and the demonstrations ceased.

Meanwhile, the civil rights upheaval had major repercussions around the state. On the last day of the 1963 General Assembly the legislature passed a controversial visiting speakers law that limited free speech on the campus and threatened the university's accreditation.

THE SPEAKER BAN LAW,

1963–1968

When the General Assembly enacted what came to be known as the Speaker Ban Law of June 1963, the university confronted the most serious attack on academic freedom since the antievolution fight of 1925. The statute itself was patterned after a law recently passed in Ohio. It denied speaking privileges on state-supported campuses to any person who "is a known member of the Communist Party" or "is known to advocate the overthrow of the Constitution of the United States" or "has pleaded the Fifth Amendment . . . with respect to Communist or subversive connections or activities." The law plainly placed restrictions on freedom of speech, in violation of the First Amendment. It was enacted in the closing hours of the session without public hearings or the knowledge of education leaders. Introduced in the House on June 25, it was immediately passed and sent to the Senate, which also passed it on the same day—a near record in parliamentary dispatch. Chancellor Aycock's wife, Grace, heard the news on the radio and notified her husband, who got in touch with President Friday, who immediately left his Chapel Hill office for Raleigh. He was too late. The bill had already been sent to the enrolling office. Efforts to have it returned proved futile as the General Assembly rolled toward adjournment the next day.

Once enacted, the law proved exceedingly difficult to amend or repeal. Anti-Communist hysteria combined with civil rights furor, and student unrest on college campuses became a powerful force. But, in fact, enactment of the law had more to do with racial policy than with political doctrine.

Students from N.C. State and Shaw University triggered the speaker ban legislation when they staged antisegregation demonstrations at the 'state legislative building and Raleigh's racially segregated Sir Walter Hotel, where many legislators roomed. "It was a terrible time," one of the authors of the bill, the veteran secretary of state Thad Eure, explained later. "They [the demonstrators] blocked the doorways and members of the General Assembly could hardly get in their rooms. The whole situation made the members mad as hell. . . . It is absolutely correct to say that the sit-ins were partly the motivation behind the [speaker ban] bill."[1]

But Chapel Hill's reputation as a liberal campus, dating from the Chase-Graham years, also influenced the legislation. State senator Robert Morgan ('48), a chief sponsor of the bill and later chairman of the board of East Carolina University trustees, argued that the frequent appearance of "radical" speakers at the university inspired the law. He listed speakers identified with such organizations as the Young Communist League, the Karl Marx Study Group, and the Chapel Hill Progressive Labor Club. He thought the university had been slow to respond to charges by the Chapel Hill chapter of the American Legion that certain speakers on the campus had criminal connections with radicals. The General Assembly, Morgan said, was "weary of waiting for an indication or acknowledgement that the problem complained of existed."[2]

As Friday and Aycock studied the statute, they realized that it was not only a grave infringement on free speech; it also would be virtually impossible to administer fairly. Aycock called the law "an insult" and "the sloppiest bit of legislation I have ever witnessed, . . . so full of ambiguities that even the author couldn't possibly explain what it means." In an analysis presented to the executive committee and later to the full Board of Trustees, Aycock documented its vagueness. "What is meant by a known member of the Communist Party?" he asked. "Known by what means?" And "Does it include overthrow by peaceful means with respect to any person using the facilities of the campus or only to invited guests? If such visitors are proscribed from speaking on the campus, why aren't they proscribed from speaking elsewhere—from a church pulpit or at a political meeting?"

After discussing the law at length at its July 8 meeting the executive committee adopted a resolution offered by Virginia Lathrop that the board "take appropriate steps to endeavor to eliminate this restriction upon academic freedom." Then, at their full board meeting on October 28, 1963, the trustees heard a similar exhaustive analysis. Chancellor John Caldwell explained how the act had already proved embarrassing at N.C. State in dealing with scholars invited to lecture on campus. President Friday declared that "already the exclusion, by law, of vital sources of knowledge from our university has begun." The standing of the university among world scholars, he said, has been damaged. Even more damaging, he added, is the implication that Communist influence exists on the state's campuses, which is untrue. The board passed a resolution deploring the legislation and appointed a committee to find ways of removing "this impairment of intellectual freedom and pre-emption of the authority and prerogatives of the board of trustees."[3]

But even as the board aroused itself to combat, many of its members recognized the law's emotional and political appeal. Governor Terry Sanford, board chairman, sensed its political potential, especially in the upcoming election year when his anointed gubernatorial choice, Judge L. Richardson Preyer, had strong opposition from racial moderate Judge Dan K. Moore and segregationist Professor Beverly Lake. Some observers thought Sanford delayed action on fighting the bill until after the Democratic primary in the spring of 1964. Sanford waited until October 21, 1964, to appoint a special trustees' study committee, chaired by William Medford. In the meantime the Moore-Lake forces combined to defeat the liberal candidate, Judge Preyer, in the Democratic primaries, and Moore went on to win the governorship in November.

On April 25, 1965, the Medford committee reported to the board that "despite a clear preference for outright repeal" the committee felt that amendment of the Speaker Ban Law was "a more practical objective to pursue." A number of amendments were introduced in the 1965 General Assembly, but none made headway.

In the meantime a representative of the Southern Association of Colleges and Schools informed the legislature that the accreditation of all state-supported colleges and universities in North Carolina might be jeopardized by the Speaker Ban Law. This annoyed some legislators, who suggested that the association was a foreign corporation unlawfully doing business in North Carolina. "A lot of people strongly feel that loss of accreditation would not mean too much and would be far more preferable than subjecting our young people to the influence of Communist speakers," said Representative Carson Gregory of Harnett County.[4]

While it took no action to amend or repeal, the 1965 General Assembly, on the advice of Governor Moore, did authorize a nine-member commission to study the law. The new commission, chaired by Representative David Britt of Fairmont, held hearings in September and heard testimony from speakers expounding a wide range of views. By late October President Friday reported that the university had been notified to appear before the executive council of the Southern Association of Colleges and Schools in Richmond on November 28.

This news coincided with the Britt commission's recommendation that the Speaker Ban Law be amended to vest power in the trustees of the institutions affected. The commission also reported that "in more than a quarter century fewer than a dozen speakers from among the thousands who have appeared [during the period 1937–1965] were specifically mentioned as extremists and not all of these were alleged to be Communists." The committee recommended that Governor Moore call a special legislative session to make changes in the law. Governor Moore called the session on November 12, 1965, and it adopted the Britt commission recommendations, on the advice of the governor.[5]

Some observers thought this would end the matter, but they were wrong. The fight had only begun. The new regulations left the door open for controversial visiting speakers, but only if their visits were "infrequent" and if the boards of trustees chose to defy the established opinion of the General Assembly.

Some called the revised policy the Little Speaker Ban. Only a few months later an organization called Students for a Democratic Society issued an invitation to two persons to speak at Chapel Hill who fell in the proscribed categories. At the trustees' executive committee meeting on January 28, 1966, President Friday informed members about the invitations and called on the newly appointed chancellor Paul Frederick Sharp, who had replaced the retiring chancellor William Aycock, to provide details. Sharp reported that he felt he could not deny permits for the two invitees, Herbert Aptheker and Frank Wilkinson; one was a well-known Marxist, and the other had taken the Fifth Amendment in connection with his opposition to the House Un-American Activities Committee.

Governor Moore, chairman of the board, had previously expressed his opposition to visiting Communist speakers. Since he left the meeting before the chancellor's recommendations, the committee adjourned in order to give the matter further study. When word spread that the speakers' invitations might be withdrawn, it evoked great excitement. Several groups asked to be heard in support of the invitations when the committee reconvened on February 7, 1966. Among them were the Faculty Advisory Committee, the president of the student body, and a group of young faculty members. Other groups also prepared resolutions, including some at Greensboro, Charlotte, and Raleigh.

At the meeting Governor Moore reiterated his position that, while he did not believe the law was necessary, he would not push for its repeal. "The Speaker Ban issue has become a symbol of resistance to Communists in North Carolina," he said. "It is our considered opinion that the present General Assembly would not be receptive . . . to any move to repeal this or to substantially amend it."

President Friday and his staff sought to find a compromise position in the widening breach, but they failed. In the end the board instructed the president and the chancellor to deny speaking privileges to Herbert Aptheker and Frank Wilkinson. During the deliberations of the full board on February 28, Paul Dickson III, president of the student body and an Air Force veteran of Vietnam, made an eloquent statement against the law and the proposed regulations. He declared that they "raise unnecessary constitutional risks for the university—risks that it does not have to take," since they are forms of prior censorship. He quoted U.S. senator Sam J. Ervin, who said that "censorship by requirement of official approval or license in advance for speaking or publishing has been condemned frequently by the courts."[6]

By this time Dickson and the Students for a Democratic Society had been joined by other student leaders, including the chairman of the Carolina Forum (George Nicholson, Jr.) and the editor of the *Daily Tar Heel* (Ernest McCrary). These students formed the Committee for Free Inquiry, which held a mass meeting at Memorial Hall and adopted a statement of principle and policy on campus speakers. More than 1,000 students marched down Franklin Street to deliver the document to President Friday's house.

The students again sought approval for the speakers from the chancellor's office. Although approval was denied, the speakers came anyway. Frank Wilkinson spoke off campus at Hillel House on March 2, 1966. A week later the students made plans for Herbert Aptheker to speak near the Confederate monument at McCorkle Place. But when campus police officer Arthur Beaumont warned that Aptheker would be subject to arrest, the assemblage moved off campus, just beyond what the *Daily Tar Heel* called Dan Moore's Wall on Franklin Street. With some 1,500 in the audience Aptheker then spoke, mostly about the Vietnam War. The audience, according to the *Greensboro Daily News* the next day, "received his short address in good-humored, almost festive mood. They cheered, clapped hands and booed a

Dan Moore's wall, Paul Dickson, and Frank Wilkinson, 1966.
(North Carolina Collection, University of North Carolina Library, Chapel Hill)

little bit too. It was, in fact, a splendid day for celebrating a Communist on campus. Sunny, springlike and almost warm." In an editorial on March 16 the *Charlotte Observer* sounded a more somber note: "Few words or pictures have been more humiliating for The University of North Carolina than the photograph of a banned speaker talking to students across a campus wall. A university cannot wall out ideas; a picture of one compelled to try was not edifying."

Paul Dickson and other students joined Aptheker and Wilkinson in filing a complaint against the Speaker Ban Law in U.S. federal court. McNeill Smith ('38), a prominent Greensboro attorney, agreed to handle the case without a fee. On February 20, 1968, a three-judge panel (Judge Clement F. Haynsworth, Jr., of the U.S. fourth circuit court, Chief Judge Edwin Stanley of the U.S. middle district court, and Judge Algernon L. Butler of the U.S. eastern district court) ruled against the Speaker Ban Law. The panel found the state statute and university regulations aimed at controlling speakers too vague to be enforceable and declared them null and void.

A few days later Governor Moore announced that the state would not appeal the decision. And so, after almost five years of controversy, the last chapter was closed. Like the antagonists in the antievolution battle of the 1920s, most of the principals were thoroughly weary and mostly relieved that the matter had been settled. University officials, many of them caught in the middle, were gladdest of all. President Friday and Chancellor Sitterson, both strong opponents, felt they could not override the action of the trustees. Both ended up as defendants in the lawsuit. President Friday said he regretted the "cost, time, energy and creative leadership" expended on the controversy but hoped "we have learned . . . that in considering legislation affecting the constitutional rights of citizens all affected parties should be heard."

The students themselves turned out to be the unquenchable force in abolishing the Speaker Ban Law. McNeill Smith, their attorney, complimented them for not resorting to sit-ins or direct action by demonstrations but by coming to the courts. "The dragon didn't just curl up and die," he said. "St. George slayed it. These students were St. George."[7]

The painful fight over the Speaker Ban Law coincided with major shifts in university leadership. In September 1963 Aycock announced his impending resignation as chancellor, following a schedule he had in mind when he took the position in 1957. "I had never intended to stay in the chancellorship beyond five or six years," he said, indicating he would return to his teaching duties at the law school.

Aycock's regime, which continued until his successor was named the following summer, had been marked by sturdy leadership in difficult areas. The chancellor's keen legal mind became an invaluable asset in the speaker ban fight. He presided over a successful long-range planning program and effective reorganization of administrative procedures, especially in the area of health affairs.

Aycock's successor, Paul Frederick Sharp, who was president of Hiram College in Ohio, had a national reputation as a "brilliant, dedicated and successful educator," President Friday declared in announcing his selection on June 17, 1964. A history professor who had taught at the University of Minnesota, Iowa State, and Wisconsin; a Guggenheim Fellow; and a Fulbright lecturer in Australia, Sharp, at age forty-six, appeared scholarly, affable, and thoroughly qualified. Being an outsider, he did not foresee the role he was destined to play.

In the beginning Sharp's administration was closely involved in the continuing furor over the Speaker Ban Law. He lost no time staking himself out as opposed to strictures on academic freedom. In an October 1965 University Day ceremony honoring him as new chancellor, he emphasized that without political independence no university can achieve greatness. Immediately after his arrival in the fall of 1964 Sharp rescinded an unpublicized regulation that white and black students would not be assigned to room together. "It was not a difficult decision to make," he said later. "It was a clear-cut issue; we took the position that any university worthy of the name must not follow a rule which discriminates against any student on the basis of race."[8]

Shortly after his arrival Sharp undertook to reorganize the administrative offices, bringing academic affairs and health affairs under one director. For this purpose he named Professor J. Carlyle Sitterson, then dean of the College of Arts and Sciences, as vice chancellor of the university. Sharp turned out to be popular among staff and students during his first year, but there were signs that he was unhappy over the multicampus organization of the university system and the shadow that the president's office cast at Chapel Hill. In December 1965, barely fifteen months after his arrival, Sharp indicated he had decided to resign and accept the presidency of Drake University at Des Moines, Iowa.

In a letter to President Friday, Sharp expressed his regret at leaving. He also voiced concern over the relationship between the consolidated office and the Chapel Hill chancellorship. He specified "the numerous and almost constant ambiguities, confusions and embarrassments surrounding the chancellor's role on this campus." He quoted a report from the Southern Association of Colleges and Schools saying the relationship is "somewhat disadvantageous."

Sharp's feelings reflected the built-in difficulties earlier chancellors had felt. But circumstances surrounding his sudden decision to resign led Friday and the trustees to conclude that other factors played a larger role in his action. At the trustees' executive committee session where he came, at Friday's invitation, to discuss his departure, Sharp revealed that he had been offered the Drake presidency earlier, shortly after he came to Chapel Hill, but had turned it down. "I felt I had an obligation to the university," he said, "and I told them I could not leave at that time. I felt I needed to remain until the issue [the speaker ban controversy] was settled."[9]

Since the Drake presidency remained open after Sharp first refused it, the trustees concluded that the chancellor had continued to negotiate with its board in the interim. Rather than agreeing that the chancellor should remain at Chapel Hill until July 1, 1966, the trustees made his resignation effective February 15, 1966. Sharp went on to serve as chief executive at Drake, moving in 1971 to the presidency of the University of Oklahoma.

When Vice Chancellor Carlyle Sitterson was named acting chancellor and later appointed as Sharp's successor, he expressed confidence in the university's administrative structure. "The administrative head of this campus is a Number 2 position," he said. "Some people work well in that situation and some don't." Chancellor Sitterson, a long-time member of the faculty, immediately addressed the serious controversies swirling around the Speaker Ban Law and other student unrest of the late 1960s.

STUDENT UNREST

AND CONSOLIDATION,

1966-1972

When several hundred members of the last pre–World War II class (1941) returned to Chapel Hill for their twenty-fifth reunion in June 1966, they were surprised by the burgeoning growth of the place. "Remember the lovely woods behind and beyond [Kenan] stadium?" Martha Clampitt Mc-Kay wrote in a special edition of the *Daily Tar Heel*. "The red earth there has been opened up and spewed forth six men's dorms, a glass and concrete cafeteria, tennis courts, a new baseball field . . . row upon row of apartments for married students and literally acres of asphalt of parking lots. . . . [The new south campus] is a complex of buildings amid a sea of Hondas, where before long at least half the student population will be living."

If the physical dimensions, and center of gravity, of the university had been changing since World War II, so had the attitudes and lifestyles of faculty and students. From the postwar conformities of the Eisenhower Fifties the nation and the university moved into the turbulent John F. Kennedy–Lyndon Johnson Sixties. The civil rights sit-ins, which first erupted at a Woolworth's lunch counter in nearby Greensboro, had reverberated in the desegregation marches of downtown Chapel Hill, culminating in the opening of all public facilities under the Civil Rights Act of 1964.

The following year the university embarked on an experimental college program, springing largely from the dissatisfaction of students with "boring classes and sermon-like lectures." Students organized voluntary, freewheeling classes, with the help of interested faculty members, offering unconventional courses with such titles as Science from Art to Bomb, Parapsychology, and Attempts at Comparative Mythology. The "college" drew 500 applicants of which 280 actively participated and about 62 percent finished the first year.[1]

The more informal, counterculture lifestyles prevailed both inside and outside the classrooms. Students wouldn't be "caught dead at a formal dance." The big prom weekends, formerly dominated by German Club dances, consisted of concerts by groups like the Supremes and myriad small, or not so small, combo parties. "A simply mad, mad time is had by all on Jubilee weekend," McKay wrote. "An outdoor concert on that weekend turns the mall between South Building and the [Wilson] Library into a sea of swinging cats. Holy Administration! It's great."

The lighter side of campus lifestyle changes gave way to a somber note as the era of peaceful, nonviolent demonstrations culminated in the assassination of Martin Luther King, Jr. In April 1968 the Black Student Movement (BSM) asked all black university employees to boycott their jobs. About 90 percent failed to show up, closing all except one dining hall.

Newly installed chancellor Carlyle Sitterson, a respected history professor, a native Tar Heel, and a Chapel Hill graduate, had already been bloodied in the speaker ban controversy. He and President Friday confronted aroused student activism and civil rights frustrations and found them fraught with difficulties.

Among lifestyle changes was the tendency of more and more of the nearly 16,000 students (only 6,000 of whom lived in dormitories) not to use campus dining halls. This augmented financial troubles for the food services. Failure to provide better menus and more attractive, up-to-date facilities played a part in the emerging controversy. When the BSM began demanding black studies programs and better salaries and working conditions for black workers, the food services, already running a deficit, faced an impasse. By December 1968 the BSM presented Chancellor Sitterson with twenty-three demands covering concerns for black student and dining hall workers. In response, the chancellor agreed to some of the demands but rejected others.

In the meantime similar controversies assailed other North Carolina campuses as a new governor, Robert W. Scott, Kerr's son, succeeded Dan K. Moore as chairman of the university trustees. Black students occupied the administration offices at A&T at Greensboro and refused to leave until their requests were granted. Similar confrontations occurred at Duke University. In February Chancellor Sitterson met with BSM leaders, but they reached no binding agreement.

Then the dining hall workers went on a prolonged strike. About 100 did not report for work, and only Lenoir Hall remained open. Strike supporters tried to disrupt food services by what they called a stall-in—going through the lines slowly, taking a glass of water, and sitting one at a table. This annoyed the student clientele. Some scuffling occurred and several participants were slightly injured. BSM members began turning over tables. They set up a soul food center in nearby Manning Hall, recently vacated by the law school and about to be renovated.

After Friday and Sitterson met with Governor Scott on March 5, 1969, the governor decided, against their advice, that a show of force was necessary. Scott released a twelve-point statement setting forth procedures to follow if attempts were made to occupy state-owned buildings. He ordered four National Guard units to assemble in Durham as a "precautionary measure" and sent five squads of highway patrolmen to Lenoir Hall with orders to reopen it. He directed that Manning Hall be cleared and that students responsible for the table-turning episode be arrested. Instead of giving the arrest warrants to highway patrolmen, Police Chief William Blake went into Manning Hall alone without a weapon and asked that the building be vacated. On the advice of Howard Fuller, one of the nonstudent black activists, it was cleared before the arrival of highway patrolmen.

University officials remained at odds with Governor Scott about use of highway patrolmen on campus. When a small group of student leaders met with the trustees' executive committee in Raleigh on March 14, 1969, President Friday noted that no confrontation, riot, fire, or student strike had taken place on the Chapel Hill campus. He commended the students for their restraint but pledged to enforce the law. The committee passed a resolution commending Friday and his associates and praising the efforts of Chairman Scott, whereupon the governor asked that his five-page statement be included in the record. The statement criticized university officials for their continued "failure to take . . . positive action."

In addressing students at Memorial Hall the following day, Chancellor Sitterson praised them for their behavior and expressed a "deep sense of sadness" over the presence of outside police on the campus. He acknowledged that auditors had found 168 cases of overtime wages due workers since February 1968 and promised that further investigation would proceed.

A few days later state senator Ralph Scott, an uncle of the governor, introduced a bill in the state Senate for an immediate 10 percent raise for all state nonacademic employees. "They've been promised a lot they've never gotten," the senator said. "They need some concrete results to get back to work." On that same day highway patrolmen began withdrawing from the campus. The food services director, George W. Prillaman, was reassigned to the accounting department. The food workers' controversy began to ease.

On March 20, 1969, Governor Scott met with three strike leaders and their lawyers and agreed that the demanded salary raises were just. Meanwhile students on the campus made plans to storm South Building and occupy it if the strike remained unsettled. More than 1,000 people had gathered in the central campus when a telephone call from Raleigh reported an agreement between the governor and the food workers' lawyer. Governor Scott announced the pay raises and said he had been assured that the strikers, about 110 of them, would return to work.[2]

After the crisis subsided, the trustees studied the rules of student and faculty discipline and overhauled the university code. The new code amendments redefined disruptive behavior and reassigned responsibilities for handling it. The board completed its revisions in October 1970 as turmoil over violence at Kent State and the Vietnam War revived campus tensions.

Frustrations over President Nixon's failure to end the Vietnam War in the fall of 1969 led to withdrawal of students from classes and to mass campus demonstrations. Thousands of students gathered to hear an address by Jack Newfield, associate editor of the *Village Voice*, against the war and the president's policies. The audience included many university officials and prominent faculty members. Class boycotts became significant in the spring of 1970 when President Nixon sent troops into Cambodia. This coincided with the confrontation of students and national guardsmen at Kent State, in which four students were killed, arousing protests across the country.

Following this outbreak, some graduate teaching assistants refused to meet their classes. They were joined by 2,000 students who marched on South Building, chanting "On strike, shut it down." The next day ninety-two Morehead scholars signed a petition supporting the strikers. Student body president Tom Bello urged students to continue to strike but to remain nonviolent. Students urged faculty members to join their protests, and some did. The situation grew tense and seemed to be slipping out of hand.

On May 7, 1970, some 4,000 students gathered outside a faculty meeting at Hill Hall to express their concern. The faculty passed a resolution reaffirming the freedom of students to be assessed only on their classroom performances and academic criteria. It permitted flexibility in grading and delays in finishing course requirements as well as rights of appeal.

When Governor Scott endorsed President Nixon's action in Cambodia, thousands of students marched on Raleigh chanting "Peace Now." The governor did not back down, although he held a conference with students at the state capitol. A group of about seventy-five students held an hour-long sit-in at South Building on May 11 to protest the university's disruption policy. Outside at a teach-in other students listened to several professors discuss the war. Students left the chancellor's office voluntarily after making their protests.

Class attendance during the period of disruption was down about 50 percent. More than 700 students and faculty went to Washington to lobby the state's congressional delegation on Vietnam. Groups of young people held extended sessions with Tar Heel congressmen. Professor John Dixon of the university's Department of Religion told the lawmakers, "These are our children. They are your children. They are the children of your neighbors. Their purpose is a deeply patriotic faith in the nation."[3]

Student activism at Chapel Hill and other campuses generated divided opinion across North Carolina. President Friday issued several statements saying that none of the campuses of the university system would be closed. None was closed, but the teaching process was sharply curtailed. These widespread protests had their effect in convincing politicians and citizens that campus discontent was not confined to the radical fringe.[4]

At a trustees' meeting on May 25, 1970, President Friday presented a detailed account of student unrest, revealing that he and several other university presidents had been invited to the White House to discuss the national crisis. He declared that few students were intent on disregarding the law, destroying property, or provoking violence. He asserted that the "university is going to remain open and the laws of the state will be enforced."

Governor Scott endorsed Friday's statement, in contrast to his action a year earlier when university administrators were at odds with him over the food workers' strike. The governor praised university officials for their devotion and diligence and congratulated them for keeping the doors of the university open "during this crucial period."

When the university reopened in the fall of 1970, interest seemed to have shifted to other issues. As the draft ended, there were no further strikes or

Carlyle Sitterson, William Aycock, Robert House (playing his harmonica),
and Ferebee Taylor.
(North Carolina Collection, University of North Carolina Library, Chapel Hill)

classroom disruptions. By the end of the 1970–71 academic year Friday declared that "there has been a perceptible change in the student community." The trustee disruption policy was invoked only once during the period of unrest. It was not included in the code adopted by the new Board of Governors in 1972.[5]

Overall, the university weathered the turmoil of the 1960s better than many of its neighbors. Student unrest exploded at Chapel Hill, as it did on most campuses. But there were no deaths and there was minimum violence, even during the dark days of the food workers' strike. In part, this relative calm stemmed from good fortune. But enlightened leadership encouraging student participation in decision making was also responsible. Student self-government as a philosophical idea got its start under President Battle in the late nineteenth century. Edward Kidder Graham gave it heavy emphasis. Then it flowered during the Harry Chase and Frank Graham regimes and was never deemphasized during the post–World War II years under Chancellor House and his successors.

Likewise the university continued to upgrade its faculty, starting with the

Mary Lily Kenan Flagler Bingham bequest establishing the Kenan professorships after World War I and continuing with the philanthropy of the same
family fifty years later. In 1966 the foundation of Mrs. Bingham's brother,
William Rand Kenan, Jr., added its own benefaction. Following Kenan's
death, his trustees underwrote twenty-five William Rand Kenan, Jr., professorships. Similar in quality and amount with the old, these new professorships almost doubled the university's ability to keep pace with distinguished academic salary levels across the nation. At the time of the 1966 gift
Chancellor Sitterson noted that "these professorships will be competitive
with the most attractive . . . in the academic world."

As these new benefactions were announced, the postwar university began
to receive recognition as a national research institution. The Second World
War had been a watershed. Before the war the curriculum had been limited
and conventional in the arts and sciences. For example, students might take
courses in American history, British constitutional history, the French Revolution, and the Napoleonic era. But after the war the curriculum broadened
greatly. In history alone, courses were introduced on Japan, China, Africa,
and the Middle East. The same kind of broadening beyond conventional
Western studies occurred in the other liberal arts as the university moved
beyond its respectable regional and national status, emulating such institutions as Michigan and California.

Likewise the university took advantage of burgeoning student growth to
improve academic standards by lifting qualifications for admission and by
offering undergraduate degrees with honors as well as interdisciplinary
studies (e.g., American Studies, International Studies, Industrial Relations,
Afro-American Studies). When the American Council on Education made
evaluations of graduate studies in American universities, UNC–Chapel Hill
usually appeared at the top of the list in the South during much of the period
from the late 1950s into the 1970s. New and innovative developments in the
1960s included the establishment of the population center and the child
development center. A $5 million Natural Science Foundation grant helped
establish the Center for Excellence in nine disciplines in mathematical,
physical, and social sciences.

Much of the new recognition centered on the four-year medical school
and the burgeoning school of public health. They gave the university indispensable ingredients for attracting research funds and distinguished faculty
members. In one of his last acts in 1944 President Franklin Roosevelt
designated Vannevar Bush, director of the Office of Scientific Research and

Development, to design a national research program against war and disease and in behalf of general scientific achievement. Bush's recommendations placed responsibility for carrying out this program—the basic research enterprise in science—on the nation's universities.

In part because of its prominence as a public health center, Chapel Hill became one of 125 national universities receiving major scientifically oriented grants. The awards stemmed in great measure from the foresight of Venable, Chase, and the Grahams in the early twentieth century. Those presidents had their academic priorities in order. They placed emphasis on top-quality scholarship and brought distinguished scholars to the campus. As one thoughtful observer wrote:

> There was not and has not been a grand design on the level of the state or in the university for these developments since 1950. There was no state or university mandate for the development of great departments of pathology, chemistry and bio-statistics and a child development center. Instead we have been, during all these years, blessed with an imaginative, creative and scholarly faculty looking for the new opportunities, an able and permissive administration structure of deans, vice chancellors and chancellors and lucky to put these together at a time of rapid growth in availability of federal funds. And from that has grown this great enterprise.[6]

As it flowered into a major research university, Chapel Hill paradoxically began to experience a slow erosion of political influence among important policymakers in Raleigh and across North Carolina. Although still the apex of state higher education, the university felt increasing competition from other state-supported institutions. The expansion of these campuses, along with the growth of Duke, Wake Forest, and others in the private sector, generated new educational loyalties. Many sons and daughters of Tar Heel families found academic homes on other campuses. Chapel Hill's high standards and popularity made it possible to enroll only a comparatively small proportion of those who sought admission. These new allegiances were naturally reflected in the General Assembly, where prior to World War II many members had been alumni or had links with Chapel Hill.

The competitive pressure became especially acute among a whole coterie of state-supported institutions, many of them former community or teachers' colleges. The university's political influence remained strong as late as the 1960s, but the number of alumni from other institutions serving in the General Assembly grew substantially. The same trend could be seen in the governor's office, where most of the chief executives for over a century had ties with Chapel Hill.

Such influence became particularly marked on the arrival in the governor's office in 1969 of Robert W. Scott, a graduate of N.C. State University at Raleigh and son of another Haw River governor, who became highly critical of what he considered the stronghold of elitist power at Chapel Hill.

Before Scott's arrival the beleaguered SBHE was repeatedly defeated when it sought to interfere with the consolidated trustees' management. Guided by the 1963 recommendations of the Carlyle Commission, the trustees brought three four-year institutions, those at Charlotte, Asheville, and Wilmington, under the consolidated university umbrella. This expanded their jurisdiction and further curbed the SBHE's authority. After the SBHE almost foundered, Governor Dan Moore and the General Assembly reorganized its membership in 1965 and sustained its mandate to coordinate the public institutions. Some of these institutions, especially East Carolina College (ECC) at Greenville under President Leo Jenkins, grew in size and increasingly made their voices heard in Raleigh.

In February 1965 ECC, through its board chairman State Senator Robert Morgan, asked the SBHE for authority to establish a two-year medical school at Greenville. It also sought "independent university status" outside the consolidated trustees' umbrella. Almost simultaneously in 1966 both Western Carolina College at Cullowhee and Appalachian State Teachers College at Boone requested regional university status.[7]

Initially the SBHE tried to slow this snowballing movement among institutions which had only recently begun offering substantial four-year degrees. But the creation of new universities at Charlotte, Asheville, and Wilmington enhanced pressure from other campuses. Political momentum for "instant universities" proved overwhelming. Some frustrated legislators even concluded that only by bestowing such labels could they force the restructuring of the whole higher education system.

Contrary to the advice of the SBHE, the 1967 General Assembly designated East Carolina College, Western Carolina College, Appalachian State Teachers College, and North Carolina Agricultural and Technical College as regional universities. Then in 1969 it so named North Carolina Central, Winston-Salem State, Fayetteville State, Pembroke State, and Elizabeth

City State, raising the total to nine campuses outside the consolidated system with the title *university*.

The management of higher education became sharply splintered. Earlier, at the suggestion of Cameron West, director of the SBHE, the General Assembly had made the governor ex officio chairman of the SBHE. It also added chairmen of the four legislative money committees as members. Later Governor Scott called this "the best move the legislature made for higher education" because otherwise there would have been "no way for me to see what a mess we [were] in."[8]

Scott, plainspoken and aggressive, favored streamlining state government. Initially he excluded higher education from this process, but after the voters ratified a 1970 constitutional amendment mandating reorganization of government and after he perceived the "instant university" tangle, he changed his mind. On December 13, 1970, Scott called together in a meeting at the governor's mansion representatives from boards of trustees of all state-supported higher education institutions. His purpose: to study devising a state board to govern all sixteen senior institutions of higher learning.

Thus began the hard-fought battle to reshape public higher education in North Carolina. Scott had no experience in education management; but he was forthright in dealing with problems, and he believed in action. Poised against him were the accumulated influence and power of the university's trustees, sensitive about their prerogatives and leery of any move that might damage the quality of the six universities in their charge.

Scott thought in terms of "starting all over again"—scrambling another batch of eggs, eliminating the SBHE and the consolidated university, and creating something new. "There will be much screaming, wailing and gnashing of teeth," he said. "I don't want this any more than you do, but I won't back down."[9]

As chairman of both the consolidated trustees and the SBHE, Scott had a foot in both camps. Bullheaded and often tactless, he forced both groups to respond to his challenges. Neither could deny that higher education was a shambles. The governor got the process started by appointing a study committee chaired by state senator Lindsay C. Warren, Jr., of Goldsboro and comprised of representatives from all the governing bodies. Initially, by a vote of 13-9, the committee adopted recommendations rejecting major structural changes but moderately enhancing the SBHE's powers. Then about a month later, on May 8, 1971, the committee reversed itself and, by a vote of 13-8, endorsed deconsolidating the university and establishing a board of regents for all sixteen state institutions.

In the meantime university trustees rallied their forces for a showdown while Governor Scott's supporters solicited political assistance from the other side. In a speech to a press association group at Wrightsville Beach on May 22 Scott abandoned his prepared text and castigated his opponents. "It's comical. It's vicious," he said. "They've got an intelligence that's unbeliev-able—Bill Friday, Leo Jenkins, Cam West. . . . They are like kids. It's sickening. It really is."[10]

At an informal meeting of the trustees' executive committee on May 13 Scott threatened budgetary reprisals if the university trustees' opposition continued. He warned that he had the votes to push the Warren plan through the legislature, that he had, in fact, a whole box full of green stamps to cash in and use on this issue. With righteous indignation, trustee Victor Bryant replied, "Governor, you use your green stamps and we will use ours, and we will see who wins."

In a forty-minute speech to the General Assembly on May 25 Scott presented recommendations of the Warren committee majority. "For some time," he declared, "we have been traveling a dangerously erratic course in public higher education in North Carolina. We are proceeding with all sail and no rudder. Wasteful and damaging forces are chipping away at the structure of our system. Disaster will follow unless it is righted, reinforced and redirected." Scott included a scathing attack on those he considered responsible for the disorder.

Lobbying grew intense as the SBHE endorsed the governor's plan 17-2. Scott himself, who was chairman of the consolidated board, declined to attend its meeting on May 28 but announced he would spend the morning talking with legislators because "that's where the votes are." At their meet-ing the consolidated trustees heard a presentation on the Warren commit-tee's minority report by President William Friday, who did not support restructuring. They gave it unanimous backing. The board's resolution emphasized that "the consolidated university . . . should not be dismantled without more objective and impartial study." In June the trustees set up a five-room lobbying command post at the Hilton Inn in Raleigh. Trustee Jake Froelich, Jr., of High Point headed the group, called Friends of Education, and Ralph Strayhorn, a Durham attorney, became one of its chief advocates. University lobbyists had plenty of potential support in the General Assembly since 45 of the 120 House members and 23 of the 50 senators were Chapel Hill alumni.

Many of Chapel Hill's loyal supporters, along with those of other units of the consolidated system, knew that higher education needed more than cosmetic revision. However, they feared that the proposed reorganization would overthrow an effective governing structure and replace it with one of unknown character, strength, and membership. All this was linked with the perception that Governor Scott, in his attack on the university's alleged elitism, acted from political as well as educational motives. Yet, as one university supporter pointed out, it was difficult to counter the argument that "if consolidation is good for six [institutions], why is it not good for 16?"[11]

Amid discussion of numerous alternatives, many thoughtful leaders came to realize that substantial structural changes—a system allocating even more centralized power than the Scott-backed system—might be desirable. This became evident as Chancellor John T. Caldwell of N.C. State University came to favor a stronger regents system—one that would govern rather than coordinate. On June 21, 1971, Dr. Cameron West, director of the SBHE, announced he could support such a system. After a long meeting of representatives from both sides, Governor Scott said he would ask the General Assembly to reconvene in the fall when he would support a more powerful board of regents than the Warren committee majority had proposed.

The governor's new plan was announced on June 28. It provided for a twenty-five member board of regents of the University of North Carolina system to govern all sixteen institutions along with a separate board of trustees for each campus. As the balance of power shifted toward a strong overall governing body, the consolidated trustees' executive committee adamantly refused to go along. Sparring among the warring camps continued through the late summer and into the fall. President Terry Sanford of Duke University endorsed the strong board plan, with some variations in detail. Former UNC chancellor William Aycock supported a regents system for planning and budgeting but giving local trustee boards substantial power.

Representative Ike Andrews and state senator John Burney, both enthusiastic Chapel Hill supporters, abandoned the Warren committee report by offering amended proposals. On September 23, 1971, Lindsay Warren told the Joint Committee on Higher Education that he favored moving beyond the coordinating board approach. Simultaneously UNC trustee George Watts Hill, Sr., an avid foe of restructuring, said he could accept some variation of the Scott plan. Trustee Victor Bryant continued to warn that if the legislature abolished the administrative offices of the consolidated university, there would be a "holy war."[12]

Governor Scott sensed that the tide was moving in his direction. In a talk to the UNC Faculty Club at Chapel Hill, he kept up the pressure by warning that the regional universities were preparing another drive to expand their graduate programs. He declared, however, that "no one is out to get the university" and that perhaps some of his earlier speeches were "too abrasive."

Chancellor Sitterson and especially President Friday, while loyal to their trustee boards, nevertheless strived without much success toward a path of accommodation. Friday offered a proposal that would gradually merge the state's nine regional university boards into the consolidated board over a period of years, but this never got off the ground.

Even as a majority began to coalesce around a strong centralized regents system, there remained considerable differences about its board membership, size, and powers. Many of these questions loomed large on the agenda of the joint higher education committee when it met before the special legislative session that fall. At their October 18 meeting the consolidated university trustees endorsed the concept of a strong central board but differed among themselves on how to put it together and who would control it.

When the General Assembly reconvened on Tuesday, October 26, 1971, there was still uncertainty about how such differences would be reconciled. After five days of hectic work, several coalitions of House and Senate members, assisted by university officials, found a consensus. Slowly they struggled to make it acceptable to all factions. Much of the trouble lay in subtle details of management and convincing various interest groups that they would have fair representation.

The project almost foundered on Friday, October 29, after the House accepted an amended Senate version of a bill that did not satisfy consolidated university supporters. Strenuous lobbying exploded in both camps. Some representatives and senators who thought the matter was settled and had gone home returned to Raleigh. One, Representative Charles Phillips of Guilford, came back from a sick bed. Representative Ike Andrews became a key leader in these activities, along with Senator Gordon Allen, Representative McNeill Smith, and Senator L. P. McLendon, Jr., all UNC–Chapel Hill stalwarts.

On Saturday morning the House, by a one-vote margin—55-54—agreed to reconsider its action of the preceding evening. This set in motion a series of amendments to give the consolidated university representation on the new Board of Governors equal to that of the ten other institutions. The amended legislation then moved smoothly through the House and Senate.

Governor Scott, still fighting to keep the regional campuses from being swallowed up in the consolidated system, explained his setback by saying, "I guess I must have dropped one of my green stamps and Ike Andrews picked it up." McNeill Smith described the scene best when he said, "It was like the Battle of Waterloo. Neither side knew for sure who had won or lost until the smoke of battle had cleared."

Despite Governor Scott's disappointment over his green stamps, his forces scored a substantial victory. At the same time the consolidated university, first by holding out and then by adroit diplomacy, protected its interests. Both sides won—not precisely what they sought but enough to give them fair representation on the new central board. John L. Sanders, director of the Institute of Government, called what had happened "the most extensive changes in the structure and governance of public higher education that this state has experienced since the adoption of the Constitution of 1868."[13]

The new system, although renamed and reconstituted, assured continuity of the old university as originally defined 180 years earlier. Any movement toward equalizing or leveling of all institutions was averted. Ten public institutions that had sought to upgrade their positions in the hierarchy of higher education succeeded and were merged into the University of North Carolina, joining six others. The new Board of Governors contained sixteen members from the old consolidated board and sixteen from the boards of the regional universities and the School of the Arts, plus two temporary nonvoting members from the dismantled State Board of Higher Education (the latter phasing out after eighteen months). After the expiration of Scott's term as governor in December 1972, the board chose its own presiding officer. This ended the chairmanship of governors, a university tradition dating from 1804. To a major extent these changes shielded the state's education system from political influences that had both helped and hindered it in the past. The General Assembly continued to select board members, but it endowed them with unprecedentedly broad powers over education policy-making and management.

Each of the sixteen institutions, including Chapel Hill, got its own thirteen-member Board of Trustees with nearly all its power delegated by the central board. The central board elected the president, who became administrative head of the university, along with chancellors of the various campuses, nominated by the president. It also had and retained full control of the programs and finances of the sixteen constituent institutions. On July 1, 1972, the revised organization became effective after a six-month period of preliminary planning undertaken by a committee composed of the same persons who became members of the new board.

The new structure appeared far superior to any proposed during the protracted struggles of the preceding year. Legally, the Board of Governors became "the Board of Trustees of the University of North Carolina writ large."[14]

One of the incidental results of restructuring harked back to the earliest period of the original university's history. The new legislation repealed statutes dating in part from 1794 that made it a crime to set up a billiard table within five miles of Chapel Hill or to conduct any kind of theatrical entertainment (including "rope or wire dancing") within that radius, without the written permission of the president of the University of North Carolina.[15] That loss pained the university scarcely at all.

CHALLENGES OF

ACADEMIC EXPANSION,

1972–1980

Even those consolidated trustees dragged reluctantly into the 1971 restructuring realized that their institutions, including Chapel Hill, fared well under the new dispensation. The revised law placed a balanced number of old trustees on the new board. It provided several built-in protective features, including staggered terms and local boards of trustees. Because of their ability and experience, UNC–Chapel Hill alumni became leading figures on the new board. They protected and enhanced the university's burgeoning academic quality.

Above all, the political struggle left unscarred the individual most capable of making the new system work. William C. Friday, the incumbent administrative chief, often found himself caught in the middle of heated impasses. But he moved so evenhandedly through the restructuring controversy that he emerged as the indispensable conciliator to head the new system.

In many respects he resembled Frank Graham, who had guided the initial consolidation of the 1930s. Also following Graham's example, Friday achieved national reputation during his first fifteen years in the consolidated presidency. In the 1970s he was named president of the Association of American Universities, comprising the top forty-eight institutions of higher learning in the United States and Canada. He became a member of the Carnegie Commission on the Future of Higher Education and served on the President's Task Force on Education and as chairman of the President's Commission on White House Fellows.

During the political infighting of restructuring, Friday and Cameron West, head of the expiring SBHE, came to distrust each other. Nevertheless the new system president did not protest the Planning Committee's decision to name West vice president for planning under the new system. Governor Scott, who had clashed repeatedly with Friday and hoped to enhance regional university influence, made sure the new law provided for a senior vice president on the Board of Governors staff. This became the spot designed for West. Friday, ever the conciliator, accepted West's appointment, though without the "senior" designation. The arrangement did not work out, and West soon resigned.

The new president's election occurred at the March 17, 1972, meeting of the Board of Governors' Planning Committee in Greensboro. Governor Scott, chairman of the personnel committee, presented Friday's nomination and, despite their recent differences, greeted him heartily after his election. During the same meeting the committee voted to locate the system's headquarters one mile east of the Chapel Hill campus in the new $1,135,000 General Administration Building of the consolidated university. Some board members found this location hard to accept since the building symbolized the old university's dominance. Similarly, some Chapel Hill partisans thought its proximity infringed on the independence of UNC–Chapel Hill. Yet Friday and the board concluded that a campus setting was important. Located in Raleigh, the General Administration might be perceived as just one more bureau of higher education subject to myriad state political pressures.

One of the last bits of business handled by the Planning Committee before its expiration on July 1, 1972, touched a matter important to Chapel Hill. President Friday announced that he and President Leo Jenkins of East Carolina University had been discussing with medical school officials at Duke, Wake Forest, and Chapel Hill the future of the existing one-year medical program at Greenville. He requested appointment of a committee to study "funding of a second year of medical education at East Carolina University." The Planning Committee accepted this recommendation, and a medical school committee was named.[1]

The Planning Committee held its final meeting in Boone as the consolidated office and the SBHE completed merging their staffs. Due to the General Assembly's foresight, members of the expiring Planning Committee on July 1, 1972, remained in place and simply took new titles as members of the Board of Governors. Thus as June ended, the old system died quietly without further transitional problems.

The Board of Governors held its first meeting on the campus of the University of North Carolina at Charlotte on July 7, 1972. At the end of the year Governor Scott finished his service as initial board chairman. The governors elected their vice chairman, William A. Dees, Jr., a Goldsboro attorney, to replace him. Meanwhile the board's committees moved to inaugurate a variety of educational missions, including selection of Chapel Hill's first local board of trustees in four decades.

The restructuring battle coincided with several end-of-the-decade transitions at Chapel Hill. Once again a scholarly chancellor who had served well, J. Carlyle Sitterson, decided to return to teaching. Sitterson, the quietly affable Kinston native who had received his A.B., M.A., and Ph.D. degrees in history at Chapel Hill, managed the chancellorship during six stormy years starting in 1966, when student unrest reached its peak. A keen administrator and an excellent teacher, he performed admirably during a time of serious campus unrest.

Sitterson's successor, another Tar Heel native, Nelson Ferebee Taylor ('42), had returned to Chapel Hill eighteen months earlier as vice president for administration in the consolidated university system after practicing law in New York City. Earlier Taylor had been a visiting professor of law at the university. When Taylor expressed a desire to come back to Chapel Hill, Friday hired him as vice president on July 1, 1970.

A native of Oxford, North Carolina, Taylor received his A.B. degree from UNC, where he was president of Phi Beta Kappa, and his LL.B. from Harvard. During World War II he served in the U.S. Navy, then became a Rhodes scholar and a partner in a well-known New York law firm. An austere, meticulous administrator, Taylor served as counselor for Friday's office during the restructuring controversy. His selection reflected the continuing emphasis on choosing chancellors with roots and experience in North Carolina.

Taylor came to the chancellorship—on February 1, 1972—at a time of striking changes in student lifestyles. A little earlier, Dean of Women Katherine Carmichael had described the typical Carolina student of 1970 as "better washed than he was two years ago." The "masculine pronoun was still much in evidence on the 1970 campus," the *Alumni Review* observed. "Men outnumbered women more than two to one among the 18,000-plus students. The women's liberation movement was introduced to the campus that year, and St. Anthony Hall became a coed fraternity—harbingers of women to come." Richard Epps served as the first black student government president, and the baseball team selected two bat girls, Mary Ann Osborne and Beth Tingley. Jubilee Weekend ended in a wild scene at Navy Field. Property was destroyed and a security guard was seriously injured, after which the holiday weekend was canceled for a decade.[2]

The splendid formal dances in Woollen Gymnasium, the chartered buses of "imports" from women's colleges and the informal hayrides and parties at Hogan's Lake—all earmarks of student life earlier in the century—had given way to other styles and fashions. But even a larger, coeducational student body could not diminish the outdoor classes some professors still held in fine weather on McCorkle and Polk places, the almost luminous appearance of the old campus at sunrise and sunset under the great trees, and the hordes of students flocking along the brick and sand paths when classes changed. Even though expansion had altered a great deal, much of the essence of the old remained.

Prosperous times had enabled the General Assembly to loosen the purse strings, and a building boom ensued in the late 1960s. The Frank Porter Graham Student Union, financed by student funds, was completed near the Wilson Library in 1968. Simultaneously, the trustees built nearby the Robert B. House Undergraduate Library, initially housing 60,000 books, and the Josephus Daniels Student Stores, a successor to the old Book-Ex in the YMCA and named for the former U.S. secretary of the navy.

The new law school building, completed near the eastern edge of the central campus in 1968, was joined by Greenlaw Hall, new home of the English department, in 1970, and the ten-story William Rand Kenan, Jr., chemistry laboratories adjoining Venable Hall in 1971. Some critics objected to the height and the warehouse style of the new laboratories, which almost overshadowed the majestic Wilson Library next door. But the new facilities enabled the department to double its graduate enrollment in chemistry. The Cary Boshamer Stadium, also dedicated in 1971 near Kenan Stadium, provided new grounds for the baseball team. Among giant new multistoried dormitories completed on the south campus during this period were Hinton James and Cameron Morrison halls.

Many areas got newly paved brick walks and freshly planted shrubs. The Old Well, symbol of alma mater for almost a century, was remodeled and freshened up. Once the center of the campus, it now stood on the northern rim of a greatly enlarged circumference as new classrooms and dormitories sprang up to the south. The area of the Bell Tower became the geographical center of the campus.

While the YMCA–South Building area once marked the focal point of student traffic, now it was The Pit, a paved sunken courtyard in the quadrangle formed by the Graham Student Union, the Daniels Building, the House Library, and Lenoir Hall. The Pit became the new "Hyde Park corner of the campus where anyone with a cause might find an audience."[3]

While the campus changed dramatically, many old haunts around the village managed to survive. Along downtown Franklin Street the Coffee Shop, Sutton's Drug Store, and Foister's Camera Store remained familiar landmarks. Even the flower ladies, who sold their wares on the sidewalk for many years, had not disappeared, although they moved into the alley between Franklin and Rosemary streets to escape crowded foot traffic. Public pressure and town planners forestalled construction of any downtown multistoried building resembling a skyscraper, in order to preserve the village ambience. Despite increased automobile traffic, by 1971 about one of every four students still rode a bicycle.[4]

In the postwar era of entertainment celebrities, several Carolina graduates attained national reputation. Robert C. Ruark ('35), the novelist, returned to visit students in the journalism school and enjoyed seeing some of his old professors, including Dean O. J. Coffin. Andy Griffith ('49), who gained fame in motion pictures and television, appeared for an interview on the university's new educational television station in Swain Hall. The university developed student celebrities, including its first black athletic star, Charlie Scott, who performed on the U.S. Olympic Team and led the Tar Heels through several outstanding basketball seasons in Carmichael Gym ("Blue Heaven") during the late 1960s. Jim Hickey coached the Carolina football team to its first postseason victory in the Gator Bowl in 1964 following an 8-2 season. Carolina's 1971 basketball team, under Coach Dean Smith, won the National Invitational Tournament in New York City in 1971.[5]

Meanwhile the journalism school, which grew out of classes taught by Professor Edward Kidder Graham in 1909–10, moved from its cramped quarters in Bynum Hall to Howell Hall in 1960 and began to achieve a national reputation. The university produced a number of distinguished journalists, including Vermont Royster, Jonathan Daniels, Clifton Daniel, Tom Wicker, Charles Kuralt, Edwin Yoder, and Jonathan Yardley.

As they took up their new duties in 1972, the new board of trustees and Chancellor Taylor confronted what became one of the more difficult issues of the decade: the sale of the campus utilities system. For lack of municipally or privately provided services, the university had developed and owned its electric power distribution, telephone, water, and sewage disposal facilities. They served the campus and later the entire community. As the town and campus expanded, management of that system became a burden, one not directly related to the university's educational mission. Joseph Eagles, a businessman and former state senator from Wilson who became vice chancellor for business and finance under Chancellor Sitterson, was among those who thought divestment essential.

Eagles, through his legislative connections, helped persuade the General Assembly to set up a commission to study the matter. Its report, recommending sale, came during the first months of the newly restructured university's operation. After considerable discussion, and quite a few differences, about who had authority to approve the sale and how the money should be distributed, the matter dragged on until the summer of 1976.

Controversy over the sale centered on efforts by the General Assembly to siphon off part of the funds for other purposes in lean fiscal times. University officials had not anticipated that the legislature would claim a share of the funds or that tax complications would tie up part of the settlement for years. Some trustees thought ownership of the utilities system should be retained as an endowment for Chapel Hill rather than sold outright with loss of funds. Trustee George Watts Hill, Sr., of Durham, who differed sharply with Chancellor Taylor and other trustees, made such a proposal.

But the General Assembly had the final word. It directed that, of the $44,065,238 received from the sale, $10 million be transferred to the state's general fund and another $4,938,520 placed in escrow to cover potential tax liability in a legal suit pending between the university and the towns of Chapel Hill and Carrboro and Orange County.

Once the university's funds became available, conflicting ideas about how they should be spent arose among trustees and faculty. Chancellor Taylor championed construction of a new central library. The Wilson and House facilities were inadequate for burgeoning student enrollment and growing collections. Wilson Library and the health affairs library also needed renovation.

Others, including trustee Hargrove (Skipper) Bowles of Greensboro, favored using most of the funds for a new sports arena. The university had recently purchased the Baity property adjoining the south campus, which was ultimately used for that purpose. The UNC Education Foundation,

Wilson Library in a snowstorm, 1978.
(Photograph by Ted Kyle, Carolina Alumni Association)

better known as the Rams Club and established to promote intercollegiate athletics, contributed $200,000 for the new arena's architectural plans.

The administration felt the pressure of athletic enthusiasts as coach Dean Smith's basketball teams excelled in ACC competition and began to star in NCAA tournaments. When Bowles failed in his 1972 campaign for the governorship, he and his friends turned in earnest toward pushing the student activities center, as the arena came to be called. Chancellor Taylor continued to support the library as his highest priority, and the trustees agreed with him.

A delay in building the new Paul Green Theatre, earlier proposed for the old Emerson Field site, proved fortunate for the library's cause. Elaborate theater building plans had to be scaled down. The chancellor's office, with trustee concurrence, redesignated the Emerson Field site for the library and earmarked $23,936,718 of the utilities sale proceeds for its construction. Another $4,660,000 went for the Wilson Library renovation and $4,730,000 for additions to the health affairs library. When the $4,938,520 set aside for potential tax liability became available in 1986, it was allocated to renovate the Ackland Art Museum and to fund planning for a new power plant.[6]

Thus the library, which Louis Round Wilson long before envisioned as the heart of a great university, got top priority. Having acquired its one mil-

William Friday and dog, Commencement, 1970.
(Photograph by William Brinkhous, Chapel Hill)

lionth book in 1960, it reached the two-million mark in 1974. On that occasion, as a special commemoration, the Hanes Foundation of Winston-Salem presented that volume to the library: *The Book of Hawking, Hunting and Heraldry,* printed in 1486.

Later, in a move initiated without consultation with the chancellor or the faculty, the trustees named the new central library for Walter Royal Davis, a wealthy trustee who had lobbied strongly in the General Assembly to save the "utilities money" for the university. A reading room in the library was named for Nelson Ferebee Taylor. Bowles, who became a generous UNC supporter, then spearheaded a drive to raise some $36 million from private sources for the student athletic center, eventually built on the south campus and named for the university's popular basketball coach, Dean E. Smith. Smith Center became a major North Carolina facility for both college athletics and other entertainment productions.

Dean Smith, who had been tapped for the basketball coaching job by Chancellor Bill Aycock to succeed Frank McGuire in 1962, became one of the campus's best-known personalities. Starting with an 8-9 record during his first year, Smith inspired his teams to win three successive ACC titles (1967–69) and coached the U.S. Olympic Basketball Team to victory in 1976. The Tar Heels won the NCAA national championship in 1957 under Frank

McGuire and again under Smith in 1982. Smith developed a host of basketball stars who went on to great success in the professional leagues. Perhaps the most outstanding was Michael Jordan, who became a folk hero and a great player for the Chicago Bulls.

Coach Smith's influence ranged far beyond the win-loss records of the basketball court. His athletes consistently scored well in the classroom. President Friday praised him as a man whose priorities were always straight. "He teaches self-discipline, he teaches organization, he teaches team play, and he teaches respect for academic excellence," Friday said.

During the 1960s and 1970s, basketball and football became multimillion-dollar businesses at Chapel Hill. Both Kenan Stadium and Carmichael Gymnasium drew record crowds, and the emerging age of televised sports brought with it more notoriety as well as headaches. Carolina's football fans got "bowl fever," and the team was selected to play in some of the major holiday games during the Christmas–New Year season. Athletic rivalry of earlier years had focused on the University of Virginia. During the 1930s and 1940s it shifted dramatically to nearby Duke, and by 1970 it was still going strong as Duke students stole Rameses IX, the celebrated ram mascot, and Carolina students retaliated by stealing the Blue Devil's uniform and spear. The matter was settled during a "fair trade" ceremony at halftime during a traditionally hard-fought game, which Carolina won.

Intercollegiate sports continued their phenomenal growth, especially among women. By the 1970s the university fielded thirteen men's and thirteen women's intercollegiate teams. For three years the men's teams won the Carmichael Cup, awarded for overall excellence in the ACC. In 1978 Dick Crum succeeded Bill Dooley as head football coach.

During this period another controversial issue moved to center stage: the continuing campaign by East Carolina University (ECU) to locate a state-supported medical school at Greenville. North Carolina's Good Health Program, launched after World War II, pinpointed the state's low per capita ratio of physicians to population, especially in the east. Chancellor Leo Jenkins and ECU leaders saw Greenville as an ideal place for training family practitioners. They also recognized that a medical school would bring economic bounties as well as medical resources to a region that had long known poverty and backwardness.

As early as 1965 the General Assembly authorized planning for a medical school at Greenville. In 1971, while Governor Scott pushed his restructuring plan, ECU and its supporters persuaded the General Assembly to appropriate $1.4 million for a first-year medical program at Greenville. It stipulated that students who completed that work would be admitted for their second year's medical training at Chapel Hill.

This one-year program created problems for Chapel Hill. The medical school, under the direction of Dr. Christopher C. Fordham III, who in 1971 succeeded Dr. Isaac M. Taylor as dean, found it necessary to set up second-year classes larger than its first-year enrollment. In order to maintain quality of instruction, the medical school had been growing at a slow and carefully controlled pace. This caused criticism. In a letter to trustee George Watts Hill, Sr., in 1970 Governor Scott questioned UNC's monopoly over state-sponsored education of physicians. "The choice of the UNC about 1965 for the medical school not to grow fast may have been right, but it should be no great surprise that pressures mounted in other areas to meet health manpower needs," Scott wrote. "One problem, at least in the past, has been that the university at Chapel Hill has had too much of a 'closed shop' attitude. . . . The university . . . continues rightfully to be a strong force in the state and the South, but it is no longer the alpha and omega of all wisdom, knowledge and power."[7]

When pressures to expand medical education continued, the Board of Governors in 1972 recommended appointment of a committee to study expanding the ECU program to two years. The committee, reporting in January 1973, suggested that a team of experienced national consultants evaluate the need for an additional degree-granting medical school in the university system. It also recommended larger classes for Chapel Hill.

The following September the evaluation panel, under the chairmanship of Dr. Ivan L. Bennett, Jr., of New York University, recommended that the Chapel Hill medical school be given supervision of the whole program at ECU and, depending on progress, proceed with establishing a second year of medical education at Greenville. The panel also championed expanding area health education centers (AHECs) for the entire state, a project that eventually became a significant source of additional health care delivery.

The Board of Governors enthusiastically supported the AHECs but questioned ECU's two-year medical program. Since enrollment capacities at Chapel Hill had already been established for the next decade, additional classes of fifty students each transferring from ECU for their third- and fourth-year work would require enormous expansion.

Despite difficulties at Chapel Hill, the General Assembly did not slow its efforts in behalf of Greenville. Numerous petitions and resolutions from towns and civic groups in eastern North Carolina supported the medical school. Even as the North Carolina Medical Society opposed the project and problems of accreditation multiplied, the General Assembly set up its own watchdog committee to monitor how the Board of Governors handled the issue. The committee reported that estimated costs of start-up had been exaggerated and concluded that the only practical way to solve North Carolina's health care problems was to provide additional facilities at Greenville.

By spring 1974 the General Assembly decided to press forward despite opposition from the Board of Governors and its study committees. On April 11, 1974, the legislature adopted a proposal drafted by Senator Ralph Scott and Representative Carl Stewart. It directed that an operating budget be authorized for expanding the program of first-year medical education at ECU as soon as possible, adding second-year instruction classes with special emphasis on family physicians and education of racial minorities. The legislation ordered the UNC–Chapel Hill medical school to work cooperatively with ECU officials toward achieving full accreditation. As a result of that directive, President Friday, the board, and the university launched a planning program with Chancellor Jenkins and ECU. After dozens of planning sessions stretching over many weeks, the difficulties of coordinating classes between Chapel Hill and Greenville became apparent. Dean Fordham reported that the heavy expenditures required would "not add to the output of doctors for the state." After a full review President Friday reported to the Board of Governors that establishing a two-year program at ECU, utilizing third- and fourth-year classes at Chapel Hill, would not produce benefits commensurate with costs. Friday, therefore, concluded that the only way to make the program worthwhile, and to achieve accreditation, would be to establish a full, four-year medical program at ECU.

The Board of Governors, after much debate and with only five dissenting votes, adopted Friday's proposal. It authorized development of a four-year, degree-granting medical school at ECU. It recommended additional appropriations of $35.2 million for capital construction projects and $1.4 million and $2.3 million for operations during the following two years. President Friday noted that if East Carolina was to have a four-year, freestanding medical school in the university system, he intended to do all he could to make it a good one. Board of Governors member Thomas J. White of Kinston observed that "at long last, I have the privilege of supporting a medical school proposal at East Carolina University without reservations."[8]

Despite budgetary stringencies, the General Assembly approved generous funding for the four-year medical school. The American Medical Association awarded its accreditation in 1976–77. Under the leadership of its first dean, Dr. William E. Laupus, and affiliation with the Pitt County Memorial Hospital the school enrolled its first four-year class in August 1977. That class of twenty-eight North Carolinians graduated in the spring of 1981 with M.D. degrees.

Many UNC trustees who had opposed the medical school for more than a decade conceded that the venture achieved a commendable degree of maturity and turned out well-trained graduates who helped upgrade North Carolina's delivery of medical care. "It ran the gauntlet of a series of experts, few of whom recommended it," declared Professor Arnold K. King, UNC system vice president. "The school was achieved out of the persistent and sometimes abrasive efforts of Chancellor Jenkins and many leaders in Eastern North Carolina who considered it essential to the further development of their region."[9]

The team of medical consultants that had been skeptical of the ECU medical school strongly endorsed another venture—the AHECs. The eight AHECs became a valuable adjunct system of medical and health care training anchored in hospitals across the state. They worked in tandem with the UNC–Chapel Hill School of Medicine, Duke University School of Medicine, and the Bowman Gray School of Medicine. The cooperative arrangement covered such varied fields as dentistry, nursing, pharmacy, and public health. In the early days major funds came from the state and federal governments; but by the early 1980s the federal government's participation had largely been phased out, and state and local resources were used. By 1984 the state was appropriating some $23 million annually for AHEC operations. AHEC programs utilized a fleet of five small planes which annually flew more than 4,200 trips serving some sixty towns and counties.[10]

During the mid-1970s one notable Chapel Hill landmark, the Tin Can, was razed to make way for the new Fetzer Gymnasium while another, Dr. Louis Round Wilson, celebrated his one-hundredth birthday. The Tin Can served as a gymnasium, but it attained more fame as the site of campus dances. Many of the nation's big bands—among them Glenn Miller's and Jimmy and Tommy Dorsey's—appeared there. A whole generation of World War II–era students and their "prom trotter" dates have vivid memories of German Club weekends at the Tin Can.

Dr. Wilson, whose life had been interwoven with the university's for all of the twentieth century, observed his centennial year in 1976. Librarians and other academic dignitaries from across the country visited the campus for two days of seminars and a gala banquet in his honor.

Chapel Hill felt the impact of the dispute between the university system and the U.S. government's Department of Health, Education, and Welfare (HEW). In 1970 HEW's Office of Civil Rights charged that North Carolina was maintaining a racially dual system of higher education. It directed that a desegregation plan be submitted in four months. The running controversy persisted not for four months but for almost fifteen years.

The unresolved problems centered on conflicting and confusing demands made on the university system by HEW and the NAACP's Legal Defense Fund. Before the turn of the century, under the racially inadequate separate but equal doctrine, North Carolina had initiated some higher education opportunities for minorities—more so than any other southern state. By the early 1970s, as the university encouraged affirmative action at its formerly all-white institutions, HEW warned it to eliminate the vestiges of racial segregation but not to wipe out racial identifiability at its five predominantly black institutions (in Greensboro, Winston-Salem, Fayetteville, Durham, and Elizabeth City).

This posed a problem: Those two goals were inherently incompatible; a fact that the courts never acknowledged. The dilemma grew in size over succeeding years as the university offered a series of plans, which HEW rejected, designed to increase minority enrollment at all institutions. President Friday's administration promoted full desegregation. But it was unwilling to install integration quota systems or to allow desegregation to disrupt efficient administration of academic programs. Noting that university and college attendance is voluntary, not mandatory (unlike grade school attendance), Friday declared, "There is no such thing as a pupil assignment plan on the university level."[11]

The controversy became more complex as HEW first accepted the university system's revised plans, then reversed its decision when a new veterinary school was placed at N.C. State rather than at A&T, the historically black land grant institution. By 1974 university campuses were generally meeting their desegregation goals, but a lawsuit filed by the NAACP revived the dispute. On April 1, 1977, Judge John Pratt of the U.S. District Court of the District of Columbia ruled that the desegregation plans of ten southern states, including North Carolina, did not "meet important desegregation requirements" and have "failed to achieve significant programs toward higher education desegregation." In order for institutions in these states to continue receiving federal funds, they were ordered to develop new criteria for eliminating racial duality.

After a new round of plan revisions, in which the Office of Civil Rights (OCR) disputed the university's "good faith" compliance, HEW secretary Joseph A. Califano, Jr., in 1978 announced his intention to begin proceedings to cut off federal funds in North Carolina. President Friday reported to the Board of Governors that he regretted HEW's "arbitrary selectivity" in its attacks on the UNC system while ignoring others. After Friday concluded that OCR's demands, which had shifted to an attack on "program duplication," would seriously disrupt the education program, the Board of Governors hired outside counsel to file a lawsuit protecting the university's interests.

Threats to cut off federal funds generated strong negative comments. The *News & Observer* declared on March 25, 1978, that Secretary Califano had "first negotiated sweetheart agreements with other states. . . . None had a problem as complex as that of North Carolina. . . . A past lack of effort in black education had left them with far fewer predominantly black institutions [than North Carolina]." HEW's demands that North Carolina's traditionally black institutions "must be enhanced while the formerly white institutions are increasing their black enrollment present an inherent contradiction." The *New York Times* warned that "HEW should be wary of crossing the line between zealous enforcement of equal rights and excessive intrusion into state higher education."

After further protracted negotiations, HEW dropped its plans to withhold funds, then revived them in 1979. At this point the university's attorneys filed suit to block cutoff. Judge Franklin Dupree of the U.S. District Court of Eastern North Carolina forbade deferment of funds pending a hearing. Further filings of motions and delays pushed the case beyond the tenure of Secretary Califano. HEW's education affairs were transferred to a new Department of Education, and Dr. Terrell Bell became education commissioner in the Reagan administration.

The marathon UNC-HEW struggle reached a settlement when the Board of Governors and counsel for the federal government submitted a consent decree to the U.S. District Court. Judge Dupree approved it on July 17, 1981. It set enrollment goals rather than fixed quotas. It directed improvements at traditionally black institutions by adding twenty-nine graduate and under-graduate degree programs. It continued efforts to integrate staff and faculty and pledged equitable salaries. Appeal efforts by the NAACP's Legal Defense Fund failed. In announcing the agreement, Secretary Bell emphasized that North Carolina "will control the destiny of its distinguished and respected university."[12]

The 1970s marked a period of enormous growth and recognized excellence for Chapel Hill in the academic world. By 1977–78 the university had risen from forty-first at the beginning of the decade to twenty-sixth among all U.S. universities in total dollars of federally sponsored research grants and contracts. The General Assembly's support for academic and health affairs grew from $43.7 million in 1971 to $76.7 million in 1977–78. Added to the new academic programs were the Institute for Environmental Studies, 1973; North Carolina Institute for Investment Research, 1974; the Cancer Research Center, 1975; the Institute for Social Service Planning, 1975; WUNC-FM Radio, 1976; the University Counseling Center, 1977; and the Center for Early Adolescence, the Government Executives Institute, the Media Center, and the Foundation Resource Center, all in 1978.

Simultaneously, the campus continued to expand its physical plant. Among new structures completed were the Paul Green Theatre, the Medical School Faculty Laboratory Office Building, the Student Health Services Building, the Botanical Garden's Totten Center, and the A. L. Brooks Building for the UNC Press.[13]

Chancellor Taylor emphasized long-range planning. He established, as an outgrowth of an elaborate self-study (1972–74), a planning council that annually prepared an updated five-year plan for the university's growth and improvement. As a result of these studies, the administration recognized the need for strengthening the university's endowment, which totaled $18.6 million in 1974.

From its founding the university had periodically been enriched by creative private bequests, starting with General Benjamin Smith's gift of 20,000 acres of Tennessee land in 1789. Yet in the early twentieth century when meager state appropriations began to improve, the university launched no organized campaign to stimulate private benefactions. Officials feared that soliciting regular or widespread gifts would encourage the General Assembly to reduce university appropriations. Other state universities, including many from the Midwest, had enlarged their private benefactions without damaging state support. In the South the University of Virginia increased its endowment beyond $100 million by the mid-1970s.

The university began to move in the same direction. After World War II, an alumni annual-giving program, featuring personal solicitations by alumni volunteers, generated new funds for academic enrichment. During the 1970s, proceeds from this program, by then called Carolina Annual Giving, more than doubled, reaching $615,932 by 1979.

On an allied front the chancellor's office created a new vice chancellorship for development and public service. Previously the university's ambassadors of good will, such persuasive individuals as William D. Carmichael, Jr., had operated largely on their own initiative. After Carmichael's death in 1961, the nonpublic money-raising efforts gradually became more professionally organized.

In 1974 the trustees, acting on authority from the Board of Governors, created a board of trustees for its endowment fund. In 1976 they set up a second vehicle for the receipt of gifts, the UNC–Chapel Hill Institutional Development Foundation, Inc.

During the same year, the university received the largest entirely unrestricted gift in its history, an $11,534,000 benefaction, virtually the entire estate of Dr. Joseph E. Pogue and Mrs. Grace N. Pogue. Dr. Pogue (A.B. 1906, M.S. 1907), a Raleigh native and well-known petroleum geologist and banker of New York, had been a generous supporter of the university. After his death in 1971 his wife continued their gifts. Prior to her death in 1973, Mrs. Pogue wrote that her husband "always felt that a good part of his work belongs to the university, and I certainly feel the same way."[14]

Using the Pogue gift as a nucleus, Chancellor Taylor in 1977 launched the Carolina Challenge, a fund-raising drive to lift the university's private endowment from $32.5 million at the end of 1976 to $100 million. Under alumnus Edward M. O'Herron of Charlotte more than 200 university supporters sought that objective. While they raised the endowment fund substantially, the goal was not attained by the end of the Taylor administration.

As part of the outreach program to the state the Board of Trustees, working under its chairman Henry A. Foscue of High Point, in 1974 established the Order of the Tar Heel One Hundred, designed to increase the university's contacts in all regions of the state. This organization mirrored the university's old 100-member board of trustees and eventually became known as the Board of Visitors.

In 1975 the university joined North Carolina State and Duke universities in forming the Triangle Universities Center for Advanced Studies, Inc. Thereupon the Research Triangle Foundation deeded to the organization 124 acres of park land. This attracted, as first tenant, the new National Humanities Center of the American Academy of Arts and Sciences. The center, housed in the Research Triangle Park, attracted renowned humanities scholars from around the world to spend an academic year in the triangle pursuing special research projects.

The university's outreach came to include the PlayMakers Repertory Company, organized by the Department of Dramatic Art in 1977. This company allowed professional actors to join students for productions, workshops, and seminars on campus, and by 1978–79 it attracted more than 33,000 a year in its audiences. The Morehead Planetarium and the Ackland Art Museum brought many more visitors to the campus, including some 40,000 schoolchildren each year.

Dean Smith.
(University News Services, Chapel Hill)

Michael Jordan.
(University News Services, Chapel Hill)

Ferebee Taylor's resignation as chancellor came in January 1980 following a serious illness. A reserved but hard-working and dedicated administrator, considered by some to be arrogant and stubborn, he returned to the law school, where he became a respected teacher. During the nearly eight years of his chancellorship Taylor presided over a period of enormous expansion. By the time of his resignation women outnumbered men in total enrollment—52.6 percent of the 21,000 students in 1979. Twelve academic programs at Chapel Hill ranked among the top 25 nationally, and 11 of the university's faculty were members of the prestigious National Academy of Sciences. The 10-story stack addition to the Wilson Library contained more than 2 million volumes, and planning had begun on the $23.8 million Davis Library, undoubtedly the most significant contribution of the Taylor administration.

A MAGIC GULF STREAM,

1980–1988

As Chapel Hill moved toward the last two decades of the twentieth century, urban growth threatened its village charm. "The unforgettable place . . . buried in a pastoral wilderness" described by Thomas Wolfe in the 1920s had given way to a vast research university with acres of diverse classroom buildings, laboratories, offices, and dormitories surrounded and even invaded by congested automotive traffic. The town's population skyrocketed. More than 20,000 students swarmed across its burgeoning campus. Dozens of suburban developments sprang up around the periphery where once only silent forests stood. By the early 1970s it was evident that without proper care, even the loveliness of the central campus and the quaintness of Franklin Street would be destroyed. "Anybody who knew the old Chapel Hill knows that it's gone to hell," James Shumaker, once editor of the old *Chapel Hill Weekly* (renamed the *Chapel Hill Newspaper*), told a *New York Times* reporter. "There's too much of everything. Too many people. Too many cars."[1]

Yet much of the ambience that had perennially attracted scholars, teachers, writers, scientists, and students—the community's intellectual ferment and individuality—survived and thrived. As the town's major industry, the university remained in the hands of administrators who recognized its uniqueness and honored its traditions. They guarded, as best they could, against encroachment on campus greenery, although the push to erect more giant buildings on the south campus proved too powerful to resist. As the Smith Student Activities Center opened along with the Kenan Center and a host of dormitories and academic halls, the congestion mounted. The small college that flowered under Chase and the Grahams in the early twentieth century struggled to hold on to its green space.

As the university grew in renown—by the 1970s and 1980s it ranked among the top twenty universities in the United States—its traditional function as a training academy for North Carolina's public leaders and its ties with a predominantly rural state weakened. Other institutions vied for college-age Tar Heel youth—most of whom, the males at least, would have headed for Chapel Hill in earlier days. To preserve educational quality, administrators made a decision after the 1971 restructuring to set an enrollment ceiling of roughly 22,000. Many Tar Heel students who sought admission (sometimes children or grandchildren of alumni) were turned away because of the enrollment cap and the campus's popularity. Concern arose that the university was losing its links with the grass roots that had nourished it for almost two centuries.

The rise of competing institutions coincided with the General Assembly's determination to heed the state constitution and keep tuition for in-state students low while limiting out-of-state enrollment to 18 percent. Debate continued over the division of emphasis between teaching and research that attracted distinguished academics and millions of dollars in grant funds. Chapel Hill's quality of life, although jeopardized by growth, continued to attract and retain a good faculty. This, in turn, enhanced its scholarly reputation.

In a study of doctoral programs in the United States sponsored by the Conference Board of Associated Research Councils and published in 1982, the university was reported to have more outstanding departments than any other southern institution. By 1986 the campus ranked thirty-eighth among all institutions in research and development expenditures and twenty-fifth among public universities. Other surveys showed that Chapel Hill, along with Duke in the South, had splendid undergraduate programs and graduate resources of distinction.

Albert Coates, founder of the Institute of Government and vigorous champion of state outreach, said shortly before his death in 1989, "The whole life of North Carolina from 1795 to today has been flavored by men and women going out from the University of North Carolina at Chapel Hill." This objective continued to receive emphasis, but meanwhile other trees had grown in the academic forest. The university's position was no longer unique in North Carolina.

Arrival of the 1980s brought another changing of the guard. Following

Chancellor Taylor's resignation, President Friday nominated another in-house successor. Dr. Christopher Columbus Fordham III, then vice chancellor for health sciences, became the university's sixth chancellor on March 1, 1980.

This Greensboro native, whose father and uncle had played on the same football team at Chapel Hill in an earlier day, came to his assignment with excellent credentials. A graduate of UNC–Chapel Hill and its two-year medical school in 1949, he finished Harvard Medical School in 1951, served his internship and residency in the U.S. Air Force, and joined the UNC medical school faculty in 1958. As an able administrator, he rapidly advanced to the associate deanship, left in 1969 to serve as dean of the Medical College of Georgia, and returned to Chapel Hill medical school in 1971, succeeding Dean Isaac M. Taylor.

An affable and collegial professional, Chancellor Fordham became popular among faculty and students, where he was already well known. But the chancellor of those years faced difficult problems. Enhanced bureaucracy and administrative pressures made the superstructure top-heavy and hard to manage. One administrator, when asked how the university was faring, replied, "The same as usual. They've just named the library for a man who's never read a book and the computer building for a man who doesn't own a typewriter."[2]

In the new era the chief headaches of administration involved not how to deal with survival but how to manage spectacular success. Burdens of management became heavy, and within ten months the new chancellor suffered a stroke, which put him on the sidelines for awhile but from which he recovered sufficiently to continue his services for another half-dozen years.

The achievements of those years were substantial. The new chancellor focused on strengthening the university's ties with North Carolina, especially its public schools. One of the first programs in this area stemmed from a $600,000 grant by the Lyndhurst Foundation of Tennessee. It aimed at enriching public school teaching, offering fellowships in science and the liberal arts. The foundation renewed its grant for a second three-year period in 1983–84, as the university also established a center for mathematics and science education and a new internship program for high school teachers of English and foreign languages. At the same time it launched the Mellon-Babcock-Reynolds Fellowships in the humanities, bringing high school teachers to the campus for a year of teaching and study.

Christopher C. Fordham III.
(University News Services, Chapel Hill)

In 1983 C. D. Spangler, Jr., president of Spangler Construction Company of Charlotte and chairman of the State Board of Education, sought improved management in the public schools. His concern centered on principals, usually ex-teachers or ex-coaches who came to their jobs with little or no administrative training. Spangler approached President Friday about establishing a training program for principals. He had in mind the model of Harvard Business School's Advanced Management Institute where "vice presidents for marketing or vice presidents for finance . . . who may not see the big picture clearly can get an overall view, suiting them for senior management." "I told Bill Friday," Spangler said later, "that . . . I did not want [the program centered] at the business school and not at the school of education and not at the law school but at the Institute of Government."[3] In 1984 the institute inaugurated the Principals Executive Program. By 1989 this intensive four-week course had graduated 847 principals and 65 superintendents from 133 of the state's 134 school districts.

Even as the university broadened its outreach, it confronted the aftermath of educational havoc wrought by the student unrest of the 1960s. The baby boom cohort encouraged unstructured permissiveness and excessive curriculum diversity. Liberal education faced a serious crisis, pressured by advancing technology and the breakdown of academic discipline. By the late 1970s the problems prompted a fresh look at the university's curriculum.

The Taylor administration set that examination in motion in 1978. After a thirty-month study, Chancellor Fordham and the Faculty Council in 1981 adopted a substantial overhaul of general curriculum requirements. They designated a new administrator and a faculty-student committee to implement it. The curriculum reaffirmed the primacy of liberal education and established strong guidelines. The General College curriculum for freshmen and sophomores defined two objectives. One fell under the head of "basic skills"—English composition, foreign languages, and mathematical sciences. The other—"perspectives"—focused on aesthetics, social and natural sciences, Western historical and non-Western or comparative studies, and philosophy.

During junior and senior years, when students transferred to the College of Arts and Sciences or to the Schools of Business, Education, Journalism, or Health Affairs, the curriculum required additional perspectives courses. While the program authorized student electives, it sought balance between "freedom and discipline." Along with the basics, it aimed at finding different "ways of looking at the world" and providing students maximum opportunities to explore them. The reforms emphasized renewed faculty interest in students along with research and outreach.[4]

Still, the dilemma over curriculum—the struggle between imposed core courses and electives and personalized attention to incoming undergraduates—continued to trouble both faculty and students. The tendency to proliferate an enormous smorgasbord of soft-core courses and to downplay information-based education left many students needing more guidance. Assailed by the information explosion, Chapel Hill's faculty felt the pressure of the controversy over course content that was fracturing academic communities everywhere.

Campus activism receded during the 1980s, reflecting the conservative upsurge of the Reagan era. Chancellor Fordham, however, encountered two sharp controversies in the public arena early in his regime.

One involved the university's ownership of stock in U.S. companies doing business in South Africa. In February 1983 student sentiment against the apartheid policies of the South African government led to a referendum supporting sale of such stocks by the university's endowment fund. Over protests from student groups the UNC Endowment Fund Board refused to change its policy. Again in November 1985 student government leaders requested divestment, without success.

On March 18, 1986, the UNC Anti-Apartheid Support Group built shanties of scrap wood and tin on Polk Place to express sympathy for black South Africans living in similar housing. University police had the shanties dismantled, but student body president Bryan Hassel persuaded Chancellor Fordham to let them be rebuilt for a stipulated time.

When the shanties had not been removed on schedule, the chancellor agreed to let them remain indefinitely. On March 28 the College Republicans and the Students for America wrote Fordham criticizing defacement of the campus. They threatened to build (and later built) a mock Berlin Wall protesting the chancellor's "indecisiveness" and the antiapartheid group's failure to address human rights violations in Marxist countries.[5]

On April 4, 1986, Fordham and board chairman J. Clint Newton failed to persuade the endowment board to approve total divestiture. Following the board's action, the chancellor ordered the shanties removed by April 7. As this was in progress, university police arrested five members of the Anti-

Apartheid Support Group, but they were later released after Fordham refused to press charges. The chancellor said they were good students and
there was no need to be punitive.

The issue was quiescent for awhile; then, at a November meeting of the
endowment board, Fordham made a motion for complete divestiture. After
the motion died, nine students observing the meeting chained themselves to
radiators in the business and finance office and were arrested. During that
same period some thirty-five students, led by the College Republicans and
the Students for America, marched to the board meeting site and waved
signs supporting U.S. involvement in South Africa.[6] The running dispute
continued into the spring as the endowment board sold some controversial
stocks and students continued to apply pressure. The university's interest in
the disputed companies had dropped from 12 percent to 4 percent of its $128
million endowment.[7]

On May 15, 1987, after a tense twenty-minute confrontation between
student antiapartheid leaders and board member Bobo Tanner, the board
appointed a committee to study the problem. After students accepted the
committee's proposed compromise, three students who had conducted an
eight-day fast decided to end it. On October 1, 1987, the endowment board
voted to sell all its remaining stocks in U.S. companies doing business in
South Africa.

Fordham's second troublesome episode in the public arena involved what
the chancellor saw as a clash of church and state. During the Christmas
season of 1982 officials of the Morehead Planetarium placed a lighted star
over the building off East Franklin Street to publicize their annual holiday
program, "The Star of Bethlehem." It offered viewers a chance to explore
astronomical explanations for the biblical story of the three wise men.

A UNC–Chapel Hill law professor, Barry Nakell, wrote Fordham ques-
tioning whether a university building was the proper place for a religious
symbol. Fordham requested the planetarium to remove the star. He told
planetarium director Lee T. Shapiro that he felt it should be removed "rather
than offend any particular segment of the community." Shapiro declared,
"We feel the star was simply an advertisement to let people know the
program was being performed and not a religious symbol." Nakell differed,
saying he wrote Fordham after several people complained to him.[8]

Fordham received numerous letters and calls, mostly protesting the re-
moval. In March 1984, after the U.S. Supreme Court ruled 5-4 that yuletide
nativity scenes displayed by local governments did not violate the Constitu-

tion, Fordham announced the star might be displayed. Shapiro said he planned to use it for the month of May, advertising a program called "Here Is Astronomy Shining in Chapel Hill," part of the planetarium's thirty-fifth birthday celebration.

By the 1980s the UNC School of Business Administration had become one of the better-known schools in the nation. The number of undergraduates enrolled increased dramatically as business job opportunities soared. In 1986 Dean John P. Evans announced a $1 million endowment named for Richard H. Jenrette, a New York investment banker and UNC–Chapel Hill trustee. Funds came from Jenrette and businesses with which he was associated. Paul J. Rizzo, vice chairman of IBM and a UNC–Chapel Hill alumnus, succeeded Evans in the deanship in August 1987 and within a short time announced plans to raise up to $30 million for a new complex housing the School of Business Administration.

Among major buildings completed during the 1980s was the $8 million Kenan Center built on the south campus to house the William R. Kenan, Jr. Fund and the Frank Hawkins Kenan Institute for the Study of Private Enterprise, the nation's first center for the study of entrepreneurship and small businesses.

In May 1985 the General Alumni Association announced plans to build an alumni center, a proposed $7 million structure to be located adjacent to the Kenan Center and the Smith Center on the south campus. The association had long occupied cramped quarters at the Carolina Inn. A year later, in May 1986, the association reported it had received an anonymous $3.5 million challenge gift along with $500,000 from the trustees of the James M. Johnston Trust. The association launched a fund-raising campaign and by July 1987 had raised $5.5 million.

Simultaneously George Watts Hill, Sr., member of a family long noted for university benefactions, was revealed as the challenge gift donor. On Hill's urging and with the administration's blessings, the association agreed to move the building site to Stadium Drive, adjacent to Kenan Stadium. The new location, one of the last wooded areas on the south campus, aroused student opposition. Criticism centered on aesthetics and the loss of parking. Douglas Dibbert, director of the General Alumni Association, emphasized that the building's design would preserve much of the area's natural beauty. Ralph Strayhorn, chief of fund raising for the project, said the center would have its own parking but would also use adjoining facilities. Officials viewed the center's proximity to the stadium as convenient for alumni and other campus visitors. Ground-breaking ceremonies for the new building, then scheduled to cost $12 million, were held in May 1989.[9]

As new buildings sprang up in every corner of the north and south campuses and traffic soared, the Fordham administration moved to devise a comprehensive land-use plan. No such plan had been drawn up since the early 1920s when President Chase originated the project to develop the wilderness behind South Building.

In the fall of 1985 the university chose the firm of Johnson, Johnson, and Roy of Ann Arbor, Michigan, to perform the task. In April 1987 the firm submitted its report, a comprehensive document recommending construction and relocation of certain streets, several of them through sensitive parts of the campus. Substantial criticism greeted the proposal to carve a new street through a residential area near the former country club and swallow up the edge of Battle Park. The thoroughfare plan, designed to improve the flow of north-south traffic on both the east and west sides of the campus, also called for relocating several streets and wiping out Odum Village's married student housing on the south campus.

The furor led Fordham and Chapel Hill mayor James C. Wallace to establish a joint university-town committee that met many times in efforts to assuage the criticism of local property owners. In December 1987 it offered a plan eliminating several of the features in the earlier plan. The report won general acceptance from the town council and the Board of Trustees.

After a hiatus caused by transitions in the chancellor's office, work on the larger land-use plan was resumed in 1989. The new plan embraced not only the 740-acre central campus but the 1,356-acre Mason Farm and Finley Golf Course; the 970-acre Horace Williams property, site of the university airport; and the University Lake tract of 575 acres.

One of the principal concerns of the planners—to avoid increasing the density and traffic of the central campus—seemed threatened by plans to construct a new School of Business building near the Kenan Center and the Dean Smith Student Activities Center on the south campus. With congestion already intense in that area, especially when some 20,000 people and their cars arrived for athletic events at Smith Center, the struggle to preserve some elements of tranquility and greenery at the heart of the campus seemed destined to continue. As one university official put it, "The conflict lay between local residents, often people with no past or present university connections, who want Chapel Hill to remain the tranquil village of earlier decades and university faculty and administrators who see the physical growth of the campus as an inevitable consequence of the evolution of the university into a major teaching and research center." Another village observer put it another way: "Chapel Hill's problem," he said, "is all those people who remember it the way it never was and want it to stay that way forever."[10]

Meanwhile, the medical school, first under the deanship of Isaac M. Taylor (1964–71) and then under Christopher Fordham (1971–80), expanded rapidly in many areas. In 1964 the National Institutes of Health selected Chapel Hill for one of its national centers for research in pharmacology and toxicology. The grant totaled $17,135,275 for a period of seven years, augmented by university funds for underwriting one-half of the costs of a new laboratory building. Also in 1964 the Sarah Graham Kenan Foundation, through its director Frank H. Kenan, made a grant to establish an endowed professorship for the medical school, the Sarah Graham Kenan professorship.

During the protracted controversy over the East Carolina medical school the General Assembly continued to fund important expansion projects for the UNC medical center. Beginning in 1965, the legislature appropriated $3,971,000 for a large addition to the basic sciences building (MacNider Hall) and for a new health sciences library. During the 1969 session it provided for some $20 million in expansion projects, the largest sum ever made available in one grant. This went for a research laboratory and clinical department additions, upgrading several facilities that had been housed in trailers. It funded new beds for the hospital in what was called the bed tower addition and financed other projects connected with expanding enrollment.[11]

North Carolina Memorial Hospital suffered setbacks in management during the late 1960s resulting in patient dissatisfaction and steps to overhaul administrative leadership. A study committee set up in 1969 submitted productive recommendations covering financial and general operation. In 1971 the hospital was placed under management of a separate board of directors and was largely separated from the control of the chancellors and trustees in an effort to restore its effective operation.[12]

The medical school also encountered management problems in the late 1960s resulting in the resignation of twenty-eight faculty members during the 1968–69 academic year. The school felt the pressures of unprecedented expansion—growth in enrollment, faculty, and academic programs.[13] During the 1970s under Dean Fordham, the school moved steadily forward, increasing total enrollment from 318 to 534 and establishing six new departments. Two of its faculty members, Dr. Kenneth Brinkhous and Dr. Carl Gottschalk, became members of the National Academy of Sciences.

By the late 1970s a study showed that the UNC medical school served as the largest single source of Tar Heel physicians. The school had awarded the M.D. degree to 1,952 students since 1954, when the first degree was granted. Some 91 percent of these students entered as North Carolinians, and 1,350 were still practicing in the state.[14]

In the post–World War II years the School of Public Health, founded in 1935 and headed for over a decade by Dr. Milton J. Rosenau, made vigorous strides. Having initiated graduate degrees in such areas as sanitary engineering, epidemiology, health administration, and parasitology, it added departments of public health nursing and education. These expansions continued under the leadership of Dr. Edward G. McGavran. In 1963 the school moved to its new quarters—Rosenau Hall—across South Columbia Street from MacNider Hall.

The school helped found the Carolina Population Center to coordinate research and education programs. It attracted the support of the Ford Foundation, the Rockefeller Foundation, the U.S. Agency for International Development, and the National Institutes of Health. The U.S. Foreign Service used the center for training diplomats for service around the world, and its influence was felt on family planning programs in India, Thailand, and Latin America.

During the 1970s and 1980s, under Deans Bernard Greenberg and Michel Ibrahim, the school developed creative ways to deal with cancer, AIDS, smoking, alcohol and drug abuse, aging, and toxic wastes. It solidified its position as one of the outstanding schools of public health in the nation.[15]

As the university's academic reputation flourished, so did its prowess in intercollegiate athletics. From the time of Edward Kidder Graham through the mid-1950s furor over the Dixie Classic, the administration had maintained firm control over athletics and demanded a high level of academic performance. Coach Dean Smith's remarkable record in basketball became the university's proof that championship teams on the playing field could fulfill their responsibilities in the classrooms. By the mid-1980s 158 of Smith's 164 scholarship athletes had won their academic degrees. Smith demanded competent classroom performance. "Athletics is to the university like the front porch is to a home," he often said. "It is the most visible part, yet certainly not the most important."

Nevertheless, the university became embroiled again in an embarrassing sports dispute in 1987 as alumni pressure forced chief football coach Dick Crum to resign because of an eroding win-loss record, recruiting difficulties, and what was described as poor interpersonal communications. The Crum affair attracted widespread attention because the coach was serving under the umbrella of a ten-year contract that provided for a stipulated settlement in case of dismissal. Word that negotiations for such a settlement were in progress reached the press toward the end of a dismal football season. Even though it was clear that pressure for Crum's departure had become intense, Chancellor Fordham, Athletic Director John Swofford, and Crum himself issued a joint statement at the end of the football season denying it and insisting that the coach was free to make his own decision. To further complicate matters Crum's attorney, Travis Porter, happened to be a member of the university's Board of Governors and a former member of the UNC–Chapel Hill Board of Trustees, thus creating a questionable conflict of interests.

As the matter became more widely publicized, the administration called on the privately financed North Carolina Education Foundation (the powerful Rams Club) for assistance. That organization agreed to underwrite an $885,000 settlement of Crum's contract, thus relieving the university of the obligation.

Crum's departure under those circumstances at the end of the year left bad feelings among members of the faculty and embarrassment on all sides, since the veteran coach had won more games than any of his predecessors during his ten-year career at Chapel Hill. Chancellor Fordham came under heavy criticism for the manner in which the resignation was handled.

The Crum controversy erupted in the wake of Chancellor Fordham's announcement in August 1987 that he would retire at the end of the 1987–88 academic year and would return to teaching in the medical school. As a search committee for his replacement was appointed, the Board of Trustees decided to conduct a management audit of the university to help in that task.

A team of nationally recognized academic consultants under the chairmanship of James L. Fisher, president emeritus of the Council for Advancement and Support of Education of Washington, D.C., conducted the study. It was based on interviews with 130 individuals across the state. The team's report recognized the university's high standing among major universities of the nation but found concern that the "institution is falling behind while coasting on its former glory." Among problem areas cited where low faculty and support salaries, overly strict state fiscal regulations, weakness in some academic departments, and an increasingly bureaucratic administration plagued by a vague decision-making process and inadequate planning. The report also incorporated criticism of the relationship between the chancellor and the president of the university system, both of whose headquarters and homes are in Chapel Hill. The report attracted attention across the state because it delved into sensitive problems facing the university as it sought new leadership. The study also mirrored unrest within the Board of Trustees over the university's evolving position in the state's education system.

In the late 1980s another changing of the guard occurred that affected not only Chapel Hill but the entire sixteen-institution system. President William Friday reached the nominal retirement age of sixty-five in 1985. Friday believed that the university's retirement-at-sixty-five policy had been soundly conceived. Having pressed it upon others, he decided to follow it himself, although he hoped there would be Board of Governors insistence on his remaining. Some factions on the Board of Governors had begun to chafe under Friday's domination, even though his skillful management had always been evenhanded and inclusive. The board resolved to push forward with the search for his successor, in the meantime asking Friday to stay on until one could be found.

That successor, C. Dixon Spangler, Jr., a wealthy, fifty-three-year-old Charlotte businessman who also served as chairman of the North Carolina State Board of Education, became the fourth president of the multicampus university on March 1, 1986. A graduate of UNC–Chapel Hill and the Harvard Business School, Spangler, like his predecessor Friday, came to his new job with no teaching experience, winning out over 150 candidates, most of them presidents of other institutions or heavily involved in academia.

Spangler's election marked another step in the gradual withdrawal of the system presidency from its formerly close links with Chapel Hill. Friday, as a protégé of both his predecessors Frank Graham and Gordon Gray, had maintained intimate ties with the university, more so than with the system's other fifteen institutions. This helped Chapel Hill's causes on the state political front but also created dual-management problems for the president and the chancellor.

William Friday's thirty-year tenure as administrator of the state's university system reflected educational statesmanship of a high order. Friday knew how to inspire associates by appealing to their better nature. An astute politician in the best sense, he nevertheless resembled Frank Graham in the generosity of his character and his instinct for the noble impulse. Like the Graham of an earlier era, he played an indispensable role in making university consolidation work. "He was the right person for the right concept for this state at the right time."[16]

The university and the state overwhelmed Friday with accolades as he retired. He became president of the William R. Kenan, Jr. Fund. He presided over its move from New York City to Chapel Hill, where it championed a host of philanthropic endeavors, many initiated by Friday, to lift the level of literacy and improve the quality of life in North Carolina.

Friday's retirement and Spangler's arrival in 1986 had almost as much significance for Chapel Hill as Fordham's departure and the arrival in 1988 of his successor, fifty-four-year-old Paul Hardin III, the Duke University graduate tapped by Spangler and the Board of Governors. Hardin was a Tar Heel Methodist minister's son who had grown up in the state and knew it well. His administrative career before coming home had been varied and tough. As an attorney who taught for ten years at the Duke University law school, he served as president of Southern Methodist University and left there after performing courageously in a controversy over athletics. Hardin came to Chapel Hill from the presidency of Drew University, a small private institution in New Jersey. A keen and warmly articulate person, he quickly and quietly grasped the reins of academic leadership and seemed to possess the qualities sought by the board.

As these new leaders arrived, the old university approached its two-hundredth birthday. It was a time for celebration and fresh planning for what seemed to be an increasingly difficult future. A rapidly tightening economy and secondary school difficulties piled budgetary problems on academic managers. How could the university continue to fulfill the mission of those farsighted individuals who had set it on its way decades before?

The Chapel Hill that had once, in the words of David L. Cohn, seemed "a rural Arcadia filled with woodsy innocence and naive delight" had vanished in the bustling bigness of the late twentieth century. Its university was still recognized as the South's celebrated "village citadel of the mind." But it was losing much of its village charm and even some of its academic vigor. Operating an institution of more than 23,000 students required prodigious administrative skills more akin to those of a large corporation than of a small academy. Retaining its topflight faculty and maintaining its individualized teacher-student relationships became vital priorities for the university.

In the 1980s the state of North Carolina itself, once known as old Rip Van Winkle and then recognized for its progressive impetus, had lost some of its enterprising sheen. Its high school Scholastic Aptitude Test scores sagged and its infant mortality and prison population soared. The university felt the threat of slashed legislative appropriations and rising interest in peripheral campus activities involving big-time athletics and mass media entertainment.

If anything jeopardized the light and liberty of Chapel Hill on its two-hundredth birthday, it was the sweet smell of success itself—the twin dangers of bigness and affluence. They had transformed a small, struggling academy into a giant conglomerate of towering classroom buildings and dormitories and a talented, research-oriented faculty rewarded by generous contributions from the government and the private sector.

For this institution there still remained saving graces. Those qualities that had always stood it in good stead in times of trouble in the past could be called on again. Chartered and opened in revolutionary times, it had hovered time after time on the edge of collapse. Shepherded for years by the remarkably gallant and energetic William R. Davie, it had weathered a succession of stormy controversies. Guided as well by strong-willed Presbyterian schoolmasters, it overcame stubborn obstacles of poverty, politics, and religious strife, even managing to reopen after the wrenching onslaughts of civil war to become one of the nation's foremost universities.

As a fortress of light and liberty in the South's backcountry, Chapel Hill had always goaded those who supported it—the people of North Carolina—to rise above their ignorance and poverty and strive toward their noble potential. Sometimes it ruffled their feathers and disturbed their complacency, but it never lost their respect and their loyalty. "I remind you," wrote journalist Vermont Royster in 1978, "that through its long history and despite all the controversies that have swirled around Chapel Hill, the people of this state have never ceased to support it and defend it, no matter how much they were disturbed by it."[17]

This remained true during the bitter struggles over religious sectarianism in the late nineteenth century and the antievolution and speaker ban controversies of the twentieth century. "Born, then, of revolution and literally cradled in liberty," David Cohn wrote earlier in this century, "this university

Polk Place, South Campus.
(Photograph by Ann Hawthorne, Carolina Alumni Association)

would be an unnatural child of its freedom-loving parents if it should become a creature of reaction."[18]

Clearly its leaders through all the decades of the twentieth century had upheld that vital tradition, very rarely stooping to compromise on major questions of independence and academic integrity. What those leaders needed to do, as the third century unfolded and as bigness and impersonality threatened its underpinnings, was to remember the sage observation of one of its flamboyantly and controversially talented sons, the Raleigh *News & Observer* editor Jonathan Daniels. Writing in his book *Tar Heels* in 1941, Daniels noted that "the university has grown in stature by getting down closer and closer to the earth and the people around it. . . . Its chief greatness now, it seems to me, lies in the fact that, in addition to the glory that was Greece and the grandeur that was Rome, the immensity of the cosmos and the infiniteness of the atom, it has looked around it at the human qualities of the State and the South."[19]

Perhaps the university must once again look to the challenges around its own doorstep and in its own garden. Certainly North Carolina and the South are in need of such homeward-looking, close-at-hand missions as the twenty-first century approaches.

Daniels referred to the distinguished research and cultural contributions of the Odums, Greens, and Kochs of his own pre–World War II era. The university of the third century might again address the manifold problems in the South's own backyard, where an old agrarianism has been too quickly urbanized. Albert Coates called the university's sense of service a "magic Gulf Stream" coursing through the region. That strength can be revived. It still gives Chapel Hill its special distinction.

NOTES

CHAPTER ONE

1. Battle, *History*, 1:62.
2. Connor, *Documentary History*, 1: front cover leaf.
3. Battle, *History*, 1:63.
4. Ibid.
5. Henderson, Phi Beta Kappa Address.
6. Connor, *Documentary History*, 1:1–2.
7. Ibid., 1:2–5.
8. Robinson, *William R. Davie*, p. 222.
9. Ibid., p. 19.
10. Gobbel, *Church-State Relationships*, p. 10.
11. Parton, *Life of Andrew Jackson*, 1:72.
12. Robinson, *William R. Davie*, p. 223.
13. Ibid., p. 224.
14. Ibid., p. 228.
15. Connor, *Documentary History*, 1:39.
16. Battle, *History*, 1:11–12.
17. Murphey, Oration.
18. Battle, *History*, 1:19.
19. Ibid., 1:21–22.
20. Henderson, *Campus*, pp. 11–12.
21. Battle, *History*, 1:27.
22. Ibid., 1:25.
23. Henderson, *Campus*, p. 25.
24. *North Carolina Journal* (Halifax), September 25, 1793.
25. Robinson, *William R. Davie*, p. 232.
26. Connor, *Documentary History*, 1:197.

27. Henderson, *Campus*, p. 16.
28. *North Carolina Journal* (Halifax), July 10, 1793.
29. Ibid., March 20, 1793.
30. Letter to Judge Spruce Macay, September 3, 1793, Davie Papers.
31. Henderson, *Campus*, pp. 17–18.
32. *North Carolina Journal* (Halifax), October 30, 1793.

CHAPTER TWO

1. Battle, *History*, 1:40.
2. Hurley and Eagan, *The Prophet*, p. 84.
3. Robinson, *William R. Davie*, p. 43.
4. Gobbel, *Church-State Relationships*, p. 10.
5. Battle, *History*, 1:60.
6. Connor, "State Experiment," p. 9.
7. Battle, *History*, 1:93–94.
8. Drake, *Education in North Carolina*, pp. 61–62.
9. Connor, *Documentary History*, 1:389.
10. Henderson, *Campus*, p. 47.
11. Connor, *Documentary History*, 1:347.
12. Henderson, *Campus*, p. 49.
13. Battle, *History*, 1:59.
14. Henderson, *Campus*, p. 40.
15. Ibid., p. 43.
16. Battle, *History*, 1:15.
17. Connor, *Documentary History*, 1:478.
18. Robinson, *William R. Davie*, p. 243.
19. Battle, *History*, 1:66.

20. Connor, *Documentary History,* 1:347.

21. Robinson, *William R. Davie,* p. 252; Battle, *History,* 1:100.

22. Battle, *History,* 1:107–8.

23. Caldwell to Thomas Y. How of Princeton University, December 5–9, 1796, University Letters.

24. John Henry Hobart to Caldwell, November 30, 1796, University Letters.

25. Battle, *History,* 1:132.

26. Connor, *Documentary History,* 2:113.

27. Ibid., 2:196.

28. Drake, *Education in North Carolina,* p. 69.

29. Connor, *Documentary History,* 2:329.

30. Ibid., 2:313.

31. Robinson, *William R. Davie,* p. 257.

32. Davie to James Hogg, August 21, 1796, University Letters.

33. Battle, *History,* 1:142.

34. Connor, *Documentary History,* 2:216.

35. Ibid., 2:190.

36. Battle, *History,* 1:155.

CHAPTER THREE

1. Anderson, Oration, p. 59.

2. Spencer, "Dr. Joseph Caldwell," p. 46.

3. Battle, *History,* 1:173.

4. Broussard, "North Carolina Federalists," p. 37.

5. Battle, *History,* 1:138.

6. Ibid., 1:146.

7. Ibid., 1:147.

8. Broussard, "North Carolina Federalists," p. 38.

9. Battle, *History,* 1:173.

10. Ibid., 1:178.

11. Eldon L. Johnson, "The 'Other Jeffersons,'" p. 135.

12. Battle, *History,* 1:176.

13. Wagstaff, *Impressions,* p. 9.

14. Russell, *These Old Stone Walls,* p. 46.

15. Henderson, *Campus,* pp. 73–74.

16. Russell, *These Old Stone Walls,* p. 34.

17. Battle, *History,* 1:208.

18. Ibid., 1:211.

19. Ibid., 1:206.

20. Anderson, Oration, p. 68.

21. Battle, *History,* 1:230.

22. Ibid., 1:231.

23. Ibid., 1:232.

24. Bailey, *Diplomatic History,* pp. 136–39.

25. Battle, *History,* 1:233–36.

26. Ibid., 1:250–53.

27. Gobbel, *Church-State Relationships,* p. 13.

28. Ibid., pp. 23–28.

29. Battle, *History,* 1:258.

30. Ibid., 1:281.

31. Ibid., 1:292.

32. Ibid., 1:295.

33. Russell, *These Old Stone Walls,* p. 35.

34. Battle, *History,* 1:336.

35. Russell, *These Old Stone Walls,* p. 13.

36. Spencer, "Old Times in Chapel Hill," *University Monthly,* May 1888, p. 329.

37. Battle, *History,* 1:233.

38. Ibid., 1:343.

39. Ibid., 1:344–45.

40. Russell, *These Old Stone Walls,* p. 43.

41. Henderson, *Campus,* p. 70.

42. Spencer, "Dr. Joseph Caldwell," p. 54.

43. Anderson, Oration, p. 57.

CHAPTER FOUR

1. Chamberlain, *Old Days*, pp. 38–39.

2. Ashe, *Biographical History*, pp. 448, 449, 452.

3. Chamberlain, *Old Days*, pp. 40–41.

4. Ibid., p. 42.

5. Ashe, *Biographical History*, p. 450.

6. Gobbel, *Church-State Relationships*, pp. 41–43.

7. Battle, *History*, 1:518–19.

8. Wagstaff, *Impressions*, p. 12.

9. Ibid., p. 11.

10. Drake, *Education in North Carolina*, p. 153.

11. Ibid., p. 242.

12. Ibid., p. 196.

13. N. V. Johnson, "Fraternities," p. 85.

14. Drake, *Education in North Carolina*, p. 212.

15. Henderson, *Campus*, pp. 92–96. The plate remains in the university archives.

16. Ibid., pp. 94–95.

17. Drake, *Education in North Carolina*, p. 219.

18. Ibid., p. 224.

19. Ibid., pp. 226–28.

20. Battle, *History*, 1:465.

21. Drake, *Education in North Carolina*, pp. 246–47.

22. Ibid., p. 112.

23. Vance, Commencement Address, pp. 14–15.

24. Henderson, *Campus*, p. 147.

25. Ibid.

26. Ibid., p. 184.

27. Ibid., p. 174.

28. Russell, *These Old Stone Walls*, pp. 109–10.

29. Battle, *History*, 1:654.

30. Ibid., 1:655–56.

31. Russell, *These Old Stone Walls*, p. 111.

32. Gobbel, *Church-State Relationships*, pp. 52, 54.

33. Battle, *History*, 1:699.

34. Chamberlain, *Old Days*, p. 69.

35. Wagstaff, *Impressions*, p. 13.

36. Battle, *History*, 1:729.

37. Weeks, "University in Civil War," pp. 16–17.

38. Wagstaff, *Impressions*, p. 12.

39. Vance, Commencement Address, p. 16.

40. Ibid.

41. Henderson, *Campus*, p. 183.

42. Russell, *Woman Who Rang the Bell*, p. 95.

43. Ashe, *Biographical History*, p. 456.

44. Chamberlain, *Old Days*, p. 88.

45. Spencer, "Old Times in Chapel Hill," *University Magazine*, May 1884, p. 21.

46. Ibid., p. 217.

47. Ibid., p. 218.

48. Chamberlain, *Old Days*, p. 99.

49. Battle, *History*, 1:754.

50. Russell, *Woman Who Rang the Bell*, p. 83.

51. Spencer, "Old Times in Chapel Hill," *University Magazine*, May 1884, p. 218.

52. Wagstaff, *Impressions*, p. 15.

53. Chamberlain, *Old Days*, p. 148.

54. Battle, *History*, 1:777.

55. Russell, *Woman Who Rang the Bell*, pp. 103–4.

CHAPTER FIVE

1. Vance, *Sketches of North Carolina,* pp. 57–58.
2. Raper, *Holden,* p. xv.
3. Chamberlain, *Old Days,* p. 151.
4. Russell, *Woman Who Rang the Bell,* p. 113.
5. Ibid., p. 112.
6. Henderson, *Campus,* p. 190.
7. Russell, *Woman Who Rang the Bell,* p. 115.
8. Vance, *Sketches of North Carolina,* pp. 57–58.
9. Chamberlain, *Old Days,* p. 156.
10. Wagstaff, *Impressions,* pp. 16–17.
11. Ibid.
12. Henderson, *Campus,* p. 198.
13. Ibid.
14. Russell, *Woman Who Rang the Bell,* p. 115.
15. Chamberlain, *Old Days,* p. 156.
16. *Wilmington Daily Journal,* June 6, 1869.
17. Chamberlain, *Old Days,* p. 158.
18. Russell, *Woman Who Rang the Bell,* p. 120.
19. *Daily Sentinel* (Raleigh), April 6, 1869.
20. Ibid., June 5, 1869.
21. *North Carolina Standard* (Raleigh), June 10, 1869.
22. Battle, *History,* 2:32–33.
23. Chamberlain, *Old Days,* pp. 163–64.
24. *North Carolina Standard* (Raleigh), June 12, 1869.
25. Russell, *Woman Who Rang the Bell,* p. 126.
26. Raper, *Holden,* p. 125.
27. *North Carolina Standard* (Raleigh), June 12, 1869.
28. Raper, *Holden,* p. 124.

29. Ibid., p. 125.
30. Russell, *Woman Who Rang the Bell,* p. 132.
31. Chamberlain, *Old Days,* p. 186.
32. *North Carolina Presbyterian,* June 22, 1870.
33. Raper, *Holden,* p. 155.
34. Russell, *Woman Who Rang the Bell,* pp. 128–29.
35. Chamberlain, *Old Days,* p. 174.
36. Russell, *Woman Who Rang the Bell,* p. 129.
37. Raper, *Holden,* pp. 158–59.
38. Russell, *Woman Who Rang the Bell,* pp. 135–36.
39. Raper, *Holden,* p. 199.
40. Russell, *Woman Who Rang the Bell,* p. 136.
41. Raper, *Holden,* p. 126.
42. Russell, *Woman Who Rang the Bell,* p. 144.
43. Battle, *History,* 2:41.
44. Ibid., 2:584.

CHAPTER SIX

1. Wagstaff, *Impressions,* p. 17.
2. Russell, *Woman Who Rang the Bell,* p. 137.
3. Wagstaff, *Impressions,* p. 17.
4. Raper, *Holden,* p. 128.
5. Chamberlain, *Old Days,* p. 116.
6. Russell, *Woman Who Rang the Bell,* p. 142.
7. Ibid.
8. *Daily Sentinel* (Raleigh), June 15, 1873.
9. *Weekly Era* (Raleigh), July 31, 1873.
10. *Daily Sentinel* (Raleigh), August 1–2, 1873.

11. Gwin, " 'Poisoned Arrows,' " chap. 2.

12. Wagstaff, *Impressions*, p. 18.

13. Battle, *History*, 2:53.

14. Ibid., 2:58.

15. Ibid., 2:60.

16. Ibid., 2:65.

17. Russell, *Woman Who Rang the Bell*, pp. 149–50.

18. Ibid.

19. Ibid., pp. 151–52.

20. Ibid., p. 153.

21. Ibid.

22. Battle, *History*, 2:90.

23. Ibid., 2:94.

24. Ibid., 2:95–97.

CHAPTER SEVEN

1. Chamberlain, *Old Days*, p. 233.

2. Battle, *History*, 2:115.

3. Toynbee, *History*, p. 316.

4. Wagstaff, *Impressions*, p. 27.

5. Ibid., pp. 28–29.

6. Battle, *History*, 2:116.

7. Wagstaff, *Impressions*, p. 30.

8. Ibid.

9. Chamberlain, *Old Days*, p. 226.

10. Ibid., p. 228.

11. Wagstaff, *Impressions*, p. 34.

12. Russell, *Woman Who Rang the Bell*, pp. 162–63.

13. Ibid., pp. 161–62.

14. Wagstaff, *Impressions*, pp. 35–36.

15. Ibid., p. 36.

16. Henderson, *Campus*, pp. 198–201.

17. Russell, *Woman Who Rang the Bell*, pp. 171–72.

18. Annual Report of the State Superintendent of Public Instruction, 1881–1882, North Carolina Archives (Raleigh), p. 68.

19. Gobbel, *Church-State Relationships*, p. 67.

20. *Biblical Recorder* (Raleigh), January 5, 1881.

21. Battle, *History*, 2:103.

22. Ibid., 2:205–13.

23. Ibid., 2:227.

24. *Carolina Watchman*, February 24, 1881.

25. *Wilmington Morning Star*, January 27, 1881.

26. Gobbel, *Church-State Relationships*, pp. 105–6.

27. Battle, *History*, 2:337–38, 379–82.

28. Gobbel, *Church-State Relationships*, p. 121.

29. Wagstaff, *Impressions*, pp. 42–43.

30. Ibid., p. 45.

31. Ibid., p. 44.

32. Ibid., p. 47.

33. Battle, *History*, 2:376–78.

34. Henderson, *Campus*, pp. 110–18, 245.

35. Ibid., pp. 245–48.

36. Gobbel, *Church-State Relationships*, p. 79.

37. Henderson, *Campus*, pp. 249–50.

38. Ibid., p. 251.

39. Ibid., pp. 252–53.

40. Battle, *History*, 2:203–4.

41. Ibid., 2:191–92.

42. Henderson, *Campus*, pp. 158–65.

43. Ibid., pp. 127–31.

44. Ibid., pp. 264–68.

45. Battle, *History*, 2:345–46; also Battle, *Memories*, p. 290.

46. Wagstaff, *Impressions*, pp. 48–49.

47. Battle, *History*, 2:404, 413, 423, 437, 449.

48. Ibid., 2:459.

49. Wagstaff, *Impressions*, p. 26.

50. Ibid., p. 31.

CHAPTER EIGHT

1. Russell, *These Old Stone Walls*, quoting Mrs. C. P. Spencer, p. 67.

2. Canada, *Life at Eighty*, p. 26.

3. Wagstaff, *Impressions*, pp. 51, 57.

4. Winston, *Far Cry*, pp. 43–44.

5. Russell, *These Old Stone Walls*, p. 74.

6. Battle, *History*, 2:466.

7. *State Chronicle* (Raleigh), June 3, 1890.

8. Wagstaff, *Impressions*, p. 58.

9. Gobbel, *Church-State Relationships*, pp. 131–34.

10. *State Chronicle* (Raleigh), February 14, 1893.

11. Wagstaff, *Impressions*, p. 61.

12. Gobbel, *Church-State Relationships*, p. 139.

13. *Tar Heel* (Chapel Hill), March 30, 1894.

14. Gobbel, *Church-State Relationships*, pp. 140–41.

15. *University Magazine* (Chapel Hill), April 1895.

16. Winston to Mrs. Spencer, April 9, 1895, Spencer Papers.

17. Gobbel, *Church-State Relationships*, p. 149.

18. Ibid., pp. 158–62; also Battle, *History*, 2:490.

19. Wagstaff, *Impressions*, p. 62.

20. Powell, *First State University*, pp. 123, 125.

21. *North Carolina Folklore*.

22. Powell, *First State University*, p. 116.

23. Ibid., p. 128.

24. Ibid., p. 144.

25. Wagstaff, *Impressions*, pp. 63–64.

26. Ibid., pp. 58–59.

27. Ibid., p. 63.

28. Russell, *These Old Stone Walls*, p. 73.

CHAPTER NINE

1. Malone, *Alderman*, pp. 3–5.

2. Ibid., p. 6.

3. E. A. Alderman, "Woodrow Wilson." Memorial address delivered before a joint session of Congress, 1924.

4. Battle, *History*, 2:535.

5. E. A. Alderman, "In Memoriam." Memorial address for Charles Duncan McIver, fiftieth anniversary volume, National Education Association, 1907, p. 311.

6. Battle, *History*, 2:536.

7. Malone, *Alderman*, p. 35.

8. Ibid., pp. 37–47.

9. Ibid., p. 53.

10. *UNC Alumni Quarterly*, October 1894, pp. 10–14.

11. Malone, *Alderman*, p. 63.

12. National Education Association *Journal of Proceedings and Addresses*, 1895, p. 981.

13. Malone, *Alderman*, p. 58.

14. Ibid., pp. 73–77.

15. Ibid., p. 78.

16. Ibid., p. 82.

17. Henderson, *Campus*, pp. 210–11.

18. Ibid., p. 212.

19. Malone, *Alderman*, pp. 88–89.

20. Gobbel, *Church-State Relationships*, p. 166.

21. Ibid., p. 171.

22. Josephus Daniels, *Editor in Politics*, pp. 318–24.

23. Alderman's Report to University

Trustees, February 21, 1900, *University Record* 5, no. 3, Minutes, pp. 123–33.

24. Malone, *Alderman*, p. 79; Louis Graves, "Memories of Edwin Alderman," *Chapel Hill Weekly*, May 8, 1931.

25. National Education Association *Journal of Proceedings and Addresses*, 1900, pp. 88–89.

26. Josephus Daniels, *Tar Heel Editor*, p. 465.

27. Malone, *Alderman*, pp. 97–98.

28. Ibid., pp. 100–102.

CHAPTER TEN

1. Henderson, *Campus*, p. 225.

2. Wilson, *University*, p. 45.

3. Wagstaff, *Impressions*, p. 85.

4. Wilson, *University*, p. 46.

5. Bursey, "Carolina Chemists," pp. 11–14.

6. Wilson, *University*, p. 19.

7. Ibid., pp. 93–98.

8. Ibid., pp. 98–105.

9. Ibid., pp. 105–7.

10. Ibid., pp. 71–76.

11. Ibid., p. 79.

12. Ibid., pp. 60–61.

13. Ibid., pp. 115–18.

14. Ibid., p. 127.

15. Ibid., p. 124.

16. Wagstaff, *Impressions*, pp. 82–83.

17. Wilson, *University*, pp. 141–45.

18. Ibid., pp. 146–52.

19. Wagstaff, *Impressions*, pp. 94–95.

20. *Tar Heel* (Chapel Hill), January 21, 1904.

21. Wilson, *University*, pp. 146–52.

22. Ibid., pp. 152–59.

23. Bursey, *Venable*, p. 66.

24. Wilson, *University*, p. 165.

25. Frank Porter Graham, "The University Today," *Alumni Review*, December 1931, p. 110.

CHAPTER ELEVEN

1. House, *The Light*, p. 8.

2. Ibid., pp. 15–16.

3. Wilson, *University*, pp. 179–80.

4. Henderson, "Edward K. Graham."

5. Albert Coates, *What the University Meant*, p. 50.

6. House, *The Light*, p. 77.

7. Coates to Professor Horace Williams, *University of North Carolina Record*, January 1919, p. 8.

8. Henderson, "E. K. G."

9. Graham, *Education and Citizenship*, pp. 13–14.

10. Wilson, *University*, p. 288.

11. Howell, *Kenan Professorships*, p. 17.

12. Ibid., p. 30.

13. Ibid., p. 35.

14. Wilson, *University*, p. 198.

15. Ibid., pp. 231–32.

16. Ibid., p. 217.

17. Ibid., p. 221.

18. Ibid., p. 219.

19. Ibid., pp. 244–50.

20. Ibid., pp. 253–59.

21. Ibid., p. 272.

22. Ibid., p. 278.

23. *University of North Carolina Record*, January 1919, p. 20.

24. Wilson, *University*, p. 290.

25. Henderson, "Two Notable Educators," p. 106.

26. House, *The Light*, p. 49.

CHAPTER TWELVE

1. Gerald W. Johnson, *South-Watching*, p. 171.

2. H. W. Chase, replying to a questionnaire sent him by the secretary of the 1904 class of Dartmouth, Chase Papers.

3. Wilson, *University*, p. 298.

4. Gerald W. Johnson, *South-Watching*, p. 170.

5. Wilson, *University*, pp. 309–13.

6. Ibid., p. 308.

7. *Alumni Review*, May 1920, pp. 263–64.

8. Wilson, *University*, pp. 320–22.

9. Ibid., pp. 325–29.

10. Ibid., pp. 331–34.

11. Ibid., pp. 413–17.

12. Ibid., pp. 425–27.

13. Ibid., pp. 430–33.

14. *University of North Carolina Record*, December 1919, pp. 27–28.

15. *Alumni Review*, February 1922, pp. 136–37; March 1927, p. 193.

16. Singal, *The War Within*, p. 115.

17. Ibid., p. 119.

18. Tindall, "Odum," p. 307.

19. Singal, *The War Within*, p. 121.

20. Ibid., p. 122.

21. Wilson, *University*, pp. 487–90.

22. Selden, *Koch*, p. 11.

23. Ibid., p. 27.

24. Wilson, *University*, p. 351.

25. April 10, 1924, Chase Papers.

26. Wilson, *University*, pp. 353–57.

27. Ibid., pp. 362, 365, 369.

28. Henderson, *Campus*, pp. 219–21.

29. Ibid., pp. 218–19.

30. Wilson, *University*, pp. 462–64.

31. Gatewood, *Preachers*, pp. 44–45.

32. Ibid., pp. 104–5.

33. Ibid., p. 94.

34. Ibid., p. 108.

35. Chase to Poteat, February 16, 1925, Chase Papers.

36. Chase to Cobb, February 7, 1925, Chase Papers.

37. Gatewood, *Preachers*, pp. 132–33.

38. Ibid., pp. 143–45.

39. *Greensboro Record*, February 21, 1925.

40. Gatewood, *Preachers*, pp. 181–82.

41. *Charlotte Observer*, June 2, 1926.

42. *News & Observer* (Raleigh), April 5, 1925.

43. Wilson, *University*, p. 385.

44. Branson to Robert L. Gray, in *Branson*, p. 23.

45. Wilson, *University*, pp. 386, 476, 477, 478.

46. Henderson, *Campus*, pp. 318–20.

47. Ibid., pp. 221–22.

48. Ibid., p. 383.

49. Wilson, *University*, pp. 387–89.

50. Ibid., pp. 396–97.

51. *Alumni Review*, December 1930.

52. Wilson, *University*, pp. 410–11.

53. Wettach, *Legal Education*, pp. 55–63.

54. Berryhill et al., *Medical Education*, p. 28.

55. Wilson, *University*, pp. 570–71.

56. Gerald W. Johnson, *South-Watching*, p. 179.

CHAPTER THIRTEEN

1. Malone, *Alderman*, p. 346.

2. Tindall, *New South*, pp. 225–26, 266–67.

3. Ibid., pp. 252–53.

4. *News & Observer* (Raleigh), June 13, 1930.

5. Ashby, *Graham*, pp. 24–25.

6. Ibid., p. 19.

7. *News & Observer* (Raleigh), April 5, 1925.

8. Ashby, *Graham*, pp. 67–68.

9. Ibid., pp. 69–70.

10. Ibid., p. 79.

11. Graham to Kemp Battle, February 18, 1930, Graham Papers.

12. Ashby, *Graham*, pp. 82–83; MacNider to Graham, February 25, 1930, Graham Papers.

13. Graham to F. O. Clarkson, June 4, 1930, Graham Papers.

14. Ashby, *Graham*, pp. 85–86; *Alumni Review,* June 1930; *Christian Science Monitor,* October 14, 1930; *News & Observer* (Raleigh), June 10, 1930.

15. *News & Observer* (Raleigh), June 13, 1930.

16. Ashby, *Graham*, pp. 87–88.

17. *News & Observer* (Raleigh), June 30, 1931.

18. *Chapel Hill Weekly,* April 9, 1931.

19. Graham to Gerald Johnson, July 17, 1931, Graham Papers.

20. Ashby, *Graham*, pp. 129–30.

21. *Greensboro Daily News,* November 12, 1931.

22. Frank Graham, Inaugural Address, November 11, 1931, Graham Papers.

23. *Greensboro Daily News,* November 12, 1931.

24. Quoted by Robert Madry, UNC News Bureau chief, in press release after Graham's inauguration, November 11, 1931, from the *Chapel Hill Weekly.*

25. Ashby, *Graham*, p. 102.

26. Ibid., pp. 108–9.

27. Ibid., pp. 110–12.

28. Graham to Leslie Weil, November 2, 1932, Graham Papers.

29. Daniels to Graham, November 7, 1932, Graham Papers.

30. Lockmiller, *Consolidation*, p. 56.

31. *Alumni Review,* June 1933, p. 283.

32. Ashby, *Graham*, pp. 115–17.

33. Ibid., p. 121.

34. Lockmiller, *Consolidation*, p. 71.

35. Ibid., p. 73.

36. Ibid., pp. 74–76.

37. *Durham Herald,* May 15, 1936.

38. Graham to Board of Trustees, May 22, 1936, Graham Papers.

39. Ashby, *Graham*, pp. 125–26.

40. Ibid., pp. 128–29.

41. *News & Observer* (Raleigh), September 10, 1934.

42. Ashby, *Graham*, pp. 131–32.

43. Ibid., p. 133.

44. *Greensboro Daily News,* editorial, January 26, 1936.

45. *News & Observer* (Raleigh), February 1, 1936.

46. *Durham Herald,* March 1, 1936.

47. *Greensboro Daily News,* letter, March 8, 1936.

48. Ashby, *Graham*, pp. 137–38.

49. Ibid., pp. 135–36.

50. Ibid., p. 140.

51. Ibid., pp. 154–61.

52. Ibid., pp. 162–68.

53. Heard, Address.

54. John Sanders, remarks at memorial celebration honoring Albert Coates, March 29, 1989, Chapel Hill, author's copy.

55. Berryhill et al., *Medical Education*, pp. 37–41.

56. Ibid., pp. 46–48.

57. William Allen White, *Defense for America*, p. 10.

58. Frank P. Graham, "The University and National Defense," convocation address, September 27, 1940, *Alumni Review,* October 1940, p. 4.

59. Ashby, *Graham*, pp. 174–80.

60. Henderson, *Campus*, pp. 312–14.

61. Ashby, *Graham*, pp. 189–91.

62. Ron Femrite, "A Long Locomotive for Choo Choo," *Sports Illustrated*, October 15, 1973, p. 48.

63. Ashby, *Graham*, pp. 197–200.

64. Berryhill et al., *Medical Education*, p. 71.

65. Robert B. House in *The Good Doctor*, ed. McLendon and Graves, pp. ix–x.

66. Berryhill et al., *Medical Education*, pp. 52–53.

67. Ashby, *Graham*, pp. 224–26.

68. Ibid., pp. 207–23.

69. Ibid., pp. 237–38.

70. Ibid., p. 243.

71. Ibid., p. 330.

72. Heard, Address.

CHAPTER FOURTEEN

1. Author's conversation with Arnold King, former UNC vice president, May 17, 1989.

2. Godfrey, "Aycock," pp. 215–18.

3. Conversation with Arnold King.

4. Radio broadcast, Robert Thompson, editor of the *High Point Enterprise*, August 1949, North Carolina Collection, Wilson Library, University of North Carolina, Chapel Hill.

5. R. M. Dobie, article in *This Week*, September 4, 1949.

6. *News & Observer* (Raleigh), June 19, 1951.

7. House to Gray, November 15, 1951, Chancellors Records, vol. 8, Southern Historical Collection, Wilson Library.

8. Conversation with Arnold King.

9. Roy Parker, "Bob House, Credentials of Excellence," *Alumni Review*, Fall 1987, p. 69.

10. Albert Coates, "Robert Burton House of Chapel Hill and North Carolina," address, June 4, 1950.

11. Taylor, *So This Is Education*, pp. 167–68, 173.

12. *News & Observer* (Raleigh), April 5, 1951; conversation with Arnold King.

13. *News & Observer* (Raleigh), April 5, 1951.

14. *Greensboro Daily News*, April 25, 1951.

15. Cheek, "Desegregation," pp. 153–58.

16. *New York Times*, April 1, 1951.

17. *Carolina Times* (Durham), March 31, 1951.

18. *Durham Morning Herald*, November 2, 1951.

19. *Daily Tar Heel* (Chapel Hill), September 29, 1951.

20. Albert and Gladys Coates, *Student Government*, p. 270.

21. *News & Observer* (Raleigh), April 7, 1952.

22. *New York Times Magazine*, March 4, 1956, p. 42.

23. Berryhill et al., *Medical Education*, pp. 78–84.

24. Ibid., pp. 88–100.

25. King, *Multi-Campus University*, p. 16.

CHAPTER FIFTEEN

1. Author's interviews with William Friday, 1985.

2. *Greensboro Daily News*, editorial, April 21, 1955.

3. King, *Multi-Campus University*, pp. 3–7.

4. Ibid., p. 8.

5. Ibid., pp. 8–9.

6. Ibid., p. 10.

7. Albert Coates, "Aycock."

8. Aycock, *Selected Speeches*, January 7, 1958.

9. Durden, "One Recumbent," pp. 445–68; *News & Observer* (Raleigh), March 27, 1945, and October 10, 1948.

10. Peter S. White, "Diversity."

11. *The First Report*, published by the John Motley Morehead Foundation, for the period November 21, 1945, to June 30, 1959.

12. King, *Multi-Campus University*, pp. 32–35.

13. Ibid., pp. 40–43.

14. *Greensboro Daily News*, June 17, 1989.

15. *News & Observer* (Raleigh), September 27, 1962.

16. King, *Multi-Campus University*, p. 51.

17. *Village Voice*, December 1963.

18. King, *Multi-Campus University*, pp. 71–72.

19. Aycock, *Selected Speeches*, pp. 107–8.

CHAPTER SIXTEEN

1. Joyce, "Reds on Campus," p. 6.

2. Ibid., p. 6.

3. King, *Multi-Campus University*, pp. 57–60.

4. Joyce, "Reds on Campus," p. 9.

5. King, *Multi-Campus University*, pp. 60–62.

6. Ibid., p. 65.

7. Joyce, "Reds on Campus," p. 11.

8. Pete Ivey, news release, UNC News Bureau, September 1965.

9. *Durham Morning Herald*, December 31, 1965.

CHAPTER SEVENTEEN

1. *Chapel Hill Weekly*, September 13, 1967.

2. King, *Multi-Campus University*, pp. 73–83.

3. Ibid., pp. 86–89.

4. Ibid., p. 89.

5. Ibid., pp. 90–91.

6. Manire, "A Research University."

7. King, *Multi-Campus University*, p. 100.

8. Ibid., p. 111.

9. Ibid., p. 112.

10. Ibid., p. 117.

11. Ibid., p. 120.

12. Ibid., p. 123.

13. Sanders, "Analysis of an Act to Consolidate," p. 1.

14. Ibid., p. 6.

15. Ibid., p. 27.

CHAPTER EIGHTEEN

1. King, *Multi-Campus University*, pp. 163–66.

2. *Alumni Review*, January 1980, pp. 6–12.

3. Powell, *First State University*, p. 296.

4. Ibid., pp. 303, 306, 307.

5. Ibid., pp. 225, 264, 276, 285, 299.

6. King, *Multi-Campus University*, pp. 176–78.

7. Robert Scott to George Watts Hill, Sr., April 13, 1970, North Carolina Collection, Wilson Library, University of North Carolina, Chapel Hill.

8. King, *Multi-Campus University*, pp. 185–91.

9. Ibid., p. 192.

10. Ibid., pp. 194–95.

11. *Greensboro Daily News*, February 7, 1978.

12. A full review of the UNC-HEW controversy appears in chapter 12 of King's *Multi-Campus University*, pp. 204–42.

13. Chancellor's Reports, 1972–1979, University Archives, Southern Historical Collection, Wilson Library.

14. Chancellor's Record, N. F. Taylor Series, subseries 1, box 8, University Archives, Southern Historical Collection, Wilson Library.

CHAPTER NINETEEN

1. Peter Range, "Capital of Southern Mind," *New York Times*, December 17, 1972.

2. Author's conversation with former university official, 1989.

3. Robert P. Joyce, "Bridging the Gaps," *Carolina Alumni Review*, Fall 1989, p. 38.

4. "A Curriculum for the 1980s," faculty publication, UNC at Chapel Hill, 1982.

5. *News & Observer* (Raleigh), March 28, 1986.

6. Ibid., November 21, 1986.

7. *Charlotte Observer*, April 28, 1987.

8. *News & Observer* (Raleigh), December 16, 1982.

9. *Daily Tar Heel* (Chapel Hill), May 23, 1985; July 2, 1987; April 20, 1988.

10. *The White & Blue*, publication of the Dialectic and Philanthropic Societies, March 1989, pp. 4–7; memorandum by John Sanders, Institute of Government, September 1990.

11. Berryhill et al., *Medical Education*, pp. 138–39.

12. Ibid., pp. 146–48, 158–59.

13. Ibid., pp. 148–49.

14. Ibid., p. 169.

15. Robert Korstad, "Fighting for Our Lives," *Carolina Alumni Review*, Fall 1989.

16. Fisher, "University Review," p. 61.

17. Vermont Royster, "A Remembrance," *Carolina Alumni Review*, Fall 1978.

18. David L. Cohn, "Chapel Hill," *Atlantic Monthly*, March 1941.

19. Jonathan Daniels, *Tar Heels*, pp. 271–72.

BIBLIOGRAPHY

MANUSCRIPTS

Southern Historical Collection, Wilson Library, University of North Carolina,
Chapel Hill, N.C.
Harry Woodburn Chase Papers
William R. Davie Papers
Frank Porter Graham Papers
Cornelia Phillips Spencer Papers
University Letters, 1796–1835

BOOKS, ARTICLES, MONOGRAPHS, DISSERTATIONS,
AND ADDRESSES

Anderson, Walker. Oration on "The Life and Character of Joseph P. Caldwell,"
1835. Chapel Hill: John B. Neathery, Printer, 1860.
Ashby, Warren. *Frank P. Graham: A Southern Liberal.* Winston-Salem: John F.
Blair, 1980.
Ashe, Samuel. *Biographical History of North Carolina.* Vol. 1. Greensboro:
Charles Van Noppen, 1905.
Aycock, William B. *Selected Speeches and Statements, 1957–1964.* Chapel Hill:
UNC-CH News Bureau, 1964.
Bailey, Thomas A. *A Diplomatic History of the American People.* New York:
Appleton-Century-Crofts, 1946.
Battle, Kemp Plummer. *History of the University of North Carolina.* Vols. 1 and 2.
Raleigh: Edwards and Broughton, 1907, 1912.
———. *Memories of an Old-time Tar Heel.* Chapel Hill: University of North Car-
olina Press, 1945.
Berryhill, W. Reece; Blythe, William B.; Manning, Isaac H. *Medical Education at
Chapel Hill.* Chapel Hill: Medical Alumni Office, 1979.
Branson, Lanier. *Eugene Cunningham Branson, Humanitarian.* Charlotte: Heritage
Printers, 1967.
Broussard, James H. "The North Carolina Federalists, 1800–1816." *North Car-
olina Historical Review* 55, no. 1 (January 1978).
Bursey, Maurice M. "Carolina Chemists, Sketches from Chapel Hill." Chapel Hill:
University of North Carolina Department of Chemistry, 1982.
———. *Francis Preston Venable of the University of North Carolina.* Chapel Hill:
Chapel Hill Historical Society, 1989.

Canada, J. W. *Life at Eighty: Memories and Comments by a Tar Heel in Texas.* La Porte, Tex.: Privately published, 1952.

Chamberlain, Hope Summerell. *Old Days in Chapel Hill.* Chapel Hill: University of North Carolina Press, 1926.

Cheek, Neal King. "An Historical Study of the Administrative Actions in the Racial Desegregation of the University of North Carolina at Chapel Hill." Ph.D. dissertation, University of North Carolina, 1973. In North Carolina Collection, Wilson Library, Chapel Hill, N.C.

Coates, Albert. *What the University of North Carolina Meant to Me.* Chapel Hill: Privately published, 1969.

———. "William Brantley Aycock—Chancellor of the University of North Carolina at Chapel Hill." *Popular Government* 25, no. 25 (October 1957).

Coates, Albert and Gladys. *The Story of Student Government in the University of North Carolina at Chapel Hill.* Chapel Hill: Privately published, [1985].

Connor, R. D. W. *A Documentary History of the University of North Carolina.* Vol. 1, *1776–1795;* vol. 2, *1796–1799.* Chapel Hill: University of North Carolina Press, 1953.

———. "A State Experiment in Higher Education." Convocation address delivered at Chapel Hill, December 4, 1946.

Daniels, Jonathan. *Tar Heels.* New York: Dodd, Mead and Company, 1941.

Daniels, Josephus. *Editor in Politics.* Chapel Hill: University of North Carolina Press, 1941.

———. *Tar Heel Editor.* Chapel Hill: University of North Carolina Press, 1939.

Drake, William Earle. *Education in North Carolina before 1860.* Bloomfield, N.J.: Carleton Press, 1964.

Durden, Robert. "One Recumbent Too Many." *North Carolina Historical Review* 65 (October 4, 1988).

Fisher, James L. "The University of North Carolina at Chapel Hill Review." McLean, Md.: James L. Fisher, January, 1988.

Gatewood, Willard B., Jr. *Preachers, Pedagogues and Politicians: The Evolution Controversy in North Carolina.* Chapel Hill: University of North Carolina Press, 1966.

Gobbel, Luther L. *Church-State Relationships in Education in North Carolina since 1776.* Durham, N.C.: Duke University Press, 1938.

Godfrey, James L. "William Brantley Aycock, University Administrator, 1957–1964." *North Carolina Law Review* 64, no. 1.

Graham, Edward Kidder. *Education and Citizenship and Other Papers.* New York: G. P. Putnam's Sons, 1919.

Gwin, Pamela Jane Blair. "'Poisoned Arrows' from a Tar Heel Journalist: The Public Career of Cornelia Phillips Spencer, 1865–1890." Ph.D. dissertation, Duke University, 1983.

Heard, Alexander. Address to Order of Golden Fleece, Chapel Hill, April 7, 1989, author's copy.

Henderson, Archibald. *The Campus of the First State University.* Chapel Hill: University of North Carolina Press, 1949.

————. "Edward K. Graham Now at the Head." *News & Observer* (Raleigh), August 3, 1913.

————. "E. K. G." *News & Observer* (Raleigh), August 10, 1913.

————. Phi Beta Kappa Address, Memorial Hall, Chapel Hill, May 17, 1950.

————. "Two Notable Educators: Edward Kidder Graham." *Sewanee Review* 27 (1919).

House, Robert Burton. *The Light That Shines*. Chapel Hill: University of North Carolina Press, 1965.

Howell, A. C. *The Kenan Professorships*. Chapel Hill: University of North Carolina Press, 1956.

Hurley, James F., and Eagan, Julia Goode. *The Prophet of Zion-Parnassus*. Richmond: Presbyterian Committee of Publication, 1934.

Johnson, Eldon L. "The 'Other Jeffersons' and the State University Idea." *Journal of Higher Education* 58, no. 2 (March–April 1987).

Johnson, Gerald W. *South-Watching: Selected Essays*. Edited by Fred Hobson. Chapel Hill: University of North Carolina Press, 1983.

Johnson, N. V. "A Sketch of Fraternities of the University of North Carolina." *North Carolina Magazine*, February 1916.

Joyce, Robert P. "Reds on Campus: The Speaker Ban Controversy." *Carolina Alumni Review*, Chapel Hill, Spring 1984.

King, Arnold K. *The Multi-Campus University of North Carolina Comes of Age (1956–1986)*. Chapel Hill: University of North Carolina System, 1987.

Lockmiller, David A. *The Consolidation of the University of North Carolina*. Raleigh: Edwards and Broughton, 1942.

McLendon, William W., and Graves, Shirley, eds. *The Good Doctor*. Chapel Hill: University of North Carolina Press, 1953.

Malone, Dumas. *Edwin A. Alderman*. New York: Doubleday, Doran and Company, 1940.

Manire, G. Philip. "Carolina: A Research University, Genesis and Consequence." The Norma Berryhill Distinguished Lecture, North Carolina School of Medicine, September 10, 1986.

Murphey, Archibald D. An oration delivered in Person Hall, Chapel Hill, June 27, 1827. Raleigh: J. Gales and Son, 1827.

North Carolina Folklore 5, no. 2 (December 1957).

Parton, James. *Life of Andrew Jackson*. 3 vols. New York: Mason Brothers, 1860.

Pleasants, Julian M., and Burns, Augustus M. *Frank Porter Graham and the 1950 Senate Race in North Carolina*. Chapel Hill: University of North Carolina Press, 1990.

Powell, William S. *The First State University*. Chapel Hill: University of North Carolina Press, 1972.

Raper, Horace W. *William W. Holden: North Carolina's Political Enigma*. Chapel Hill: University of North Carolina Press, 1985.

Robinson, Blackwell. *William R. Davie*. Chapel Hill: University of North Carolina Press, 1957.

Russell, Phillips. *These Old Stone Walls.* Chapel Hill: Chapel Hill Historical Society, 1972.

———. *The Woman Who Rang the Bell.* Chapel Hill: University of North Carolina Press, 1949.

Sanders, John L. "Analysis of an Act to Consolidate the Institutions of Higher Learning in North Carolina." Chapel Hill: Institute of Government, 1971.

Selden, Samuel. *Frederick Henry Koch: Pioneer Playmaker.* Chapel Hill: University of North Carolina Library, 1954.

Singal, Daniel Joseph. *The War Within: From Victorian to Modernist Thought in the South.* Chapel Hill: University of North Carolina Press, 1982.

Spencer, Cornelia Phillips. "Dr. Joseph Caldwell: A Study." *University of North Carolina Magazine* 12, no. 2 (1892).

———. "Old Times in Chapel Hill." *University Magazine,* no. ix (May 1884).

———. "Old Times in Chapel Hill." *University Monthly,* May 1888.

Taylor, George Coffin. *So This Is Education.* New Bern: Owen G. Dunn Company, 1980.

Tindall, George Brown. *The Emergence of the New South.* Baton Rouge: Louisiana State University Press, 1967.

———. "The Significance of Howard W. Odum to Southern History." *Journal of Southern History,* Fall 1958.

Toynbee, Arnold W. *A Study of History.* New York and London: Oxford University Press, 1947.

Vance, Zebulon Baird. Commencement address at the University of North Carolina, June 7, 1877. Durham, N.C.: W. T. Blackwell and Company, 1878.

———. *Sketches of North Carolina.* Norfolk, Va.: The *Norfolk Landmark,* 1875.

Wagstaff, Henry McGilbert. *Impressions of Men and Movements at the University of North Carolina.* Chapel Hill: University of North Carolina Press, 1950.

Weeks, Stephen B. "The University of North Carolina in the Civil War." *University Magazine* 28, no. 2 (November 1910).

Wettach, Robert H. *A Century of Legal Education.* Chapel Hill: University of North Carolina Press, 1947.

White, Peter S. "Leading the Way for Diversity." *Carolina Alumni Review* 78, no. 2 (Summer 1989).

White, William Allen, ed. *Defense for America.* New York: Macmillan, 1940.

Wilson, Louis Round. *The University of North Carolina, 1900–1930: The Making of a Modern University.* Chapel Hill: University of North Carolina Press, 1957.

Winston, Robert Watson. *It's a Far Cry.* New York: Henry Holt and Company, 1937.

INDEX

Page numbers in italics refer to illustrations.